T0348396

International Investments in Private Equity

International Investments in Private Equity

Asset Allocation, Markets, and Industry Structure

Peter Cornelius

ELSEVIER

AMSTERDAM • BOSTON • HEIDELBERG • LONDON • NEW YORK • OXFORD
PARIS • SAN DIEGO • SAN FRANCISCO • SINGAPORE • SYDNEY • TOKYO

Academic Press is an imprint of Elsevier

Academic Press is an imprint of Elsevier
30 Corporate Drive, Suite 400, Burlington, MA 01803, USA
525 B Street, Suite 1800, San Diego, CA 92101-4495, USA
84 Theobald's Road, London WC1X 8RR, UK

First edition 2011

Library of Congress Cataloging-in-Publication Data
Cornelius, Peter, 1960-
  International investments in private equity : asset allocation, markets, and industry structure /
  Peter Cornelius. – 1st ed.
      p. cm.
  Includes bibliographical references and index.
  ISBN 978-0-12-375082-2
  1. Private equity. 2. Investments, Foreign. I. Title.
  HG4751.C75 2011
  332.67'3–dc22

                                    2010038319

British Library Cataloguing in Publication Data
A catalogue record for this book is available from the British Library

ISBN: 978-0-12-375082-2

For information on all Academic Press publications visit
our website at books.elsevier.com

Contents

For Heike and Paul

For Heide and Paul

Foreword

After the recent dramatic events in the private equity industry—such as the boom of the mid-2000s and the collapse in the wake of the financial crisis and the attendant recession—its future remains uncertain along many dimensions. Nonetheless, two predictions about the industry's evolution can be made with confidence.

First, much of the future growth in venture capital and private equity activity is going to take place outside its traditional hubs of the United States and continental Europe (especially Great Britain). In particular, it is likely that the industry's focus will be increasingly on the emerging markets. The trend toward increased globalization of the private equity industry was evident from the first days of the 21st century. The industry downturn has only accelerated this trend, and although there will be growing pains in many markets, there are many reasons to conclude that private equity investing will increasingly be a global enterprise.

A related change will be a shift in the ranks of who is raising private equity. According to the Emerging Market Private Equity Association, 26 percent of the total amount invested by private equity funds in 2009 went to companies based in emerging markets, but only 9 percent of funds was raised by groups based in these markets. Going forward, it is likely that emerging market-based groups will gain a much larger share of the global private equity pool.

Second, the model of "loose governance" by limited partners, who have traditionally relied on incentive compensation to ensure that the general partners "do the right thing," may have reached its limits. The disappointments brought about by the bursting bubbles of the late 1990s and mid-2000s have opened the door to tough questions about the behavior of general partners, and whether carried interest still serves as a sufficient spur to good behavior. As a result, we are likely to see increased attention—and perhaps a fundamental rethinking—of the way in which private equity groups are governed and rewarded. In particular, there is likely to be a much greater emphasis on performance measurement and evaluation.

This book is a very timely one along both these dimensions. First, unlike so many texts that implicitly take a national view of the industry, *International Investments in Private Equity* assumes a global perspective throughout. Second, the volume emphasizes an analytic view throughout, highlighting cutting-edge research and quantitative methodologies that can address many of the concerns raised by current and potential investors in the asset class.

It is also worth noting that it is hard to think of a more perfect author for a text like this than Peter Cornelius. Peter combines many years of experience grappling with thorny global macroeconomic questions, a substantial understanding of the practicalities of the private equity industry, and a deep interest in the sometimes fascinating, sometimes befuddling realm of academic research into this arena. (Peter is one of the few practitioners I know who is interested and engaged after 2 days of presentations of academic papers, a task I often struggle with!) As such, this book can build a bridge between perspectives that are not often seen in conjunction with each other.

Josh Lerner

Harvard Business School, Boston, Massachusetts

June 10, 2010

Acknowledgements

This book could not have been written without the generous help of a large number of individuals in the private equity industry and in academia. Many ideas in this book have been developed or refined in numerous conversations with my colleagues at AlpInvest Partners, investment professionals at other limited partner organizations, general partners of private equity funds, representatives of private equity associations, and researchers teaching private equity courses at leading business schools around the globe. Some have served as informal sounding boards throughout the process of writing this book, others have commented on early drafts of the manuscript. To all of them, I am extremely grateful for their invaluable insights and the time they have made available so generously.

At AlpInvest Partners, I am particularly thankful to Volkert Doeksen and Paul de Klerk for encouraging me to undertake this project. Their continued support throughout the entire process has been even more important, given the huge uncertainties the private equity industry has been facing in the aftermath of the deepest financial crisis in several generations. I also thank the members of AlpInvest Partners' Research and Allocation Committee for very helpful discussions, namely Wim Borgdorff, Iain Leigh, Wouter Moerel, Elliot Royce, and George Westerkamp. Having read individual chapters or the manuscript in its entirety, they provided me with detailed comments, identified inconsistencies and made extremely useful suggestions to make the book more readable. Similarly, I have greatly benefited from conversations with, and concrete comments by, Erik Bosman, Tjarko Hektor, Sander van Maanen, Maarten Vervoort, and Erik Thyssen, to whom I am also deeply indebted. I also thank my colleagues Karlijn Juttmann, Broes Langelaar, Maarten van Rossum, and Robert de Veer. Some of the ideas in the book have been developed jointly in previous research projects with them, whose contributions are gratefully acknowledged. I am also grateful to Marleen Dijkstra who carefully read the manuscript, cross-checked the data, and helped me clarify the flow of some arguments. Finally, my special thanks go to my assistant Petri de Jong who kept me organized during the intense period of finalizing this project.

At APG, AlpInvest Partners' lead investor, I thank Reitze Douma, Rob van den Goorbergh, Roderick Molenaar, John Rekema, and Jan van Roekel for discussing alternative investments in the broader context of portfolio construction and asset-liability management. Furthermore, John provided me with detailed comments on the manuscript for which I am particularly grateful.

In the general partner community, I am greatly indebted to Max Burger Calderon of Apax Partners; Adiba Ighodaro and Peter Schmid of Actis; Henry Kravis of KKR; Omar Lodhi of Abraaj Capital, Daniel O'Connell of Vestar Capital Partners; Brian Powers of Hellman & Friedman; and Stephen Schwarzman of The Blackstone Group. They have generously made available their precious time to be interviewed for this book. The strategic conversations with these leading private equity investors, which are presented in the final chapter of this book, provide invaluable insights in GPs' global expansion strategies and risk management practices in an international context. Others have provided feedback on specific ideas or portions of the manuscript. I am especially grateful to Joost Hollemann, Prime Technology Ventures.

In the limited partner community, I have received extremely helpful comments from John Breen of the CPP Investment Board, Haydee Celaya of the International Finance Corporation, Christian Diller of Capital Dynamics, Suzie Kwon Cohen of the Government Investment Council (GIC) of Singapore, and Ernest Lambert of EMAlternatives. Many other industry insiders provided valuable comments, critiques, and suggestions. I thank in particular Jennifer Choi, Emerging Markets Private Equity Association; Heino Meerkatt, Boston Consulting Group; and Thomas Meyer, European Venture Capital and Private Equity Association. Furthermore, I am thankful to Christopher Ward of State Street Investment Analytics for sharing and discussing their data on private equity fund returns.

Written predominantly for practitioners, this book takes into account the growing academic literature on private equity investing. Many in academia have been extremely generous with their time and ideas, greatly helping me make the book more rigorous. First of all, I am extremely grateful to Josh Lerner, Harvard Business School, for writing the foreword to this book. In fact, many ideas developed in this study go back to Josh's extensive contributions to the literature on private equity. The same applies to Steven Kaplan, Booth School of Business at the University of Chicago, with whom I had several conversations on many key subjects in this book. His comments on an earlier paper on cross-border private equity capital flows (coauthored with Karlijn Juttmann and Broes Langelaar) proved extremely helpful in drafting parts of this book. Furthermore, my former coeditor of *Corporate Governance and Capital Flows in a Global Economy* (Oxford University Press, 2003), Bruce Kogut, Columbia Business School, deserves special thanks for his availability and feedback over the years. As always, his observations and suggestions have provided extremely useful guidance in undertaking this project. Other academics I am highly grateful to are Francesca Cornelli, London Business School; Heinrich Liechtenstein, IESE; Roger Leeds, Johns Hopkins University; Ludovic Phalippou, University of Amsterdam; and Peter Roosenboom, Rotterdam School of Management, for their comments on the manuscript. I am also thankful to Ulf Axelson, London School of Economics and Political Science, and Per Strömberg, Swedish Institute for Financial Research, with whom I have discussed various aspects of performance measurement and portfolio and risk management in private equity.

At Elsevier/Academic Press, I thank Karen Maloney. As the former publisher of Elsevier's Economics and Finance series, Karen was extremely supportive right from the beginning. Her enthusiasm was shared by Scott Bentley, who took over from

Karen as my editor, guiding me through the entire production process of this book. Without his continuous encouragement, support, and assistance, this book would not exist. Many other professionals at Elsevier have been involved in this project. My special thanks to Anjana Jeyan, Cindy Minor, Karthikeyan Murthy, Kathleen Paoni, and Stacey Walker stand for my general appreciation of the excellent work of the entire Elsevier crew.

Finally, I owe a deep debt of gratitude to my wife Heike and my son Paul. As anyone who has ever written a book will confirm a project like this substantially tilts the author's work–life balance (even more) to the former. Sincerely appreciating the support and the time my family has given me to write this book, I would like to dedicate it to them.

Karen as my editor, guiding me through the entire production process of this book. Without his continuous encouragement, support, and assistance, this book would not exist. Many other professionals at Elsevier have been involved in this project. My special thanks to Anjana Jeyan, Cindy Minor, Kathie... and Stacey Walker stand for my special appreciation of the excellent work of the entire Elsevier crew.

Finally, I owe a deep debt of gratitude to my wife Heike and my son Paul. As anyone who has ever written a book will confirm a project like this substantially cuts the author's work–life balance lever in the family. Sincerely appreciating the support and the time my family has given me to write this book, I would like to dedicate it to them.

About the author

Peter Cornelius

Peter Cornelius is heading economic and strategic research at AlpInvest Partners, one of the world's largest investors in private equity. Prior to his current position, he was the group chief economist of Royal Dutch Shell, chief economist and director of the World Economic Forum's Global Competitiveness Program, head of International Economic Research of Deutsche Bank, and a senior economist with the International Monetary Fund. Dr. Cornelius is the chairman of the European Venture Capital & Private Equity Association's working group on private equity risk management. A visiting professor at the Vlerick Leuven Gent Management School, he has been a visiting scholar at Harvard University and an adjunct professor at Brandeis University.

List of abbreviations

ADB	Asian Development Bank
ADIA	Abu Dhabi Investment Authority
AfDB	African Development Bank
AIF	Alternative investment fund
AIFM	Alternative Investment Fund Manager
AIFMD	Alternative Investment Fund Manager Directive
ALM	Asset-liability management
AMF	Autorité des Marchés Financiers
APG	Algemene Pensioen Groep
ARD	American Research and Development
ASEAN	Association of Southeast Asian Nations
AUD	Australian dollar
AUM	Assets under management
BRIC	Brazil, Russia, India, and China
BRL	Brazilian real
BV	Besloten vennootschap met beperkte aansprakelijkheid
CA	Cambridge Associates
CAD	Capital Adequacy Directive
CanD	Canadian dollar
CAPM	Capital asset pricing model
CAGR	Compound annual growth rate
CalPERS	California Public Employees' Retirement System
CDC	Commonwealth Development Corporation
CDO	Collateralized debt obligation
CEE	Central and Eastern Europe
CEIOPS	Committee of European Insurance and Occupational Pensions Supervisors
CIC	China Investment Corporation
CIS	Commonwealth of Independent States
CLO	Collateralized loan obligation
CPIS	Coordinated Portfolio Investment Survey
CPPIB	Canadian Pension Plan Investment Board
CSR	Corporate social responsibility

(*Continued*)

CV	Commanditaire vennootschap
DCF	Discounted cash flows
DEG	Deutsche Entwicklungsgesellschaft
DPI	Distributed to Paid-In
EBITDA	Earnings Before Interest, Taxes, Depreciation, and Amortization
EBRD	European Bank for Reconstruction and Development
EC	European Commission
ECB	European Central Bank
EIF	European Investment Fund
EMPEA	Emerging Markets Private Equity Association
EMS	European Monetary System
EMU	European Monetary Union
ESG	Environmental, social, and corporate governance
EU	European Union
EUR	Euro
EVCA	European Private Equity and Venture Capital Association
EWS	Early warning system
FASB	Financial Accounting Standards Board
FDI	Foreign direct investment
FCPI	Fonds Commun de Placement dans l'Innovation
FCPR	Fonds Commun de Placement à Risques
FCR	Fundos de Capital de Risco (Portugal); Fondos de Capital de Riesgo (Spain)
FIP	Fundos de Investimento em Partipações
FMIEE	Fundos Mútuos de Investimentos em Empresas Emergentes
GBP	British Pound
GCR	Global Competitiveness Report
GDP	Gross Domestic Product
GIC	Government Investment Council (of Singapore)
GmbH	Gesellschaft mit beschränkter Haftung
GmbH & Co KG	GmbH & Co Kommanditgesellschaft
GP	General Partner
HH	Hirschman-Herfindahl (index)
HNWI	High net worth individual
IASB	International Accounting Standards Board
ICR	Investidores em Capital de Risco
ICAPM	International capital asset pricing model
IFC	International Finance Corporation
IFI	International Financial Institution
IFRS	International Financial Reporting Standards
ILPA	Institutional Limited Partners' Association
IMF	International Monetary Fund

INR	Indian Rupee
IOSCO	International Organization of Securities Commissions
IPO	Initial public offering
IT	Information technology
IRR	Internal rate of return
JPY	Japanese Yen
KG	Kommanditgesellschaft
KKR	Kohlberg Kravis Roberts & Co
KPCB	Kleiner Perkins Caufield & Byers
LBO	Leveraged buyout
LIBOR	London Interbank Offered Rate
LP	Limited partner
LPA	Limited partnership agreement
LQ	Lower quartile
LTCB	Long-Term Credit Bank (of Japan)
LVCA	Latin American Venture Capital and Private Equity Association
M&A	Mergers and acquisitions
MM	Money multiple
NAV	Net asset value
NIAC	Newly industrialized Asian country
NOK	Norwegian Krona
NPV	Net present value
NV	Naamloze vennootschap
NVCA	National Venture Capital Association
OECD	Organization for Economic Co-operation and Development
OMERS	Ontario Municipal Employees Retirement System
OPIC	Overseas Private Investment Corporation
OTC	Over-the-counter
PAYG	Pay-as-you-go
PE	Private equity
PIPE	Private Investment in Public Equity
PME	Public market equivalent
PPP	Purchasing power parity
PREQIN	Private Equity Intelligence
RMB	Renminbi (Chinese)
RPPP	Relative purchasing power parity
RVPI	Residual Value to Paid In
SA	Société par actions (France); Sociedades Anónimas (Spain)
SAS	Société par actions simplifée
SCA	Société en Commandite par Actions
SCR	Société de Capital Risque (France); Sociedades de Capital de Risco (Portugal); Sociedades de Capital Riesgo (Spain)

(Continued)

SEC	Securities and Exchange Commission (USA)
SEK	Swedish krona
SHE	Sand Hill Econometrics
SWF	Sovereign Wealth Fund
TVE	Thomson VentureXpert
TVPI	Total Value to Paid In
UQ	Upper quartile
USD	US Dollar
VaR	Value at risk
VC	Venture capital
VY	Vintage year
WCY	World Competitiveness Yearbook
ZAR	South African Rand

1 Introduction

Private equity is subject to boom and bust cycles. Private equity cycles are driven by both macroeconomic conditions and return expectations by investors. In a downturn, inflows to private equity funds fall, which forces fund managers to be highly selective in identifying the most attractive investment opportunities. As a result, private equity returns tend to rise. However, as returns increase, investors adjust their return expectations and raise their commitments to private equity funds. As more capital chases a finite number of deals, the surge in fund inflows sows the seeds for the next bust. In the most recent cycle, which coincided with the worst economic and financial crisis since World War II, leveraged buyouts were hit particularly hard: From its peak in 2007, the global buyout volume fell at a compound annual rate of more than 50 percent in the 2 subsequent years, while commitments to buyout funds declined at a compound annual rate of almost 45 percent during this period.

As we go to press, there are signs that the sharp downturn in private equity investing and fundraising has finally bottomed out amid improved macroeconomic and financial market conditions. However, there remains exceptional uncertainty as to the near- to medium-term outlook for private equity. A clear indicator is the recent sovereign debt crisis in the peripheral countries of the euro area, which has reminded market participants that fiscal support for global growth is strictly time limited. The risk of renewed market turbulences is still high, suggesting that the expected recovery in private equity activity could be bumpy.

To be sure, private equity has been in similar situations before. Arguably, the uncertainties about the future of leveraged buyouts had not been less after the collapse of the junk bond market in the early 1990s. Investors did not face less uncertainty after the bursting of the tech bubble, the terrorist attacks on September 11, 2001, and a series of corporate governance scandals that led to significantly more stringent legislation under the Sarbanes-Oxley Act of 2002. Yet, private equity has recovered every time, resuming its long-term growth and reaching nearly US\$ 1.4 trillion in assets under management in 2009 from just a couple of billions in 1980. There are no signs that the private equity model is broken, as some have claimed. In fact, although the debris from the crisis will be known only when the dust has fully settled, so far

International Investments in Private Equity. DOI: 10.1016/B978-0-12-375082-2.10001-1

private equity seems to have weathered the storm considerably better than had been feared (Thomas, 2010). In buyouts, there is ample evidence of the model's long-term success in creating value through superior governance, efficient capital structures, and operational improvements. In venture capital, it is well documented how the model solves a difficult mismatch in a market economy—entrepreneurs with a good idea but no money and investors who have money but no good ideas (Kaplan and Lerner, 2009).

1.1   From a closed to an open market view

As dramatic as the recent cycle has been, both in terms of the huge built-up of private equity assets and the subsequent decline in new commitments and investment, it confirms a pattern we were already familiar with prior to this cycle. And yet, the last cycle has been fundamentally different in one important aspect. Whereas previous private equity cycles had largely been confined to the United States, the last cycle has been a global phenomenon. In both the United States and Europe, buyout volumes had risen at a compound real annual growth rate of more than 35 percent between 2003 and the middle of 2007, and both markets fell in tandem when debt financing became unavailable. In Asia and in other parts of the world, which had also seen a significant pick up in private equity transactions, the market correction was less extreme, in part because transactions were much less dependent on the availability of debt. Nevertheless, as the global economic cycle turned out to be highly synchronized, no private equity market was immune to a much harsher investment environment. Today, the US market accounts for less than 60 percent in terms of private equity assets domestic funds manage. In 1990, when the first buyout boom came to an end, the US market still had a share of more than 80 percent. During this period, European funds have expanded their global share to more than one quarter, while funds in the rest of the world are catching up quickly.

As private equity has begun to migrate from being an alternative asset class to mainstream investing, the literature on this subject has expanded appreciably. There are already numerous books in print and even more in preparation. MBA students who plan a career as a general partner find several textbooks on their reading lists covering subjects ranging from company valuations and acquisitions, capital structures and debt financing to the design of venture capital contracts, and the process of initial public offerings. For portfolio managers and limited partners in private equity funds, the literature has grown equally rapidly. In these studies, readers find answers to many questions ranging from the performance characteristics in individual market segments to the due diligence process in selecting private equity funds and the planning of an investment program. How does private equity create value? How are private equity markets organized? How is the relationship between private equity fund managers and investors governed? And what are the alternative channels through which investors can get exposed to the asset class? Several studies treat private equity on a stand-alone basis, while other books put private equity in the broader context of a multiasset investment strategy pioneered by Swensen (2009) of the Yale University

Endowment. However, most of these treatises have in common that they take a national or regional perspective.

The US private equity market has attracted by far the greatest amount of attention. As the cradle of modern private equity, the US market has the longest history, the largest size, and the best data researchers can work with. However, as a growing number of economies have imported the private equity model over time and more empirical evidence outside the United States has become available, there is an increasing body of literature analyzing the European private equity market and, more recently, new markets in emerging economies. At the same time, the growing importance of private equity in financial intermediation around the globe has allowed researchers to undertake comparative studies, examining the drivers of private equity activity and returns in a cross-section of countries.

Nevertheless, the globalization of the private equity model, and the opportunities and risks that arise from it, is still well ahead of what investors in private equity may find in the literature on the subject. Analyses of cross-border investments and trade in financial services in private equity have remained surprisingly rare—as if markets outside the United States had developed largely in isolation.[1] As market participants know, this of course has not been the case. Instead, private equity funds raise substantial amounts from investors who are domiciled outside their home market. Large US pension funds, such as CalPERS, have committed around one third of their private equity allocations to non-US funds. AlpInvest Partners, Europe's largest private equity investor, holds, on a commitment basis, more capital abroad than in its home region. To the extent that sovereign wealth funds in emerging market economies seek exposure to private equity, they often commit capital to foreign fund managers.

Private equity funds have not only an increasingly internationally diversified investor base, many of them also hold a regionally or even globally diversified portfolio of companies. To identify attractive investment opportunities, they rely on an international network of offices or have engaged in cross-border joint ventures with local partners. Cross-border capital transactions and trade in financial services raise a new set of important issues for investors in private equity, however, which have remained underexplored in the existing literature. How integrated is the private equity market, both globally and regionally? What are the opportunities that come with the globalization of the private equity model? How can investors exploit these new opportunities? What are the main risks in cross-border investing and how can investors mitigate these risks? This book focuses on these topics. In essence, it aims to open the "closed economy" for private equity investors, an approach that hitherto has been the dominant model for most studies on the subject.

The growing internationalization of private equity does not make the existing literature less relevant or even obsolete, of course. For example, whether investors hold internationally diversified portfolios, limited partners in private equity funds must understand the structure of partnerships and the terms and conditions under which they commit capital to such funds. They need to know how private equity

---

[1] A notable exception is Cumming and Johan (2009) and the collection of articles in Cumming (2010).

returns are calculated, which potential pitfalls exist and how fees and carried interest affect the net performance of private equity funds. And they must be aware of the specific cash-flow dynamics of private equity funds to manage liquidity risk effectively.

This book is written predominantly for investment professionals who are assumed to be familiar with these and other key characteristics of private equity. Readers will thus find only a brief overview, which covers in particular those fundamentals that are of direct relevance for the main focus of the book—cross-border investments in globally and regionally integrated private equity markets. Accordingly, the book is divided into four parts: Part I discusses the risk and return profile of private equity in the context of diversified investment portfolios; Part II analyzes the growth dynamics in individual markets and geographies, examines investment flows between them, and evaluates different types of risk arising from international transactions and how such risks may be managed; Part III provides an outlook for global private equity in light of the macroeconomic and structural factors that drive the supply and demand dynamics in individual markets; and finally, Part IV contains conversations with leading private equity fund managers on their global expansion strategies and risk management.

1.2   Private equity fundamentals

Part I contains four chapters. In setting the scene for the rest of the book, Chapter 2 starts by defining what we mean by private equity. This is necessary as there remains a surprising degree of disagreement among practitioners, academics, and policy makers. Although some equate private equity strictly with leveraged buyout trans-actions, others—including this book—take a broader view and consider private equity as an asset class consisting of different segments. These segments—in the investment world sometimes referred to as "buckets"—reflect the different forms of private equity financing companies may turn to over their entire life cycle. Besides leveraged buyouts, our definition of private equity also encompasses venture capital, growth capital, mezzanine, and distressed and turnaround capital. Note that our definition emphasizes the demand for private equity capital by firms. This excludes private investments in areas such as infrastructure, real estate, or energy, which some also consider as a form of private equity.

On the supply side, the most important investors are pension funds, insurance companies, banks, endowments, and family offices. There are different ways for them to get exposed to private equity. This book focuses on the most common form, that is, commitments to private equity funds, which are typically organized as limited part-nerships and targeting different investment stages. However, there are alternative routes investors can pursue, including, for example, investments in a listed private equity vehicle or a listed management company, or capital commitments to a fund of funds. Furthermore, a secondary market has emerged where investors may acquire stakes in private equity funds, which were raised in previous years and have typically already deployed a significant part of their capital. Investments in publicly listed private equity, funds of funds, or secondary funds are subject to different risk and return characteristics, which we do not explicitly cover in this book.

With these clarifications in mind, Chapter 2 then turns to the question of value creation in private equity. More specifically, this discussion focuses on two aspects: How do private equity investments create value? And how do the investment returns arising from value creation get distributed between the general partner and their limited partners? This distinction is critical, given the substantial fees general partners charge to their investors. In this book, we take the perspective of a limited partner who assesses the performance of his private equity investments solely on the basis of net-of-fee returns—as opposed to the overall (gross-of-fees) profits a buyout or a venture capital transaction might have generated.

Net-of-fee returns to investors still do not tell us the full picture about the attractiveness of the asset class. For this, we need to compare the performance of private equity funds to alternative investments, such as public stocks. Such comparisons are far from trivial, which explains why this issue continues to attract a substantial amount of attention of academics and investment professionals alike. A review of the existing literature tells us why. First of all, private equity data are, as the term suggests, private. As chapter 3 discusses in greater detail, there are no universally agreed benchmarks in private equity, even in the most mature market segments, such as US and European buyouts and US venture capital. True, there are several data providers who report private equity returns, which are typically expressed as internal rates of return (IRR) per vintage year or as horizon IRRs. The average IRR in a given vintage year and the distribution of returns across individual funds are generally interpreted as "market" returns. As we show, however, there is a considerable variation of reported returns across individual data suppliers. For example, for the US buyout market, which is by far the world's largest private equity segment in terms of fund-raising and investment, we find on average differences in reported returns of around 500 basis points (and in some vintage years significantly more) between Thomson VentureXpert and Cambridge Associates, two of the most widely used sources in the industry. In other market segments, such as mezzanine or distressed investing, investors face even greater challenges. However, as our review of global benchmarks shows, the biggest challenges exist in emerging economies, where in the absence of historical data and the limited depth of the market, investors often have to rely on relatively crude yardsticks.

The private character of private equity data raises another issue. Although data providers report IRRs and other return measures, they usually do not publish the underlying cash flows of individual funds and the precise dates when such flows occurred. However, unless we know the exact cash flows and their dates, we are unable to make performance comparisons. Luckily, a few academic researchers (Kaplan & Schoar, 2005; Phalippou & Gottschalg, 2009) have been able to get access to cash-flow data on an anonymous basis for a large sample of funds, which has enabled them to calculate public market equivalents. However, such studies have remained rare and exist only for the more mature markets.

An even thornier issue concerns risk. Unless investors know the risk they have to accept to generate a given level of returns, they are unable to draw any meaningful conclusions about the relative attractiveness of an asset class. But what exactly do we mean by risk in private equity investments? One risk category is illiquidity. Investors in private equity funds typically demand an illiquidity premium to compensate them for the fact that their investments are locked in for the lifetime of the partnership, which is normally 10 years, sometimes even longer. During this period, the general partner in a private equity fund draws down the capital that his limited partners have committed. However, the drawdown dates are unknown. Although investors typically run sophisticated cash-flow models to minimize the risk of not being able to meet their commitments, a significant number of limited partners have faced serious liquidity issues in the recent crisis as their cash-flow models failed to cope with the sudden jump in correlations.

Another risk in private equity stems from the leverage in buyouts. In a typical buyout transaction in the last cycle debt accounted for around two-thirds of the financing, and in the late 1980s the typical ratio was closer to 85 to 90 percent. Debt amplifies returns, but risk increases proportionally. Conversely, less debt (and more equity) in a deal not only reduces returns but also risk. Although this would suggest that investors should be neutral with regard to leverage being used in private equity, portfolio companies tend to be significantly more leveraged than public companies. As we discuss in the following chapter, this means that private equity returns are strictly speaking not comparable with public equity returns, unless the former are corrected for higher leverage risk.

Finally, there have been several attempts to measure market risk in private equity and to estimate its cost of capital. In empirical applications, such attempts have faced substantial challenges, however, which, on the one hand, arise from the highly restrictive assumptions of standard approaches, such as the Capital Asset Pricing Model, and, on the other hand, the special characteristics of private equity investments and returns. One of the most important problems to overcome is stale pricing. In Chapter 4, we show that, unless corrected for, stale prices may lead to a significant underestimation of risk and hence to an overallocation of capital to private equity, given an investor's return expectations and risk aversion.

Differing risk and return preferences are not the only reason, however, why allocations to private equity vary considerably across different investor classes and even within individual classes. As we discuss further in Chapter 4, investment strategies by pension funds, for example, must take into account the structure and duration of their liabilities. Banks' decisions to invest in private equity may be driven not only by expected (risk-) adjusted returns but also by other objectives, such as the cross-selling of their services. Furthermore, different classes of investors are subject to different regulations affecting their allocations to different asset classes. Looking forward, regulations look set to be tightened, not least in response to the recent financial crisis, which could force investors to restructure their portfolios. Finally, practical considerations matter. While scalability and sufficient access to outperforming funds are important factors in determining the ceiling for private equity allocations, especially for large investors, at the lower end allocations need to be sizeable enough to "move the needle" and to justify a dedicated investment team.

In Chapter 5, finally, we turn to the design of private equity investment programs, given an overall allocation of capital to this asset class. Generally, private equity portfolios are diversified along four dimensions, namely (i) the different investment stages (venture capital, buyouts and mezzanine, distressed and turnaround capital); (ii) vintage years; (iii) industries; and (iv) geographies. Investors who have no particular view on individual market segments and are not constrained by any access restrictions to individual funds may well hold the market portfolio. However, such an allocation is likely to lead to some inevitable surprises. For instance, investors holding the market portfolio will be overexposed to vintage years that tend to underperform, given the inverse relationship between capital inflows and market returns. Deviations from market neutrality require investors to formulate their own return expectations for individual market segments and specify the degree of confidence they have in their own views. In a Black–Litterman (1992) framework, the optimal portfolio is then simply a set of deviations from neutral market capitalization weights in the direction of portfolios about which views are expressed. In formulating specific views, Chapter 5 advocates a combined top-down and bottom-up approach that take into account macro variables, such as interest rates, specific industry cycles, and country and currency risk, as well as market factors such as the track record of individual fund managers and expected coinvestment opportunities.

1.3 Global markets and investment flows

The emergence of private equity markets outside the United States and Europe has significantly broadened the scope for portfolio diversification. At the same time, however, the growing importance of private equity in nontraditional markets has substantially increased investors' knowledge requirements. Such requirements may be an important impediment to international investing. In fact, in public markets, investors are still found to be significantly home biased, despite the progressive dismantling of investment barriers, an observation, which is at least in part attributable to persistent information gaps about foreign markets. Arguably, filling such gaps in private markets represents an even greater challenge. How developed is the market in terms of the role private equity funds play in intermediating capital? Is there a sufficiently developed ecosystem (e.g., law firms, accounting firms, placement agents, and banks) in place to support the private equity market? How important are the individual market segments in terms of different investment stages? What does the industry structure look like? What role do international private equity funds play? Is there a market benchmark against which the performance of individual funds can be measured? And how dispersed are the returns? These are just a few examples of questions investors need to answer when venturing into foreign private equity markets.

The second part of the book is therefore devoted to issues arising in the context of international portfolio diversification. This part is divided into five chapters. In Chapter 6, we kick off with a brief sketch of the size of the global private equity market in terms of fund-raising and investment volumes and assets under management. This discussion is followed by an analysis of regional trends. In this context, we pay particular attention to the catch-up process in the emerging markets where private equity is assuming an increasingly important role in financial inter-mediation as their economies grow and their prosperity rises. However, this process has been uneven, and while some countries show rapidly increasing penetration rates as they transition through the different stages of economic development, in others this process has been much more gradual. This suggests that economic and financial development is a necessary but not a sufficient condition for private equity to play a more prominent role. Instead, there must be additional factors at work, a hypothesis that is consistent with the observed substantial variation in penetration rates in the industrialized countries. Which path will today's emerging markets follow—the United States where private equity investing has accounted for almost 2.5 percent of GDP in the last cycle, or Japan where the rate of penetration has remained in the range of 0.5 percent of GDP?

To shed more light on this important question, Chapter 6 discusses existing approaches to assessing the quality of the business environment for private equity. These approaches are generally based on a complex system of factors, which are identified as important drivers for private equity activity. Individual factors are then aggregated to a summary index, which allows one to rank countries according to their attractiveness for private equity investing.

Measurement matters, and what matters is what gets measured. Some elements of the investment decision process are, however, inescapably issues of judgments or values, rendering a purely quantitative process not only impossible but also unwise. Presumably, this is an important reason why few investors follow a strict permissible markets approach that excludes markets below a predetermined rank or threshold from the investment universe. For the majority of investors, broader market classi-fications of the type we propose in Chapter 6 are of greater relevance than the numerical ranking of an individual country. When contemplating foreign investments, notably coinvestments alongside funds, many of them pursue a case-by-case approach that focuses on the underlying drivers of market attractiveness within broader groups of countries.

While market attractiveness rankings may be a good starting point, they suffer from two important shortcomings: first, although the rankings reflect variables that are relevant from a risk management stand point, they are not designed as a tool to assess macro risk. For instance, high income tax rates render a market less attractive for private equity investors, but as long as the tax system is predictable high rates per se do not cause investment risk. Second, market attractiveness rankings do not give investors the level of granularity they require in their risk analysis. Take regulatory risk, for example, a category that can fundamentally change the economics of a private equity investment. To the extent that market attractiveness rankings capture this risk, the evidence is typically based on national and international surveys. However, regulatory risk often varies substantially across sectors, and while some industries may be particularly susceptible to regulatory changes, others may be significantly less sensitive. In the final section of Chapter 6, we present a "risk heat map" that helps address these shortcomings. As a risk management framework, the "heat map" allows investors to categorize different types of macro risks, assess these risks from the viewpoint of a given transaction, and compare them across different economies and markets in a consistent fashion.

However, the fact that private equity markets have emerged in an increasing number of countries does not say much about the degree to which they are integrated. Anecdotal evidence tells us that national or regional private equity markets have not emerged completely independently. For instance, we know that several US buyout funds have led some of the largest transactions in Europe. We also know that some European investors and sovereign wealth funds in Asia and the Middle East are among the most important limited partners in some US partnerships. On the regional level, London's role as the major hub for Europe's private equity market is equally well known. However, apart from the anecdotal evidence we have got, few studies have looked systemically at cross-border transactions and their implications for market integration, asset prices, and investment opportunities for limited partners. For instance, the regional and global expansion of a growing number of private equity firms has broadened the scope of diversification for their limited partners whose international investment strategies would otherwise be restricted to commitments to local funds in their target countries or regions. However, this expansion into new territories has brought about new challenges for limited partners in terms of portfolio construction, bottom-up due diligence, and currency risk management, which have remained largely unexplored in the literature.

Chapters 7 and 8 aim to narrow this gap. Our analysis starts by examining cross-border acquisitions by private equity funds. More specifically, we use a proprietary dataset for buyout partnerships, which helps us track international fund investments between major regions. Our analysis confirms the anecdotal evidence. In fact, we find buyout funds on average to be less home-biased than mutual funds. What explains this seemingly surprising result? As we discuss in greater detail, one important factor is likely to be the lower governance risk in financial sponsor-led acquisitions, which typically involve the transfer of significant, and often controlling, stakes in a company.

Market integration is also driven by cross-border commitments by limited partners, the focus of Chapter 8. In principle, cross-border investments by limited partners may be hindered by the same factors (e.g., capital barriers, informational gaps, behavioral biases) as cross-border acquisitions made by their general partners. In perfectly segmented markets, GPs raise capital only from domestic investors and deploy the funds exclusively in domestic transactions. This was basically the situation in the early days of private equity, and for smaller funds, it is still a more or less accurate description. For larger funds, however, this is no longer the case. Instead, as our analysis in Chapter 8 reveals, the investor base of large buyout and venture capital funds has become substantially international. In the future, their investor base is set to include to an even larger extent investors from emerging market economies, which are expected to continue to run sizeable current account surpluses. In recycling these surpluses, sovereign wealth funds from Asia and the Middle East will play a pivotal role.

Finally, Chapter 8 focuses on the new challenges limited partners face in their due diligence work when they examine investment opportunities abroad. A key issue foreign investors face lies in the substantially greater information requirements, both at the macro- and micro levels, to assess investment risks relative to the expected returns. This applies especially to investments in emerging markets. Are local private equity firms, which tend to have better local market knowledge but often have less investment experience, better suited to deal with such risks than global players, whose track record has been largely gained through transactions in the more mature markets? A useful approach to address this question are real options, which we present in the final section of this chapter.

In Chapter 9, we turn to regional integration in the European private equity market. Although we find a significant degree of integration in terms of intraregional investment flows, much of the integration process seems to have already occurred in the 1990s. Surprisingly, this process appears to have slowed considerably in the past decade, despite the introduction of a single currency in the countries forming the European Monetary Union. Cross-border commitments have also proliferated, with London serving as a global as well as regional hub. However, market integration appears less pronounced than it could be, with the legal, tax, and operating environment of private equity still being largely determined at the national level. Important impediments to greater regional integration are seen in particular in the area of fund structuring and selling funds across borders. While the *European Alternative Investment Fund Managers Directive*—whose final form was still under discussion when we went to press—has raised serious concern with regard to its potentially isolating effects on Europe's private equity market *vis-à-vis* the rest of the world, little suggests that such initiatives help foster market integration within Europe.

A key risk in international investments is currency risk. Currency risk occurs at different levels in the investment process. At the beginning of the process, limited partners face currency risk between the point in time when they make a commitment to a fund raised in a different currency and the time when they receive capital calls. Distributions are made in the fund's currency, and to the extent that the exchange rate between the fund's currency and the limited partner's home currency moves, it will affect the performance of the fund seen from the perspective of the latter. However, not only limited partners make international investments involving currency risk. Private equity funds have also become more international, and to the extent that they deploy their capital in transactions, which are denominated in foreign currencies, investors face additional currency risk.

Chapter 10 looks at the empirical evidence and finds that currency movements have indeed a material impact on the performance of private equity funds. Given that currency movements are largely unpredictable, hedging foreign exchange risk appears to be advisable. Unfortunately, as we shall show, existing hedging instruments are inappropriate in an asset class in which cash outflows and inflows are unknown both in terms of their size and timing. What then? For large institutional investors whose private equity exposure is usually small relative to their total assets under management foreign exchange risk is usually treated from the perspective of the entire portfolio, for example, through currency overlays. For smaller investors with significant exposures to private equity and other illiquid assets, this issue is more relevant. As we shall argue in Chapter 10, however, this should not lead investors to abandon international investing. Rather, currency risk should be embraced, in the same way as investors face other investment risks. This entails, for example, incorporating foreign exchange risk in the due diligence process and benchmarking approaches, thus increasing transparency and helping improve investment decisions.

1.4   What's next?

In Part III of this book, we discuss the medium-term outlook for private equity in the era of deleveraging. More specifically, we discuss the prospects for a "New Normal" in private equity, consistent with the view of a flatter trajectory in global economic growth. We then debate possible structural changes in private equity that could occur in a *New Normal* scenario. Of particular interest is the outlook for the credit markets, which play a pivotal role for leveraged buyouts. As we see it, during the next few years the supply of leveraged finance will be influenced by a number of factors that work in different directions. On the one hand, although substantial progress has already been made in writing down risky assets, going forward new regulatory initiatives aiming to strengthen the capital base of banks are expected to shift pressures to the liability side of bank balance sheets. New regulations on securitization and resecuritization have already been put in place, potentially affecting banks' ability to provide leveraged finance. On the other hand, in a New Normal scenario investors will be faced with anemic returns in low-risk asset classes. In search for yield, investors' demand for high-yield bonds, and, to a lesser extent, leveraged loans, has already picked up appreciably. Should risk-free interest rates remain low, the demand for corporate debt could gain further momentum.

Although the supply of credit should become a less constraining factor, the recovery is likely to be relatively gradual and uneven. At the individual deal level, we anticipate continued derisking, with a greater share of equity fostering GPs' emphasis on operational improvements to achieve superior returns. At the same time, with less leveraged finance available, GPs are expected to engage to a larger extent in minority deals and private investments in public companies. Furthermore, as the importance of financial leverage as a value driver diminishes in the more mature markets, the New Normal scenario could see a further push into emerging economies where debt financing has traditionally played a relatively limited role.

A New Normal scenario would also have important implications for the industry structure in private equity. Importantly, global deleveraging could accelerate the recent trend of private equity firms going public and floating public vehicles to rely less on capital raised through traditional fund structures. At the same time, as transactions involve more equity capital, private equity firms would have a strong incentive to redouble their efforts to raise funds internationally. Moreover, under this scenario, an increasing number of private equity firms would be likely to aim to become asset managers or merchant banks. Some of the largest private equity firms have already made substantial progress in this direction—in fact, to an extent that private equity operations no longer represent their main source of revenues. What has so far remained limited to a few cases could become a broader trend over the next few years.

These changes, if they occur, should be seen as evolutionary rather than revolutionary. In its progression from a small cottage industry to a trillion-dollar asset class in just a few decades, private equity has been subject to important structural changes. Many of these changes have been triggered or fostered by boom-bust cycles. It would be surprising if this time is different.

1.5 Strategic conversations with general partners

The final part of the book includes strategic conversations with seven leading general partners on their global expansion strategies and risk management. Four of the general partners interviewed for this project are of US origin, namely The Blackstone Group, Hellman & Friedman, Kohlberg Kravis Roberts & Co (KKR), and Vestar Capital Partners. Two of the world's largest private equity firms, Blackstone and KKR, are well known for having been involved in some of the largest buyouts in history. Both firms have been at the forefront of global investing, and both have a highly international investor base. However, their expansion strategies have differed markedly. Hellman & Friedman and Vestar Capital Partners have also undertaken important efforts to leverage their substantial experience in foreign markets. Thus far, however, these efforts have focused primarily on Europe whose private equity market shares relatively more similarities with their home market.

In Europe, the four firms interviewed for this book compete with Apax Partners, one of Europe's leading private equity houses. However, they also compete with Apax Partners in third markets, notably in Asia, a region that has attracted substantial private capital inflows in recent years. Our strategic conversation with Apax Partners brings in a European perspective on global expansion strategies, which contrasts in some important aspects with their US peers. Actis and Abraaj Capital, finally, are two leading firms focusing on emerging markets. While the former takes a global perspective, with their investments spanning virtually all emerging market regions, the latter concentrates on the Middle East, North Africa, and South Asia.

While all firms we have interviewed for this project differ fundamentally in terms of their roots and history, assets under management, investment focus, and organization, they are all internationally operating financial intermediaries who raise capital and invest across borders. These conversations provide invaluable insights in a number of key issues this book is concerned with. Among others, readers will find answers to the following questions: Which business model have GPs chosen in penetrating new markets? How are investment decisions taken at the regional or global level? How do GPs assess the competitive landscape in different markets where they compete with local as well as international players? To what extent does due diligence in emerging markets differ from that in more traditional markets? How do GPs deal with corporate governance risk in minority deals? And how do they manage foreign exchange rate risk? It is the answers to these questions that transform the skeleton provided in the earlier parts of the book into a living body.

Part One

Private Equity as an Asset Class

2 Organization, value creation, and performance

Chapter Outline head

Private equity has emerged as a separate asset class since the early 1980s. Although investments in private equity funds had been made before, US institutional investors remained severely restricted in committing capital to high risk and illiquid asset classes. This changed in 1979 when the US Department of Labor clarified the "Prudent Man" provision of the Employee Retirement Income Security Act, a decision that significantly broadened the spectrum of investment opportunities for pension funds and allowed private equity funds to absorb a growing share of investors' assets under management (AUM).

What constitutes an asset class remains subject to discussion. While assets should have distinct risk-return properties to qualify as separate classes, in practice asset classes are often defined on the basis of functional attributes. As David Swensen (2009, p. 101) explains, investors often use broad characteristics to identify individual asset classes in their portfolio construction, such as debt versus equity, domestic versus foreign, liquid versus illiquid, and public versus private. On this basis, investments in private equity funds are generally classified as a separate asset, although some investment vehicles closely resemble marketable securities with highly correlated returns. Private equity managers who can lay the strongest claim to managing a separate asset class are generally perceived to be those focusing on value creation through operational improvements, combined with superior governance and financial engineering. In Chapter 4, we will be returning to this issue when we discuss the allocation of capital to private equity in a broader investment portfolio.

Although private equity is often considered as meaning an investment of an equity nature in an unlisted company, this definition is neither completely exhaustive nor

International Investments in Private Equity. DOI: 10.1016/B978-0-12-375082-2.10002-3

does it adequately reflect the complexity of different forms of private equity investments that have emerged over the years. Therefore, this chapter starts by presenting the major segments in private equity and describing their key characteristics. Much of this is already covered in great detail in standard textbooks on private equity (Fraser-Sampson, 2007; Lerner, Hardymon & Leamon, 2009; Mathonet & Meyer, 2007; Metrick, 2007; Meyer & Mathonet, 2005) so that a brief overview will suffice. Turning to the organization of the private equity market, this chapter discusses how capital is intermediated between firms that require financing and investors. Financial intermediation in private equity comes at a significant price, which, as we will see in the following section, has an important impact on investors' net returns. Finally, this chapter examines the menu of options investors may choose from in getting exposure to private equity as an asset class.

2.1   Forms of private equity

Private equity is a form of financing to which companies may turn to for their entire life cycle. In their start-up phase, when firms have little or no access to bank loans, venture capital may be the only source of funding. As companies expand and seek growth capital, private equity plays an important catalyst in this process. In the more mature phases of a company, private equity provides buyout financing to private middle-market firms as well as to larger publicly listed corporations. Some buyout transactions involve "mezzanine financing," a term that refers to unsecured debt sitting between the equity and senior layers of a buyout structure. For firms that are experiencing economic difficulties, the private equity market serves as an important source for turnaround capital aiming to re-establish prosperity. This form is often associated with distressed investing in companies, whose securities are trading at substantial discounts in anticipation of a possible default or whose debt has already defaulted. Although some private equity investors in this asset class seek an influential role in the restructuring process by purchasing a company's debt without necessarily aiming to be involved post-reorganization, others seek outright ownership through distressed debt or equity securities in pursuing a longer term value creation strategy. What all these approaches in distressed investing have in common with other forms of private equity is that they are "active," which distinguishes them from the more passive trading-oriented strategies that the hedge funds are typically pursuing.

For each investment stage different private equity funds are raised by General Partners (GP) who are typically specialized in particular private equity market segments. In addition to funds focusing on different investment stages, capital is also raised for sector-specific investments, for example, in infrastructure, real estate, energy, and forestry. While investments in these areas share several characteristics with private equity investments in portfolio companies, there are also important differences. Most obviously, they all invest in different things. For example, real estate funds invest in various classes of property and sometimes property-related securities, while the investment universe of energy funds ranges from investments in the exploration and production of conventional resources, new technologies to develop unconventional resources (e.g., solar and wind energy and biofuels, often referred to as "clean-tech") to midstream and downstream activities. From a portfolio modeling and asset allocation standpoint, many institutional investors, therefore, do not treat commitments to such funds as part of their private equity exposure. Rather, these investments are usually combined with other investments in infrastructure, real estate, or commodities as part of a broader portfolio of alternative investments. The present book follows this practice, concentrating on private equity investments in companies over their life cycle.

Buyout funds represent by far the largest category, with global commitments during the six-year period from 2004 to 2009 totaling around US$ 1 trillion, or two-thirds of all capital flows to private equity funds (Fig. 2.1). In terms of capital raised, venture capital funds are the second largest category, accounting for about 15 percent of total commitments between 2004 and 2009. Whereas the bulk of venture capital has traditionally been invested in information technology (IT) and life sciences, more recently a growing number of special clean-tech funds have been raised. Although some venture capital funds provide seed financing at the early stages of a company, others invest in firms who are already more developed and require capital to grow. In fact, some funds focus exclusively on providing growth capital, a relatively small market segment.

Buyouts and venture capital transactions are fundamentally different in terms of the stage of their investments (mature vs. young and emerging companies), the industry focus (broad coverage of the economy vs. concentration on technology-driven sectors) and hence the risk profile of deals. Buyout and venture capital transactions are also different with regard to the financing and the control of investments. In a buyout transaction, the private equity firm and the management team purchase or "buy out" all or the vast majority of the shares in the company. As the

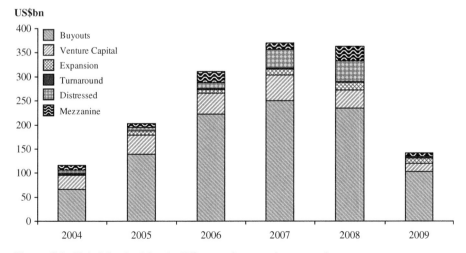

Figure 2.1 Global fund-raising in different private equity categories.
Source: PREQIN.

companies involved in a buyout transaction are more mature and stable, it is common for such transactions to be financed with a significant amount of debt to minimize the amount of equity capital commitments, thereby increasing returns. While in the second half of the 1980s debt typically accounted for about 90 percent of the buyout capital structure, in the most recent buyout cycle between 2004 and 2007 the share of debt averaged only about 65 percent. As a result, debt multiples (of EBITDA) were considerably higher in the 1980s, despite higher purchase prices in the most recent cycle (Fig. 2.2). Although the use of debt in private equity transactions has moderated over time, leverage is still significantly higher than that in publicly listed companies, explaining why transactions involving private equity firms—sometimes labeled as "financial sponsors"—are known as *leveraged* buyouts (LBOs).

While LBOs generally involve a change of control, venture capitalists usually acquire minority stakes. Thus, somewhat confusingly, the term "private equity" is sometimes used only in reference to LBOs, with venture capital being considered as a separate asset class rather than a segment of a broader private equity market (Kaplan & Strömberg, 2009). This book will follow the broader definition.

However, not all buyout transactions involve the acquisition of the majority of a company's stake. In fact, some transactions do not even involve private companies. Sometimes, private equity firms acquire minority stakes in public companies in what is known as a private investment in public equity, or *PIPE*. In such a transaction, publicly traded common shares or some form of preferred stock or convertible security is purchased by private investors, who generally seek contractional protection against dilution and board presentation. PIPE transactions typically gain momentum when debt capital markets are unable to provide sufficient financing for acquirers to obtain a controlling stake in the company and when equity capital markets do not provide alternatives for an issuer.

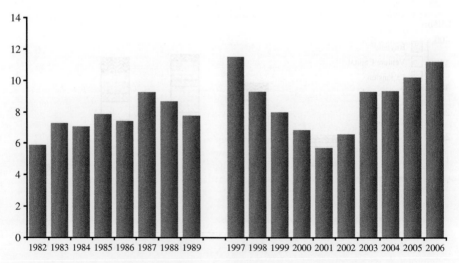

Figure 2.2 Enterprise value to EBITDA in large US public-to-private buyouts.
Source: Kaplan and Strömberg (2009); Guo, Hotchkiss, and Song (2009).

PIPE deals become less attractive when debt and equity capital markets are liquid. In this environment, LBO transactions tend to involve increasingly larger companies, some of which are publicly listed. In these public-to-private transactions, companies are delisted, which allows management to restructure them in a framework that is not subject to the same set of reporting requirements and regulations. Once restructured, private equity firms often seek to take the company public again in what is known as a reverse buyout.

2.2 Capital demand, capital supply, and market organization

The bulk of private equity capital is intermediated through an institutional market,[1] in which private equity funds raise capital to invest in closely held private firms. In raising capital, private equity funds are typically organized as limited partnerships, a structure, which is also common in other high-risk areas such as oil exploration.[2] In a limited partnership, the private equity firm serves as the general partner who raises and manages a fund. Investors in private equity funds are mainly public and corporate pension funds, insurance companies, banks, endowments, and wealthy individuals (Fig. 2.3). Appendix 2.1 provides an overview of principle structures around the world.

As limited partners (LPs) in the fund, investors promise to provide a certain amount of capital. These commitments are firm, and only in exceptional circumstances may GPs and LPs agree on ex post adjustments.[3] Their capital commitments are normally drawn down at the discretion of the GP who makes "capital calls" when needed. Private equity funds normally have a fixed life span of 10 years. The GP usually has five to six years ("the investment period") to invest the capital committed to the fund in companies they normally hold for around four to seven years before

---

[1]Nonorganized markets include the market for angel capital, that is, investments in small, closely held companies by wealthy individuals, and the informal markets, in which unregistered securities are purchased by institutional investors and accredited individuals. For details, see Fenn, Liang, & Prowse (1997).

[2]The first private equity limited partnership was formed in 1958 by Draper, Gaither & Anderson, a venture capital firm based in Palo Alto. The limited partnership sowed the seeds for a substantially larger role of private equity in financial intermediation as it represented the institutional solution to the problems with closed-end funds. Limited partnerships were open only to financially qualified investors, that is, institutions and high net worth individuals who were assumed to be familiar with the investment risks involved in private equity (Kogut, Urso, & Walker, 2007). By contrast, closed-end funds, which were modeled after American Research and Development (ARD), the first venture capital fund established in 1946, were publicly traded. While in principle shares in ARD could be held by any class of investors, in practice they were marketed mostly to retail investors who were often lurked into buying shares by unscrupulous brokers promising immediate profits. Institutional investors showed little interest in what they considered an unproven style of investing with incalculable risks (Gompers & Lerner, 2001, p. 146).

[3]For example, as investment opportunities were perceived to have worsened significantly relative to the size of their funds, in the first half of 2009 TPG gave their investors the option to cut commitments by a certain percentage. As far as TPG's US$ 4.25 billion Asia V fund is concerned, investors are reported to have been allowed to reduce their commitments by up to 10 percent (PEI Asia, June 2009, Issue 31, p. 6).

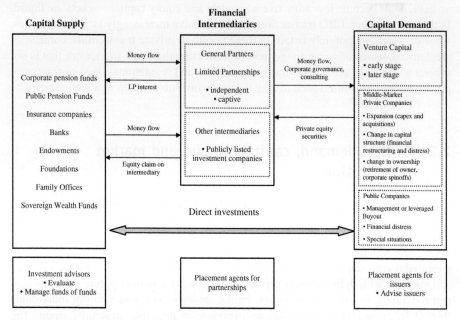

Figure 2.3 The organization of the private equity market.

returning the capital to the investors through "distributions." There is little, if any opportunity for investors to redeem their capital before the end of the fund's lifetime, which makes private equity a highly illiquid asset class. However, to meet investors' need for greater liquidity, a secondary market has emerged over time. The secondary market provides the opportunity for LPs to sell their fund investments to other LPs. This may include already funded investments as well as still unfunded commitments. However, the transfer of investments in private equity funds through a secondary transaction requires the consent of the general partner. As we shall see later, buyers in the secondary market may be motivated by different considerations. Apart from return expectations, the secondary market enables especially new LPs to get access to older vintages, thus providing greater portfolio diversification in terms of the age of the funds invested in.

Private equity funds are blind pools of capital. The limited partnership agreement (LPA) defines the broad investment objectives of the fund in terms of stages, industries, and geographies and includes basic covenants, for example, with regard to the maximum percentage of the fund's capital that can be invested in a single portfolio company and types of securities the fund can invest in. The covenants typically leave considerable investment flexibility for the GP; however, as long as the covenants are adhered to, LPs have only limited control over how the manager deploys the fund's capital. In fact, an overly activist LP runs the risk of being reclassified as a GP and hence losing his limited liability status, according to the laws governing LPAs.

Though there are good reasons to retain a sufficient degree of flexibility, it is important to minimize potential agency conflicts between the fund manager and investors. Efficient governance structures are therefore critical. These include advisory boards, audit and valuation committees as well as special provisions, such as the "key man clause," which allows an LP to suspend or even terminate his contributions in case a key person of the fund's management team departs (for details on corporate governance structures in private equity funds, see Meyer & Mathonet, 2005). Furthermore, the fund manager is generally expected to invest a significant portion of his personal wealth in the fund to discourage excessive risk taking.

Conflicts of interest are particularly pertinent in "captive" funds, which are linked to a bank or other financial institution. Unless the management team is completely independent, there is risk that investment decisions are driven by the objective to maximize profits of the parent organization, which may or may not be fully consistent with the objective to maximize profits for the fund and its investors.

Fund-raising is a time-consuming exercise, and successful GPs normally raise a new fund every three to four years to ensure that there is always at least one fund from which they can make investments. In raising a fund, many GPs make use of placement agents who serve as brokers. In particular, GPs who do not already have an established LP basis often rely on the agents' extensive networks of contacts with investors who seek exposure to private equity. Similarly, some LPs seek advice from specialized investment advisors ("gatekeepers") with regard to their allocation to private equity and the selection of individual funds.

To raise permanent capital, as opposed to having to go through periodic fund-raising cycles, a small number of private equity firms have decided to list special investment vehicles on the stock exchange.[4] Investors typically include institutions such as hedge funds that seek exposure to private equity but are unable or unwilling to make long-term commitments to otherwise illiquid private equity funds. Listed investment vehicles need to be distinguished from the listing of the private equity firm (or the "management company") itself, an issue we return to in Section 2.5.

2.3   Terms and conditions

The LPA also determines the fund's terms and conditions. While the fee structure for private equity funds is often complex and varies considerably, generally speaking GPs are compensated in three different ways (Kaplan & Strömberg, 2009): first, the GP earns an annual management fee that is typically set at approximately 1–2 percent of committed capital during the initial investment period, which lasts for about five years. Thereafter, these payments fall to a percentage of the net asset value (NAV) of investments which the fund holds. Second, the GP earns a share of the profits of the

---

[4]The largest investment vehicle of this kind was, until recently, Kohlberg Kravis Roberts (KKR) Private Equity Investors (KPE). Listing KPE in an initial public offering on the Euronext exchange in Amsterdam in May 2006, KKR raised US$ 5 billion to be invested in KKR's private equity funds. In 2009, KKR agreed to a business combination with KKR Private Equity Investors, which was renamed KKR & Co. (Guernsey) L.P. On July 14, 2010, KKR & Co. (Guernsey) L.P. dissolved, and on July 15, 2010, the common units of KKR & Co. L.P. began trading on the New York Stock Exchange under the symbol "KKR".

fund. Commonly referred to as "carried interest," or just carry, this performance-related fee typically amounts to 20 percent of capital gains, although some funds charge even higher carried interest. While in the United States carry is usually determined on a deal-by-deal basis, in Europe carry is not normally paid out until all LPs' capital has been returned and an internal hurdle rate (usually 8 percent) has been met. Thereafter, normally 100 percent of additional returns go to the GP. This catch-up period ends when the agreed carried interest split is reached, after which point distributions are shared according to the agreed split.[5] Finally, some GPs charge transaction and monitoring fees to the companies they have acquired. These fees are quite opaque as they are taken directly out of the portfolio companies and hence are not easily visible to investors.

Phalippou (2009) presents an interesting example of a representative buyout fund. Under plausible assumptions, he finds that the representative fund's gross internal rate of return is reduced by nearly 40 percent.[6] In his example, management fees, carried interest, and portfolio company fees are nearly the same. This is broadly consistent with a recent empirical study by Metrick and Yasuda (2007) who find that on average about 60 percent of a GP's compensation is due to nonperformance-related management, transaction and monitoring fees.

Although the complexity of private equity funds' fee structures makes fund-to-fund comparisons difficult, two structural observations can be made: First, smaller funds tend to charge higher management fees relative to the capital they raise. As fund sizes grow, management fees as a percent of assets normally decline. However, this reduction is typically smaller than the economies of scale the management of larger funds brings about. Other things being equal, GPs thus have an incentive to raise more capital. Second, the compensation of GPs is relatively inelastic over the cycle. This is particularly true for the performance-related part of a GP's compensation structure. In fact, GPs virtually never use carried interest as a parameter to compete in the fund-raising market, because a reduction below the industry standard of 20 percent is feared to be perceived as a signal of inferior fund management skills. While nonperformance-related management fees appear to be somewhat more flexible, investors have been pushing for greater transparency and alignment of interests in the recent downturn. Their efforts have followed the Private Equity Principles issued by the Institutional Limited Partners' Association (ILPA) (2009), a best practice document, which calls, among other things, for limiting management fees to a GP's normal operating costs; ensuring that transaction and monitoring fees accrue to the benefit of the fund; and subjecting fee and carry calculations to an LP and independent auditor review and certification.

---

[5]Most LPAs include a "claw-back provision," which ensures that managers will not receive a greater share of the fund's distributions than they are entitled to. If the final carried interest due to the GP is lower than what he has actually received, the difference is returned to the investors. Claw-back clauses are relevant in situations where early investments have performed well, while investments at a later stage of the fund have performed relatively poorly.

[6]LPs who are offered coinvestment opportunities for individual investments may reduce their costs significantly, as no fees are charged on coinvestments made alongside the fund. Invitations to coinvest are often limited to the fund's largest and/or most capable investors.

2.4   Value creation and returns

2.4.1   Buyouts

While carried interest and fees determine how profits are distributed between the fund manager and investors in the fund, the more basic question concerns the returns private equity investments generate in the first place. As far as buyouts are concerned, value creation can generally be attributed to three different sets of measures: (i) strategic measures, (ii) operational measures, and (iii) financial measures. While strategic measures generally aim at enhancing EBITDA growth, they often also result in multiple expansions. Such measures include, for example, buy-and-build initiatives, divestments of noncore business units, as well as the development of new products and markets. Operational measures usually focus on improving product quality and sales effectiveness; reducing overhead costs; and optimizing the company's value chain. Financial measures, finally, aim at maximizing capital efficiency and optimizing the company's capital structure. Typically, financial measures—often referred to as financial engineering—entail using significant leverage. Leverage serves multiple functions. While it amplifies gains (as well as losses), debt serves as a powerful disciplining device in the sense that the increased debt burden of the portfolio company forces management to run the firm efficiently to avoid default. Increasing required debt payments reduce free cash flow available to management, which might otherwise be used in value-reducing investments (Jensen, 1986). Furthermore, debt used to finance the buyout generates increased tax benefits (Kaplan, 1989).

In implementing strategic, operational and financial measures, buyout firms put great emphasis on execution and hence on effective governance structures. Specifically, substantial attention is generally paid to management incentives to ensure that their interests are fully aligned (Jensen & Meckling, 1976). This is achieved by giving management teams of portfolio companies a large equity upside through stock and options. That management is also exposed to the downside is ensured by requiring executives to make a meaningful investment in the company. Furthermore, boards of portfolio companies tend to be smaller and meet more frequently, with the private equity investors playing a more active role than is usually the case in public firms of a similar size (Acharya, Hahn, & Kehoe, 2010; Cornelli & Karakas, 2008).

Over time, there has been a shift in emphasis from financial engineering to strategic and operational measures. Although financial engineering skills remain important, most larger private equity firms are increasingly hiring professionals with operating backgrounds and are organized around industries. As Acharya et al. (2010) and Gadiesh & MacArthur (2008) explain, these shifts aim at putting deal teams in a better position to identify cost-cutting potential and possible productivity improvements, introduce management changes and upgrades, and develop the potentially necessary strategic repositioning of the portfolio company.

There is a substantial body of empirical studies on buyout transactions from the 1980s that finds considerable gains in operating performance and increases in firm

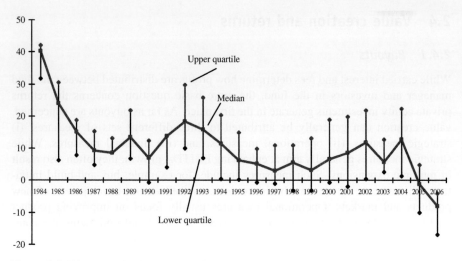

Figure 2.4 US buyout funds: IRRs by vintage year (as of September 30, 2009). *Source*: Thomson VentureXpert.

values or both (for a review, see Kaplan & Strömberg, 2009). This evidence has been interpreted as providing support for the hypothesis that LBOs create value by reducing agency costs through the disciplining effects of leverage and better governance. There is less evidence regarding LBO transactions from the 1990s and the most recent buyout boom. One exception is a study by Guo, Hotchkiss, and Song (2009) who review 192 buyout transactions completed between 1990 and 2006. While the authors find that returns to either pre- or post-buyout capital are positive and significant,[7] their results suggest that gains in operating performance were substantially smaller than documented for deals of the 1980s. This result may seem surprising, given the growing importance private equity firms attach to operational engineering. Clearly, more research is needed to explain this apparent contradiction.

Creating value though leveraged buyouts does not necessarily mean that private equity partnerships represent attractive investments for LPs. First of all, private equity firms often purchase companies in competitive auctions. In public-to-private deals private equity firms generally pay a meaningful premium to public shareholders. As a result, sellers may capture a significant amount of the value the private equity firm creates through financial, governance, and operational engineering. Second, as we have discussed above, GPs receive significant compensation from their limited partners. From the LP's perspective what solely matters, of course, are the fund's distributions net-of-fees and carried interest.

What does the empirical evidence tell us? In Figs 2.4 and 2.5, we show the performance of US and European buyout funds. Compiled by *Thomson VentureXpert* (TVE; formerly Venture Economics) these figures depict the IRRs of the median

---

[7]Guo, Hotchkiss, and Song (2009) calculate median market and risk-adjusted returns to pre- (post-)buyout capital of 72.5 percent and 40.9 percent, respectively.

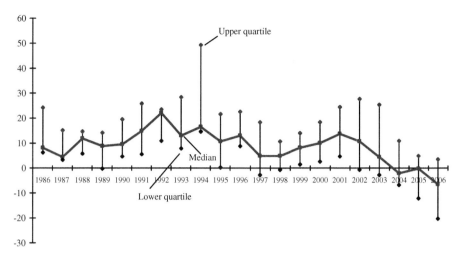

Figure 2.5 European buyout funds: IRRs by vintage year (as of September 30, 2009).
Source: Thomson VentureXpert.

funds as well as the returns of the upper and lower quartiles for the *vintage years* from 1984 (United States) and 1986 (Europe) to 2006, as of September 30, 2009 (Box 2.1 summarizes standard return measures in private equity). Before we interpret this evidence, two health warnings are in order: First, while we have decided to show TVE data as a standard industry benchmark, readers should note that there are alternative yardsticks, whose performance sometimes deviates markedly from TVE. As benchmarks play an important role in helping investors allocate capital to different asset classes and monitor their performance relative to the market, a more detailed assessment of different benchmarks is provided in Chapter 3.

Second, the term "vintage year" refers to the year when a fund is raised, not when the fund begins to deploy its capital by acquiring companies. We choose 2006 as the cutoff year, because a significant share of capital raised by buyout funds after that date had yet to be invested, and those investments the funds had already made by the end of the third quarter of 2009 were to a considerable extent still held at cost. As a result, these vintages are too "young" to be meaningful in terms of generating returns for investors. However, while the cutoff date we choose reduces the well-known *J-curve effect*, it does not eliminate it. This effect describes the typical path of private equity returns: In the first few years private equity funds show negative returns due to capital outflows. Since it takes several years for value to be created, which is mirrored in valuation adjustments, funds normally show positive returns only after a number of years (Mathonet & Meyer, 2005, pp. 12–14). Hence the typical return pattern in private equity that resembles a "J" (or, in the view of some observers, a hockey stick). While GPs report net asset values of their portfolio companies on a quarterly basis, such valuations are necessarily subjective. The final performance of a fund can only be determined once all portfolio companies are fully divested and the capital is returned to the investors. This is not the case for the more recent vintage years shown

---

Box 2.1 Measuring Private Equity Returns

Private equity returns are generally expressed in terms of the *internal rate of return* (IRR). The IRR for a sample of funds is usually calculated per vintage year, which is the compound return for all constituent funds formed during a particular year until a given cutoff point. IRRs are usually reported as a simple as well as a capital-weighted average of the constituent funds. Furthermore, IRRs are calculated for the median, upper quartile and lower quartile funds, which provides important information on the distribution of returns among the funds.

By contrast, *pooled IRRs* are calculated by combining the cash flows of all funds, treating them as one huge fund.

Finally, most sources also report *horizon IRRs* for different periods, usually one, three, five, and ten years. This concept uses the funds' net asset value at the beginning of the period as an initial cash outflow and the residual value at the end of the period as the terminal cash flow. The IRR is calculated using those values plus any cash actually received into or paid by the fund from or to investors in the defined time period (i.e., horizon).

While the IRR is the most common performance indicator, there are a number of other measures, which are widely used in the industry. The *money multiple* (MM) is the simple ratio between the capital returned to the investor and his invested capital. For example, an MM of 2 means that the private equity fund has doubled its capital, however, without saying anything about the investment period. More specifically, the *Distributed to Paid-In* (DPI) is a measure of the cumulative distributions returned to the limited partners as a proportion of the cumulative paid-in capital. Another realization ratio is *Residual Value to Paid-In Capital* (RVPI). Finally, the *Total Value to Paid-In* (TVPI) is the sum of the DPI and the RVPI. The realization measures are generally net-of-fees and carried interest. Although popular, each of them has their own important pitfalls, as discussed in standard textbooks on private equity (e.g., Fraser-Sampson, 2007; Meyer & Mathonet, 2005).

---

in Figs 2.4 and 2.5, which implies that the performance of the funds raised during these years remains subject to change.

With these qualifications in mind, three observations are particularly important:

(1) Vintage year returns vary considerably over time. In part, this cyclicality is driven by macroeconomic factors; in part it is a particular characteristic of the private equity market (Fig. 2.6). The best vintage years have been typically those following an economic recession and a market correction. In these years, capital inflows to private equity funds tend to be comparatively small, limiting the amount of capital fund managers can deploy. Thus, less money is chasing a given number of attractive deals (Diller & Kaserer, 2009; Gompers & Lerner, 2000). Furthermore, purchase prices tend to be low when the economy leaves its cyclical trough, and as economic growth begins to recover, earnings start to improve. At the same time, interest rates still tend to be low during this period, and as risk appetite returns, yield spreads typically narrow, permitting debt refinancings at cheaper cost and dividend payments to investors. Conversely, poor returns have generally been

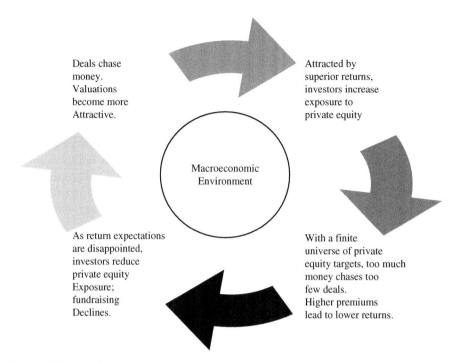

Figure 2.6 The private equity cycle.

achieved in vintage years when capital inflows to private equity funds were strong.[8] Cyclical increases in commitments have usually been accompanied by easy conditions in the debt capital markets, allowing private equity firms to compete aggressively for deals. High acquisition prices and highly leveraged capital structures make LBOs vulnerable to changes in economic and financial market conditions, undermining returns and raising significantly the risk of defaults.[9]

(2) Buyout returns in the United States and Europe are imperfectly correlated. In the 1990s, buyout returns in Europe were higher than those in the United States, which is sometimes attributed to the less mature status in the former at that time, which gave rise to market

[8]Regressing vintage year IRRs on fund inflows expressed as a percent of the stock market capitalization, Kaplan (2009) finds the following relation for the US buyout market: IRR VY = 35% − 25 × capital inflows in the current and the prior year as a percent of the stock market capitalization at the beginning of the year. Given the record fund-raising levels in 2006–2008 (see Fig. 2.1), Kaplan projects significantly negative returns for these vintage years. Whether this will actually be the case will be known only when the funds are fully deployed and their investments completely exited. By the end of 2009, a substantial amount of capital raised in 2007 and 2008 had remained uninvested, propelling the dry powder of buyout funds to US$ 500 billion (see Fig. 6.2) and severely dampening the flow of capital to new partnerships.
[9]For a discussion on the first LBO wave in the United States and the subsequent surge in bankruptcies, see Kaplan and Stein (1993a, 1993b). While early fears (e.g., Boston Consulting Group & IESE, 2008a) about a jump in bankruptcies of portfolio companies acquired during the most recent private equity boom have probably been too pessimistic (Thomas, 2010), debt defaults did increase noticeably in 2009.

imperfections (Fraser-Sampson, 2007). More recently, however, the European market appears to have underperformed relative to US buyout funds.

(3) There are substantial performance differentials among funds. While in good years the tide tends to lift all boats, upper-quartile funds have outperformed their lower-quartile peers by as much as 20 percentage points in certain vintage years. For top-decile funds (which are not reported in Figs 2.4 and 2.5) the performance differentials are considerably larger.

Unfortunately, the return history of private equity outside the United States and Europe is considerably shorter. Figure 2.7 shows vintage year returns for private equity funds in the "rest of the world" raised between 1992 and 2006. Based on data compiled by Private Equity Intelligence (PREQIN), another data vendor, average annual returns of already liquidated private equity funds (i.e., those raised in the 1990s) fluctuated around 10 percent (net-of-fees). However, the "rest of the world" is just too heterogeneous for this regional benchmark to provide any meaningful guidance for investors. Clearly, private equity markets in developed market countries, such as Australia and Japan, show a fundamentally different risk profile compared with investments in emerging market economies, and even within the universe of emerging markets there are profound differences.

Figure 2.8 presents IRRs for emerging markets funds reported by Cambridge Associates (CA). Given the limited number of funds raised in some years, IRRs are shown for four different four-year periods. Unfortunately, there is no breakdown according to the stage of investments of the funds, although it is reasonable to assume that the majority of funds have targeted growth capital transactions.

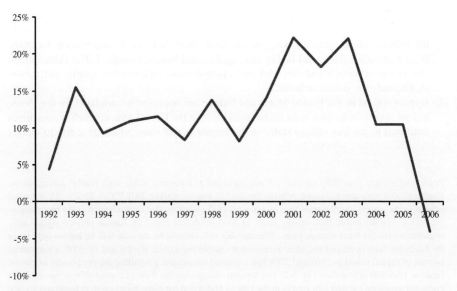

Figure 2.7 Mean vintage year IRRs for all private equity in "the rest of the world", 1992–2006 (as of September 30, 2009).
Source: PREQIN.

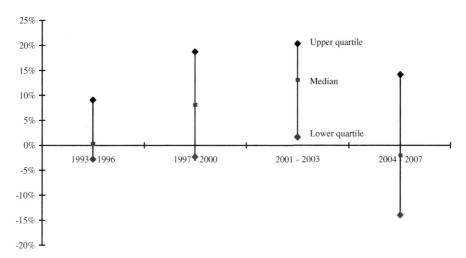

Figure 2.8 Vintage year statistics for emerging market funds (as of September 30, 2008).

In the 1990s, the performance of emerging markets funds has been clearly disappointing, both in absolute terms and relative to the returns an investor would have achieved by committing capital to US and European funds (Leeds & Sunderland, 2003). In fact, even if an investor had been able to put all his capital into top-quartile funds in emerging markets funds, he would have been worse off than investing in the median US and European funds. More recently, however, the performance gap appears to have narrowed. This conjecture is supported when we look at pooled end-to-end returns instead of vintage-year IRRs (more on this in Chapter 3). In fact, Cambridge Associates reports five-year pooled IRRs of emerging market funds (buyout and venture capital funds combined) that exceeded US buyout and venture capital funds by around 1.5 percent and almost 6 percent, respectively, as of September 30, 2009.[10] Although the performance of private equity funds remains subject to change until all investments are exited, the seemingly improved performance of emerging markets funds has presumably been a catalyst for larger capital inflows. In the second part of this book, we shall come back to the recent catch-up process in the emerging economies in the context of a globally integrated private equity market and its implications for portfolio diversification.

The preceding analysis still does not tell us whether buyouts are an attractive asset class for investors. This is a question of private equity's performance relative to other asset classes, with public equity representing the obvious benchmark. In addressing this question, Kaplan and Schoar (2005) examine the performance of

[10]The pooled five-year net IRR for emerging market funds was 12.8 percent, compared with 11.1 percent and 4.9 percent, respectively, for US buyout and venture capital funds. On a one-year basis, Cambridge Associates reports a positive pooled IRR of 0.3 percent for emerging market funds, compared with −8.9 percent and −12.4 percent for US buyout and venture capital funds, respectively, as of September 30, 2009.

individual private equity funds using a data set collected by Thomson Ventur-eXpert. Their sample is restricted to funds raised before 1995 to ensure that it includes only funds that are largely liquidated, given that there is no true market value for fund investments until the investments are exited.[11] There are 169 buyout funds in their data set. For these funds, the authors calculate IRRs using the funds' cash flows as well as the public market equivalent (PME), a measure to compare an investment in a private equity fund to an investment in the public stock market, as benchmarked by the S&P 500. The PME is calculated by investing (or discounting) all cash outflows of the fund at the total return to the S&P 500 and comparing the resulting value to the value of the cash inflows (all net-of-fees) to the fund invested (discounted) using the total return to the S&P 500. The PME has a value of 1 if an investment in a private equity fund achieves exactly the same returns as an investment in the public stock market. It is larger (smaller) than 1, if an investment in a private equity fund outperforms (underperforms) an investment in the public stock market.[12]

Kaplan and Schoar's (2005) results indicate that, net-of-fees, buyout funds have slightly underperformed the public market. On an unweighted basis, the authors calculate a PME of 0.97. If buyout funds are weighted according to their size, their average PMEs are 0.93.

Although compensation structures vary across funds, these results imply that on average buyout funds have outperformed on a gross-of-fees basis, which is consistent with the observation that LBOs have indeed created value through strategic and operational measures as well as financial engineering. Under plausible assumptions about management fees and carried interest, Kaplan and Schoar (2005) explain that gross PMEs would be at least 13 percent higher than the estimated net PMEs. Thus, gross PMEs would be well above 1, both on an equal and size-weighted basis.

Phalippou and Gottschlag (2009) who use a slightly updated version of the Kaplan and Schoar data set, obtain qualitatively similar results. In fact, their findings suggest an even greater degree of underperformance of private equity, net-of-fees, once the data set is corrected for a possible sample selection bias. More specifically, Phalippou and Gottschalg (2009) assume that the market value of nonliquidated mature funds equals zero (complete write-off), whereas Kaplan and Schoar (2005) set the market

---

[11]While the secondary market may reveal true market values before the liquidation of the fund, the market has remained relatively small, and transaction prices are generally not observable.

[12]Using the PME circumvents a common problem with IRRs. This problem lies in the reinvestment hypothesis of the underlying cash flows. In presenting their performance, funds implicitly assume that cash proceeds have been reinvested at the IRR over the entire investment period. For instance, if a fund reports a 40 percent IRR and has returned cash early in its life, it is assumed that the cash proceeds were invested again at a 40 percent annual return. In practice, however, such opportunities are rarely found. If one works with the more realistic assumption that cash proceeds are invested at a fixed rate of return (e.g., the long-term total return of the S&P 500), the average performance of private equity funds drops significantly. Recalculating the performance of the top 25 percent of 1184 private equity funds, Phalippou and Gottschalg (2009) find a decline in their average IRR from 35.32 percent to 18.56 percent.

value of non-liquidated mature funds equal to the reported final NAV, effectively treating the final NAVs as a final cash flow.[13]

From the Kaplan and Schoar (2005) and Phalippou and Gottschalg (2009) studies, we still do not know how buyout funds generate their returns. Importantly, we do not know the extent to which the funds' measured performance is attributable to leverage as opposed to other factors. Leverage amplifies returns, but it also amplifies risk, and in order to compare private and public equity returns one would need to estimate the performance of buyouts at a level of leverage, which is comparable to that of publicly traded companies in the same industries.[14] However, such a comparison requires very detailed information about the capital structure in individual buyout transactions, which is normally not available. Nevertheless, even without this deal-specific information, the substantially greater reliance on leverage in private equity (McKinsey Global Institute, 2008, p. 133) reinforces Kaplan and Schoar's (2005) and Phalippou and Gottschalg's (2009) conclusion that the average/median buyout fund underperforms public equity.[15]

2.4.2 Venture capital

In contrast to buyout transactions, venture capital investments are generally unleveraged. In examining how value is created in venture capital deals, academic studies have focused on a wide range of issues, including agency conflicts and the design of contracts (Kaplan & Strömberg, 2004); the involvement of venture capitalists in their portfolio companies (Bottazzi, Da Rin, & Hellmann, 2008); and the importance of human versus nonhuman assets of VC-backed firms (Kaplan, Sensoy, & Strömberg, 2009). While these studies have been based on relatively small samples of VC-backed firms, other research has focused on the performance

---

[13]More positive results are obtained, for example, by Ljungqvist and Richardson (2003), who use cash flow data from a large data set of private equity funds raised between 1981 and 2001. Their data set, which was made available to them by an unidentified LP, contains 73 partnerships classified as mature funds (1981–1993). Of these, one quarter are venture capital funds, the rest are buyout funds and a small number of generalist private equity and mezzanine funds. Net-of-fees, the mature funds are calculated to have achieved an average IRR of 19.81 percent, compared with public market returns of 14.1 percent under an identical time schedule of cash outflows.

[14]In principle, investors should not care about the cyclical variation in the availability of debt for private equity. In economic slumps it becomes increasingly difficult to obtain leveraged loans or to issue high-yield bonds. As a result, expected returns on any given deal decrease. But so does the risk to them. In practice, however, GPs tend to take a different view, as highlighted by Axelson, Strömberg, and Weisbach (2009) in a fictitious conversation between a practitioner and an academic: "We don't think that way at our firm. Our philosophy is to lever our deals as much as we can, to give the highest returns to our limited partners."

[15]While LBO debt has on average accounted for around two-thirds of the capital structure in the most recent buyout cycle, in S&P 500 companies debt represents only about 20 percent to 25 percent. In adjusting returns for leverage risk, Phalippou and Gottschalg (2009) assume that each portfolio company has the same unlevered beta as the average publicly traded stock in the industry. Further, they assume that the leverage of portfolio companies decreases over the investment life to the leverage that prevails in the industry at exit. Under these assumptions, they show that risk-adjusted returns for buyout funds drop by almost a quarter compared with "raw" returns.

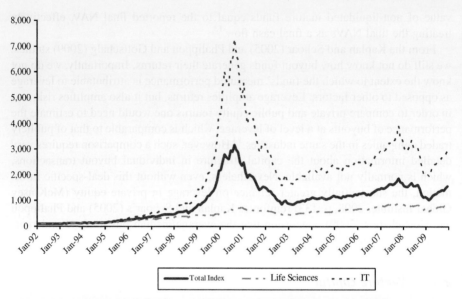

Figure 2.9 Sand Hill Econometrics venture capital index (January 1992 = 100).
Source: Sand Hill Econometrics.

of VC investments using substantially larger data sets. One frequently cited study is
Cochrane (2005) whose data set is a subset of that used by Hwang, Quigley, and
Woodward (2005). The latter is particularly interesting, as it represents the basis
for a venture capital return index, which is constructed bottom-up and calculated
monthly for the US market by Sand Hill Econometrics (SHE).[16] During the 20-
year period from its inception in December 1988 to December 2008, the SHE
index has increased by more than 1000 percent, implying a compound annual
growth rate of 12.3 percent. However, much of the SHE index's performance
happened during the bubble period between 1997 and 2000, when the index rose
by 340 percent (Fig. 2.9). More recently, gross VC returns have been considerably
more moderate. During the six-year period between the trough in December 2002
and December 2008, the index gained only 17 percent, implying a compound
annual growth rate of only 2.6 percent.

In Fig. 2.10, we take a top-down perspective and look at the performance of US
venture capital funds per vintage year. The best funds were clearly those raised in the
mid-1990s. With many of their portfolio companies exited between 1998 and the first
half of 2000 at highly inflated prices, these funds are essentially responsible for the

---

[16]The SHE index calculates its monthly returns bottom-up, gross-of-fees. The index is available only for
the US venture capital market, combining data from VentureOne and Thomson VentureXpert, other
industry sources and Sand Hill Econometrics proprietary database. The index tracks over 20,000 portfolio companies and more than 70,000 financing rounds. In 2010, Sand Hill Econometrics licensed its
methods for building a VC index to Dow Jones. The former SHE index is now published by Dow Jones
as the Dow Jones Index of Venture Capital and built with data from Dow Jones' Venture Source.

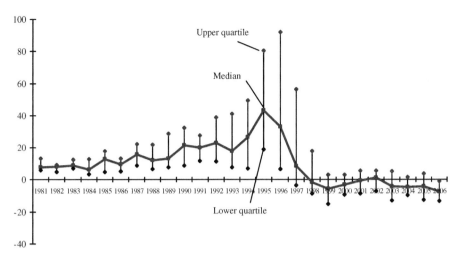

Figure 2.10 US venture capital funds: IRRs by vintage year (as of September 30, 2009).
Source: Cambridge Associates.

performance peak shown in Fig. 2.9. But when we compare the gross-of-fee SHE index with quarterly end-to-end, net-of-fee fund returns something strange happens. Net-of-fee fund returns are higher than gross-of-fee returns for extended periods of time (Fig. 2.11), contrary to what logic would dictate! For instance, this is the case during the bubble years 1999 and 2000, and it is also the case post-2004. Although there is no clear solution to this puzzle, one explanation could be that the net-of-fees fund returns are subject to a sample selection bias.

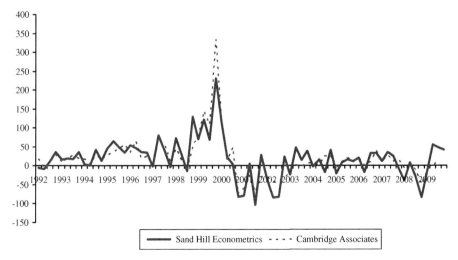

Figure 2.11 Comparing venture capital returns, net-of-fees and gross-of-fees (quarterly returns, annualized, Q1 1992–Q3 2009, in %).
Source: Cambridge Associates; Sand Hill Econometrics.

How do venture capital returns, net-of-fees, compare to the public market? Based on the 577 US venture capital funds in their data set, Kaplan and Schoar (2005) calculate an equally weighted PME of 0.96. When they weigh funds according to their size, they obtain a PME of 1.21. With larger VC funds on average outperforming smaller funds, they find that the VC funds in their sample actually outperformed the public market, even on a net-of-fees basis. However, we need to remind ourselves that the Kaplan–Schoar data set includes only funds raised before 1995. As the SHE index indicates, gross-of-fees venture capital returns appear to have been considerably lower in the post-bubble period. In fact, during this period they have been lower than the total returns an investor would have received by investing in the S&P 500 or NASDAQ, implying an even greater underperformance net-of-fees.

2.4.3 Performance differences, persistence, and selection skills

Our results so far can be summarized as follows: While gross-of-fees buyout funds have outperformed the public market, there is considerable evidence that net-of-fees the average investor would have been better off by investing his capital in public equity. As far as venture capital funds are concerned, academic research finds that private equity investments did achieve superior returns compared with the public market. However, this evidence refers to funds raised before 1995, whereas more recently formed venture capital partnerships appear on average to have under-performed the public market. These findings provide an important puzzle: why do investors commit capital to private equity funds if, net-of-fees, private equity funds on average underperform the public market? This question is all the more relevant as investments in private equity funds are essentially illiquid, requiring a premium for investors to tie in their capital for around 10 years.

One possible explanation could be that lower average private equity returns reflect a lower level of systematic or market risk. Unfortunately, there is little empirical support for this hypothesis. Few studies have made an attempt to correct private equity returns for risk, and those studies that do exist differ significantly in terms of the betas they find. We will return to this issue in Chapter 4 in the context of private equity as an asset class in a broader portfolio.

The more plausible explanation lies in the upside risk private equity funds provide. Investors do not consider themselves as the "average" investor. When making investment decisions, LPs do not target average or median returns. Rather, they aim at committing capital to funds that achieve returns above the median, ideally funds that fall into the upper quartile. So how would have an investor done if he had managed to put all his capital in the 75th percentile fund? As far as buyouts are concerned, Kaplan and Schoar (2005) report PMEs for buyout funds at the 75th percentile of 1.12 and 1.03, depending on whether the funds are equally or seize-weighted. For VC funds, the respective PMEs are 1.13 and 1.40. These results imply that the LP would have indeed been better off investing in private equity, even considering the hefty fees private equity funds charge.

While individual investors may target upper-quartile funds, collectively this target is inconsistent and substantial amounts of capital will inevitably end up in funds that underperform the public market. For the 25th percentile buyout fund, Kaplan and Schoar (2005) calculate net PMEs of 0.62 and 0.72, depending on whether funds are equally or size-weighted. Comparable estimates for VC funds are even lower, with PMEs of 0.43 and 0.55, respectively, for the 25th percentile. This greater dispersion of VC returns across funds mirrors a significantly more skewed distribution of returns among portfolio companies within individual funds. Compared with buyout funds, there tend to be considerably more write-downs and write-offs of portfolio companies. What distinguishes the outperforming VC funds is not so much that they have fewer unsuccessful deals than their competitors. Rather, the substantial outperformance of a small number of funds can generally be attributed to a few exceptionally successful deals, often called "home runs" or "grand slams," achieving returns of 10 times the invested capital and sometimes even (substantially) more.

These results suggest that fund selection is critical. One guiding principle LPs typically use is a GP's track record. Indeed, the empirical evidence appears to support this view. Several industry studies suggest that private equity returns are persistent. For example, examining the performance of 3400 funds managed by 1159 private equity firms, a recent study by McKinsey (2007, p. 140) finds that a GP managing a top-quartile fund has a 43 percent probability of seeing his next fund in the top quartile as well (McKinsey Global Institute, 2007, p. 140). This compares with a 25 percent probability if the distribution of returns across GPs were perfectly random and the track record of individual fund managers were completely irrelevant. By contrast, a manager of a fund in the lowest quartile has only a 16 percent probability that his next fund is in the top quartile. That his successor fund is again in the lowest quartile has a 35 percent probability. Importantly, according to a recent study by Boston Consulting Group & IESE (2008b), the persistence of returns in private equity is found to be considerably higher than that in other asset classes.

In explaining the apparent persistence of returns, these studies point to the importance of experience in managing a private equity fund. As fund managers become more experienced, the performance of their funds improves, which, in turn, allows them to raise more capital. In fact, empirically we observe that the fund-raising market has become considerably more concentrated over the past few decades (Cornelius, Langelaar, & van Rossum, 2007). In the last cycle, a small group of private equity firms has raised double-digit billion dollar buyout funds, a multiple of their predecessor funds (Table 2.1). For example, Blackstone's Capital Partners V Fund, the world's largest fund to date, closed at almost US$ 22 billion in 2007. Four fund generations, or nearly two decades ago, Blackstone's first Capital Partners Fund closed at US$ 800 million.

Additional support for the persistence hypothesis has come from academic research by Kaplan and Schoar (2005), who control for investment overlap (the current and previous fund of a particular GP have some investments in common) and time overlap (the time periods overlap across funds). At the same time, however, there appear to be significant diseconomies of scale in managing private equity funds (Lopez de Silanes, Phalippou, & Gottschalg, 2009). As funds become larger and manage more and larger (more valuable) portfolio companies, the funds' performance tends to deteriorate. In regression analysis, the impact of the scale measures (number of investments held in

Table 2.1 Growth in fund sizes of today's largest fund managers

	Last fund raised in	Most recent main fund size ($bn or €bn)	Time since last fund (years)	Δ_{-1} (%)	Time since last fund (years)	Δ_{-2} (%)	Time since last fund (years)	Δ_{-3} (%)	Time since last fund (years)	Δ_{-4} (%)
US ($bn)										
Blackstone	2007	21.7	4	236	5	71	4	197	6	59
GS CP	2007	20.3	2	139	5	62	2	89	3	59
TPG	2008	17.8	2	19	3	183	4	55	2	37
KKR	2007	17.6	6	193	5	0	3	209	6	−38
Apollo	2008	14.8	2	45	6	215	2	−11	3	140
Carlyle	2008	13.7	3	173	5	103	4	193	...	...
Providence	2007	12.1	3	181	5	54	2	193	2	158
Bain Capital	2008	10.0	2	25	2	129	4	40	...	...
Silver Lake	2007	9.3	4	90	5	64	...	...	...	...
Hellman & Friedman	2009	8.0	3	135	4	59	6	47	3	82
Europe (€bn)										
Apax	2008	11.2	3	160	4	−2	2	144	...	...
CVC Europe	2008	10.8	3	11	4	51	3	19	2	296
Permira	2006	9.6	2	88	4	47	3	289	...	...
Cinven	2006	6.5	5	49	3	81	2	470	...	...
KKR Europe	2009	6.0	5	33	5	50	...	...	...	...
Carlyle Europe	2007	5.3	4	194	6	80	...	...	...	...

Source: PREQIN; private equity firms' Web sites

parallel and value of investments held in parallel) is large and robust with regard to investment characteristics, firm characteristics, various fixed effects (e.g., firm, fund, country, industry, and time), and other factors explaining performance. For LPs, these findings have important implications for their due diligence approach. Instead of being primarily guided by a GP's past performance, investors are well advised to take into consideration the growth of the funds a GP raises.

Interestingly, some institutions are found to be better than others in selecting private equity funds. In fact, as much as individual private equity funds differ in their performance, as much do the portfolio returns differ that institutional investors realize from private equity investments. This is by no means obvious, given that large institutional investors sometimes hold hundreds of private equity funds in their portfolios, some of which may be in the upper quartile while others are under-performing the median fund. This suggests that something more systematic is going on here. Using detailed data from fund investors, Lerner, Schoar, and Wongsunwai (2007) show that there is enormous heterogeneity in the performance of funds in which different classes of institutions invest. Overall, funds selected by endowments tend to outperform by a wide margin. Public pension funds are found to be the second best class of investors in private equity funds, followed by insurance companies and corporate pension funds. By comparison, funds that are selected by banks lag sharply. In interpreting their results, the authors attribute the observed performance differences to differing degrees of sophistication across different classes of LPs but also point to potential differences in investment objectives. For example, this might be the case for banks where the cross-selling of services to portfolio companies of a fund could justify accepting a lower return on the initial LP investment.

However, two important caveats are in order. First of all, the empirical evidence presented by Lerner et al. (2007) refers to the period before the recent economic and financial crisis that hit many endowments particularly hard. Future research will show whether their findings remain valid post-crisis. Second, endowments' superior selection skills are entirely driven by venture capital funds. Importantly, Lerner et al. show that their results are not primarily due to endowments' greater access to established funds, because they also hold for young or under-subscribed funds. As far as buyout funds are concerned, however, public pension funds are found to be as good as endowments, leaving other institutional investors far behind.

2.5   Getting exposure to private equity

The default option for investors seeking exposure to private equity is to commit capital to newly raised, or primary, funds, which explains why our preceding discussion has concentrated on the primary market. However, there may be important reasons for investors to pursue alternative routes into the asset class.

Gaining access to private equity funds, particularly the top performing ones, may be an issue for some investors. This applies in particular to some US venture capital funds, sometimes called the "Golden Circle" (Fraser-Sampson, 2007, p. 160), which tend to be notoriously over-subscribed. Their investor base is typically dominated by smaller endowments and foundations, and new clients are rarely accepted. To the extent that large institutional investors have access to these funds, their commitments are usually extremely small relative to their overall private equity program. Although the "Golden Circle" firms have an outstanding track record, the strict access limitations imply that their returns do not really move the needle for large investors, an issue we return to in the next chapter.

However, access restrictions are not confined to the "Golden Circle." Prior to the recent market correction, many institutional investors increased their target allocation to private equity capital, while others who had no exposure hitherto decided to enter the asset class. In mid-2009, Private Equity Intelligence's database included 5415 LPs worldwide (Table 2.2), compared with just 3195 organizations in 2006. Although part of this huge increase is due to the improved statistical coverage of the private equity investor base, it helps to explain why the push of institutional capital was so great that a significant number of funds, including some of the largest funds, were unable or unwilling to accommodate fully their investors' target allocations.

Access restrictions to individual funds are one reason to seek alternative routes. The lack of experience is another. Constructing a robust private equity portfolio requires considerable market knowledge and expertise, and many new investors hope to accelerate their learning process by outsourcing the management of their private equity investments to a specialist. This can be done via a dedicated account or by committing capital to a pool of assets with other investors. As regards the latter, the universe investors can choose from is large. Worldwide, there are more than 500 funds of funds. Between 2004 and 2009, funds of funds accounted for around 8 percent of the capital committed to private equity funds.

Table 2.2 Limited partners in private equity funds (as of June 2009)

	Western Europe	North America	Rest of the World	Total
Public Pension Funds	142	335	55	532
Corporate Pension Funds	283	269	153	705
Insurance Companies	129	85	106	320
Corporate Investors	75	109	136	320
Banks/Investment Banks	216	109	251	576
Investment Companies/Asset Managers/Trusts	276	223	217	716
Endowments	32	372	15	419
Family Office/Foundation	61	531	30	622
Fund of Funds Manager	198	196	132	526
Secondary Fund of Funds Manager	11	18	8	37
Government Agencies	27	32	64	123
Sovereign Wealth Funds	2	7	58	67
Other	115	128	209	452
Total	1567	2414	1434	5415

Source: PREQIN Database

However, two issues need to be considered: First, funds of funds are often set up as limited partnerships, and commitments to funds of funds add an additional layer of management fees and carried interest. Second, as David Swensen of the Yale Endowment argued in an interview with the *Wall Street Journal* (13 January 2009), "(if) an investor can't make an intelligent decision about picking managers, how can he make an intelligent decision about picking a fund-of-funds manager...?" A similar argument applies to consultants, of course, who are hired by inexperienced investors. In the same interview, Swenson goes on by arguing that "...consultants make money by giving advice to as many people as possible. But you outperform by finding inefficiencies most of the market has not yet uncovered. So consultants ultimately end up doing a disservice to investors..."

Second, experienced investors with a sufficiently large private equity program may seek to enhance their exposure to the asset class through coinvestments alongside private equity funds they commit to. While coinvestments are rarely subject to the typical compensation structures in limited partnerships and thus represent a way to reduce costs of the investor's private equity program, this route is often limited to the largest investors in a fund. Furthermore, coinvesting in private equity transactions requires deal-specific due diligence skills that are fundamentally different from those required in the fund selection process. Moreover, coinvestments are concentrated bets on individual companies in specific sectors, requiring enhanced risk management skills at the portfolio level.

A third avenue into private equity is the secondary market. Unlike commitments to primary funds, buying in the secondary market is not investing in a blind pool of capital. An exception is so-called early secondaries, sometimes also called purchased primaries, where the buyer purchases commitments to private equity funds that have been raised only recently. A substantial part of these commitments are still unfunded—hence the name of this sub-segment of the market, which has gained in prominence in the wake of the recent market correction as a considerable number of investors faced mounting liquidity issues.

Apart from early secondaries, the market norm, however, is that the funds that the seller has invested in have typically already deployed a significant percentage of their capital. Thus, the potential buyer is able to examine the value of the underlying portfolio companies relative to the asking price. In this process, information asymmetries play a critical role. Typically, the seller knows much more about the quality of his portfolio than the potential buyer, an issue which has been intensively discussed by economists ever since Akerlof's (1970) influential paper on the market for lemons.[17] Potential buyers who have made commitments to the same funds

---

[17] Akerlof was awarded the Nobel Memorial Prize in Economics in 2001 for his research on asymmetric information, together with Michael Spence and Joseph Stiglitz. In his original paper, Akerlof uses the market for used cars as an example of the problem of quality uncertainty. There are good used cars and defective used cars ("lemons"). Since the buyer of a car does not know beforehand whether it is a good car or a lemon, his best guess is that the car is of average quality. Thus, he will be willing to pay for it only the price of a car of known average quality. This means that the owner of a good used car will be unable to get a high enough price to make selling that car worthwhile. As a result, owners of good cars will not place their cars on the used car market.

a seller wants to sell are in a much better position to evaluate the quality of the portfolio compared with other investors. Thus, on the buyer's side, the secondary market is dominated by large LPs whose portfolios allow them to exploit their informational advantages. Investors with relatively smaller private equity portfolios who lack the informational advantages of large LPs have the option to commit capital to a specialized fund of funds, which, of course, raises the same issues as we discussed in the context of primary fund of funds managers.

There are different reasons for LPs to pursue the secondary route (Meyer & Mathonet, 2005). First of all, LPs are attracted by the returns secondary transactions may offer. Excess returns in the secondary market are a function of the discount the buyer is able to get, which in turn, is a function of the overall business and private equity cycle. For example, in downcycles investors are more likely to sell parts of their private equity portfolios because of liquidity needs that opens up opportunities for potential buyers with the ability to assess the quality of the underlying assets. Furthermore, a secondary buyer gets his investment back considerably faster. Typically, a secondary acquisition of a 4-year old fund reduces the time to break even to around 3 years, thus mitigating the well-known J-curve effect of an LP's primary portfolio. Finally, secondary acquisitions may be used as a portfolio diversification tool by providing access to past vintages.

Sometimes, transactions in the secondary market are "stapled" in the sense that the investor (i) acquires an interest in an existing fund in combination with (ii) a blind-pool commitment to a fund managed by the same GP that is aimed at making new investments. Through a stapled transaction the secondary investor thus becomes an LP in an existing pool of assets as well as an investor in a new fund (Moerel, 2008).

Between 2001 and 2008, the secondary market has expanded 10-fold, with the volume of transactions estimated to have increased to US$ 20 billion (Fig. 2.12). In part, this substantial growth reflects the rapid growth in the primary market, with a delay of 2–3 years. However, it also mirrors the emerging role of the secondary market as an instrument to help LPs manage their liquidity needs and design robust private equity portfolios. It is estimated that on average around 5–7 percent of fund interests trade on the secondary market (Fig. 2.13). Efforts are intensifying to increase market transparency by creating web-based information services and networks of potential sellers and buyers, and some even anticipate online exchanges for secondary private equity interests in the next few years. Although the secondary market is unlikely to fundamentally alter the liquidity characteristics of private equity, it does extend the tool set for managing private equity portfolios.

Fourth, some institutional investors have chosen to buy stakes in the management company of a private equity firm. Institutional investors who have been particularly active in this field are the Sovereign Wealth Funds (SWFs). Important examples include China Investment Corporation's (CIC) decision to take a US$ 3 billion nonvoting minority stake (9.4 percent) in Blackstone's management group, prior to Blackstone's IPO in mid-June 2007;[18] Mubadala's investment in The Carlyle Group (7.5 percent valued at US$ 1.35 billion) in September 2007; and Abu Dhabi

---

[18]In October 2008, CIC raised its stake to 12.5 percent.

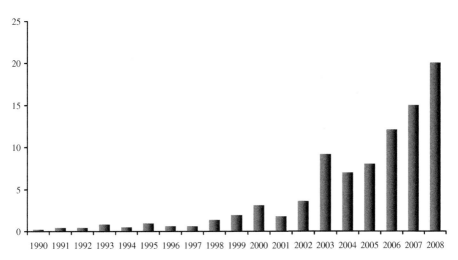

Figure 2.12 Transactions in the global secondary market (US$ bn).
Source: Lexington Partners, UBS.

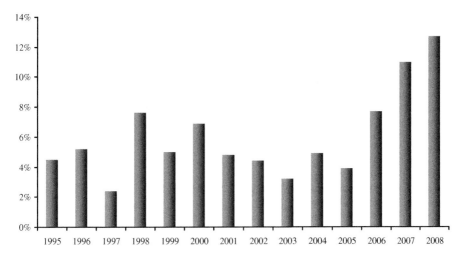

Figure 2.13 Percentage of fund interests that trade on the secondary market.
Source: StepStone Group LLC (June 2009).

Investment Authority's (ADIA) investment in Apollo Management in November 2007. However, investments of this kind are not confined to SWFs. For example, CalPERS, America's largest pension fund, holds significant stakes in Apollo Global Management, Silver Lake Partners, and The Carlyle Group.

There are various reasons for investors to seek exposure to private equity through direct investments in private equity firms, a route that is typically open only to large investors. To begin with, direct investment may enhance key relationship benefits, such as preferred fund allocations, coinvestments as well as secondary opportunities. Furthermore, investors may gain additional insights in the private equity firm's investment strategies, allowing them to undertake a more detailed bottom-up valuation of the GP. Moreover, investors may receive a predictable income stream from management fees and other nonperformance-related fees. Further, as many large GPs are also active in other alternative asset classes, investors may gain access to diversified income streams across a variety of alternative asset classes, investment strategies, vintages and geographies, and smoother cash return patterns through annual dividend distributions. Finally, investors may see potential for gain from the eventual IPO of the management company.

However, investing in the management company of a GP brings about important challenges as well. These lie in particular in potential conflicts of interest. Traditional incentive structures benefiting LPs are weakened by the increased focus on management fees and "indirect" stock-based incentives instead of carried interest. Further, there are potentially opposite interests with regard to hurdle rates, fee levels, fund sizes, and timing of new fund raises/exits. Moreover, re-up decisions may be distorted if an LP holds a significant share in the private equity firm. Finally, investments in management companies tend to be large, which increases an investor's exposure to a particular GP, his underlying assets, and the GP's investment strategy.

For reasons of completeness, we finally refer to investments in publicly listed private equity firms, a route that is also open to retail investors. In this context, a distinction must be made between (i) investments in publicly listed vehicles giving investors direct exposure to the underlying portfolio companies and (b) investments in the management company of private equity funds. Investments in publicly listed vehicles are fundamentally different from commitments to private equity funds under limited partnerships we have focused on in this chapter. In contrast to commitments to private equity funds, which are typically priced on a quarterly basis, listed private equities are substantially more liquid and can be traded on an intra-day basis. Private equity funds express their returns as internal rates of returns, which are not generally comparable to time-weighted returns.

There are about 100 listed private equity businesses trading on developed market exchanges, the largest ones being The Blackstone Group (Ticker: BX), Kohlberg Kravis Roberts & Co (KKR), 3i Group (III), and the Fortress Investment Group LLC (FIG). Some of them are not just private equity managers, however, but have mutated over time into alternative asset managers. Publicly listed private equity firms are tracked by different benchmarks, such as the LPX index (Fig. 2.14) and the S&P Listed Private Equity Index. The market capitalization of the LPX index was about EUR 35 billion as of March 31, 2010.

2.6 Summary and conclusions

This chapter has provided a general overview of the organized private equity market, its market segments, the performance of buyout and venture capital funds, and the different avenues through which institutional investors can get access to the asset

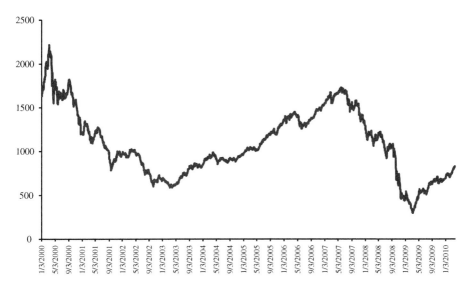

Figure 2.14 LPX 50 total return index of publicly listed private equity, January 3, 2000–March 31, 2010.
Source: Bloomberg.

class. As an introduction to the chapters that follow, none of these topics have been covered exhaustively, and readers interested in a deeper understanding of the issues discussed here are referred to the rapidly growing body of textbooks and academic papers cited in the preceding presentation. However, the following points should be regarded as important takeaways:

- Private equity is a challenging asset class that requires particular investment skills. Investing in private equity is based on long-standing relationships between limited partners and the general partner managing a private equity fund. Given that investors cannot easily enter and exit the market, investing in private equity requires a long-term commitment to the asset class.
- Private equity is a highly illiquid asset class. Notwithstanding the emergence of a secondary market, investors essentially commit capital for the life span of the fund, which is normally a minimum of 10 years.
- Private equity is a cyclical industry thanks to the supply–demand dynamics of the market, which can be amplified by macroeconomic shocks.
- Private equity is an expensive asset class. Fees and carried interest going to the fund manager take away a significant part of the value creation. Fees and carried interest have been largely immune to private equity cycles.
- Private equity is found to achieve returns that are comparable with public equity. Once we factor in that private equity is essentially illiquid and riskier due to the significant amount of leverage in buyouts, on average private equity is likely to underperform public markets. So why bother? The answer lies in the significant performance differences across private equity funds. To the extent that investors are able to select the top-performing funds, they may enjoy returns exceeding public equity by a considerable margin.
- There are different ways to invest in private equity. While commitments to funds in the primary markets remain the standard option, coinvestments, investments in the secondary

market, direct investments in the management companies of GPs, and investments in listed private equity provide alternatives in constructing a private equity portfolio.

Whatever the avenue is through which investors seek exposure to private equity, their investments should not be seen in isolation. Rather, investing in private equity should be considered from the standpoint of constructing a diversified portfolio, the issue we turn to in Chapter 3.

Appendix 2.1: Private equity fund structures around the world[19]

1. Main Markets
   a. United States
      The most common structure for domestic private equity funds is a limited partnership under the law of the state of Delaware. A Delaware Limited Partnership is a separate legal entity that continues as such until it is dissolved and winds up its affairs pursuant to the partnership agreement. Typically, this is the case after 10 years. Limited Partnerships organized in Delaware are not generally required to register with any regulatory authority. However, if the fund, or its promoter, maintains an office in a state other than Delaware, the fund, or its promoter, may be subject to the regulatory requirements of that state. The management company of the fund is normally organized as a separate entity, which may be subject to registration as an investment advisor.
   b. United Kingdom
      Funds organized as limited partnerships must be registered in England under the Limited Partnerships Act 1907.[20] The limited partnership must have a general partner with a principal place of business in England. The liability of the limited partners is limited to the amount of capital in the partnership as long as they do not take part in its management. While the English Limited Partnership is the most common structure in the United Kingdom for private equity funds, some vehicles are organized as investment trusts, which invest in securities and are quoted on the London Stock Exchange PLC. A variation of the investment trust is the venture capital trust, a form that provides tax-free income and capital gains to individual investors but is restricted with regard to the amounts and types of company in which a venture capital trust can invest.
2. Other Mature Markets
   a. Canada (Quebec)
      Private equity and venture capital funds are organized as limited partnerships, which are generally aimed at investors meeting the regulatory definition of accredited investors. Capital is normally raised through confidential offering memorandums. However, private equity funds may also choose to raise capital from retail investors, in which case a prospectus must be filed. In such cases, funds often register their securities on a public exchange, a step that subjects them to stock exchange supervision and securities regulation and hence public disclosure.

[19]This appendix is based on information collected by the International Organization of Securities Commissions (2009) and by the European Private Equity and Venture Capital Association (2006).
[20]For a detailed discussion of the legal framework for private equity funds under the Limited Partnerships Act, see Financial Services Authority (2006).

A less common form are labor-sponsored or development capital investment funds, which are designed for retail investors, providing them with additional tax benefits. Such funds are subject to their own individual legislation.

b. France

There are two common fund structures. While the Fonds Commun de Placement à Risques (FCPR) is defined by law as a joint ownership of securities, it itself is not a separate legal entity and hence does not have the legal capacity to enter into contracts. This right falls exclusively to the Management Company, which must have its registered office in France and must be authorized by the Authorité des Marchés Financiers (AMF). In contrast to the custodian (dépositaire) in the fund, the Management Company has sole responsibility of the management of the FCPR, which includes all decisions to buy and sell company shares. As a specific form of French collective investment schemes, FCPRs are eligible to certain tax advantages, which, however, accrue only to natural persons. There are various subtypes of FCPRs. While Fonds Commun de Placement dans l'Innovation (FCPI) specialize in the financing of innovating, nonlisted companies, Fonds d'Investissement de Proximité focus on investments in a specific region. While some FCPRs are open for retail investors, two types may be offered to qualified investors only and hence are exempt from the AMF authorization requirement, the FCPR allégés and FCPR contractuels.

Alternatively, private equity funds may be formed as a Société de Capital Risque (SCR). Unlike in FCPRs, there is no management company. Instead, SCRs are managed by a board of directors or by one or two managers. All investors are eligible to subscribe in an SCR, including individuals. Unit holders may qualify for tax benefits, provided that the SCR's sole purpose is to invest in a portfolio of investments. SCRs may be formed as a Société par Actions (SA), a Société en Commandite par Actions (SCA), or a Société par Actions Simplifée (SAS).

c. Germany

The Limited Liability Company (Gesellschaft mit beschränkter Haftung, GmbH) and the Limited Partnership (Kommanditgesellschaft, KG) with a GmbH as the sole general partner (GmbH & Co Kommanditgesellschaft, GmbH &Co. KG) are the most common structures today. Shareholders in the GmbH, whose liability is limited to the amount of their respective subscriptions, may be partnerships, corporations, or individuals. KGs have a general partner (Komplementär) and one or more limited partners (Kommanditisten), whose liability is limited to the amount of their respective capital subscriptions. Funds are generally set up as closed-end funds.

d. Italy

Private equity activity is usually based on closed-end funds (fondo chiusu). Funds are managed by a management company (Società di Gestione del Risparmio), which must be registered and authorized by the Bank of Italy. Bylaws regulating the funds have to be approved by the Bank of Italy, too. Investments in a fund are usually reserved to qualified investors. Assets of the fund are legally distinct from the management company and the investors. Thus, creditors of the SGR cannot make claims against the fund, and creditors of the investors of the fund can only make claims with regard to the shares of the specific investors.

e. Japan

Many Japanese fund structures are based on structures employed in other markets. Some fund structures take the form of tax transparent partnerships (Japanese General Partnerships, Japanese Limited Liability Partnerships and Cayman Islands Limited Partnerships), with investment incomes being taxed at the members' level rather than the fund level. Furthermore, some funds take the form of corporate entities or are akin to corporate entities, such as investment trusts. Such forms are usually chosen to take advantage of tax benefits.

f. Netherlands

The principal structures available for private equity funds are the (i) Dutch limited liability company, (ii) the limited partnership, and (iii) the investment or mutual fund. As far as the Dutch limited liability company is concerned, there exist two basic types of company structures, the naamloze vennootschap (NV) and the besloten vennootschap met beperkte aansprakelijkheid (BV). Only the former can qualify as an investment company with variable capital, may be listed on the Amsterdam Stock Exchange and can issue registered as well as bearer shares. A limited partnership is known as a commanditaire vennootschap, or CV. There needs to be at least one managing partner who is fully and personally liable for all obligations of the partnership. Furthermore, the CV must have at least one limited partner who has no further liability than up to the level of what he or she has contributed to the partnership. In contrast to the Dutch limited liability company and the limited partnership, investment funds do not provide limited liability for their investors. An investment fund provides its investors with joint ownership of the underlying investments that are made in the name of the fund's investors. However, the investment fund itself does not constitute a vehicle that can act and enter contracts in its own name.

g. Portugal

There are three common structures. Venture Capital Companies (Sociedades de Capital de Risco, SCRs) are corporate vehicles taking the form of public limited companies. Venture Capital Funds (Fundos de Capital de Risco, FCRs) are closed-end funds representing autonomous assets. They do not have legal personality, and, as a result, are not responsible for the debts of the unit holders, depositaries, managing entities, or other FCRs. Finally, Venture Capital Investors (Investidores em Capital de Risco, ICRs) provide the opportunity for individual investors ("business angels") to carry out private equity activities. The ICR acts as an individual entrepreneur but must be incorporated under the specific corporate type of a sole partner private limited liability company. Only natural persons may be considered sole partners. There are other structures, such as public limited companies and private limited companies, but only the afore-mentioned forms benefit from a favorable tax treatment.

h. Spain

Private equity companies (Sociedades de Capital Riesgo, SCRs) must take the form of a Public Limited Company (Sociedades Anónimas, SA). Private equity funds (Fondos de Capital Riesgo, FCR) do not have legal personality and must be managed by a management company (Sociedad Gestora de Entidades de Capital Riesgo). The incorporation of FCRs and SCRs must be approved by the securities regulatory authority. Once approved, FCRs and SCRs must be registered both with the commercial and public registry.

i. Sweden

In a limited partnership all partners and the partnership itself must be registered in Sweden with the Swedish Companies Registration Office. Limited partnerships consist of one or more limited partners and at least one general partner. A limited partner has no obligation for the debts and liabilities of the limited partnership in excess of the amount which it has committed to the limited partnership. The general partner is solely responsible for the limited partnership's debts and liabilities, which exceed the responsibility of the limited partners.

A Swedish consortium is a private equity investment vehicle where the investors invest directly and in parallel in the investee company. Although the consortium does not constitute a separate legal entity, a managing company will act as nominee for the investors for investment activities. In addition to the limited partnership and the consortium, there are also foreign structures and vehicles organized as a foreign company or a foreign limited partnership. These foreign structures differ in particular with regard to the way they are taxed in Sweden.

j. Switzerland

Investments in private equity are usually based on a limited partnership for collective investments. In a limited partnership, which is a closed-end structure, at least one member bears unlimited liability (general partner). The general partner must be a public limited company with its registered office in Switzerland. While the general partner may only be active as a general partner in one limited partnership, he may delegate investment decisions and other activities to a third party. The other members, who are the limited partners, are liable only up to a specified amount. The limited partnership is restricted to qualified investors (institutional investors and HNWIs). The limited partnership requires authorization by the Swiss supervisory authority.

3. Emerging Markets

a. Brazil

Private equity funds (Fundos de Investimento em Participações, FIP) are closed-end funds with no redemptions. They are restricted to qualified investors (institutional investors and HNWIs). FIPs are managed by an independent manager and registered and supervised by the Securities and Exchange Commission of Brazil. Seed and Venture Capital Funds (Fundos Mútuos de Investimentos em Empresas Emergentes, FMIEE) are similar to FIPs, with the notable exception that nonqualified investors are allowed to invest in the former. In practice, however, investors in FMIEEs are almost exclusively qualified investors.

b. India

Venture capital funds can be set up as a Trust, a Company or a Body Corporate. In addition, the Limited Partnership Act of 2008 allows venture capital funds to be structured as a limited liability partnership. Venture capital funds enjoy certain tax benefits and are regulated by the Securities and Exchange board of India. The funds are required to have a minimum overall commitment from investors as well as minimum commitments per individual investor.

3 Global benchmarks

Chapter Outline

Benchmarks serve important functions in investment decisions. They help investors determine their allocations to individual asset classes and different market segments within particular asset classes. In-house investment teams who are responsible for investment decisions are generally appraised against agreed benchmarks. To the extent that external fund managers are mandated, their selection is usually based on market benchmarks. Those who select external managers are judged against such yardsticks, sometimes with direct implications for their compensation.

In public markets, there exist a number of well-established benchmarks, such as the S&P 500 for US equities, the DJStoxx 600 for European equities, or the MSCI World for global equities. As private equity has attracted a rising share of investors' portfolios, there is an important need for an unbiased benchmark, too. Fraser-Sampson (2006, p. 167) argues that this need is already satisfied: "We are fortunate indeed that for private equity a widely accepted and respected set of benchmarks exists, namely the Thomson Financial Venture Xpert system (formerly known as, and still frequently referred to colloquially as, Venture Economics)." As a matter of fact, Thomson VentureXpert's database is widely used in the industry as well as in academic research in private equity. In Chapter 2, and throughout the book, we frequently refer to this source.

Thomson VentureXpert competes with a rising number of other data providers who have emerged in recent years. However, neither Thomson VentureXpert (as Fraser-Sampson admits) nor any other benchmark provider has yet been able to achieve the same level of acceptance as their counterparts in the public markets. In the investor community, concerns remain about the quality of the underlying data. One reason for such concerns lies in the private nature of return data in private equity. As far as Thomson VentureXpert is concerned, their database essentially relies on voluntary reporting by the general partners and limited partners. Other data providers use data they have access to, thanks to their role as gatekeepers or custodians, while a third group has populated their databases on the basis of legal obligations arising, for

International Investments in Private Equity. DOI: 10.1016/B978-0-12-375082-2.10003-5

example, from the US Freedom of Information Act. In all these cases, however, there remain questions as to whether the different samples are representative of the market and provide unbiased information about market returns.

Another reason is the relatively short time period for which private equity benchmarks exist. In the more mature markets in the United States and Europe, this concern is gradually vanishing as we now already have nearly 30 years of data. In the emerging markets, however, investors continue to face substantial challenges in identifying appropriate market benchmarks.

Against this background, this chapter reviews the major existing private equity benchmarks in terms of their sample sizes, geographic coverage, and the periods for which they are available. Furthermore, we examine the performance of private equity as reported by the different benchmarks. Finally, we discuss alternative yardsticks that investors may use, especially in markets where private equity benchmarks have yet to be developed.

Our analysis is limited to those benchmarks that are generally available, either free of charge or for a fee. We do not consider proprietary benchmarks that only clients of a custodian or gatekeeper have access to. For example, this excludes the European indexes calculated by Cambridge Associates, a gatekeeper who only publishes their US buyout and venture capital benchmarks. It also excludes data reporting and management platforms, such as the Burgiss Group's Private iQ, where only clients have access to aggregate performance data. We also ignore indexes of publicly listed private equity. Although such indexes exist for a range of regional markets, we know from Chapter 2 that the return characteristics of publicly listed private equity vehicles differ fundamentally from those a limited partner in a traditional fund structure is confronted with. Finally, taking the perspective of a fund investor who is interested in private equity returns net of fees, we do not consider benchmarks based on deal data, which excludes providers such as Private Equity Insight, VentureOne (Dow Jones), Sand Hill Econometrics and CEPRES.[1]

3.1 Benchmark characteristics

3.1.1 Benchmarks for mature private equity markets

Our focus on publicly available, net-of-fees fund-based return indexes leaves us with four main benchmark suppliers, Cambridge Associates (CA) (US markets only); State Street, PREQIN; and Thomson VentureXpert. PREQIN's and TVE's data sets are

---

[1]Thomson VentureXpert also provides information on portfolio company investments, in addition to calculating benchmarks at the fund level. In fact, most researchers in venture capital have used TVE or VentureOne, to study VC financings. Examining the quality of the two primary databases, Kaplan, Sensoy, and Strömberg (2002) compare the actual contracts in 143 VC financings to their characterizations in the databases. Although the two databases are found to provide unbiased measures of financing amounts, they are missing valuations for a substantial fraction of the financing rounds they report. This applies in particular to TVE, which oversamples larger rounds. VentureOne, by contrast, is found to oversample valuations for highly valued firms.

based on voluntary reporting, information released by investors due to legal obligations and proprietary research. By contrast, CA, an independent investment consulting firm, and State Street, a leading custodian, have built their databases from information on private equity funds their clients have invested in. PREQIN, TVE, and State Street make their data available for a subscription fee, whereas CA's benchmarks are freely downloadable from the firm's public Web site. All four data sets are widely used by investment professionals and academics, and much of the empirical evidence we present in this book is based on these sources.

Given the particular challenges in developing benchmarks in an asset class where data are essentially private, users should be aware of the special characteristics of the different data sets. As Table 3.1 shows the individual benchmarks vary considerably in terms of their underlying partnerships. As of September 2009, CA's US private equity benchmark included 741 partnerships formed between 1990 and 2009 (and another 57 formed between 1986 and 1989). However, this sample includes an unspecified number of growth capital and mezzanine funds. By comparison, State Street's US buyout return index is based on 569 partnerships, 70 percent of which were formed between 2000 and 2009. The relatively smallest sample used to calculate a benchmark index is TVE's data set. Surprisingly, TVE's subsample of 2000–2009 is considerably smaller than that of the 1990s. This is in stark contrast to TVE's competitors who have been able to increase the number of partnerships they use for benchmarking purposes. It is also in stark contrast to actual developments in the market, which saw the number of US buyout funds to increase significantly in the recent cycle. For benchmark users interested in the consistency of performance measurement over time, these observations raise important questions.

How representative are the individual benchmarks we consider here? Unfortunately, we do not know for sure, since different data sources vary in terms of the number of partnerships they report as having being formed in individual years. Recognizing that there is uncertainty about the true denominator, we take data on individual funds reported by PREQIN, whose database appears particularly

Table 3.1 Number of constituent buyout partnerships forming the benchmark
(as of September 30, 2009)

	Cambridge Associates[a]	PREQIN	State Street[b]	Thomson VentureXpert
US buyouts				
1990–1999	295	249	176	263
2000–2008	446	433	399	187
1990–2008	741	682	575	450
European buyouts				
1990–1999	n/a	100	34	186
2000–2008	n/a	214	157	218
1990–2008	n/a	314	191	404

[a]Includes an unspecified number of mezzanine and growth capital funds.
[b]European buyout funds include a small unspecified number of funds targeting the rest of the world.
Source: Cambridge Associates, PREQIN, State Street, and Thomson VentureXpert

comprehensive on a global scale. For the most recent fundraising cycle from 2003 to 2007, PREQIN identifies more than 400 US buyout funds having had their final close. Cambridge Associates provides the most representative benchmark, covering 72 percent of the thus defined market universe. While State Street and PREQIN are not too far behind, TVE's benchmark is the least representative one, with a ratio of only about 22 percent (Fig. 3.1).

These estimates ignore of course that individual fund sizes vary substantially. Unfortunately, not all data providers provide information about the constituent funds of their benchmarks. From those who do (PREQIN and TVE), it appears that larger funds are over-sampled, implying that the capital-weighted ratios are higher than those calculated on an unweighted basis. However, there is no reason to assume that on a capital-weighted basis the ranking of the individual benchmark providers would be different from an unweighted basis.

The European sample size is generally considerably smaller. The notable exception is TVE, whose benchmark for European buyouts for the subperiod 2000–2008 actually includes more constituent funds than its counterpart for the US market. When we compare the number of funds used in the individual benchmarks with the total number of funds raised in the market, two observations are particularly important. First, the European benchmarks are generally less representative than the US benchmarks. Second, there is much less variation across individual benchmarks, with the respective ratios varying between 34 and 42 percent. While TVE provides the least representative benchmark for the US market for the last cycle, its benchmark for the European buyout market is the most representative one of all available indexes.

Figures 3.2 and 3.3 depict the number of benchmark partnerships in individual years from 1990 to 2009. Generally, the number of partnerships constituting the different benchmarks varies in line with the overall fund-raising cycle. In the United States, CA's benchmark has the largest number of constituent funds in most individual vintage years, although PREQIN and State Street have been catching up in recent years. The clear outlier is TVE, whose benchmark for US buyouts has progressively

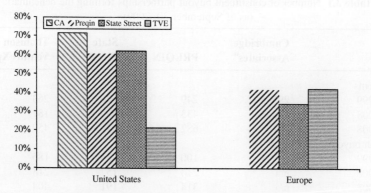

Figure 3.1 Ratio of constituent buyout funds in benchmarks relative to buyout funds raised in the market, 2003–2007.
Source: Individual benchmark suppliers.

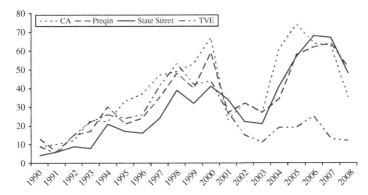

Figure 3.2 Number of constituent US buyout partnerships forming the benchmark, 1990–2008 (as of September 30, 2009).   Note: CA data include mezzanine and growth capital funds. *Source*: Individual benchmark suppliers.

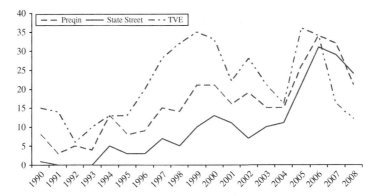

Figure 3.3 Number of constituent European buyout partnerships forming the benchmark, 1990–2008 (as of September 30, 2009).
Source: Individual benchmark suppliers.

lost ground against its competitors. In fact, from the number of constituent funds in TVE's database it would be difficult to identify the most recent private equity cycle, which saw a huge increase in the number of partnerships formed and capital raised.

In the European buyout market, benchmarks have converged considerably in terms of the number of their constituent funds. Although TVE was widely considered to be the only benchmark provider in Europe in the 1990s, today it competes with State Street and PREQIN whose benchmarks have become similarly representative. Potentially, the sample of their benchmark funds may continue to increase in size not only for future vintage years but also for past ones. In fact, all benchmark suppliers make important efforts to backfill their data sets, including through acquisitions of other data providers. As a result, the number of benchmark partnerships in the individual benchmarks continues to change even for early vintages. Users should be aware, however, that backfilling may result in an upward bias in reported returns. To the extent that benchmark providers need the authorization of their clients, investors in better-performing private equity funds are probably more willing to give that authorization. In the future, commercial benchmark suppliers in Europe will also compete with the EVCA, which until 2007 provided market and performance data in association with Thomson. Since then, however, it reports data based on *PEREP_ Analytics*, a centralized noncommercial pan-European private equity database, which aspires to transform itself into a private equity research exchange platform.

Turning to venture capital, Cambridge Associates has by far the largest number of US venture capital funds that serve to benchmark this market segment. With more than 1000 partnerships formed between 1990 and 2009 (and another 241 partnerships formed in the 1980s not considered here), the CA benchmark includes about twice as many funds as PREQIN and State Street. Compared with TVE, CA has around 25 percent more benchmark funds (Table 3.2). Although we do not know whether CA's benchmark is also more representative on a capital-weighted basis, there is nothing that would suggest otherwise. In August 2009, the National Venture Capital Association (NVCA) announced a strategic partnership with Cambridge Associates as a provider of US venture capital performance data. Hitherto, the NVCA had endorsed TVE's return numbers. In the joint press release (August 4, 2009) announcing the change, Mark Heesen, NVCA's president explained: "After assessing multiple providers of US venture capital performance statistics it became clear that Cambridge Associates has the most robust sample size and comprehensive method-ology for providing industry information."

Although CA possesses the most comprehensive data set to benchmark the US venture capital market, it is significantly less representative than the firm's buyout database. Focusing on US venture capital funds with a final close in 2003–2007, CA shows a coverage ratio of about 47 percent (Fig. 3.4)—some 10 percentage points higher than its closest competitor, State Street, but considerably below the 72 percent we estimated for the US buyout market (see above). Again, all percentages are on an unweighted basis as we do not know the constituent funds in all cases. While

Table 3.2 Number of constituent venture capital partnerships forming the benchmark (as of September 30, 2009)

	Cambridge Associates	PREQUIN	State Street	Thomson VentureXpert
US VC				
1990–1999	483	188	165	479
2000–2008	563	265	383	335
1990–2008	1046	453	548	814
European VC				
1990–1999	n/a	60	11	237
2000–2008	n/a	113	84	442
1990–2008	n/a	173	95	679

Source: Cambridge Associates, PREQIN, State Street, and Thomson VentureXpert

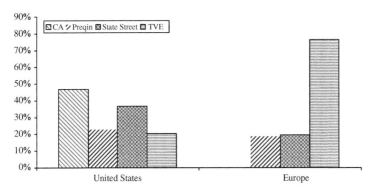

Figure 3.4 Ratio of constituent VC funds in benchmarks relative to VC funds raised in the market, 2003–2007.
Source: Individual benchmark suppliers.

anecdotal evidence suggests that on a capital-weighted basis the individual benchmarks are comparatively more representative in terms of the actual market size, there is a priori no reason to assume that a capital weighting would change the ranking of the benchmark providers.

In the European VC market, the leading benchmark provider remains TVE. For the entire period under consideration from 1990 to 2008, TVE uses nearly four times as many VC funds to calculate market returns as its closest competitor, PREQIN. For the subperiod 2003–2007, the most recent cycle in the global private equity market, TVE's benchmark funds account for nearly 80 percent of all European VC funds with a final close during these five years. This compares with less than 20 percent for PREQIN and State Street.

Figures 3.5 and 3.6 show the number of constituent benchmark funds for the US and European VC markets in individual years. In the United States, where all

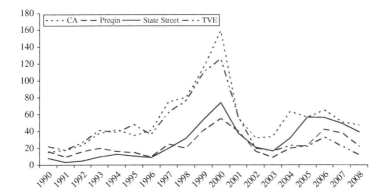

Figure 3.5 Number of constituent US venture capital partnerships forming the benchmark, 1990–2008 (as of September 30, 2009).
Source: Individual benchmark suppliers.

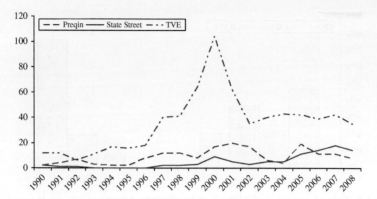

Figure 3.6 Number of constituent European venture capital partnerships forming the benchmark, 1990–2008 (as of September 30, 2009).
Source: Individual benchmark suppliers.

benchmarks mirror the fund-raising cycle, PREQIN and State Street appear to significantly undersample the huge spike in fund-raising activity in 1998–2000. In virtually all years, CA has the largest number of constituent benchmark funds. In the European VC market, where CA does not have a publicly available benchmark, the leading provider is TVE. One may go even further: In fact, TVE seems to be the only source as alternative benchmarks have largely failed to reflect the actual cyclicality in the fund-raising market.

Within venture capital, investors are able to drill even deeper and use benchmarks for different investment stages (seed, early-stage, balanced, and later-stage). Such benchmarks are provided by TVE and, somewhat less nuanced, by PREQIN. Although there is no differentiation at the fund level in terms of industry focus (life sciences, IT, and clean-tech), CA does provide industry-specific benchmarking data at the company level.

While buyouts and venture capital represent the dominant segments in the private equity market in terms of the number of funds and the capital they raise, investment benchmarks are also needed for smaller asset classes in an investor's private equity portfolio. Commitments to mezzanine and distressed partnerships are often motivated by the assumption that such investments show distinct risk-return characteristics. Whereas the risk-return properties of mezzanine financing mirror its special position in a portfolio company's capital structure (between equity and debt), distressed investing is generally driven by the default cycle, thus following different macro-dynamics than buyouts and venture capital.

Between 2003 and 2008, 172 US and European mezzanine funds are reported (PREQIN) to have raised US$ 88 billion. While most funds have raised less than US$ 1 billion, there have been some multibillion dollar partnerships, led by *Goldman Sachs Mezzanine Partners V*, which closed in 2008 at US$ 13 billion. Distressed funds raised between 2003 and 2008 were on average larger, with investors reported to have committed about US$ 103 billion to 68 partnerships. In both market segments, US partnerships account for the vast majority of funds raised. This is especially true for distressed funds, with US partnerships accounting for 96 percent of the capital raised. In mezzanine, the dominance of US funds is less extreme, but with 76 percent it is still significant.

Finding appropriate benchmarks for mezzanine and distressed is considerably more challenging than for buyouts and venture capital. Although Cambridge Associates does not publish any benchmarks other than for US buyouts and venture capital, State Street's global database includes just 17 mezzanine and distressed partnerships formed between 2001 and 2008. There are no data for older vintage years. As far as more recent years are concerned, some include only one fund. Furthermore, users are unable to tell mezzanine from distressed funds as both market segments are lumped together. Similarly frustratingly, TVE reports benchmarks neither for distressed investments nor for the European mezzanine market. Although TVE does calculate a benchmark for the US mezzanine market, several vintage years include fewer than three funds. As of September 2009, the sample of benchmark funds totaled 51 for all vintage years from 1990 to 2008, raising considerable doubts whether the database is a sufficiently accurate mirror image of actual market developments.

This leaves us with PREQIN. On a global scale (including a small number of partnerships formed in non-US, non-European markets), there are 119 mezzanine and 146 distressed partnerships formed between 1996 and 2008, which are used as constituent benchmark funds (Fig. 3.7). However, a significant percentage of these funds have been raised in 2005 or later. Their cash flow-based returns will not be known for several years, implying that investors have little guidance in examining the relative attractiveness of these asset classes and benchmark their own investment decisions against the market. In the absence of industry-specific benchmarks, some investors have looked for alternative yardsticks that may be used as rough approximations. As far as mezzanine is concerned, one candidate that is sometimes proposed is the total return of high-yield debt. Although various high-yield indexes are readily available, they are of course imperfect given the differing positions in the capital

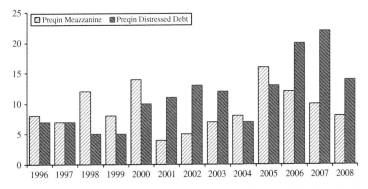

Figure 3.7 Number of constituent mezzanine and distressed partnerships forming PREQIN's global benchmarks (as of June 30, 2009).
Source: PREQIN.

structure and the associated risk differentials. Investors are thus faced with an unsatisfactory trade-off between the availability of information and its relevance. In this situation, qualitative factors will play a larger role for investors contemplating commitments to particular fund managers in these asset classes.

3.1.2 Benchmarks for nontraditional private equity markets

As we have already indicated in Chapter 2, investors in private equity funds targeting nontraditional markets are confronted with even bigger challenges. Neither State Street nor TVE publishes separate benchmarks for markets outside the United States and Europe. PREQIN's database does include a separate geographic category labeled "rest of the world," a region that is essentially identical with our definition of nontraditional markets (see chapter 6). At the beginning of 2010, this category encompassed 66 buyout funds and 128 VC funds formed between 1990 and 2006. However, the majority of these partnerships were formed only in the 2000s, implying that their final returns will not be known until the second half of the next decade. Because there are often only a handful of funds (sometimes even fewer) for older vintages, there is no information on the distribution of returns across funds. Finally, given that all non-US, non-European funds are lumped together, the "rest-of-the-world" is a mélange that is of little use for private equity investors seeking guidance on fund investments in particular regions targeting specific stages in the life cycle of companies.

Cambridge Associates does provide performance benchmarks for individual emerging markets regions, including Asia, Central and Eastern Europe, and Latin America. Nonclients have to be members of the Emerging Markets Private Equity Association (EMPEA) to access this information. However, investors remain in the dark as to how many constituent funds are included in the different regional benchmarks. Furthermore, as we discuss later, only end-to-end pooled average horizon IRRs are available. Vintage year returns, and the return distribution across funds, remain unknown.

In the absence of private equity benchmarks in nontraditional markets, investors generally use public benchmarks as an approximation. Although public benchmarks may help investors form return expectations with regard to individual markets and determine capital allocations, they are unable to give investors guidance regarding the selection of individual fund managers. That there is very little return history against which investors could benchmark individual investment opportunities is of course explained by the fact that private equity has begun to play a more meaningful role in financial intermediation in these markets only recently. To be sure, the current situation in nontraditional markets is comparable with the one investors were confronted with in Europe in the 1990s or in the United States in the 1980s and before. Perceiving investments in private equity as real options, early investors in the United States and Europe had to rely to a substantial extent on rough approximations and qualitative factors in their valuation approaches. Given that today's investors in nontraditional markets are in a similar position, we will discuss the real options concept in greater detail in Chapter 8.

3.2 Benchmark performance

3.2.1 Benchmarking returns in mature markets

The most common measure of private equity returns is the pooled mean IRR of partnerships formed in the same year in the same geography. Let us look first at US buyout partnerships (Fig. 3.8). Two sources—Cambridge Associates and Thomson VentureXpert—provide data from 1986. While PREQIN's time series starts in 1989, State Street's database goes back to 1990. Overall, we find that the four benchmarks follow a similar pattern. Pooled mean returns are relatively high in the early 1990s, fall in the subsequent years, and recover substantially in the early 2000s. As we have already discussed in Chapter 2, this pattern is inversely related with the amount of capital commitments to private equity funds. Although more recent vintage years see a sharp drop in pooled mean IRRs, at least in part, this decline is due to the well-known *J*-curve effect.

Notwithstanding the same pattern that the four benchmarks follow, there is considerable variance between them. TVE shows the lowest returns in most vintage years. Between 1986 and 2000—vintage years whose returns can be considered as more or less realized—TVE's benchmark is on average more than 4 percent per annum below the comparable index calculated by CA. While PREQIN is on average closer to CA, State Street's benchmark falls in between. Obviously, the performance differences measured by the individual benchmarks reflect the underlying samples of constituent funds. However, since we know neither the constituent funds of all individual benchmarks nor the individual partnerships actually formed in a given vintage year, we are unable to say which benchmark is the least biased one. Thus, the choice of a benchmark remains arbitrary and is usually driven by factors such as accessibility, investment focus, and the period for which a benchmark is available.

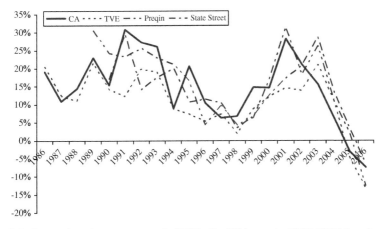

Figure 3.8 Comparing vintage year pooled IRRs for US buyouts, 1986–2006 (as of September 30, 2009).
Source: Individual benchmark suppliers.

However, investors should be aware that their benchmark choice may have important implications: Other things being equal, an investor would tend to allocate more capital to private equity the higher the benchmark returns of this asset class are. At the same time, if an LP's compensation is defined relative to a benchmark, he would obviously prefer one that makes it easier for him to outperform.

This brings us to the distribution of returns. While pooled-mean vintage year IRRs are generally considered as "market" returns—just as standard public market indexes—for benchmark purposes private equity investors are also interested in the dispersion of returns across individual funds. The dispersion of performance is generally expressed in terms of IRRs at the median, and the 25th and 75th percentiles.[2] The crux is that, as Table 3.3 indicates, there are also considerable differences between individual benchmarks. Interestingly, the reported dispersion of returns does not seem to be simply explained by the number of constituent funds in the benchmark. PREQIN shows the relatively widest dispersion of US buyout returns, which is mainly due to comparatively higher upper quartile returns in their sample. By comparison, State Street reports a relatively narrower bandwidth of returns between UQ and LQ funds. However, the IRR of the median fund in both databases is similar.

The benchmark an investor chooses determines not only his overall allocation to private equity and in many cases his compensation, but it also impacts the allocation of capital to different market segments within the broader asset class of private equity investments. One of the most basic portfolio decisions an LP has to take concerns his allocation of capital to private equity funds targeting different investment stages. Let us turn therefore to US venture capital funds, a market segment that in the late 1990s actually attracted more capital than buyout partnerships. As Fig. 3.9 shows, all data providers report remarkably similar pooled average IRRs, except for the bubble period in the second half of the 1990s. During this period, CA indicates an even stronger market performance than other benchmark providers. To the extent that investors are not entirely immune to a belief in "new era" stories and other behavioral biases, following the CA benchmark might have prompted LPs to allocate even greater amounts of capital to the venture capital market than other benchmarks would have signaled.

Table 3.4 shows the distribution of VC returns as reported by the different data providers. As we already know from Chapter 2, the difference between UQ and LQ returns in venture capital is considerably larger than in buyouts, an observation which is consistent across all databases. However, there is significant variance with regard to the reported distribution of returns. PREQIN has considerably fewer US venture capital funds in its database than CA and TVE, and the reported dispersion of returns is greater than shown by any other data provider. More specifically, PREQIN's database indicates both comparatively greater upside and downside risk of VC

---

[2]As Phalippou (2008) points out, the reported dispersion of returns may be misleading, as the performance of funds measured by their IRRs depends critically on the reinvestment rate of intermediary cash flows. Under plausible assumptions, he shows that the performance of private equity funds appears more dispersed than is likely to be the case. Although the dispersion of returns shown in Tables 3.1 and 3.2 may overstate the true situation, appropriate adjustments would still be likely to leave significant differences across individual benchmarks.

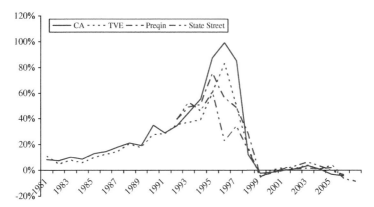

Figure 3.9 Comparing vintage year pooled IRRs for US venture capital, 1981–2006 (as of September 30, 2009).
Source: Individual benchmark suppliers.

investing in the US market. Depending on the risk function of individual investors, which benchmark they choose could have important implications for their allocations to venture capital.

Turning to the European private equity market, the universe of benchmarks is more limited. In the European buyout market, TVE has the longest time series of returns. For the post-1997 period, for which we also have data from PREQIN and State Street, we find that the individual benchmarks follow the same pattern. However, there is considerable variation across these benchmarks, with TVE consistently reporting the lowest pooled average IRRs and PREQIN showing the comparatively highest benchmark returns. To be sure, the difference between the two benchmarks is far from trivial—in most years it varies between about 5 and 10 percentage points, that is, a magnitude that should fundamentally affect investors' views about the attractiveness of this asset class.

Similar observations apply to the European venture capital market (Figs 3.10 and 3.11). In this market, investors can only choose among two data providers, with TVE's pooled mean IRR benchmark consistently underperforming PREQIN's.

An alternative approach to measuring the performance of private equity funds is based on horizon IRRs. While academic studies almost invariably focus on vintage year returns, horizon IRRs tend to be a more commonly used performance measure among practitioners—despite the methodological concerns raised about them (Phalippou, 2008). Horizon IRRs are generally calculated for 1 year, 3 years, 5 years, 10 years, and 20 years; some data providers also report since-inception IRRs. These IRRs are calculated by summing the NAVs of all funds in the database at the beginning of the "investment horizon" (i.e., 1 year, 3 years, etc.), computing the aggregate net cash flows until the final date (e.g., September 30, 2009), and adding the sum of all NAVs at the final date to the last cash flow.

In Figs 3.12 and 3.13, we show horizon IRRs for the US buyout and venture capital markets. The different benchmarks show a similar pattern—significantly negative

Table 3.3 Comparison of return distribution in US buyouts as reported by different data providers, 1986–2006 (as of September 30, 2009)[a]

	Cambridge Associates					PREQIN					State Street					Thomson VentureXpert				
	# Funds	UQ	Median	LQ	UQ–LQ	# Funds	UQ	Median	LQ	UQ–LQ	# Funds	UQ	Median	LQ	UQ–LQ	# Funds	UQ	Median	LQ	UQ–LQ
1986	10	17.7	11.0	6.6	11.1	8	62.7	33.8	18.0	44.7	...	...	...	...	...	10	18.7	15.1	7.8	10.9
1987	13	18.0	14.7	8.6	9.4	8	30.5	20.5	11.4	19.1	...	...	...	...	...	25	15.2	9.3	4.8	10.4
1988	16	15.2	13.0	10.0	5.3	12	20.1	13.1	10.0	10.1	...	...	...	...	...	14	13.1	8.6	...	...
1989	18	29.2	23.0	12.6	16.6	10	47.6	31.9	24.9	22.7	4	21.3	16.9	14.3	7.0	23	21.7	13.5	6.7	15.0
1990	9	20.0	16.0	10.8	9.2	13	31.7	15.3	8.8	22.9	6	34.7	27.9	21.4	13.4	9	12.3	7.0	−0.7	13.0
1991	10	42.0	28.2	12.6	29.4	6	...	22.1	...	...	9	21.7	19.5	8.2	13.5	5	13.9	13.8	4.0	9.9
1992	12	27.6	23.3	12.7	14.8	15	45.7	21.2	−0.8	46.5	8	21.6	17.9	13.4	8.2	15	29.8	18.3	10.0	19.8
1993	23	32.9	23.2	11.3	21.6	17	27.7	20.0	12.2	15.5	21	20.9	16.4	7.7	13.2	22	25.8	15.8	6.9	18.9
1994	22	21.6	10.6	0.3	21.3	30	25.7	17.9	8.8	16.9	17	18.1	9.9	0.8	17.3	26	20.4	11.4	0.4	20.0
1995	33	30.9	18.7	0.6	30.3	21	29.9	11.0	5.1	24.8	16	13.0	7.3	0.2	12.8	24	14.9	6.2	0.2	14.7
1996	37	13.8	9.6	−0.2	14.0	24	20.7	9.3	0.2	20.5	24	13.9	9.3	3.5	10.4	26	9.9	5.2	−0.6	10.5
1997	47	12.5	6.3	−1.7	14.2	35	14.3	7.2	−0.5	14.8	39	12.3	6.1	−3.5	15.8	41	11.0	3.0	−1.0	12.0
1998	49	14.4	11.0	1.2	13.2	48	13.0	6.9	−1.0	14.0	32	13.1	8.1	−1.1	14.2	53	10.9	5.5	−3.1	14.0
1999	53	18.4	13.2	7.6	10.9	40	15.0	7.9	−2.0	17.0	41	18.1	9.2	4.6	13.6	42	13.1	3.1	−3.2	16.3
2000	67	20.7	12.4	5.0	15.7	59	21.4	13.8	7.1	14.3	34	23.4	12.7	3.3	20.1	44	18.8	6.5	−0.7	19.5
2001	23	39.6	24.5	10.0	29.6	27	27.9	22.3	10.0	17.9	22	24.3	13.0	5.7	18.6	27	19.8	8.6	−1.9	21.7
2002	32	28.7	19.3	11.5	17.2	32	27.5	17.2	8.6	18.9	21	30.3	17.3	9.0	21.3	15	21.8	11.8	0.5	21.3
2003	27	19.2	13.7	5.0	14.2	27	18.6	9.5	3.2	15.4	41	15.1	7.7	0.4	14.7	11	12.7	5.7	2.6	10.1
2004	61	11.3	7.1	−0.3	11.7	34	19.7	7.3	0.9	18.8	57	7.9	2.2	−3.9	11.8	19	22.4	12.7	1.3	21.1
2005	74	6.4	−1.2	−11.1	17.5	58	11.3	2.0	−3.4	14.7	68	6.5	−7.9	−16.9	23.4	19	4.7	−1.1	−10.0	14.7
2006	64	5.2	−5.8	−15.0	20.2	62	0.1	−9.9	−16.7	16.8	...	...	...	...	...	25	−4.0	−8.1	−17.0	13.0
1986–2006[b]	700	21.2	13.9	4.7	16.5	586	25.6	14.3	5.2	20.3	...	...	...	...	...	495	15.6	8.2	0.4	15.3
1986–2000[b]	419	22.3	15.6	6.5	15.8	346	29.0	16.8	7.3	21.7	...	...	...	...	...	379	16.6	9.5	2.3	14.6
1990–2006[b,c]	643	21.5	13.5	3.5	17.9	548	21.9	11.8	2.5	19.4	460	18.6	11.4	3.9	14.7	423	15.2	7.4	−0.7	15.9
1990–2000[b,c]	362	23.2	15.7	5.5	17.7	308	24.5	13.9	3.8	20.7	217	19.0	13.5	6.3	12.7	307	16.4	8.7	1.1	15.3

[a] Net to LPs (%), unless specified otherwise.
[b] Unweighted annual average, except for number of funds, which is the sum of partnerships formed during specified period.
[c] Includes largely unrealized values.
Source: Cambridge Associates, PREQIN, State Street, and Thomson VentureXpert; author's calculations.

Table 3.4 Comparison of return distribution in US VC funds as reported by different data providers, 1986–2006 (as of September 30, 2009)[a]

	Cambridge Associates					PREQIN					State Street					Thomson VentureXpert				
	# Funds	UQ	Median	LQ	UQ–LQ	# Funds	UQ	Median	LQ	UQ–LQ	# Funds	UQ	Median	LQ	UQ–LQ	# Funds	UQ	Median	LQ	UQ–LQ
1986	31	13.0	9.5	5.4	7.6	15	14.3	8.9	5.5	8.8	...	...	...	...	...	43	11.1	6.2	2.2	8.9
1987	34	22.2	15.7	8.7	13.5	17	22.1	15.9	7.2	14.9	...	...	...	...	...	63	17.6	7.7	-0.3	17.9
1988	27	21.9	12.0	6.7	15.2	20	32.1	23.1	10.3	21.8	...	...	...	...	...	44	21.0	9.5	1.6	19.4
1989	37	28.8	13.3	7.8	21.0	25	33.5	14.7	6.4	27.1	8	26.6	19.3	15.8	10.8	54	17.7	10.8	0.8	16.9
1990	15	32.2	21.5	9.0	23.2	16	27.4	20.6	2.2	25.2	3	...	...	...	...	22	29.3	14.0	-0.1	29.4
1991	18	27.8	20.0	11.8	16.0	9	48.9	28.7	16.0	32.9	5	38.9	25.5	25.1	13.8	18	25.5	17.8	4.4	21.1
1992	24	38.9	23.0	11.4	27.5	17	38.5	19.0	2.8	35.7	10	34.1	10.2	-15.4	49.5	27	38.9	13.7	11.1	27.8
1993	38	41.1	17.7	7.9	33.2	25	44.8	36.5	1.4	43.4	13	40.3	25.9	7.2	33.1	41	39.1	12.5	0.7	38.4
1994	42	49.3	26.5	7.1	42.2	25	54.8	28.5	-0.8	55.6	11	51.1	15.9	1.1	50.0	39	41.0	15.6	3.2	37.8
1995	35	80.6	43.2	18.8	61.8	28	84.9	20.0	0.3	84.6	9	24.3	10.2	5.1	19.2	48	66.4	20.3	3.0	63.4
1996	41	92.1	33.2	6.7	85.4	23	66.1	14.6	-0.1	66.2	20	59.9	7.2	-4.2	64.1	36	113.9	33.0	1.3	112.6
1997	75	56.1	8.6	-3.3	59.4	36	79.3	22.0	-2.1	81.4	32	17.3	2.2	-8.9	26.2	62	59.6	20.0	-0.9	60.5
1998	80	18.0	-1.6	-8.5	26.5	40	14.6	0.2	-12.7	27.3	54	0.6	-4.9	-10.9	11.5	76	10.6	1.2	-4.7	15.3
1999	115	2.9	-5.5	-14.9	17.8	57	3.5	-6.3	-15.9	19.4	74	1.5	-3.1	-10.2	11.7	110	0.6	-5.8	-14.3	14.9
2000	159	3.0	-3.2	-9.3	12.3	73	5.1	-2.9	-9.0	14.1	38	6.7	-0.6	-7.4	14.1	126	1.9	-3.0	-6.9	8.8
2001	55	5.5	-0.6	-8.6	14.1	45	5.6	-1.4	-6.9	12.5	21	3.3	0.4	-4.1	7.4	57	7.3	-0.7	-4.2	11.5
2002	32	5.4	1.1	-7.0	12.4	29	7.3	2.3	-5.2	12.5	17	6.3	1.6	-6.9	13.2	20	2.4	-1.2	-3.1	5.5
2003	34	5.4	-4.2	-13.0	18.4	23	10.1	2.0	-3.4	13.5	32	6.5	-3.9	-8.7	15.2	17	8.6	2.9	1.1	7.5
2004	63	1.6	-4.4	-9.5	11.1	27	3.9	-4.4	-13.4	17.3	57	7.1	-2.2	-11.3	18.4	23	5.5	-1.7	-6.1	11.6
2005	57	3.9	-4.1	-12.6	16.5	37	4.3	-2.9	-7.0	11.3	56	0.4	-5.8	-14.9	15.3	22	6.2	-0.7	-7.8	14.0
2006	65	-0.9	-7.3	-13.4	12.5	48	0	-10.5	-17.7	17.7	...	...	...	...	...	33	1.4	-5.2	-13.3	14.7
1986–2006[b]	1,077	26.1	10.2	0.1	26.1	635	28.6	10.9	-2.0	30.6	...	...	...	...	...	981	25.0	7.9	-1.5	26.6
1986–2000[b]	771	35.1	15.6	4.4	30.8	426	38.0	16.2	0.8	37.2	...	...	...	...	...	809	32.9	11.6	0.1	32.9
1990–2006[b,c]	1,106	27.2	9.6	-1.6	28.8	558	29.4	9.8	-4.2	33.6	460	27.1	20.3	6.1	23.3	777	27.0	7.8	-2.2	29.1
1990–2000[b,c]	642	40.2	16.7	3.3	36.8	349	42.5	16.4	-1.6	44.2	239	21.7	19.9	5.2	24.2	605	38.8	12.7	-0.3	39.1

[a]Net to LPs (%), unless specified otherwise.
[b]Unweighted annual average, except for number of funds, which is the sum of partnerships formed during specified period.
[c]Includes largely unrealized values.
Source: Cambridge Associates, PREQIN, State Street, and Thomson VentureXpert; author's calculations

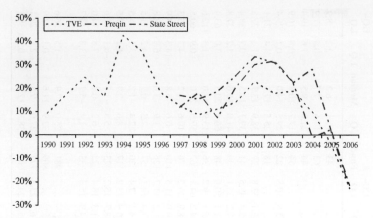

Figure 3.10 Comparing vintage year pooled mean IRRs for European buyouts, 1990–2006 (as of September 30, 2009).
Source: Individual benchmark suppliers.

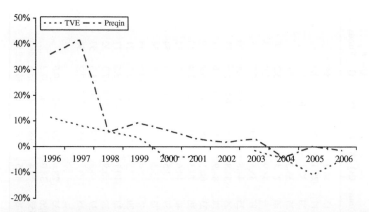

Figure 3.11 Comparing vintage year pooled mean IRRs for European venture capital, 1997–2006 (as of September 30, 2009).
Source: Individual benchmark suppliers.

returns on a 1-year basis and improving returns as we extend the horizon. In venture capital, returns increase substantially when we take a very long-term view that encompasses the last 20 years, that is, partnerships formed prior to the tech bubble. Notwithstanding the similar pattern in horizon IRRs, there are meaningful differences in the magnitude of reported returns across different data providers. This is particularly evident in the US buyout market, where on a 5-year horizon IRRs reported by TVE and CA differ by almost 5 percentage points.[3]

[3]Given that reported NAV is subject to GP discretion, while reported cash flows are significantly less so, older vintages have more reliable IRR calculations than younger vintages (less reliant on reported NAV). Thus, the weighted average age of funds within the benchmarks will be different. Controlling for this might explain some of the difference in horizon returns.

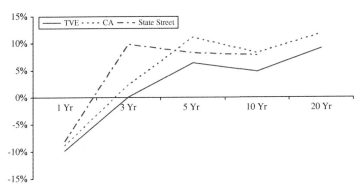

Figure 3.12 US buyouts: horizon IRRs (as of end-September 2009).
Source: Individual benchmark suppliers.

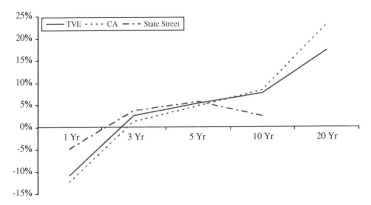

Figure 3.13 US venture capital: horizon IRRs (as of end-September 2009).
Source: Individual benchmark suppliers.

3.2.2   Benchmarking returns in nontraditional private equity markets

In nontraditional markets, the universe of available vintage-year benchmarks boils down to just one (PREQIN). As we already discussed in Chapter 2, however, this benchmark is too broad to provide any meaningful guidance in terms of individual geographies and market segments. Private equity investors in emerging markets may find more granularity in the Cambridge Associates database. However, for earlier vintage years there are not enough private equity funds in the database to calculate benchmark returns for each year. Furthermore, as we have stressed before, CA benchmarks for emerging markets (and other non-US markets, Fig. 3.14) are restricted to CA clients. The exceptions are horizon IRR benchmarks, which CA has made available to a broader audience via the EMPEA.

Three observations are particularly worth noting. First, when we compare the CA pooled end-to-end returns for emerging markets funds with those for the US market,

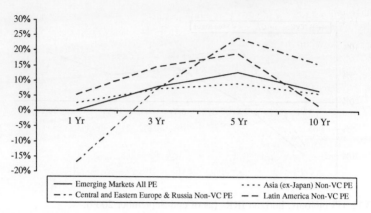

Figure 3.14 Emerging markets: pooled end-to-end returns by region (as of September 30, 2009).
Source: Cambridge Associates, EMPEA.

we find that the former have relatively outperformed for horizons of up to 5 years. Second, when we take a longer-term perspective that encompasses various economic and financial crises in emerging market economies in the late 1990s and early 2000s, the performance of emerging markets funds drops, both in absolute terms and relative to mature markets. Third, there is substantial variation across different regions. While Latin American funds show significantly positive returns on a 1-year horizon (as of end-September 2009), buyout funds targeting central and eastern Europe and Russia, a region that has been hit particularly hard by the global economic and financial crisis, report substantially negative returns. Clearly, these observations suggest that a "rest-of-the-world" benchmark is too crude to reflect the heterogeneity of nontraditional markets, which look set to attract increasing investment flows in the future.

3.3 Summary and conclusions

Benchmarks play a critical role for investment decisions. They help investors determine their capital allocation to individual asset classes, select individual fund managers, and monitor their performance relative to the market. In public markets, investors have a choice of well-established benchmarks that are constructed to provide unbiased information about asset prices and investment returns. As investors have allocated a rising share of their capital to alternative asset classes, there has been a growing need for more information about the risk-return properties of such investments. In response to such needs, a number of new benchmarks have emerged over the last two or three decades. However, as these benchmarks are based on private data, many investors remain concerned about possible sample biases, resulting in distorted investment decisions.

In this chapter, we have compared four benchmarks that are widely used by practitioners and academics. These benchmarks have two things in common—they are based on net-of-fees fund data, as opposed to deal data, and they are generally available to investors. Our analysis allows us to make the following observations:

- The availability of benchmarks is a function of the depth and breadth of individual markets. The longer a market exists and the greater the fund-raising and investment volumes, the wider the choice of different benchmarks and the greater the number of funds constituting a benchmark.
- The universe of benchmarks for the US buyout and venture capital markets is the greatest. At the other end of the spectrum are nontraditional markets where long-term benchmarks are largely nonexistent.
- Similarly, investors in mezzanine and distressed funds face substantial challenges in benchmarking their allocations and analyzing the risk-return characteristics of these market segments. Although this chapter has only considered investments in the primary private equity markets, the same applies to commitments to secondary funds where benchmarks are yet to be developed.
- Where alternative benchmarks exist, they are broadly comparable in terms of changes in market returns. Importantly, for example, they all show an inverse relationship between (pooled average) market returns and the volume of capital committed to private equity funds.
- However, in individual vintage years the reported performance of private equity funds varies significantly across different benchmarks. This is particularly true for buyout funds, where the IRR reported by individual benchmarks vary by as much as 10 percentage points in some vintage years. There is no guarantee that the benchmark based on the largest sample provides the least biased information.
- We find a significant variation not only in terms of pooled average IRRs but also with regard to the reported dispersion of returns. Although all sources find that returns in venture capital are generally more dispersed than buyout returns, some benchmarks indicate considerably larger upside and downside risk in manager selection than others.
- The reported dispersion of returns is not simply a function of the number of constituent funds forming a benchmark. The benchmark based on the smallest number of constituent funds does not show the widest distribution of returns (and vice versa).

So what are the implications? With the existing private equity benchmarks suffering from different deficiencies, many investors have decided to benchmark their performance against an absolute return target, such as public equity, plus a premium of, say, 2 percent to compensate them for the illiquidity of private equity. However, while absolute return targets may be used for performance monitoring and compensation purposes, they provide no guidance in terms of allocating capital to different market segments.[4] Inevitably, then, we are looking for second-best solutions that use all available information to track market developments. This suggests using different benchmark providers not only for different markets, but also, to the extent they exist, for the same markets, instead of limiting oneself to just one yardstick. Where the use of benchmarks goes beyond market monitoring, choosing a single yardstick should be done in a transparent way that carefully reviews all alternatives. Again, there is no reason to use the same benchmark provider for all markets, if there are better

---

[4]Benchmarking private equity investments against public markets raises additional methodological issues. See Day and Diller (2010).

yardsticks available. The biggest challenge exists in markets where there are no fund-based benchmarks at all. Inevitably, investors sometimes have to work with rather crude approximations. This may entail using benchmarks developed on the basis of deal-specific data and/or public market indexes, such as high-yield bond indexes for mezzanine, distressed bond prices for distressed fund investments, and public equity indexes for emerging markets. While none of these approximations are ideal, they are still better than investing blindly in the market. In the future, stricter disclosure requirements may help improve the availability of more appropriate benchmarks. For the time being, however, investors will need to live with second-best solutions.

4 Private equity in diversified investment portfolios

In constructing their investment portfolios, many investors follow a two-step approach. In a first step, portfolio managers determine the share of capital they want to allocate to broadly defined asset classes, such as public equity in mature markets and emerging markets, fixed income, real estate, hedge funds, and private equity. Once the overall asset mix is determined, in a second step investors need to decide how much capital they want to allocate to individual market segments within an asset class.

In this chapter, we concentrate on the first step. Asset allocations are generally based on econometric models, which have their roots in Markowitz' (1952) work on modern portfolio theory and the CAPM developed by Treynor (1962), Sharpe (1964), Lintner (1965), and Mossin (1966). Although the range of asset classes has broadened substantially during the past four to five decades, and several alternative approaches have been developed during this period,[1] the CAPM is still widely used as a framework for thinking about investments. Its basic idea is that the expected rate of return of an asset should reflect the *systematic*, or *nondiversifiable*, risk of the asset in a broader investment portfolio. However, while the CAPM has remained the "workhorse" for computing the cost of capital and determining the share of individual asset classes in a multiasset portfolio (Metrick, 2007), the specific return and risk characteristics of many alternative assets classes, including private equity, raise important challenges for asset managers. A key challenge we discuss in this chapter

---

[1]The development of alternative approaches has been motivated by the limitations of the CAPM and its restrictive assumptions (Roll, 1977). In practical applications, the CAPM sometimes leads to counterintuitive results, as optimal allocations are highly sensitive to changes in expected returns. Small changes in input variables can cause large changes in the weighting schemes and hence result in extremely unstable portfolio weights. Alternative approaches include, for example, Ross's (1976) Arbitrage Pricing Theory and Fama and French's (1993) Three-Factor Model and its extension by Pastor and Stambaugh (2003), which explicitly takes into account liquidity risk.

are stale prices, which—if left uncorrected—lead investors to underestimate risk in private equity.

However, correcting for stale prices is not enough. As the recent financial crisis has shown an important part of risk is not stationary in the sense that "normal" correlations of returns among asset classes may shift rapidly upward in times of a financial crisis. Standard asset allocation models, such as the CAPM, are essentially static and unable to handle dynamic risk. As we discuss further in this chapter, this important shortcoming has caused considerable cash-flow distress especially in portfolios with a sizeable allocation to illiquid asset classes.

This is particularly true for some endowments, some of which have allocated up to 20 percent of their capital to private equity alone, and in individual cases even more. While some endowments were hit particularly hard by the recent dislocations in the financial markets, few observers expect a wholesale shift in strategy back to traditional publicly traded assets. Conversely, we shall argue in the final part of this chapter that it is equally unlikely that allocations to private equity by other institutional investors will converge toward endowment levels. Instead, allocations look set to continue to differ across different investor classes, reflecting differing investment objectives, risk preferences, and regulatory constraints.

4.1 Returns, risk, and correlations

Why do investors commit capital to private equity, an asset class that, on average, is not only found to underperform public equity but is also highly illiquid? In Chapter 2, we argued that this puzzle is likely to be explained by the substantial dispersion of private equity returns and the overconfidence of investors believing that they are able to select, and have access to, the best-performing funds. While each investor may thus consider private equity to be attractive, collectively a substantial share of their investments will inevitably end up in funds achieving returns, which are worse than those equivalent investments in a public market index would have achieved.

Our analysis thus far has considered private equity investments largely from an isolated perspective. In reality, however, private equity investments are part of a broader asset mix, and allocations to each asset class are generally determined on the basis of their expected returns and their level of risk. In this context, risk usually refers to the variance of returns. The more the returns of an asset vary over time, the riskier an investment is. Other things being equal, asset classes whose returns are more stable will receive a larger portion of an investor's portfolio (and vice versa).

So how risky is private equity? Let us look at the empirical evidence in the way an investor would typically see it. In Figs 4.1 and 4.2, we show IRRs for the US buyout and venture capital markets, respectively, which are calculated on a quarterly basis by summing distributions and remaining values at the end of each quarter and comparing them with the sum of beginning-period values.

Between the first quarter of 1986 and the fourth quarter of 2008, annual US buyout returns averaged 12.7 percent, compared with 16.6 percent in the venture capital market. At the same time, however, buyout investments were comparatively less

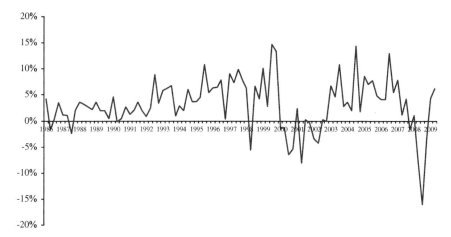

Figure 4.1 US buyout quarterly returns (end-to-end net to LPs) (as of September 30, 2009).
Source: Cambridge Associates.

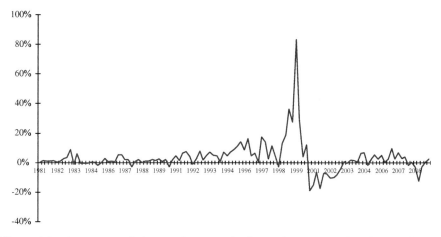

Figure 4.2 US venture capital quarterly returns (end-to-end net to LPs) (as of September 30, 2009).
Source: Cambridge Associates.

risky. While buyout returns had a standard deviation of 20 percent, venture capital returns had a standard deviation of 48 percent.[2] In Table 4.1, we compare the return and risk characteristics of the US buyout and VC markets with US treasury bonds, Aaa- and Baa-rated US corporate bonds and the public equity market. As shown by

---

[2]Venture capital is still riskier if we take out the bubble years 1999–2000. Although the standard deviation of VC returns drops to 25.04 percent, this is still considerably higher than that for buyouts. Average net-of-fee returns fall to 8.68 percent, significantly below buyout returns, implying a decline in the Sharpe ratio.

Table 4.1 Performance and risk in different asset classes, 1986–2008

	Mean (%)	Standard deviation (%)	Sharpe ratio (%)
US Buyouts	12.69	19.96	41.5
US VC	16.57	48.07	25.4
S&P 500	6.95	30.79	32.5
NASDAQ	9.73	53.95	9.7
US 10-year treasury bonds	6.04	1.69	132.7
US Aaa corporate bonds	7.28	1.43	246.5
US Baa corporate bonds	8.21	1.45	206.1

Source: Cambridge Associates; Bloomberg; author's calculations

a higher *Sharpe ratio*, private equity has generated superior risk-adjusted returns than public equity.[3] At the same time, however, private equity has underperformed fixed-income assets as higher nominal returns in private equity have not fully compensated investors for significantly higher risk compared with bonds.

However, what matters in the portfolio context is not just the variance of returns of individual asset classes. To the extent that risk is *diversifiable* (or *idiosyncratic*), it should not play a role in determining the cost of capital. Rather, what matters is the extent to which asset returns are correlated. Table 4.2 presents the correlation matrix for the six assets we consider here. The significantly less-than-perfect correlation between US buyout returns, as published by standard data vendors, and the S&P 500 suggests that there are considerable diversification gains to be had from adding private equity to a portfolio. This is true to an even larger extent for venture capital, especially with regard to the S&P 500 and also with respect to the NASDAQ. Although private equity returns show very low—in fact, even negative—correlations with sovereign and corporate bonds, buyout, and venture capital returns show limited degrees of correlation even among themselves.

Table 4.2 Correlation matrix for selected US Assets, 1986–2008

	Buyouts	VC	S&P 500	NASDAQ	10-Year treasuries	Aaa bonds	Baa bonds
Buyouts	1.00	0.63	0.66	0.66	0.05	-0.11	-0.25
VC		1.00	0.41	0.60	0.12	0.05	-0.04
S&P 500			1.00	0.83	0.21	0.08	-0.03
NASDAQ				1.00	0.10	-0.05	0.01
10-Year treasuries					1.00	0.96	0.90
Aaa bonds						1.00	0.97
Baa bonds							1.00

Source: Cambridge Associates, Bloomberg; author's calculations

---

[3]The Sharpe ratio is calculated by dividing (1) the historical excess return over the riskless rate of interest (3-month treasury bills) by (2) the standard deviation of its excess return.

Because we know the mean returns, their variance, and their correlations with other asset classes, it would seem to be straightforward to estimate efficient portfolios in a CAPM framework, which can be found in any finance textbook. Appendix 4.1 provides a brief overview of this model and summarizes the empirical literature on market risk in private equity. Unfortunately, as many of the studies we survey in the appendix have pointed out, using the raw data presented in Figs 4.1 and 4.2 would give us highly misleading results. Let us just focus on the most critical issues.

To begin with, the CAPM assumes that asset returns are (jointly) normally distributed random variables. This assumption is generally found to be violated in equity markets. Instead, equity returns are usually assumed to follow log-normal distributions. This is also the case in private equity. The probability density function of private equity transactions has a fat left tail with a zero bound (total write offs) and a long right tail, reflecting a low likelihood of very high returns (so-called "home runs"). Unfortunately, non-normality leads to biased estimates of the portfolio's risk and returns and hence the optimal weights of individual assets. Second, private equity funds express their returns in terms of IRRs, which are not generally comparable to time-weighted returns on public market assets. Finally, private equity returns are based on the quarterly reports made by the GPs, which include estimates of the values for unrealized investments. Although recent regulatory changes require GPs to mark-to-market their portfolio companies, stale values in private equity funds remain an important issue potentially distorting the results of the CAPM.

Investors use different tools to address these issues. As far as the log-normal distribution of private equity returns is concerned, the standard approach is to determine portfolio weights on the basis of Monte Carlo simulations. An example is given by Metrick (2007, pp. 368–371). Furthermore, Artus and Teïletche (2004) show how IRRs and time-series returns can be reconciled under certain assumptions.

4.2 The stale price problem

The stale price problem has probably attracted the greatest amount of attention both by academics and practitioners. To see why, consider the following example of three assets, with their standard deviations, expected mean returns, and correlations shown in Tables 4.3 and 4.4.[4]

Table 4.3 Expected returns and risk in a simple 3-asset example

	Mean (%)	Standard deviation (%)
Asset A	20	20
Asset B	15	10
Asset C	18	15

[4]Thanks to my colleague Broes Langelaar for the calculations.

Table 4.4 Correlation matrix in a simple 3-asset example

	Asset A	Asset B	Asset C
Asset A	1.00	0.50	0.50
Asset B		1.00	0.50
Asset C			1.00

In this simple example, we assume that assets A, B, and C have correlation coefficients of 50 percent. Figure 4.3 depicts the familiar efficient frontier for portfolios consisting of our three assets. Randomly chosen portfolios shown as grey points below the frontier are inefficient in the sense that it is possible to reduce portfolio risk at a given level of expected returns or, alternatively, achieve higher expected returns at a given level of risk by changing the weights of each asset.

What happens if asset returns are more or less correlated than shown in Table 4.4? The entire efficient frontier moves, as depicted in Fig 4.4. To the extent that the true correlations are lower, our portfolio is less risky at any given level of expected returns (or, alternatively, expected portfolio returns are higher at any given level of risk). However, to the extent that we have underestimated the true degree of correlations, our portfolio is riskier at any given level of expected returns (or, alternatively, our expected returns are lower at any given level of risk).

As far as publicly traded assets are concerned, portfolio models rely on observable market data. In private equity, however, such market data do not exist. Alternatively, investors may use return data provided by commercial data vendors and other institutions (see Chapter 3). However, as Conroy and Harris (2007) show, relying on

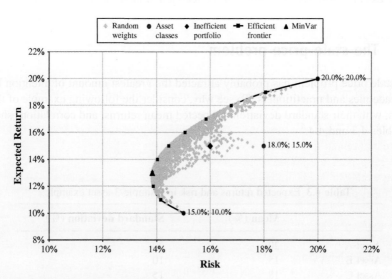

Figure 4.3 Efficient Frontier for three assets.
Source: AlpInvest Research.

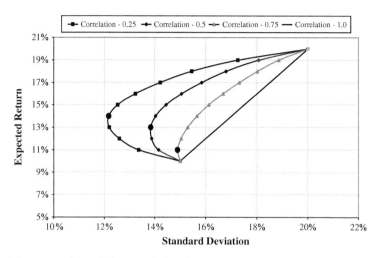

Figure 4.4 Impact of correlation on efficient frontier.
Source: AlpInvest Research.

published private equity returns may result in a significant underestimation of systematic risk, causing investors to become considerably overexposed to private equity. More specifically, Conroy and Harris estimate efficient portfolios consisting of private equity (buyout funds), public equity (S&P 500 for large firms and NASDAQ for smaller firms), and bonds. Quarterly private equity returns are calculated on the basis of data, which are taken directly from Thomson VentureXpert, a database that is widely used by practitioners (see chapter 3).

Given the standard variation of returns and their correlation with other assets, Conroy and Harris (2007) calculate optimal allocations to private equity, given alternative levels of expected returns. For example, if the representative investor targets annual returns of 10 percent, the optimal allocation to private equity would be 20 percent (left column in Table 4.5). With this allocation, the investor's overall portfolio would have an estimated standard deviation of 5.8 percent. At 12 percent expected returns, the optimal allocation to private equity increases to 50 percent, with the standard deviation rising to 6.6 percent. In the absence of private equity, the investor would need to accept significantly higher levels of risk. Given expected portfolio returns of 12 percent, the standard deviation of a portfolio consisting only of the S&P 500, the NASDAQ, and bonds would be nearly twice as high. Thus, it seems that private equity indeed possesses excellent diversification properties.

But is this really true? In a second step, Conroy and Harris (2007) "de-smooth" reported private equity returns, which rely on general partners' estimates of remaining values rather than market prices. Those estimates represent "smoothed" series as market value changes usually feed only gradually through the reported data. So even if the mean return figures are correct, they understate true economic risk.

In "de-smoothing" the reported return data, Conroy and Harris (2007) use a standard Dimson (1979) approach, which takes the current observed reported return as

Table 4.5 Private equity allocations using raw and adjusted data

Portfolio expected return (%)	Private equity allocation based on raw data[a] (%)	Private equity allocation based on adjustments for stale pricing[b] (%)
9	4	2
10	20	14
11	36	26
12	50	37
13	62	48
14	75	61

Return and risk estimates are annualized based on quarterly data, 1989–2005. Reported private equity returns are from Thomson VentureXpert.
[a]Initial standard deviations and correlations are not adjusted for smoothing in private equity returns.
[b]Standard deviations and correlations are adjusted for smoothing using Dimson's beta approach. Correlations with both the S&P 500 and NASDAQ are adjusted. The estimate of private equity's standard deviation is the simple average of the standard deviations implied by the S&P 500 and NASDAQ results.
Source: Conroy and Harris (2007, p. 104)

a weighted average of current and past true returns. On this basis, the authors recalculate the variance–covariance of private equity, which they use as input for reestimating efficient portfolios with and without private equity. The true risk of private equity is found to be significantly higher. While the standard deviation jumps from 13 to 25 percent, the correlation with the S&P 500 increases from 63 to 74 percent. As a consequence, the beta more than doubles from 0.53 to 1.17. With private equity being considerably riskier than naïve estimates imply, the weight of private equity in an investor's portfolio is considerably smaller, given alternative levels of expected returns. As shown in the right column in Table 4.5, private equity would have a share of only 14 percent in a portfolio whose expected return is 10 percent. With an expected portfolio return of 12 percent, an investor would hold 37 percent in private equity, around one-quarter less than estimated on the basis of raw return data. Importantly, the efficient portfolio would be riskier at any given level of expected returns. For instance, targeting portfolio returns of 12 percent, the investor would need to accept a standard deviation of around 11.5 percent, much higher than that suggested by the unadjusted raw data.

Conroy and Harris' (2007) findings are broadly in line with other academic studies on risk-adjusted returns of private equity, which are summarized in Appendix 4.1. Although these studies generally find that private equity does play an important role in a diversified portfolio, they support the warning of Gompers and Lerner (1997) that "...the stated returns of private equity funds may not accurately reflect the true evolution of value, and the correlations reported by Thomson Economics and other industry observers may be deceptively low. To ignore the true correlation is fraught with potential dangers."

Therefore, sophisticated investors adjust their portfolio models for stale prices. For instance, while Yale's Investment Office employs a standard mean-variance approach as described above, it makes subjective adjustments to the observed historical return and risk characteristics in private equity. Swensen (2009, p. 115) who introduced

Yale's rather groundbreaking approach to endowment management in the mid-1980s explains: "Assuming that private equity investments generate 12 percent returns with a risk level of 30 percent represents an appropriately conservative modification of the historical record of 12.8 percent returns with a 23.1 percent risk level." Similarly, informed judgments are used to make adjustments to the observed correlation with other asset classes. These judgments are periodically reviewed in order to take into account expected changes in correlations, for example, due to changes in the market structure, macroeconomic policies or regulation.

A more realistic assessment of risk in private equity reinforces the importance of manager selection. While, other things being equal, adjustments for stale prices imply lower portfolio weights, such weights are typically derived from average return data. Although stale pricing is a phenomenon affecting reported returns across the entire distribution, superior selection skills could at least in part offset the implied decline in risk-adjusted returns, justifying greater portfolio weights than CAPM and similar models suggest.

4.3 Managing dynamic risk

The phenomenon of stale prices in private equity became particularly obvious in the recent financial crisis when valuations of portfolio companies were adjusted only with a lag relative to public markets. In fact, it was not until Q3 2008, the quarter in which Lehman Brothers filed for bankruptcy, that net asset valuations of portfolio companies started to fall markedly. With exit markets essentially shut and distributions to LPs having disappeared, a large number of investors thus found themselves overexposed to private equity relative to their allocation targets. Over time, this *denominator effect* gradually weakened as private equity valuations were catching up with public asset prices (or, in some cases, LPs increased their allocation targets to private equity).

While stale prices may lead portfolio managers to underestimate risk already under normal market conditions, correlations between asset prices are unstable over time. In periods of financial stress they tend to jump. As Spence (2009) argues, traditional portfolio models, such as the CAPM, are essentially static and ignore that an important component of risk is not stationary. This risk is systemic, and when the risk in the system as a whole rises, "normal" correlations of returns among asset classes shift rapidly upward. In this situation, diversification and hedging models and risk mitigation strategies are bound to malfunction. Major systemic disruptions occur infrequently, but when they happen portfolio losses can be substantial. In a hypothetical example, Spence assumes that a period of nine years of "normal" average returns at various rates is followed by a "bad year" caused by a jump in systemic risk. For different levels of returns and sizes of the shock (expressed as the percentage decline in returns), he calculates the total impact of the shock on the returns over the 10-year period. For example, with an assumed 14 percent annual return in normal times, Spence estimates that a 15 percent shock reduces the average 10-year returns by 3.3 percentage points to 10.7 percent. A 25 percent shock, which has more resemblance with the recent economic and financial crisis, would have reduced the average 10-year returns by 4.67 percentage points to 9.33 percent.

At the same time, dynamic risk caused havoc with investors' cash-flow models, and when the parameters of these models suddenly shifted due to reduced distributions, the suspension of redemptions, increased capital calls and collateral, some investors were faced with an acute lack of liquidity.[5] University endowments were hit particularly hard thanks to their relatively high allocations to alternative investments, including private equity, hedge funds, commodities, and timber. Given their payout requirements, several endowments were forced into distressed sales of assets, amplifying the negative returns. Others were able to avoid, or at least limit, fire sales at hugely discounted prices by borrowing in the debt capital markets. For instance, although Harvard Management Company, Harvard University's endowment, sold assets of around US$ 1 billion, they also issued a bond in December 2008, raising US$ 2.5 billion. However, borrowing inevitably affects the leverage and hence the risk profile of the portfolio. According to the Wilshire Trust Universe Comparison Service, the average large US university endowment fell by 17.2 percent in 2008, but some suffered even larger losses.

Based on Spence's simulations investors are well advised not to take short and medium term returns as accurate signals of long run returns. Instead, investors should factor in a dynamic risk component associated with systemic risk. This is especially relevant for illiquid investments, such as private equity. Such investments should have a complementary part of liquid investments in the portfolio, with liquidity being valued for avoidance of cash-flow distress, flexibility in restructuring the portfolio in response to rising systemic risk and for the option value it creates in the aftermath of the shock (Spence, 2009).

The existence of dynamic risk requires important changes in investors' risk budgeting, a risk management approach that aims at better understanding the total portfolio risk borne by decomposing it into various risk exposures. In allocating risk to each asset class, risk is usually measured using passive benchmarks. Within individual asset classes, risk is then budgeted to generate alphas relative to the benchmark. As far as traditional assets are concerned, risk is usually proxied by the volatility of returns. For nontraditional assets, however, other risk proxies are required. The standard approach is to use value at risk (VaR) to allocate capital to strategies with option-like returns. VaR has two important shortcomings, however: first, it is based on the historical volatility of asset returns and their correlations with other assets. As a result, VaR may underestimate the risk of extreme events. Therefore, VaR is usually combined with stress tests to budget and allocate risk.

[5]As we discussed in Chapter 2, cash flows in private equity are uncertain. In managing the liquidity of their portfolios investors typically rely on models, which are based on historical liquidity streams arising from capital calls and distributions. While investors want to be compensated for accepting liquidity risk in private equity, attempts to quantify the risk premium have remained rare. One exception is based on a model developed by Pastor and Stambaugh (2003). Employing Pastor's and Stambaugh's Four-Factor Model, Metrick (2007) estimates the illiquidity premium for US venture capital at around 1 percent. In practice, many investors use in their allocation models a required premium of 2 percent, which still appears too low for the tail risk private equity investments are subject to.

Second, and potentially more importantly, VaR does not capture all the risks that exist in the market. This includes, for example, liquidity risk and leverage risk, two components, which have proved to be of critical importance especially for the portfolios of endowments with their relatively high allocations to alternative assets. Their experience has highlighted the need for an alternative risk budgeting model, shifting the focus from the volatility of returns to the risk of outright loss and hence from a static risk approach to a dynamic one.

4.4   Why do allocations to private equity vary so much?

The substantial amount of distress that many investors have experienced during the recent financial crisis has raised profound questions about portfolio construction. More specifically, there is considerable uncertainty as to how much capital investors will be allocating to illiquid asset classes in the future, among them private equity. As far as endowments are concerned, an investor class hit particularly hard due to their relatively high exposure to illiquid asset classes, few expect a wholesale shift in strategy back to traditional public markets. Swensen of the Yale University endowment explains (*Financial Times*, October 10/11, 2009): "There have been some articles that have criticized the Yale model and my role in managing the endowment. And I think that's odd…What's the alternative? Aside from the heroic impossible alternative of being 100 percent in treasury bills?" Conversely, there a few signs that other investors with relatively low allocations to private equity will substantially raise their allocations to this asset class, as some had suggested prior to the recent financial crisis (Fraser-Samson, 2007, xvi). Instead, the most plausible assumption is in our view that allocations will continue to differ substantially across and within different investor classes, reflecting their individual objectives, risk appetite, and regulatory requirements.

The broadest possible benchmark for individual allocations to private equity is the average share of private equity in global investors' portfolios. At the end of 2008, pension funds, mutual funds, and insurance companies around the world are estimated to have held total AUM of US$ 60 trillion, around 20 percent less than the year before (McKinsey Global Institute, 2009a). Taking into account assets held by sovereign wealth funds in Asia and the Middle East (US$ 9.5 trillion) and assets managed by hedge funds (US$1.4 trillion), institutional investors' AUM stood at around US$ 71 trillion. To this amount, we add AUM held by family offices and high net worth individuals (HNWIs), which are estimated to have totaled $32.8 trillion at the end of 2008 (CapGemini & Merrill Lynch, 2009). Excluding capital allocations to hedge funds to avoid double counting, total AUM held by institutional investors and HNWIs thus amounted to about US$ 103.5 trillion. In Chapter 6, we estimate private equity AUM at almost US$ 1.4 trillion, which implies that private equity had a share of somewhat more than 1 percent at the end of 2008.

Figure 4.5 depicts the percentage of capital the 10 most important private equity investors in individual investor groups had allocated to this asset class as of the middle of 2009. As we can see, allocations to private equity do vary widely. By far, the

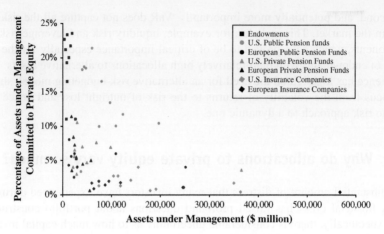

Figure 4.5 Commitments to private equity by large institutional investors (10 most important private equity investors in each investor class, measured by their committed capital to private equity funds).
Source: PREQIN.

highest relative allocation is found to be among endowments, averaging 19 percent. Endowments are followed by US public pension funds, with the 10 most important private equity investors in this group having on average committed 14.9 percent to the asset class. US private pension plans and US insurance companies are substantially behind, with respective exposures of 5.9 and 1.8 percent. In all categories, European investors show considerably lower degrees of exposure to private equity than their US counterparts. For instance, the 10 most important private equity investors among European public pension funds have on average allocated only 5.5 percent of their capital to private equity, or only around one-third of the average allocation by US public pension funds.

Investors' exposure to private equity varies not only across different groups of investors but also across individual institutions. As far as endowments are concerned, individual allocations range from 11 to 23.5 percent. Exposure ranges are similarly broad among pension funds and insurance companies. While the lowest exposure of a top 10 private equity investor of US public pension funds was 9.9 percent, the highest exposure was 21.3 percent. Recall that in Fig 4.5 we consider only the largest private equity investors in each category. In fact, in each category, we have a nontrivial number of institutions that have no exposure at all to private equity— which explains why private equity still accounts for only around 1 percent of the world's AUM.

In a pure mean-variance world, it would be easy for an investor to choose an efficient portfolio consistent with his own preferences. The real world is more complex, however, and other factors play an important role as well. As far as pension funds are concerned, investment strategies must take into account the structure and duration of their liabilities. Over the past decade or so, several factors have forced investors to reevaluate their traditional approaches to asset-liability management

(ALM). Among those, a low-return environment, the market-consistent valuation of assets and liabilities and risk-based capital, and the emergence of new asset classes have played a particularly important role in this process. With the focus shifting from the behavior of assets to the behavior of assets versus liabilities, investment strategies of pension funds have generally become more rigorous and dynamic. These strategies are driven to a greater extent by absolute returns rather than relative returns, giving more weight to alternative asset classes and trading strategies. As a result, solvency shortfalls have gained in importance as a key risk measure, whereas tracking errors have become less important.

Other investors pursue different objectives. Banks, as we have discussed in Chapter 2, are likely to take into account the potential cross-selling of their services to fund managers when determining their optimal allocation to private equity. For university endowments, the preservation of purchasing power and the provision of sustainable support are key factors determining their investment strategies (Swensen, 2009, p.122).

Furthermore, different classes of investors are subject to different regulations. As far as banks are concerned, the Basel II framework allows banks to use their own internal VaR approach, subject to approval by the regulators. However, there is a minimum risk weight, or "floor," which is set at 300 percent. This translates into a minimum capital requirement of 24 percent for private equity exposures, 8 percentage points higher than the floor set for public equity. Banks that do not run internal VaR models are faced with higher capital requirements for their private equity investments. Under the simple risk weighting approach, Basel II prescribes to use a capital requirement of 32 percent of the economic value of an investment as capital.[6] These rules are subject to change, however, as new regulatory proposals aim to strengthen the capital base of banks as a consequence of the recent financial crisis (for more details, see Chapter 11).

Insurance firms operating in the European Union could also become subject to a considerably higher solvency capital requirement. Under Solvency II, which is planned to take effect from October 2012, the minimum capital requirement for private equity could be as high as 55 percent, if the most recent proposal (January 2010) of the Committee of European Insurance and Occupational Pensions Supervisors (CEIOPS) were to be adopted.[7] This proposal is based on a standard formula that considers private equity as "other equity," together with emerging market equity, hedge funds, and commodities. For each asset class within the broader category of

[6]According to the European Union's Capital Adequacy Directive (CAD) III, which serves to transpose the Basel Accord into EU legislation, banks using internal risk models are subject to different floors for the minimum capital requirements for private equity. These floors vary between 13 and 17 percent, depending on the size and the annual turnover of portfolio companies included in diversified portfolios. Under the simple risk weighting approach, capital requirements are set at 15.2 percent, less than half the level under Basel II (32 percent). Using a proprietary dataset, Bongaerts and Charlier (2008) argue that while the capital requirements proposed under Basel II appear too high, the particular risk characteristics of private equity would suggest higher capital requirements than specified under CAD III.

[7]Initially, the Committee of European Insurance and Occupational Pensions Supervisors (2009) proposed a capital requirement of 60 percent.

"other equity," different risk factors are calculated. In the case of private equity, this calculation is based on the statistical properties of the LPX50 Total Return index.[8] To avoid undue complexity, CEIOPS proposes to apply a minimum capital requirement of 55 percent across the board for "other equity," which would be more than twice as much as the minimum capital requirement under Basel II. While the final outcome of the consultative process on Solvency II remains uncertain at the time of writing, it is likely that the European insurance and banking industries will be subject to significantly different capital requirements (the same could of course be true for firms in the same industry operating in different jurisdictions).

Finally, size matters. Although most university endowments manage assets of less than US$ 20 billion, some public pension funds, such as CalPERS in the United States and ABP in the Netherlands, have AUM 10 times that amount. Finding a good home for, say, US$ 40 billion in private equity funds is certainly a much bigger challenge than finding a place for US$ 4 billion. Thus, while allocation models, investment objectives and regulations determine the range of commitments to private equity, the actual degree of exposure often mirrors pragmatic considerations. On the upper side, scalability, access to outperforming funds, and management fees typically play an important role. On the lower side, investors' private equity allocations need to be sizeable enough to "move the needle" and to justify putting in place a dedicated investment team. The costs of recruiting and retaining an experienced team, whose objectives are fully aligned with the rest of the organization, are generally a key factor in this decision.

4.5   Summary and conclusions

In this chapter, we have presented the broad contours of the mean-variance approach as the core of modern portfolio theory. We have shown that private equity may play an important role in enhancing a portfolio's expected returns at a given level of risk thanks to the low correlation with other asset classes. However, we have immediately warned that the portfolio benefits calculated on the basis of publicly available information are likely to overstate private equity's real contribution to a portfolio's risk-adjusted returns by a considerable margin. As we discussed, this overstatement is due to the stale price problem, which arises from the lagged adjustment in valuations in private equity. Once we correct for the stale price problem, the true risk of private equity is found to be significantly higher and risk-adjusted returns lower.

However, correlations between asset prices are not stable over time. Instead, they tend to rise in periods of financial stress, causing diversification and hedging models

[8]Not surprisingly, CEIOPS' approach has prompted sharp criticism from the private equity industry, arguing that investments in private equity funds are far less risky than a public index suggests. In its comments to the CEIOPS proposal, the EVCA made it clear that it "... considers this approach to modeling private equity risks as fundamentally flawed. Institutional investing in private equity is predominantly through funds that have a contractual lifetime of 10 years and follow a very distinct lifecycle. In such cases it is meaningless to view risk as the volatility of a time series over short horizons."

and risk mitigation strategies to malfunction—whether adjustments were made for stale prices in the portfolio. In the recent financial crisis, this dynamic risk proved disastrous especially for portfolios with a significant exposure to alternative asset classes, such as private equity. As the parameters of the portfolios' underlying cash-flow models suddenly shifted due to reduced distributions, the suspension of redemptions, increased capital calls and collateral, some investors were faced with an acute lack of liquidity. A nontrivial number of investors had to liquidate some of their portfolio positions, including in private equity due to their inability to honor their unfunded commitments. Trying to avoid the steep discounts in the secondary market, other investors preferred to raise fresh capital in the bond markets.

The recent financial crisis has revived the debate about the role of alternative investments in diversified portfolios. As we have argued in this chapter, we do not anticipate a wholesale shift back to traditional public markets in portfolios where private equity and other alternatives represent a sizeable share of total AUM. Instead, a key lesson for investors with substantial exposures to illiquid investments is to hold a complementary part of the portfolio in liquid assets to avoid cash-flow distress and to retain flexibility in adjusting their asset allocation. Nor do we see signs that the share of private equity in portfolios with a moderate exposure to alternatives will progressively converge toward levels seen in some endowment portfolios, as some had predicted before the crisis. As we have argued in this chapter, there are good reasons why allocations to private equity vary substantially, both across and within different investor classes. Individual investors have different utility functions, they operate under different regulatory requirements, the size of their portfolios varies, and their access to top-performing funds may be sufficiently heterogeneous. Despite these fundamental differences, overall private equity has gained substantial importance over the last few decades. Having emerged into a trillion dollar industry, today private equity funds manage around 1 percent of the world's financial assets under management. In the following chapter, we focus on the second step of investors' portfolio construction—the allocation of capital to different segments of the private equity market.

Appendix 4.1   Measuring market risk in private equity

Several academic studies have used single-factor models to estimate market risk in private equity. These models are based on the well-known Capital Asset Pricing Model. According to the CAPM, the risk of an asset is equivalent to its beta, which reflects the covariance of an asset's returns with the returns on the overall portfolio. Beta risk is also called *market risk*, *systematic risk*, or *nondiversifiable risk*—as opposed to diversifiable or idiosyncratic risk, which is the variance of the asset's returns. Differences in the average returns generated by different assets should be entirely explained by differences in their betas. Formally, the CAPM can be derived as follows:

$$\frac{[E(R_i) - R_f]}{\beta_i} = E(R_m) - R_f \quad (1)$$

where $E(R_i)$ is the expected return for asset i, R_f is the risk-free rate for borrowing and lending, and R_m is the return on the whole market portfolio. The term $(R_m - R_f)$ is called the market premium. β_i is the level of risk for asset i, which can be expressed as follows:

$$\beta_i = \frac{Cov(R_i, R_m)}{Var(R_m)} \quad (2)$$

According to Eqn (1), the market reward-to-risk ratio equals the market risk premium. By rearranging (1), we obtain the CAPM:

$$E(R_i) = R_f + \beta_i(R_m - R_f) \quad (3)$$

In empirical applications, realized returns on asset i are usually used for R_i. For R_m, researchers usually take the realized returns on a portfolio of all publicly traded stocks. R_f is generally assumed to be the realized returns on short-term US treasury bills. After rearranging Eqn (1), the CAPM can then be estimated in an ordinary least squares regression:

$$R_{it} - R_{ft} = \alpha + \beta(R_{mt} - R_{ft}) + \varepsilon_{it} \quad (4)$$

The term α is the regression constant and ε_{it} represents the regression error term. Thus, the return on an asset should be consistent of an appropriate risk-free benchmark return plus an additional return, the market-risk premium, which compensates an investor for the additional risk of the asset relative to the risk-free benchmark rate of return.

More recently, researchers have also applied multifactor models in estimating market risk in private equity (for an overview, see Fleming, 2010). Essentially, multifactor models augment the single-factor CAPM through the inclusion of additional factors that are assumed to have systematic relations with expected returns. These models are generally based on the Fama–French model, which relates equity returns to market, company size, and value/growth characteristics. Equity risk is estimated as the summation of three betas measuring the relation between returns to a private equity investment and (i) public equity return premia (the difference in returns between the public equity market and the risk-free rate); (ii) the difference in returns across company size; and (iii) the difference in returns between value and growth companies.

One of the earliest contributions to the literature on market risk in private equity comes from Gompers and Lerner (1997), who examine the investments of one private equity firm (Warburg Pincus) between the first quarter of 1972 and the third quarter of 1997. Using "raw data," they find an arithmetic average annual return (gross of fees) of 30.5 percent, with a beta of 1.08. In a second step, the authors then mark-to-market the portfolio. Specifically, in quarters where there is neither an investment nor a write down, they adjust the portfolio value by the change in the matched industry public market index. Finally, they regress these "refreshed" returns on market returns. While the intercept (the alpha) is still positive, the beta in the CAPM regression increases to 1.44.

Using cash-flow data from a unique data set of buyout and venture capital funds raised between 1981 and 1993, Ljungqvist and Richardson (2003) follow a three-step procedure to estimate the risk of each fund in their sample. First, they identify each portfolio company held by a fund. Second, they assign portfolio companies to (one of 48) broad industry groups chosen by Fama and French (1997). For each of these industries, Fama and French provide estimates for an equity beta over the 5-year period from 1989 to 1994. Finally, they assign the industry beta to the portfolio company and compute the average equity beta of the fund using the capital disbursements as weights. The authors calculate an average IRR of 19.81 percent, implying excess returns of almost 6 percent relative to investments in the public market under an identical time schedule. Buyout funds are estimated to have generated even higher excess returns, with an IRR of 21.83 percent and a Fama–French beta of 1.08. These excess returns appear high, and as Ljungqvist and Richardson show, on a leverage-adjusted basis excess returns disappear completely when the average debt-to-equity ratio in buyout deals reaches 2:1, a level, which was common in the last cycle.

Jones and Rhodes-Kropf (2004) use a dataset from Thomson Venture Economics, containing (after some filtering) 1245 venture capital and buyout funds formed from 1969 to 1999. For the 866 VC funds they calculate an annualized value-weighted average fund IRR of 19.31 percent, substantially larger than the 4.57 percent they obtain for the 379 buyout funds in their sample. The estimated returns of buyout funds are rather low, especially in light of the strongly positive average stock market excess returns over the sample period. This is explained by the fact that their sample includes more recent funds that have not been wound up. Regressing returns on contemporaneous and lagged market returns, Jones and Rhodes-Kropf find that funds mark-to-market with a substantial lag. Summing up the betas on current and lagged factor returns, the portfolio of VC funds has an estimated "long-run" beta of 1.80, whereas buyout funds are estimated to have a long-run beta of only 0.65. Although the buyout beta appears to be surprisingly small, especially taking into account that this is an unlevered equity beta, the authors argue that their results are consistent with the conventional wisdom that buyout funds typically acquire companies with steady cash flows that are relatively insensitive to changes in aggregate conditions.

Kaplan and Schoar (2005) use essentially the same data set. However, in contrast to Jones and Rhodes-Kropf, they work only with cash flows and do not rely on interim IRRs of a fund that are necessarily based on subjective valuations by the fund manager. Instead, they attempt to adjust for market risk by including the average annual returns to the S&P 500 in the 5 years after the fund is raised and excluding year-fixed effects. While the authors are unable to calculate "true" betas, they find a coefficient on the S&P 500 of 1.23 for VC funds and 0.41 for buyout funds. The 1.23 for VC funds is lower than the one found by Jones and Rhodes-Kropf (2004) but higher than that found by Ljungqvist and Richardson (2003). As far as buyouts are concerned, Kaplan and Schoar's results are comparable with Jones and Rhodes-Kropf but significantly lower than the coefficient reported by Ljunggqvist and Richardson.

Driessen, Lin, and Phalippou (2009) use cash-flow data from 958 mature private equity funds between 1980 and 2003. Provided by Thomson Venture Economics, their sample includes 686 venture capital funds and 272 buyout funds. Using a GMM-style methodology, they estimate the alpha and beta of (a portfolio of) private equity funds in a way that gets the net present value closest to zero. In the CAPM specification, the authors obtain a market beta for venture capital funds of 3.21, and given the equity premium over the sample period, they calculate the cost of capital for venture capital (after fees) to be 31 percent per annum. With an alpha of -15 percent per annum, they find strong negative abnormal performance. Materially, their findings are the same when they use a Fama–French model instead of the CAPM (although the estimated underperformance is somewhat less). For buyout funds, they find a relatively low market beta of 0.33 (after fees), implying that these funds have a risk below that of public equity. Although abnormal performance is found to be slightly positive, both in the CAPM and Fama–French frameworks, the results are mostly statistically insignificant.

Cochrane (2005), Korteweg and Sorensen (2009), Peng (2001), and Quigley and Woodward (2002) all use company-level venture-capital deal data (private rounds of funding, IPOs, acquisitions, and write downs). Taking a maximum-likelihood approach, Cochrane finds a mean log return of about 15 percent, an arithmetic average return of 50 percent, and a beta of about 1. By contrast, extending a standard dynamic asset-pricing model by adding a selection process to correct for the endogenous selection of the observed returns, Korteweg and Sorensen find betas that are consistently above 2.2, with an average of 2.8.

Finally, as far as listed private equity vehicles are concerned, Bilo, Christophers, Degosciu, and Zimmermann (2005) consider an equally weighted portfolio of liquid private equity assets that is fully rebalanced on a weekly basis. Using data from 1986 to 2003, the authors calculate mean returns of 15.99 percent, a standard deviation of 19.34 percent, and a beta of 0.6. However, when they adjust their estimates for autocorrelation, the standard deviation and the beta increase to 33.67 percent and 0.99, respectively. As a result, the Sharpe ratio drops from 0.57 to 0.33.

5 Designing private equity programs in open markets

Once investors have determined their overall allocation to the broad asset classes, they need to decide on strategies to implement the allocation by filling the individual pieces (Sharpe, 2007, p. 207). As far as private equity is concerned, this decision entails allocating capital along four dimensions, that is, (i) the different stages of private equity investing (buyouts, venture capital, and distressed funds); (ii) vintage years; (iii) industries; and (iv) geographies. Some investors leave this decision to external advisors or fund-of-funds managers, but those who manage their private equity portfolios in-house are usually guided by a combined top-down and bottom-up analysis. From a top-down perspective, capital allocations generally take into account factors such as economic growth, interest rates, industry cycles, and country and currency risk. From a bottom-up perspective, investors factor in, among other things, the return distributions in individual market segments, fund-raising cycles, access to (historically) outperforming fund managers, and expected coinvestment opportunities. At the end of this process, the two perspectives should converge to one consistent view as to how the individual private equity "buckets" should be filled. If an investor has no particular views on individual market segments and is not constrained by any access restrictions, the outcome of this process may well be that he holds the market portfolio. As we discuss in this chapter, however, his top-down and bottom-up analyses may lead him to formulate return expectations, which result in market weights that differ from the market portfolio.

5.1 Bottom-up versus top-down planning

How should an investor determine the composition of his private equity portfolio once the allocation to this asset class is known? Instead of worrying too much about market

International Investments in Private Equity. DOI: 10.1016/B978-0-12-375082-2.10005-9

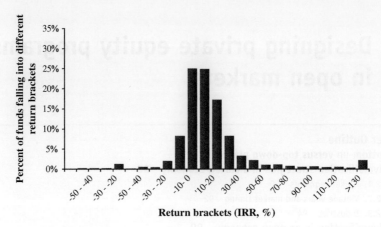

Figure 5.1 Histogram of US venture capital returns (net-of-fees).
Source: TVE; AlpInvest Research.

segments, geographies, fund styles, and the correlations of returns between them, it might be argued that investors should be solely concerned about the past and expected performance of individual fund managers (Meyer & Mathonet, 2005, p. 84). As we have seen in Chapter 2, private equity is characterized by a substantial degree of dispersion of returns between lower-quartile and top-quartile funds. This is particularly true for the US venture capital market. In fact, when we look at the distribution of fund returns, we see that venture capital has a substantially longer tail on the right-hand side distribution than buyouts (Figs 5.1 and 5.2). The skewness of the VC distribution is 3.65, around three times larger than the return distribution for buyouts. At the same time, the return distribution for the US venture capital funds is leptokurtic with a parameter of 18.58, compared with 5.18 for the US buyout market.[1] Thus, the VC market seems to provide considerably more upside risk for investors with the right selection skills.

Looking at the historical performance of a small group of US venture capitalists, an investor might well decide to allocate a substantial share of his capital to these funds.[2] However, such a strategy would be overly naïve. To begin with, much of the evidence on the performance of venture capital funds dates back to the period before the tech bubble. As far as the post-bubble period is concerned, it seems that few, if any, venture capitalists have been able to return to their pre-bubble track record. Home runs, such as *Google* or *YouTube*, have been rare, and, as we have seen in Chapter 2 (Fig. 2.9), even

---

[1]A normal distribution has a skewness of zero. Positive skewness means that a distribution is skewed to the right, whereas a negatively skewed distribution is skewed to the left. Kurtosis measures whether the data are peaked or flat relative to the normal distribution. Leptokurtic distributions (kurtosis > 3) are both peaked and have fat tails. Platykurtic distributions show the opposite properties.

[2]There is a surprising degree of agreement as to who the best venture capitalists are. Metrick's (2007, p. 88) subjective A-list of top-tier US venture capital firms include Accel Partners, Benchmark Capital, Charles River Ventures, Kleiner Perkins, Caufield & Byers, Matrix Partners, and Sequoia Capital. All these firms are also on Fraser-Sampson's (2007) *Golden Circle* list.

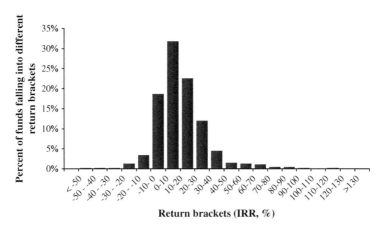

Figure 5.2 Histogram of US buyout returns (net-of-fees).
Source: TVE; AlpInvest Research.

the top-performing funds could remain well below their historical performance. As of September 30, 2009, the upper-quartile funds that were raised in 2002 and 2003 had IRRs of only around 5.5 percent, a fraction of the performance of funds raised in the aftermath of recession in the early 1990s. Although the final returns of the 2002 and 2003 vintages will be known only when all transactions are exited, the relatively poor post-bubble performance has raised concerns that the venture capital might be fundamentally broken.[3] However, in a recent paper Kaplan and Lerner (2009) reject such concerns, emphasizing that returns to VC funds in the first decade do not seem to have been unusually low relative to the overall stock market.

Second, even if the level of performance and its distribution had remained largely unchanged post-bubble, an investment strategy focusing predominantly on venture capital would hardly be feasible in practice. Although some university endowments have enjoyed high returns thanks to their early support of the top VC funds, the majority of investors are in a different position. In particular, new investors with sizeable assets under management will encounter severe access restrictions, especially in the US venture capital market. In the unlikely event that a top-performing venture capital fund was willing to accept capital from a new investor at all, the amount would be pitifully small. Interviewing Swensen for a recent Harvard Business School Case Study on the Yale Investments Office, Lerner (2007) reports that "…Swensen mused that if he were starting an investment program today, he might avoid venture capital entirely. He reasoned that obtaining access to the best firms was nearly impossible and that, even if successful, the endowment was unlikely to receive an allocation that would be meaningful to an $ 18 billion portfolio."

Such constraints favor a more balanced approach, taking into account a top-down view on individual market segments. In a top-down approach, investors start with

---

[3]Such concerns were, for example, expressed in a *New York Times* article on October 7, 2006, entitled "A Kink in Venture Capital's Gold Chain."

a general macroeconomic analysis of business cycle fluctuations and inflation, industry-specific trends, developments in the equity and debt capital markets, economic, financial, and regulatory policies, and country risk. The strategic asset allocation is followed by the planning of commitments to funds that are identified to match the defined portfolio composition. In practice, of course, few investors rely solely on a top-down approach—just as few investors would follow exclusively a bottom-up approach. Advocates of a top-down approach would hardly commit capital to funds they classify as mediocre, just to be in compliance with their target allocation. Nor would the proponents of a bottom-up strategy entirely forego the potential benefits of diversification and construct a highly concentrated portfolio based on historical performance. Thus, the most common approach is a mixed strategy combining top-down diversification and risk-control objectives and bottom-up selection skills.

5.2   Diversification strategies in a closed economy

5.2.1   Market segments

The most fundamental decision in the allocation process concerns the stage of companies private equity funds focus on. How much capital should be allocated to venture capital, growth capital, buyout, and distressed funds? And within the buyout segment, should investors differentiate between funds focusing on small, mid-sized, and large transactions?

Generally speaking, defining target allocations for different stages and deal sizes makes sense only if the risk-return properties of these market segments are sufficiently different. Besides, as we have argued earlier, individual market segments need to provide sufficient investment opportunities in terms of their absorptive capacity and accessibility. As far as venture capital and buyouts are concerned, they are generally considered as two distinct forms of private equity, with their performance and risk driven by sufficiently different factors (see Chapter 4, especially Section 4.1). Whereas venture capitalists provide financing for companies at the early stages of their life cycles, buyout funds typically target mature firms. Most venture capital deals are technology focused, in IT, life sciences, or clean-tech, with uncertain cash flows. By contrast, buyout transactions are found across a wide spectrum of industries, with a particular focus on predictable cash flows. Venture capitalists normally use no debt, whereas buyouts tend to be substantially leveraged and are, therefore, highly susceptible to changes in debt market conditions. The fundamentally different characteristics of buyouts versus venture capital are mirrored in their relatively low correlation. When we look at vintage year returns—as opposed to end-to-end quarterly returns we showed in Figs 4.1 and 4.2—we find a correlation coefficient of 38 percent for the median US buyout and VC funds. As far as upper-quartile funds are concerned, their (vintage year) returns are even less correlated, as evidenced by a coefficient of 18.9 percent.

However, the degree to which investors can diversify their private equity portfolios across buyouts and venture capital is limited by their fundamentally different market

sizes. Although the number of buyout and venture capital funds are broadly similar—
in 2007, at the peak of the last cycle, 225 buyout funds and 296 venture capital funds
had their final close worldwide—the capital they raise and invest differs substantially.
Broadly speaking, as we have discussed in Chapter 2, the buyout market is about four
to five times larger than the VC market. Furthermore, VC returns are substantially
more skewed, with the best funds being subject to severe access restrictions. Thus,
asset allocation targets derived from portfolio models may be difficult to implement,
a challenge in particular large investors face.

As far as other market segments are concerned—turnaround capital, distressed
funds, and mezzanine—quantitative allocation approaches are even more severely
restricted by the quality of data. The sample of funds for which performance data exist
is often small, and the time series of returns is considerably shorter than in buyouts
and venture capital. As a result, we face even greater uncertainty with regard to their
risk-return properties and their correlations with other forms of private equity, making
it extremely difficult to draw any meaningful conclusions with regard to their desired
weight in a well-structured private equity portfolio.

Within the buyout market, many investors distinguish between middle-market
and large transactions, and some even have a third allocation, the mega category.
In fact, the performance of buyout funds with different amounts of capital is
imperfectly correlated (Fig. 5.3). However, it is less clear to what extent the less-
than-perfect performance correlation is driven by different deal sizes the funds are
targeting. Although it is true that small funds invest virtually exclusively in small
companies, middle-sized and some large buyout funds are less focused on the size
of transactions but pursue opportunities across a wider range of deal sizes.
Regressing deal sizes on fund sizes, we find a correlation coefficient between deal
sizes and fund sizes of only 42 percent (Cornelius, Langelaar, & van Rossum, 2007,
p. 110).

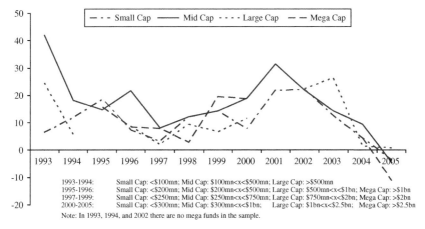

Figure 5.3 US buyout returns based on fund capitalization pooled mean net to LPs (%).
Source: Cambridge Associates.

5.2.2 Vintage years and market timing

In Chapter 2, we already observed that vintage year returns vary considerably over time. Vintage year IRRs are inversely related to inflows to private equity funds, which are generally a function of the business cycle. Given the relation between fund inflows and vintage year performance, private equity investors are usually advised to invest anticyclically. An example may help illustrate the potential gains that are at stake. Suppose an investor were able to time the US buyout market by varying his capital commitments according to the deviation of total inflows in individual vintage years relative to their long-term trend (Fig. 5.4). In years when total fund commitments "overshoot" their long-term trend, investments are reduced proportionally, resulting in a decline in the investor's market share. Conversely, when total fund commitments fall short of their long-term trend, the investor increases his absolute commitments and extends his market share. Alternatively, assume that an investor pursues a market-neutral strategy by maintaining exactly his market share in the fund-raising market in each vintage year. Considering an entire private equity cycle, this implies that a substantially larger amount of capital is invested in funds raised in underperforming vintage years. On the basis of Thomson VentureXpert data on commitments to US buyout funds and their mean returns per vintage year, the market-timing strategy would on average have generated excess returns of around 4.5 percent!

A market-timing strategy in the primary private equity market could be coupled with an anticyclical strategy in the secondary market. At a time when the primary market overheats, the investor could sell (funded and unfunded) commitments at a premium. Conversely, in a slump, he may purchase funds in the secondary market at steep discounts.

Unfortunately, in practice, this strategy is much more difficult to implement than it may seem. To begin with, to time the market an investor needs to be able to predict

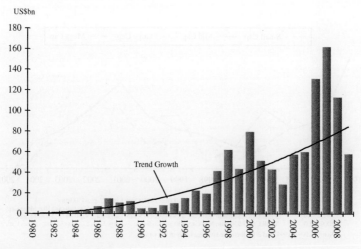

Figure 5.4 United States: fund-raising by buyout funds, 1980–2009.
Source: TVE; AlpInvest Research.

turning points. Although there is usually broad agreement about market troughs—as in the first half of 2009, when fund-raising and investing in virtually all markets had fallen to multiyear lows—there is much less agreement about an imminent turning point in an upswing. For example, who had predicted at the beginning of 2007 that the volume of global buyout transactions would fall by more than 90 percent between the first half of that year and the same period of 2009? And who had predicted that global commitments to private equity funds would decline by 60 percent between their peak in the last quarter of 2007 and the first of 2009 (and by 70 percent as far as buyout funds are concerned)? Obviously, had investors and private equity fund managers foreseen the dramatic dislocations in the financial markets and the deepest economic recession in postwar history, commitments to private equity funds and the deployment of capital would have been substantially less, potentially avoiding the severe market overheating that actually took place.

The second point to make is that although it is relatively easy to identify recessions and market troughs—which should set the stage for good vintage year returns— investors are often constrained precisely during such periods. Typically, recessions are associated with a broad adjustment in asset prices (with few exceptions, such as sovereign bond yields and, in the recent recession, gold) and hence a decline in investors' overall assets under management. To the extent that valuation adjustments in private equity lag publicly traded assets, investors are subject to a "denominator effect" (see Chapter 3). Other things being equal, the share of private equity in the portfolio rises, prompting asset allocation models to signal reducing private equity investments in line with the targeted composition of the portfolio. Potentially, this effect can be compounded by regulatory requirements, given private equity's exposure to liquidity risk. In this situation, investors may find it increasingly difficult to honor existing commitments to funds, let alone to make new ones. As a result, in the most recent market correction, a considerable number of investors decided to sell (part of) their private equity holdings, which generally included uncalled commitments.

Investors who are fortunate enough not to be liquidity constrained nor to see their asset allocation targets being violated by the denominator effect face a third challenge. In economic recessions, GPs tend to raise fewer funds, and the limited number of funds that do raise new capital typically target smaller amounts. This means that there are fewer investment opportunities for LPs, whether or not they are able and willing to provide new capital.

Overall, perfect market timing seems elusive. While it is notoriously difficult, if not impossible, to predict the turning points of the cycle, there are important supply-side and demand-side factors constraining investment opportunities precisely when return expectations improve. Hence, what are the alternatives?

A market-neutral strategy aiming at maintaining a constant market share in the fund-raising market leads to the worst outcome. Instead, the investor may pursue a rules-based strategy allocating (more or less) the same amount of capital to each vintage year. This strategy has some important advantages. First, it would imply a rising market share in troughs when returns are good and a falling market share in boom periods when vintage year returns tend to be poor. Furthermore, this strategy does not require investors to predict the cycle but frees them from potential behavioral biases, such as herd behavior, overconfidence, and the belief in "new era" stories (Shiller, 2005).

The disadvantage is, of course, that a strict rules-based strategy forces investors to ignore potentially valuable information that could be used to form a probabilistic view of market developments. Although the exact timing of the end of a buyout boom and the speed and depth of the subsequent market downturn may not be known, indicators, such as interest rates and spreads, valuations, fund inflows, investment volumes, and defaults, may flag a rising probability of an imminent market correction before it actually happens. Investors following a rules-based diversification strategy would continue to allocate the same amount of capital, despite the progressive increase in perceived risk. Moreover, investing the same amount of capital in each vintage year requires a sufficient number of attractive investment opportunities in each part of the cycle. Although rules-based investors may be less demand constrained than investors trying to time the market, for large institutional players it may nevertheless be challenging to identify enough assets that meet their return expectations.

A final alternative lies in trend investing. Avoiding the market exuberance in boom periods and the subsequent "valley of tears" the majority of investors go through, this strategy takes into account that the asset class is growing over time. As can be shown, trend investing generates considerable excess returns relative to a market-neutral strategy, albeit to a lesser extent, of course, than perfect market timing. However, despite its apparent simplicity, this strategy is not entirely trouble-proof. By definition, implementing this strategy requires that a trend can be identified. Although there is already a considerable history in the US and European buyout markets and in the US venture capital market, the track record in most other markets is substantially shorter. Furthermore even where a historical trend can be identified, there is no guarantee that this trend will actually hold. Structural breaks, for example, due to regulatory changes, such as the clarification of the "Prudent Man" provision in the United States in 1979, may have a profound impact on the attractiveness of private equity relative to other asset classes and lead to significant shifts in fund-raising and investments.

In practice, therefore, investors are likely to choose a combination of rules-based and discretionary strategies. Consistent with their top-down and bottom-up analyses, they will not only "right-size" their commitments to private equity funds over the cycle but will also adjust their mix of different asset categories. For instance, at a time when market signals suggest reducing commitments to buyout funds relative to the fund-raising market, investors may decide to increase their exposure to distressed funds and to secondary funds. Although the cyclical performance of these funds has attracted much less attention by academics, the focus and the nature of their investments suggest that they may offer interesting diversification benefits.

5.2.3 Industries

Related to the cyclical variation of private equity commitments is the diversification across industries. In venture capital, many funds are specialized either in information technology (Internet, software, telecom, etc.) or in life sciences (biotechnology, pharmaceuticals, healthcare devices, services, and systems), but there are some generalist funds that invest in both areas. In buyouts, generalist funds are the norm, with GPs usually being organized around a number of individual industries. However, there are some highly specialized GPs such as *Providence Equity Partners*, who invest only in the areas of media, entertainment, communications, and information. This industry-focused organization aims to ensure that informational advantages are accumulated, which GPs seek to exploit in identifying assets with superior value potential and unleashing this potential through a combination of financial leverage, operational improvements, and multiple arbitrage.

Industries matter from a fund investment point of view and to an even greater extent from the standpoint of a coinvestor, who can choose among the investment opportunities offered to him by a GP. Although industries tend to follow the overall business cycle, their returns are imperfectly correlated and, thus, offer diversification benefits. Cornelius, Juttmann & de Veer (2009) present correlation coefficients for total stock returns in 33 Fama–French industries in the United States for the period from 1970 to 2008. Although in several cases total returns are highly correlated [e.g., the household goods sector relative to the automotive industry (92.0 percent), clothing relative to retail (91.8 percent), and building materials relative to construction (88.3 percent)], in other cases, correlations are considerably lower [e.g., publishing relative to pharmaceuticals (43.2 percent) and utilities versus health care (46.4 percent) or versus computers (28.1 percent)].

Understanding industries and their cyclicality is found to be an important differentiator in public markets. Kacperczuk et al. (2005) shows that specialist mutual funds outperform more generalist funds, after controlling for risk and style differences, which is attributed to superior market timing skills. Table 5.1 suggests that market timing skills matter for private equity investments as well, and not only from the standpoint of the overall cycle but also with regard to individual industries. In Table 5.1, dollar-weighted IRRs are shown for 6828 portfolio companies acquired by US private equity funds between 1996 and 2006. Compiled by Cambridge Associates, these IRRs refer to the pooled *gross* mean of companies receiving initial investment in individual years. Overall, the data confirm the already well-known inverse relationship between vintage year performance and the business cycle.

Individual industries tend to follow a similar pattern in the sense that their vintage year performance deteriorates as the business cycle matures and improves as real economic activity picks up again. For example, this is the case in the consumer goods and retail industries. However, in some cases, performance swings tend to be significantly more pronounced than the overall return cycle. Take chemicals, for instance: In the second half of the 1990s, its performance worsened significantly more than the average performance of buyouts, whereas it led the recovery in the upswing between 2002 and 2005. Similarly, gross returns in manufacturing underperformed in the more mature phases of the 1990s cycle but increased more or less in line with the overall market. By contrast, in some industries, returns seem to be less susceptible to the business cycle. For example, gross IRRs in healthcare show comparatively less variance across different vintage years. However, while individual industries differ considerably in terms of the variance of their performance, private equity investors in individual

Table 5.1 US buyout dollar-weighted IRR on vintage year companies (as of September 30, 2009). Pooled gross mean of companies receiving initial investment in

	1996	1997	1998	1999	2000	2001	2002	2003	2004	2005	2006	Average	Standard deviation
Chemicals/materials	−19.1	−2.2	−11.4	−3.4	1.1	30.4	27.1	54.9	135.5	25.4	−19.8	19.9	45.0
Consumer/retail	12.0	11.6	9.5	4.7	23.9	30.7	39.1	28.3	28.6	7.5	4.1	18.2	12.2
Electronics	35.0	34.1	−42.6	15.3	−0.8	86.0	28.5	21.0	39.5	15.6	−38.3	17.6	36.0
Energy	17.2	20.1	21.2	12.6	25.8	30.5	64.5	76.5	151.6	42.4	8.1	42.8	42.0
Environmental	...	2.3	8.1	1.8	18.5	13.5	16.5	40.6	45.9	128.2	9.3	28.5	38.1
Financial services	60.7	0.8	30.9	1.1	19.5	25.7	22.3	−5.6	14.8	24.4	5.9	18.2	18.5
Hardware/systems	−0.2	−16.0	2.6	79.0	38.2	26.3	609.8	...	5.1	23.9	80.0	84.9	187.2
Healthcare	12.1	21.6	18.6	17.4	15.4	14.7	43.7	31.1	27.1	22.3	6.3	20.9	10.2
Industrial	89.6	8.1	6.7	30.3	17.4	42.6	10.8	27.8	23.6	35.2	2.2	26.8	24.5
IT	43.0	98.0	21.0	1.8	−8.9	10.9	10.5	37.2	91.1	29.1	−7.6	29.6	36.2
Manufacturing	−0.4	14.6	6.2	10.1	1.1	−4.3	22.4	38.5	20.1	23.5	9.1	12.8	12.6
Media/communications	37.9	15.0	1.7	3.6	−3.8	9.2	40.2	33.9	7.5	23.1	2.2	15.5	15.8
Software	43.9	93.9	17.0	8.8	1.0	25.2	37.6	32.2	26.1	10.2	16.9	28.4	25.2
All companies	17.7	27.6	13.4	7.1	6.6	21.7	33.9	36.4	40.1	21.6	1.7	20.7	12.9
Number of companies	373	474	554	804	1,166	421	391	479	631	707	828	...	...

Source: Cambridge Associates

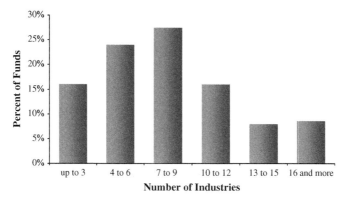

Figure 5.5 Number of industries in buyout funds.
Source: AlpInvest Research.

industries get compensated for higher risk: Those industries that show the greatest variability of returns across vintage years tend to have the highest average returns.

Given the importance of industry selection, the question arises whether an LP should commit to specialist funds according to the industry cycle or leave the industry selection to the GP by committing capital to generalist funds. A priori, there are two competing hypotheses: First, more specialized funds may possess informational advantages to generate excess returns. Alternatively, high concentration limits a fund's flexibility to invest in different industries as a function of the business cycle. Thus, more concentrated funds may be more likely to underperform and subject to considerably greater fluctuations in their investment volume—or performance—over time.

In a research project at AlpInvest Partners (Cornelius, Juttmann & de Veer, 2009), we examined the industry focus of 131 individual European and US buyout funds raised between 1997 and 2006. Overall, we found that most of them are relatively diversified across industries. As shown in Fig. 5.5, one-third of the funds had made investments in at least 10 different industries, whereas another 28 percent of the funds were diversified across at least 7 industries.[4] However, the funds had not deployed their capital equally across different industries. In several cases, a significant share of the fund's capital was absorbed by just one sector—in some extreme cases even more than 50 percent. This is reflected in the Hirschman-Herfindahl (HH) index.[5] As Fig. 5.6 shows, almost 50 percent of the funds included in the sample had a HH index

[4]Based on two-digit industries following the North American Industry Classification System (NAICS). Manufacturing is disaggregated at the three-digit level.
[5]The HH index is defined as: ΣS_i^2, with S_i denoting the share of the ith industry in a buyout fund. If the entire capital of a fund is deployed in just one industry, the index reaches its maximum value of 10,000 (100^2). Consider two examples: Fund 1 invests in 10 different industries, whereby 8 industries absorb equal shares of 10 percent of the fund's capital, one industry absorbs 15 percent of the capital, and one industry receives 5 percent. Fund 2 invests 50 percent of its capital in one industry, 10 percent in another industry, and divides the remaining 40 percent in equal parts of 5 percent across eight industries. Although the HH index is 1050 for Fund 1 ($8 \times 10^2 + 1 \times 15^2 + 1 \times 5^2$), it is 2800 for Fund 2 ($1 \times 50^2 + 1 \times 10^2 + 8 \times 5^2$).

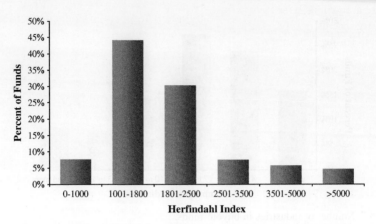

Figure 5.6 Industry concentration in buyout funds measured by Herfindahl index.
Source: AlpInvest Research.

value of more than 1800, which is generally considered as an indicator for the presence of concentration. Interestingly, fund size does not seem to play a role—large funds are as concentrated across industries as smaller funds.[6]

Not all funds are concentrated, however, and we (Cornelius, Juttmann & de Veer, 2009) found a considerable degree of variation across our sample. We also found that the degree of concentration was largely uncorrelated with the performance of the funds in our sample. When we ranked funds according to the extent to which they are concentrated with regard to different industries and rank them according to their performance (IRRs or money multiples), we obtained a Spearman rank correlation coefficient of -0.08 (with a t statistic of -0.92).[7] This result might reflect the fact that most private equity firms have dedicated industry teams, regardless of the number of industries they include in their investment universe. Interestingly, recent academic research on the specialization in the US venture capital industry finds that specialist US venture capital firms, which typically have more concentrated portfolios, tend to outperform generalist firms (Gompers et al., 2005). However, this research also finds that performance differentials between specialist and generalist venture capital firms largely disappear to the extent that the latter comprise of specialists.

Although our evidence remained inconclusive with regard to the relation between private equity funds' degree of industry specialization and their performance, we did

---

[6]Industry specialization tends to be sticky, given that the acquisition of superior expertise in particular industries is costly. Changes in a GP's industry focus are, therefore, infrequent and usually mirror secular shifts in the structure of the national or global economies. Examples of such structural shifts include the software and Internet industries, hotels and restaurants, healthcare services, business services, education, and infrastructure, whose shares in the buyout market in period from 2000 to 2007 at least doubled compared with the 1970s and 1980s, albeit from a low level. The expansion of these industries has mainly come at the expense of retail, chemicals, industrial materials, and household durables (Strömberg, 2008).
[7]The Spearman rank correlation coefficient ranges from -1 (perfect inverse correlation of ranks) to 1 (perfect correlation of ranks).

find strong support for the hypothesis that fund performance is, among other factors, a function of industry selection. More specifically, upper-quartile funds in our sample were found to have chosen industries at a stage of a cycle, whose dynamics had supported their performance. Conversely, funds whose performance had put them in the second, third, or lower quartiles were found to have chosen industries whose stage in the cycle had been less conducive to good returns. These results were statistically significant, suggesting that acquiring assets in an industry at the wrong time of the cycle will make it considerably harder for the fund manager to achieve good returns.

What are the implications for the construction of private equity portfolios? Focusing on the past performance of a fund and the persistence of its (risk-adjusted) returns, its performance is usually scrutinized with a view to a GP's skills to identify underperforming assets and generate value through a combination of operational and strategic improvements and financial engineering. Industry selection normally enters the process only to the extent that excessive industry concentration is seen as potentially risky. From an LP's risk management standpoint, the limited degree of diversification of buyout funds on a dollar-weighted basis should not cause too much worry, however, as long as funds include industries that produce relatively stable and predicable cash flows, such as food and beverages, healthcare, and utilities. Although the risk-mitigating effects of including defensive industries are sometimes offset by comparatively higher degrees of leverage in such deals, most LPs invest in a number of buyout funds, so that their portfolios are usually well diversified across industries, even if an individual fund's portfolio of companies is not. Beyond this, a fund manager's ability to time the industry cycle seems to be of secondary importance from a due diligence standpoint.

However, because the timing of the industry cycle is a necessary—although not a sufficient—condition for funds to generate upper-quartile returns, LPs should look carefully at a GP's market timing performance as an integral part of their due diligence process. Industry-specific knowledge matters even more for LPs who not only commit capital to primary funds but are also active as coinvestors and in the secondary fund market. First, LPs with a well-diversified primary fund program may choose to construct a more concentrated coinvestment portfolio, selecting industries they expect to have above-average upside potential given the stage of the cycle. Second, LPs may use their industry-specific expertise in valuating portfolios in the secondary market. Given that individual industry cycles are not fully aligned with the overall business cycle, but may lead or lag a downturn as well as an economic recovery, this knowledge should produce superior results compared with the cruder but popular approach of using GDP growth as a proxy for the earnings outlook for companies in a secondary portfolio.

5.3 Diversification in an open economy

Thus far, we have considered portfolio construction only from the perspective of the closed economy. This is an important shortcoming, however, as it ignores the growing investment opportunities that are brought about by the emergence of private equity around the globe, a process we shall be discussing in detail in the second part of this book. Generally speaking, by investing abroad, an investor can add another dimension to the menu of options he can choose from. For example, in each market segment (LBOs, mezzanine, venture capital, and distressed opportunities), an LP may decide to commit capital to funds investing in different regions and countries. The same is true for different fund styles and vintage years.

For some investors, getting exposure to private equity as an asset class or to particular market segments almost inevitably implies committing capital to foreign funds. For instance, sovereign wealth funds in the Middle East and in Asia deploy most or even all their private equity allocations abroad, as their home markets have remained largely embryonic. Another, somewhat less extreme, example is the European venture capital market whose size provides insufficient opportunities for large European investors seeking exposure to this market segment. Size constraints are often aggravated by the substantial dispersion of returns, which imply that only a relatively small number of funds are of interest from a portfolio standpoint.

However, even in mature private equity markets where size constraints do not necessarily matter—for example, the US and European buyout markets—investors may choose to commit part of their private equity allocations to foreign funds. To the extent that private equity returns at home and abroad are less-than-perfectly correlated, international investing reduces portfolio risk—just as adding a domestic asset to the portfolio whose returns are imperfectly correlated with other assets. Graphically speaking, the entire efficient frontier shifts upward in the mean-variance framework we introduced in the previous chapter. There is substantial empirical evidence in the public equity and bond markets that investors benefit from diversifying their portfolios internationally, an observation that also applies to cross-border investing in private equity.

Let us take the case for international portfolio diversification from the perspective of a US private equity investor. Specifically, our representative investor considers adding commitments to European buyout funds to his hitherto entirely domestic portfolio. In determining his potential portfolio gains, suppose that the investor first compares the vintage year IRRs for the median fund in the US and European buyout markets as reported by Thomson VentureXpert from 1987 to 2005.[8] During this period, the median US buyout fund generated on average slightly lower IRRs than the median European buyout fund. At the same time, however, the vintage year IRRs of the US median fund varied comparatively less over time (Table 5.2). In fact, the lower variance of vintage year IRRs more than offset the lower average returns in the US market, as indicated by the higher Sharpe ratio (with 3-month treasury bills generating a risk-free return of 3.75 percent). Does the historically superior risk-return trade-off in the US buyout market mean that our US private equity investor should hold a purely domestic portfolio? Absolutely not. Given that US and European mean

---

[8]Note that this approach is different from our analysis in the preceding chapter where we treated private equity as an ordinary asset class in a standard CAPM framework. In this framework, the cost of private equity capital was derived from quarterly return data. However, given the unique properties of private equity as an illiquid asset class, we focus here on the vintage year performance of buyout funds and the variance of returns across individual vintage years.

Table 5.2 Returns, risks, and Sharpe ratios for US and European buyouts, 1987–2005

	Average returns (%)	Standard deviation (%)	Sharpe ratio (%)
US buyout funds	9.3	4.4	127.3
European buyout funds	9.5	5.5	105.9
Equally weighted portfolio	9.4	4.4	129.0

Source: Thomson VentureXpert; author's calculations

returns have a correlation coefficient of 60 percent, a US investor could have increased his Sharpe ratio by allocating part of his capital to the European market (in our example, we assume equal weights).[9] From the perspective of a European investor, the diversification gain would have been even higher, given the comparatively high risk in the European buyout market.

The return history in other markets is still too short to examine the extent to which their performance is correlated with the US and European markets. However, differing business and industry cycles, economic structures, and fiscal and monetary policies suggest that investing in these markets may further enhance the risk-adjusted returns of an investor's portfolio.

However, there are a number of important caveats. To begin with, the returns, the standard deviations, and the correlation coefficient we have calculated for the US and European buyout markets are expressed in local currencies. This ignores currency risk, which may affect the potential diversification gains a US investor may reap from committing capital to European buyout funds (and, of course, vice versa). How important is currency risk from a portfolio diversification standpoint? Not much, one would be tempted to conclude from the evidence in the public markets. For example, as far as monthly US and European stock markets returns between 1997 and 2007 are concerned, Solnik and McLeavey (2009) find a correlation coefficient of 76 percent. When the foreign investments are fully hedged against currency risk by selling the foreign currency forward for an amount equal to that of the foreign stock investment, the correlation coefficient increases marginally to 77 percent. For the US and Japanese markets, Solnik and McLeavey find an unhedged coefficient of 43 percent, which drops to 41 percent if investors hedge their currency risk. Similar conclusions are reached for bond investors. However, as we have already repeatedly emphasized, private equity investors make long-term commitments, which are essentially illiquid. The evidence from the public markets is, therefore, of limited relevance, which is why we come back to the issue of currency risk in Chapter 10.

Second, simply looking at the statistical measure of risk as defined by the volatility of recent-past asset returns may underestimate country risk. This seems especially important for investors in illiquid assets who have to make commitments over many

[9]As is well known the standard deviation of a portfolio, σ_p, is given by $0.5^2[\sigma_d^2 + \sigma_f^2 + 2\rho_{d,f} (\sigma_d + \sigma_f)]$, where σ_d^2 is the standard deviation of the domestic asset, σ_f^2 is the standard deviation of the foreign asset, and $\rho_{d,f}$ is the correlation coefficient between the two assets. Here, we assume an equally weighted portfolio consisting of a domestic and a foreign asset.

years. Assessing country risk is particularly critical in emerging markets whose institutions, including their legal frameworks, are still emerging. In the past, there have been numerous examples of different types of country risk foreign investors are facing, including unanticipated changes in tax regimes, product and factor market regulations, or capital controls. How investors may assess country risk is discussed in Chapter 6.

Third, investors in foreign private equity funds face heightened governance risk in their due diligence work. Gathering information about foreign fund managers is costly and GPs' track records, especially in emerging markets, tend to be shorter. Some investors, therefore, prefer internationally operating funds they already know. However, there are doubts whether their performance in their traditional markets can be taken as a good predicator for their performance in new markets. We will return to this topic in the second part of Chapter 8.

Finally, it is sometimes argued that correlations rise as markets become increasingly integrated due to the dismantling of capital and trade barriers, financial deregulation and innovation, and major advances in information technology. However, to the extent that asset prices become more correlated, the potential gains from diversifying internationally decline and may eventually disappear. At the same time, industry factors look set to gain in relative importance. Indeed, several studies confirm that industry factors have a growing influence on stock returns relative to country-specific factors (for an overview, see Solnik & McLeavey, 2009, p. 418). Despite this, however, there remains considerable idiosyncratic risk in purely domestic portfolios. Country factors still have a significant influence in publicly traded assets. A priori, one would expect country factors to play an equally, if not more important, role in private equity as well. An ideal test case is the European Union where goods, labor, and capital markets are largely integrated. We will leave this analysis to Chapter 9.

5.4 Determining the asset mix

In the preceding analysis, we have discussed four major dimensions of diversifying a private equity portfolio. Individually, each dimension helps investors build a more robust portfolio, but how should a portfolio be constructed across all dimensions? One approach a private equity investment team could think of is to employ a mean-variance framework of the type we discussed in the previous chapter or alternative asset pricing models, such as Fama and French's (1993) Three-Factor Model. However, using a mean-variance approach to distribute a given overall allocation to private equity to the different buckets within that asset class magnifies the problems we discussed in the preceding chapter. Apart from making appropriate adjustments for stale pricing, non-normal returns, and so on, expected returns would need to be specified for every component of the relevant inverse. In practice, expected returns are typically defined by a broad benchmark, but which benchmark should investors use for venture capital in Asia or distressed investments in Europe? Furthermore, investors often find that their specification of expected returns produces output portfolio weights, which, given the complex mapping between expected returns and portfolio weights, may not make sense. Small changes in expected returns can lead to rather dramatic changes in portfolio weights, which, however, are difficult, if not impossible, to implement, taking into account the long-term nature of private equity investing and the very different investment opportunities in individual market segments.

These issues have motivated Black and Litterman (1992) to develop an alternative model of portfolio selection, which is based on a Baysian approach. Although Black and Litterman's model was originally designed for diversified portfolios of different asset classes, its fundamental ideas can usefully be applied to the narrower context of constructing a robust private equity portfolio. Importantly, the Black–Litterman model takes into account that investment managers tend to think in terms of weights in a portfolio rather than balancing expected returns against the contribution to portfolio risk—the relevant margin in the traditional mean-variance optimization process. In essence, their approach can be conceived as an attempt to make the mean-variance approach more applicable for investment professionals. The starting point of the Black–Litterman approach is the market equilibrium returns, which provide a neutral reference point, in the sense that they clear the market if all investors have identical "views" (i.e., specific opinions about asset returns). As Black and Litterman show, the unconstrained optimal portfolio is the market equilibrium (capitalization weights) portfolio. For example, in a pure private equity portfolio, an investor would hold 20 percent of his assets in US buyouts, if this market segment accounted for 20 percent of the global private equity market in a given vintage year.

A market-neutral allocation assumes that the investor has no particular views about individual market segments. The beauty of the Black–Litterman approach is that it allows investors to deviate from the (neutral) market equilibrium in a very intuitive way. To deviate from market neutrality, investors must formulate their own return expectations and specify the degree of confidence they have in the stated views.[10] In the model, this information is translated into symmetric confidence bands around normally distributed returns. The optimal portfolio is simply a set of deviations from (neutral) market capitalization weights in the directions of portfolios about which views are expressed. The major contribution of the Black–Litterman model lies in its ability to derive a consistent weighting scheme between the (neutral) equilibrium view and the subjective view of the investor, with the extent of deviations from the equilibrium view being determined by the degree of confidence the investor has in each view. In other words, the higher (lower) the degree of confidence, the more (less) the revised expected returns are tilted toward the investor's particular views. The major steps in the Black–Litterman model can be summarized as follows (Fig. 5.7).[11]

[10]In implementing the Black–Litterman approach, the investor has to express his views in terms of a probability distribution. The model can handle both relative views ("I expect that US buyouts outperform European buyouts by x percent") as well as absolute views ("I expect that Asian venture capital funds raised in 2010 will generate a mean IRR of 20 percent").

[11]An empirical exposition of the Black–Litterman model is given, for example, in He and Litterman (1999).

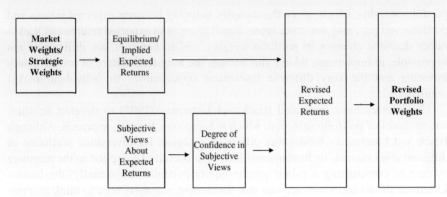

Figure 5.7 The Black–Litterman optimization process.
Source: Black and Litterman (1992).

If an investor has no particular views on individual assets, he will not deviate from the market capitalization-weighted portfolio, and the structure of his private equity portfolio will then look like the global private equity market as depicted in Fig. 2.1. However, based on his top-down and bottom-up research, which takes into account factors such as supply and demand dynamics in the fund-raising and M&A markets, interest rates, and deal fundamentals (e.g., industry-specific valuations, equity and debt multiples, and earnings expectations), the investor may decide to deviate from a market-neutral allocation. For example, from a top-down perspective, he might have concluded that large buyout funds raised in 2006 and 2007 were likely to under-perform, an input the Black–Littman approach would have translated into an underweighting, relative to the market, of this market segment. At the same time, the investor might have had superior return expectations with regard to secondary and distressed funds, leading him to overweight these segments. In terms of emerging geographies, his return expectations might have led him to invest a relatively greater share of his private equity capital in Latin American growth funds than market neutrality would have suggested. Conversely, in a Black–Litterman approach, his relatively more cautious return outlook on Central and Eastern Europe might result in lower-than-market-neutral weights for this region.

Deviations from market-neutral weightings may also result from an investor's bottom-up analysis. This is particularly possible in market segments where returns are highly dispersed. Consider US venture capital, for example, where access restrictions to top-performing funds are particularly prevalent. Although the investor's return expectations may be consistent with a market-neutral exposure to this asset class, his bottom-up analysis may lead him to conclude that there are too few investment opportunities in a given vintage year relative to the size of his target allocation. The opposite may also be true: If the investor is confident that he can identify, and has access to, the few highly successful funds that are raised in a given vintage year, he may adjust his return expectations upward relatively to the market, with the Black–Litterman approach providing the revised portfolio weights for the individual private equity assets.

What remains to be done once the portfolio weights are determined is to decide on the number of fund managers in each segment. As Meyer and Mathonet (2005, pp. 95–113) show, the portfolio's standard deviation declines as more funds are added to the portfolio. However, on the basis of Monte Carlo simulations (with 100,000 runs of randomly chosen funds), they find that most of the diversification gains occur with fewer than 20 funds; they become minor at 30 funds or more. In determining the optimal number of funds in a private equity portfolio, Meyer and Mathonet factor in the costs of running a private equity portfolio, which they assume to be a (decreasing) function of the size of the portfolio. As the optimization criterion, they choose the *Sertino ratio*, which is a modification of the well-known Sharpe ratio.[12] On this basis, they conclude that while for an investment portfolio of € 300 million the optimal number of funds is reached between 25 and 30, for a portfolio of € 500 million the optimal number of funds lies between 35 and 40. Multibillion dollar (euro) portfolios typically include many more funds. Large LPs such as AlpInvest Partners or CalPERS have made commitments to around 300–400 private equity funds.

The optimal number for the overall private equity investment portfolio needs to be allocated to individual market segments, styles, and geographies, which depends on their respective probability density functions. There may be good reasons for being underdiversified relative to what the Sertino ratio suggests. For example, in venture capital where the function has a long right tail, it may make sense to invest only with a small number of funds that are expected to provide particular upside risk. In large buyouts, it might be argued that the probability density function has become more compressed, making coinvestment opportunities an increasingly important criterion for the selection of individual funds. However, as coinvestment opportunities are generally reserved for the largest investors in a fund, LPs may decide to make more concentrated bets.

5.5 Summary and conclusions

In this chapter, we have discussed the allocation of capital across market segments, vintage years, industries, and geographies, given an overall allocation to private equity as an asset class. Each dimension may provide important diversification gains—subject to a number of investment constraints. In constructing a robust private equity portfolio along these dimensions, we have proposed a Black–Litterman approach whose starting point is a market-neutral allocation. Although the market portfolio reflects the market view on returns in individual market segments, deviations from that view result in different portfolio weights. For example, given the inverse relationship between the overall inflow of capital to private equity funds and their performance, a market-neutral allocation would inevitably result in a concentration of

---

[12]Similar to the Sharpe ratio, the Sortino ratio measures the risk-adjusted return of an asset or portfolio. However, unlike the Sharpe ratio, it penalizes only those returns falling below a user-specified target or required rate of return. The Sortino ratio, S, is calculated as: $S = (R - T)/DR$, with R denoting the asset or portfolio realized return; T the target or required rate of return for the portfolio, and DR the downside risk defined as the target semideviation or the square root of the target semivariance.

capital in underperforming vintage years. As we discussed, a more balanced distribution of capital across individual vintage years would help investors enhance returns relative to the market benchmark. Similarly, there may be important reasons for investors to overweigh or underweigh individual market segments, industries, or geographies. Such reasons may be grounded in both top-down and bottom-up analyses. In this chapter, we have favored a combined approach, ensuring that an investor's macro perspectives on factors such as economic growth, corporate earnings, interest rates, and exit markets are consistent with the perceived investment opportunities at the micro level, which are determined, among other things, by the fund-raising cycle and access to individual funds.

Part Two

Markets, Investment Flows, and Due Diligence

6 Global markets, regional penetration, and country risk

In Chapter 5, we have argued that global investing may help increase risk-adjusted returns of private equity portfolios. Until recently, the potential for international portfolio diversification was largely confined to two markets, the United States and Western Europe. Today, however, investors have a much wider choice as private equity markets are emerging around the globe. In this chapter, we provide an overview of the size and the regional structure of the global private equity market and ask why some national and regional markets are playing catch-up considerably faster than others. Distinguishing between mature markets, nontraditional markets in advanced economies, and emerging and frontier markets, we then discuss attractiveness indexes that have been developed as a tool for investors to assess the quality of the business environment for private equity in individual economies. In reviewing such efforts, we also debate the feasibility for LPs to a priori restrict their investment universe to a predefined universe of "permissible" markets. Attractiveness indexes provide useful input in assessing country risk, an issue we turn to in the final part of this chapter. More specifically, we present a framework that can be used to classify different types of country risk and examine such risks in a consistent way across different markets. An appendix provides a brief overview of statistical sources and information to help quantify country risk.

6.1 Global private equity and the size of regional markets

Although commitments to private equity vary substantially across different classes of investors as well as across individual investors within such classes, overall

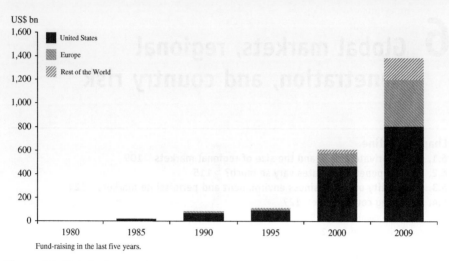

Figure 6.1 Global private equity assets under management.
Source: McKinsey (2007, 2008); PREQIN.

private equity AUM (as defined in Section 2.1) has risen substantially over time. Conventionally measured as the sum of private equity funds raised over the last 5 years,[1] AUM stood at almost US$ 1.4 trillion at the end of 2009 (Fig. 6.1). Of this amount, around US$ 950 billion was due to commitments to buyout funds. Over the 20-year period between 1990 and 2009, private equity AUM rose at a CAGR of more than 15 percent, considerably faster than AUM in most other asset classes. However, two important qualifications are in order. First of all, since AUM are measured as the cumulative amount of committed capital to private equity funds, they do not reflect any NAV changes with regard to the portfolio companies these funds have acquired. Given the substantial decline in asset prices in the wake of the financial crisis, on a marked-to-market basis AUM defined as portfolio company holdings may be lower than valued at cost.[2] Second, AUM shown in Fig. 6.1 include undrawn commitments to private equity funds, which are estimated to have amounted to around US$ 740 billion at the end of 2009 (Fig. 6.2). Obviously, this part would not be subject to mark-to-market adjustments. Thus,

[1] This takes into account that private equity funds hold on average their portfolio companies for a period of 5 years.

[2] As asset prices have recovered significantly following their trough in the spring of 2009, some of the losses have been recouped. However, estimates of private equity AUM on a marked-to-market basis are subject to considerable uncertainty. Requirements to mark-to-market portfolio companies vary substantially across countries, and even within individual jurisdictions there remains considerable variation as to how GPs report their holdings, despite important efforts to implement more transparent and consistent rules to reflect fair market values. Intertemporal comparisons of AUM valued on a marked-to-market basis are further aggravated by the fact that until recently adjustments to the fair market value of private equity funds occurred relatively infrequently, with portfolio companies often held at cost for a prolonged period of time.

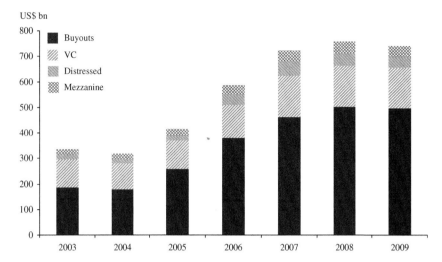

Figure 6.2 Global dry powder of private equity funds, end of period.
Source: PREQIN.

under reasonable assumptions private equity AUM would still have grown at double-digit annual rates over the past two decades.

As we have discussed before in the context of the US market, the substantial growth in private equity AUM over the last few decades has not been linear but instead has been subject to pronounced cycles around the long-term trend. As institutional investors and HNWIs have increased their allocations to private equity, they have enabled fund managers to acquire substantially more and larger assets. Lerner, Sørensen, and Strömberg (2009) estimate that during the period from 1990 to 2007, the peak of the last private equity cycle, the value of transactions worldwide totaled almost US$ 5.5 trillion (deflated to 2008 dollars).[3] During this period, the global value of transactions increased at a compound annual growth rate of about 23.5 percent (Fig. 6.3). Leveraged buyouts accounted for the bulk of the total value of transactions. However, in terms of the number of deals, venture capital saw almost twice as many transactions as LBOs between 1990 and 2007.

In terms of geographies, the United States remains the most important market, followed by Western Europe. However, other regions are catching up as shown in Figs 6.4 and 6.5, which compare the amount of private equity transactions between 1990 and 1999 and between 2000 and 2008 (in constant 2008 dollars) in

---

[3]Their estimates are based on transactions recorded by Capital IQ. For those transactions where transaction values are missing, values are imputed by a fitted value from a regression of the log transaction-value-on-year dummies, dummies for the 10 main industry groups, dummies for the main transaction types given in Capital IQ (VC, LBO, growth capital, PIPEs, other acquisitions, and other private placements) and 123 country dummies.

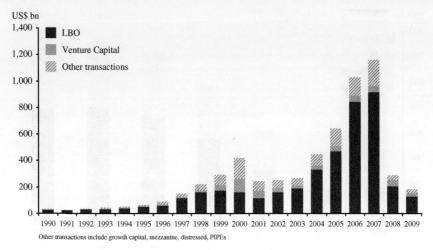

Figure 6.3 Global transaction volume, 1990–2009 (in 2008 US$).
Source: Strömberg (2008, 2009), Capital IQ, TVE, EVCA, NVCA, and other national and regional venture capital and private equity associations.

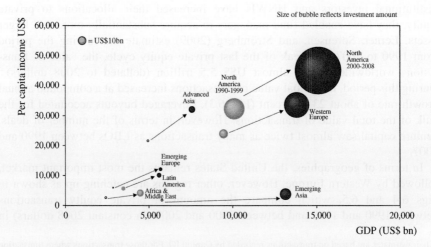

Figure 6.4 Evolution of regional venture capital markets, 1990–2008. Venture capital transactions relative to size of the economy and stage of development.
Source: Strömberg (2008); IMF, Capital IQ, TVE, EVCA, NVCA, and other national and regional venture capital and private equity associations and author's calculations.

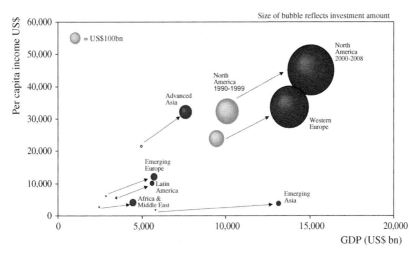

Figure 6.5 Evolution of regional buyout markets, 1990–2008. Buyout transactions relative to size of the economy and stage of development.
Source: Strömberg (2008), IMF, and author's calculations.

the venture capital and buyout markets, respectively.[4] In these figures, the catch-up process is shown as a function of two variables, the size of a region's economy (typically expressed by a region's GDP) and its stage of development, which we approximate by the region's per capita income. Broadly speaking, three different stages can be identified (Porter, 1990): In the *factor-driven stage*, a country's competitive advantages are driven by basic factor conditions, such as low-cost labor and unprocessed natural resources. In the second, or *investment-driven stage*, the dominant source of competitive advantage lies in the efficiency in producing more advanced but still largely undifferentiated goods and services. In the final stage of development, the *innovation-driven stage*, a country's firms compete on the basis of their ability to produce innovative goods and services at the global technology frontier using the most advanced techniques. Progressing through the different stages of development is a function of a complex set of factors (e.g., macroeconomic stability, education, infrastructure, quality of institutions, depth and breadth of financial markets), which are tried to be captured by the annual competitiveness rankings of the World Economic Forum (see also Barro, 1998).

As Figs 6.4 and 6.5 show, private equity markets have expanded around the world as regional economies have grown and become more sophisticated (in the diagram they move along the horizontal and/or vertical axes). In venture capital, however, the catch-up process has been relatively gradual, with the United States remaining by

---

[4]Buyouts include growth capital transactions that dominate in emerging markets. It is not always easy to distinguish growth capital transactions from venture capital deals. As a result, Figs 6.4 and 6.5 may be subject to some misclassification.

far the world's most important market. Between 2000 and 2008, US firms still attracted more than two-thirds of all venture capital investments. By contrast, European firms received less than 25 percent of global venture capital (measured in US$), a share which would have been even lower in the absence of the substantial appreciation of the euro during this period. In absolute terms, European venture capital investments averaged less than US$ 10 billion during the 4-year period from 2005 to 2008, and at this level, they continue to fall considerably short of what economic policy makers have envisioned with a view to providing support for early stage and high-tech firms. In fact, the creation of active venture capital markets has received high policy priority both at the Pan-European and national levels. In 2001, the European Commission catapulted the European Investment Fund (EIF) into Europe's largest venture capital investor with a capital injection of more than € 2 billion. Motivated by the objective to increase the supply of risk capital to foster innovation, this approach has been shared by similar schemes in individual member countries. In essence, these programs have in common that they are trying to replicate the diffusion and success that venture capital has achieved in the United States—thus far, with limited results (Da Rin, Nicodano, & Sembenelli, 2006; Lerner, 2009).

Emerging Asia's catch-up process in the global venture capital market has been comparatively faster. This is particularly true with regard to China, whose enterprises received on average more than US$ 4 billion per annum between 2005 and 2008, a tenfold increase since the beginning of the decade. As in Europe, an important driver of this substantial growth has been public policies, with the government investing as a limited partner in venture capital funds along with other investors. Today, China is the world's second most important national VC market. By comparison, India's and Israel's VC markets have remained considerably smaller, although their shares have also increased appreciably.

The real outlier is Advanced Asia, whose stage of development and the size of economy would suggest a significantly larger role for venture capital. Although Advanced Asia has become more penetrated in recent years, it continues to lag substantially behind North America and Western Europe. Obviously, there are other factors at work that have severely limited the expansion of the region's venture market, an issue we discuss in the following section.

Buyouts have proved to be comparatively more successful in penetrating economies outside the United States. True, the United States has remained the largest buyout market in terms of transaction volumes. However, Europe is not far behind, although its indigenous private equity industry began to emerge only in the early 1980s. Between 2000 and 2008, the volume of Western European buyouts amounted to 70 percent of the North American market, up from about 40 percent during the preceding 10 years. Other regions have also increased their market shares. Buyout activity has picked up considerably in Advanced Asia-Pacific, quite in contrast to the region's rather gradual catch-up process in venture capital. Much of this growth in buyouts has occurred in Australia, mirroring a rise in the number of deals as well as larger average deal sizes. By contrast, the Japanese buyout market has been dominated by relatively small deals. Although transactions with an enterprise value of more than US$ 1 billion have remained the exception, the number of Japanese buyouts has also increased significantly over the last decade.

Buyout activity in emerging economies has also increased appreciably. This is particularly true for Emerging Europe where mature industries have required substantial amounts of capital in their transformation process. Although buyout transactions have also gained momentum in Emerging Asia, this process has been comparatively more moderate, given the region's industry structure, which is dominated by relatively young companies seeking capital to expand and grow. In growth capital transactions, it is the norm that financial sponsors are able to acquire only a minority stake in the company. However, even in buyout transactions of more mature companies it is often difficult to acquire a controlling stake, which represents another limiting factor for the development of a buyout market in these economies.

6.2   Why do penetration rates vary so much?

As impressive as the recent catch-up process outside the United States and Western Europe has been (Fig. 6.6),[5] there remains a substantial degree of variance across regions and, indeed, individual countries in terms of their market penetration—even if we take into account differences in terms of their respective stage of development. In the 1990s, it had already looked as if penetration rates in what is often labeled the *rest of the world* would rapidly converge toward those in the mature markets. As Leeds and Sunderland (2003) explain, private equity had appeared like a clear winner in the developing world when a broad global consensus emerged that the private sector, rather than the state, should be the primary driver for new investment and economic growth. As long as private firms played a limited role in the economy, many relied on "friends and family." However, as the private sector expanded, an increasing number of firms had to move beyond their traditional financing model. But how? Given their risk profile and the lack of a track record, many firms found it very difficult, if not impossible, to obtain bank financing or raise equity and debt capital in the securities markets. While private equity seemed to provide an important alternative for firms requiring capital to grow, on the supply side investors were attracted by the potentially lucrative returns amid low valuations. As it turned out, however, investors' expectations were soon disappointed, causing the pickup in private equity activity to be a temporary phenomenon.

---

[5]In Fig. 6.6 we compare the 4-year periods 1993–1996 and 2003–2006. These periods have been chosen to focus on "normal" years as opposed to "bubble years" or "market troughs." For example, during the Great Recession from 2007 to 2009, investment-to-GDP ratios fell across all regions. However, in the mature markets in the United States and Western Europe the decline was considerably more pronounced as the dominance of leveraged buyouts made private equity activity particularly susceptible to the turmoil in the debt capital markets. In 2009, which saw the lowest level of global private equity investing since 2002, the penetration rate in mature markets averaged only 0.2 percent. This was hardly more than that in the emerging markets whose lesser dependence on debt allowed them to gain market share.

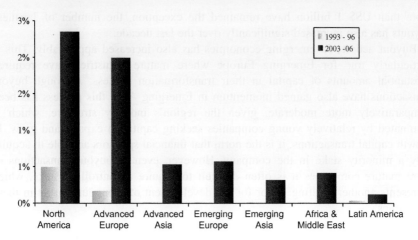

Figure 6.6 Private equity penetration in individual regions. a. Penetration measured as private equity investments (in 2008 dollars) in percent of GDP
Source: Lerner et al. (2009), IMF WEO Database, and author's calculations.

Given the heterogeneity in private equity markets, we suggest a country classification that is more granulated than the standard differentiation between "advanced" and "emerging economies" or the "United States and Europe" on the one hand and the "rest of the world" on the other. Instead, in this book we differentiate between truly mature private equity markets and "nontraditional markets," with the latter showing some emerging market characteristics, despite the advanced stage of their economies (Table 6.1). As far as emerging markets are concerned, the degree of heterogeneity is even greater. Coined in 1981 by then World Bank official Antoine van Agtmael (2007), the term "emerging markets" has been widely adopted by international investors to refer to all developing countries rather than the few that have relatively developed domestic financial markets (Leeds, 2006). The same applies to private equity markets in emerging market economies. While some countries have already enjoyed considerable growth in private equity investing—notably the BRICs (Brazil, Russia, India, and China), some Central and Eastern European economies, South Africa, and Turkey—others are still at a more embryonic stage. As a result, we distinguish between emerging markets and what we call "frontier markets." In these frontier markets international financial institutions often play the lead role in getting private equity activity off the ground.[6] By contrast, we define emerging private equity

---

[6]International Financial Institutions (IFIs) investing in private equity funds include, for example, the International Finance Corporation (IFC), the African Development Bank (AfDB), the Asian Development Bank (ADB), or the European Bank for Reconstruction and Development (EBRD). National development organizations providing private equity capital include, for instance, America's Overseas Private Investment Corporation (OPIC), Britain's Commonwealth Development Corporation (CDC), and Germany's Deutsche Entwicklungsgesellschaft (DEG). An - admittedly extreme - example of a frontier market benefiting from public capital in private equity funds is Afghanistan. Raised in 2004 and managed by ACAP Partners, the Afghanistan Renewal Fund invests in small- and medium-sized firms between US$ 500,000 and US$ 5 million.

Table 6.1 Market typology

	Mature markets	Nontraditional markets in advanced economies	Emerging markets	Frontier markets
Economic structure	Sophisticated	Sophisticated	Relatively developed	Comparatively early stage of economic/financial development
Economic stability	High	High	Track record is being established	Track record still short
Size of the economy and growth	Large/high level of prosperity	Varies	Significant size of the economy and/or growth prospects or part of larger economic area	Small size; growth from a comparatively lower level
Debt markets	Highly liquid	Liquid	Emerging	Still embryonic
Exit markets	Developed public equity markets with high market capitalization	Developed public equity markets with significant market capitalization	Relatively developed public equity markets with sufficient market capitalization	Underdeveloped
Global private equity firms	Investing	Investing	Investing	Very limited, if any, investments
Domestic private equity industry	Developed	Emerging	Emerging	Rudimentary

(continued on next page)

Table 6.1 Market typology—*cont'd*

	Mature markets	Nontraditional markets in advanced economies	Emerging markets	Frontier markets
Private equity exits	Considerable history	Track record being established	Visible exits already occurred	Very limited, often yet to happen
Role of international financial institutions	None	None	Diminishing	Active
Key markets	United States, EU-15, Switzerland	Australia, Canada, Hong Kong (SAR), Singapore, Japan, New Zealand	Argentina, Brazil, China, Czech Republic, Egypt, Hungary, India, Mexico, Poland, Russian Federation, Slovak Republic, Slovenia, South Africa, South Korea, Taiwan (ROC), Turkey	Bulgaria, Colombia, Indonesia, Jordan, Kazakhstan, Morocco, Nigeria, Pakistan, Philippines, Romania, Saudi Arabia, Thailand, Tunisia, Ukraine, Vietnam, UAE

markets as those where an indigenous private equity industry is already developing and visible exits have begun to attract a growing amount of interest among international investors.

What explains the degree of variance of market penetration and why do some countries have played catch-up more rapidly than others? The observation that the role of private equity in financial intermediation continues to vary significantly across countries—even when corrected for variations in the countries' stages of development—has attracted considerable interest in academic research. Initially, most cross-country studies have focused on the role of venture capital in high-income countries. Generally, these studies have identified the existence of a robust market for initial public offerings (IPO) as the single most critical factor for venture capital investing. Comparing the US and German venture capital markets, Black and Gilson (1999) conclude that venture capital can flourish especially, "and perhaps only" if the venture capitalist can exit from a successful portfolio company through an IPO, which requires an active stock market. In bank-financed systems, like in Germany, but also Japan, equity markets tend to be significantly smaller relative to the size of their economies, which Black and Gilson (1998) interpret as the key reason why venture capital has remained much less important than in market-based systems like the United States. Jeng and Wells (2000) who study venture capital investments in 21 developed economies confirm the explanatory power of the IPO market for venture capital activity. Similarly, Da Rin et al. (2006) find strong evidence that the creation of "new" stock markets in Europe targeted at entrepreneurial companies helped increase the "innovation" ratio of early stage investments to total venture investments.

Although a well-functioning IPO market is found to be particularly critical for venture investing, it is not a sufficient condition. In Japan, for example, several stock markets have been created (e.g., Mothers, Hercules, and JASDAQ), albeit with limited success measured by VC activity in this economy. This suggests that other factors may play an important role as well. Empirical studies have looked at a large number of variables, including the tax treatment of venture capital funds and investments, the quality of labor market institutions, and a country's capacity to innovate. Among the variables potentially explaining cross-country differences in VC investing, particular attention has been paid to different corporate governance structures and the quality of legal institutions in individual economies. Motivated by the rapidly growing "law and finance" literature (La Porta, Lopez-de-Silvanes, & Shleifer 1999; La Porta, Lopez-de-Silvanes, Shleifer, & Vishny, 1997, 1998, 2002), most studies in this field have focused on contractional arrangements in individual deals. For example, Lerner and Schoar (2005), who study 210 developing country private equity investments (mainly expansion and venture capital transactions) find that deals in low-enforcement countries are based to a comparatively larger degree on equity and board control as opposed to convertible preferred stock with covenants, a more common form in high-enforcement countries. Their finding is broadly consistent with what the "law and finance" literature predicts. Studying venture capital investments in 16 countries (mostly in Asia), Allen and Song (2003) show that venture capitalists seem to rely to a much larger degree on implicit relationships as opposed to explicit contracts in countries where the rule of law is relatively weak. Somewhat surprisingly, they find a negative relation between the rule of law and venture capital activity, suggesting that relationships can substitute for contracts with this type of financing. However, relying on implicit relationships or majority ownership rather than contractional provisions is found to only partially alleviate legal enforcement problems, as evidenced by significantly higher firm valuations in economies with superior legal enforcement mechanisms.

In the most comprehensive cross-country study to date, which includes almost 33,000 venture capital deals in a large sample of countries, Lerner et al. (2009) confirm that institutions matter. Specifically, they show that minority shareholder rights are important for venture (as well as for growth capital) deals. In their view, the linchpin between the protection of minority rights and venture capital activity is the IPO market: Unless venture capital firms are able to exit via an IPO, they will need to convince new shareholders to buy the stock of their portfolio companies. However, investors are likely to be reluctant to purchase stakes in firms where private equity groups have major holdings—a reluctance that may be overcome only through the effective protection of minority rights. Similarly, Lerner et al. (2009) find that countries where investors are better protected, for example, through disclosure requirements and liability standards, typically enjoy more venture capital trans-actions. Again, they interpret their finding as evidence for the critical role of well-functioning exit markets.

As far as LBOs are concerned, the empirical evidence is less conclusive. According to Lerner et al. (2009), IPO markets do not seem to matter much for buyout activity. Nor does the provision of debt, suggesting that buyout firms do not need to rely on domestic capital markets but may borrow and raise debt capital internation-ally.[7] And unlike in venture capital deals, minority shareholder rights play little, if any, role in explaining cross-country variations in LBOs.

Instead, what matters for buyout transactions is the potential for operational engineering, that is, measures to improve portfolio companies' production processes, working capital management, and their marketing and production mix. Operational and strategic improvements require appropriate corporate governance standards. Corruption is generally found to hamper operational improvements and is therefore associated with fewer buyouts. Similarly, barriers to entrepreneurship—often proxied by the number of procedures required to start a business and the costs associated with them—is found to be inversely related to the volume of buyout transactions in a cross-section of countries. Finally, the freer an economy with respect to international trade, the larger tends to be the role of buyout funds in financial intermediation. Conversely, high regulatory trade barriers, international capital market controls, and high taxes on international trade are generally associated with fewer LBOs.

---

[7]This applies to large buyouts, whereas cross-border borrowing for transactions at the smaller end of the market is generally more difficult. Raising debt internationally entails currency risk. As our conversations with leading GPs confirm (Chapter 12), this risk is usually hedged.

6.3 The quality of the business environment and permissible markets

Taking into account the factors that are found to explain cross-country differences in private equity investing, there have been several attempts to develop private equity country attractiveness indexes. Examples include Apax Partners (2007), Latin American Venture Capital Association (2010), and Groh and Liechtenstein (2009). Groh and Liechtenstein's *Global Venture Capital and Private Equity Country Attractiveness Index* appears especially valuable for investors as its country coverage is particularly comprehensive (66 economies); the country rankings are updated annually, which allows the user to track improvements and slippages over time; and the results are accessible on the Internet (http://vcpeindex.iese.us/).[8] Distilling information from a large variety of sources, including some described in more detail in Appendix 6.1, the index is comprised of 62 indicators. These indicators are grouped into six broad categories: economic activity, depth of capital markets, taxation, investor protection and corporate governance, human and social environment, and entrepreneurial culture opportunities. In aggregating the individual indicators, the index employs equal weights. The overall index is then split into sub-indices for venture capital and buyouts by eliminating indicators that are deemed to be unimportant for the respective market segment. For example, while the depth and efficiency of the debt and credit markets are critical for buyouts, the index assumes that they are largely irrelevant for venture capital. Conversely, the sub-index for buyouts ignores an economy's level of innovation, a criterion that plays an important role for venture capital investments.

The rankings correspond more or less to the degree to which individual economies are penetrated (Table 6.2). As far as the mature markets are concerned, the most attractive business environment for private equity is found to be in North America and the United Kingdom. In non-UK Europe, Scandinavia is generally identified as comparatively attractive, whereas important disadvantages are found in the Southern markets, Greece, Italy, Portugal, and Spain. In the emerging world, markets in Central and Eastern Europe and Asia appear on average more attractive than those in Latin America and Africa. These observations are largely consistent with other rankings (e.g., Apax Partners, 2007) that are based on similar models.

From an investor's standpoint, the analysis gets particularly interesting when the perceived degree of attractiveness deviates from actual capital flows. For instance, private equity and venture capital still play a relatively rudimentary role in Japan, although it scores among the top-ten markets on the attractiveness index. Conversely, countries such as Brazil and Egypt have recently attracted considerable interest from both domestic and foreign private equity funds, despite their comparatively poor rankings. Luckily, the index allows the user to identify the sources of such discrepancies on the basis of a SWOT (strengths/weaknesses, opportunities/threats) analysis for individual economies. Arguably, the most

---

[8]The foundations of the index are explained in greater detail in Groh and Liechtenstein (2009) and Groh, Liechtenstein, and Lieser (2010).

Table 6.2 The global venture capital and private equity country attractiveness index, 2009–2010

	Overall index	Economic activity	Depth of capital markets	Taxation	Investment protection and corporate governance	Human and social environment	Entrepreneurial culture and opportunities
US	1	4	1	53	10	12	3
Canada	2	10	3	52	9	6	7
UK	3	9	2	33	6	14	11
Australia	4	7	4	41	11	5	13
Hong Kong	5	19	5	9	3	8	18
Singapore	6	25	13	6	1	1	10
Japan	7	6	7	48	18	18	8
Switzerland	8	2	11	4	23	3	5
Netherlands	9	3	16	29	15	16	6
Germany	10	5	14	16	14	19	14
Sweden	11	15	17	38	12	10	4
Denmark	12	14	29	27	4	2	2
Korea	13	23	9	13	26	30	12
Norway	14	1	24	35	8	15	9
Finland	15	17	28	32	5	7	1
France	16	11	10	44	19	25	22
Belgium	17	16	27	47	17	11	16
New Zealand	18	29	40	54	2	4	15
Austria	19	8	37	36	16	9	19
Spain	20	22	12	46	24	38	26
Ireland	21	28	41	5	7	13	17
Israel	22	24	26	43	21	24	21
Taiwan	23	30	19	31	25	31	24
Luxembourg	24	12	42	11	13	22	20

Malaysia	25	38	15	21	28	28	32
UAE	26	20	22	3	38	17	38
Portugal	27	31	33	25	30	32	28
China	28	35	6	62	52	42	50
Italy	29	18	21	49	46	47	27
Saudi Arabia	30	36	30	1	37	35	41
Poland	31	27	32	30	39	34	35
Chile	32	44	34	39	22	27	42
Slovenia	33	33	52	24	33	29	23
Czech Republic	34	26	44	28	35	20	33
Estonia	35	60	50	14	20	26	25
Thailand	36	43	25	42	42	41	52
Hungary	37	41	54	17	31	45	30
India	38	55	8	58	44	39	64
Greece	39	21	35	26	45	50	39
Lithuania	40	48	58	10	32	40	29
Slovakia	41	37	56	20	36	37	34
Kuwait	42	13	38	64	40	33	45
South Africa	43	58	20	34	27	63	48
Turkey	44	47	36	18	50	46	44
Croatia	45	46	49	15	48	43	31
Oman	46	52	53	2	34	21	56
Romania	47	39	47	60	41	44	40
Russian Federation	48	40	23	19	61	54	47
Mexico	49	32	39	40	47	62	46
Latvia	50	64	60	7	29	36	36
Brazil	51	34	18	65	54	56	57
Uruguay	52	50	63	56	43	23	43
Peru	53	45	48	22	51	55	54

(continued on next page)

Table 6.2 The global venture capital and private equity country attractiveness index, 2009–2010—*cont'd*

	Overall index	Economic activity	Depth of capital markets	Taxation	Investment protection and corporate governance	Human and social environment	Entrepreneurial culture and opportunities
Indonesia	54	54	31	57	63	51	61
Bulgaria	55	53	64	8	53	49	37
Morocco	56	51	46	50	59	60	53
Egypt	57	59	45	23	49	61	58
Colombia	58	49	51	45	58	64	49
Argentina	59	42	59	37	64	53	51
Vietnam	60	62	55	55	62	52	55
Philippines	61	56	43	59	60	58	65
Nigeria	62	57	62	51	57	57	62
Ukraine	63	63	61	66	56	48	59
Kenya	64	66	57	63	55	59	60
Paraguay	65	61	66	12	65	66	63
Venezuela	66	65	65	61	66	65	66

Source: Groh and Liechtenstein (2009)

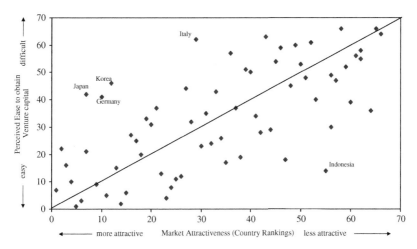

Figure 6.7 Venture capital market attractiveness and perceived ease to obtain venture capital in 66 markets.
Source: Groh and Liechtenstein (2009) and World Economic Forum (2009).

important value for investors lies in the rankings of emerging markets where important informational deficiencies persist. This is particularly true for the "second generation" emerging markets, or frontier markets, where a private equity ecosystem has just begun to develop. Though their overall score on the index provides useful guidance as to where individual countries stand relative to others, it is the individual components that help investors form their expectations about the risks and returns in investing abroad.

How does the picture look like from the demand side? Other things being equal, we would expect entrepreneurs who operate in a business environment that is conducive to private equity investments to find it relatively easier to obtain capital (and vice versa). Every year, the World Economic Forum asks in its Global Competitiveness Survey the following question: "In your country, how easy is it for entrepreneurs with innovative but risky projects to find venture capital (1 = very difficult; 7 = very easy)?"[9] In Fig. 6.7, we plot the country rankings according to Groh and Liechtenstein's (2009) sub-index for the attractiveness of venture capital markets and the country rankings that result from the World Economic Forum's survey. As expected, we find a positive correlation between the attractiveness of individual markets and the perceived ease at which entrepreneurs can obtain venture capital. However, this correlation is far from perfect (if it were, all observations would fall onto the diagonal). In countries that lie in the area above the diagonal access to venture capital is more difficult than the measured market attractiveness suggests. This applies, for example, to Japan and Korea and to Germany and Italy. Below the diagonal lie countries where access to venture capital is perceived to be easy relative to challenges their business environments pose for investors.

[9]In 2009, more than 13,000 executives from 133 countries participated in the survey.

Market attractiveness rankings may provide useful input for investors in their macro due diligence work to assess country risk. This applies to the allocation of capital to private equity funds operating in different regions of countries, and it is especially relevant for coinvestors who contemplate an investment alongside a private equity fund. As a limited partner in a private equity fund or a coinvestor, am I comfortable with the level of country risk I have to accept in different markets? Given the perceived level of risk, what is my required return that compensates me for the risk I take? How risky is a particular investment universe relative to an alternative group of countries?

One approach is to identify countries where investments are in principle permissible and distinguish such markets from others where the LP is not allowed to invest. The emphasis is on "in principle"—whether or not investments are actually made in countries that are classified as permissible still depends on the investor's specific risk/ return analysis. Such an approach has been pursued by CalPERS between 2002 and 2007 with respect to its public equity emerging markets portfolio. CalPERS (2007a) "permissible markets" approach was based on a seven-factor model, which included three country factors (political stability, transparency, and productive labor practices) and four market factors (market liquidity and volatility, market regulation/legal system/ investor protection, capital market openness, and settlement proficiency/transaction costs). Each group of country factors and the market factors was given a weight of 50 percent, with equal weights attached to the individual factors within the two categories. Each factor was based on a number of indicators, which were quantified using publicly available information, for example, the World Bank's *Doing Business Report or* the World Economic Forum's *Global Competitiveness Report*. The individual indicators were scaled from 1 to 2. Aggregating the individual indicators, all countries were ranked according to their overall score. To qualify as permissible, a minimum score of 2 was required. Of the 27 emerging markets included in the 2007 analysis, 20 economies fell into this category. Among the seven markets that did not make the cut were, for example, China, Egypt, and Russia—as well as all other countries that were not even included in the analysis, such as Vietnam and Saudi Arabia.

Conceivably, Groh and Liechtenstein's attractiveness index for national private equity and venture capital markets could be employed in a similar fashion to identify permissible private equity markets. Since the index is a numeric ranking of markets based on quantifiable indicators—many of which are also employed in CalPERS' former approach to public equity investing—in principle it would allow users to determine a cutoff separating markets that are deemed to have a sufficiently attractive risk-return balance, from those markets whose expected risk-adjusted returns are viewed to be unattractive. The motivation behind drawing a demarcation line would be the same as in CalPERS' case, namely to rationalize the investment process in an increasingly complex market environment.

However, there are some fundamental problems with the permissible markets' approach. First of all, country rankings are much less objective than they might appear. Individual country scores are highly sensitive to the selection of individual indicators and the weights that are used to aggregate these indicators. Although the rankings are based on quantitative data complied by reputable institutions, such as the World Bank or the World Economic Forum, many indicators are actually based on surveys and expert views that necessarily introduces some degree of subjectivity.[10] Take corruption, for instance, an indicator that is employed in both the global venture capital and private equity attractiveness index and CalPERS' permissible markets approach. The standard source for this indicator is Transparency International, which itself ranks a large sample of countries (for details, see Appendix 6.1). The rankings are based on scores derived from various surveys, which is why Transparency International has—quite appropriately—labeled its index as the *Transparency International Corruption Perceptions Index*.

The second fundamental problem with the permissible markets approach is this: Even if a fully objective (hard-data based) ranking of countries could be established, where would one draw the line between permissible and non-permissible countries? This decision is necessarily arbitrary, presumably an important reason why CalPERS (2007a, 2007b) decided in late 2007 to replace its permissible markets' approach by a principles-based one. Although the factors to evaluate emerging markets have remained largely unchanged,[11] the new approach gives fund managers considerable more discretion. In explaining its decision, CalPERS (2007b) "… recognizes that emerging markets countries and companies are in different developmental stages and that CalPERS' internal and external portfolio managers will need to exercise their best judgment after taking all relevant factors, principles, and trends into account. CalPERS requires managers to consider these principles among the decision factors employed in the investment process but does not necessarily require managers to invest in accordance with each individual principle."

CalPERS' policy switch is very much consistent with our earlier assessment of the global venture capital and private equity index. What gets measured gets attention, and in that sense the index is a welcome tool for private equity investors. But it is the more nuanced picture behind the overall rankings investors should look at when accessing country risk and taking investment decisions in emerging markets.

6.4   Assessing country risk

A third reason is that "attractiveness" and "risk" are two fundamentally different investment concepts. As regards the latter, there is no universal definition of risk, but from an investor's standpoint risk generally concerns the expected value of one or more results of one or more future events. Thus, risk may be defined as the probability that an investment's actual return will be different than expected. Deviations of actual from expected returns may be positive and negative, but it is generally

---

[10]This is not to say that these indicators are useless in cross-country comparisons. Kaufmann et al. (2009), who compile governance indicators around the world, report the margins of error accompanying each country estimate. These reflect the inherent difficulties in measuring governance using any kind of data. However, they show that even after taking margins of error into account, their rankings permit meaningful cross-country comparisons as well as monitoring progress over time.

[11]While the market factors on liquidity/volatility and regulation/legal system and investor protection have been streamlined and merged, two new factors focus on corporate social responsibility and long-term sustainability as well as on appropriate disclosure on environmental, social, and corporate governance issues.

the latter investors are most concerned about. In that sense, risk may be assessed in terms of an expected after-the-fact level of regret (Dembo and Freeman, 1998).

Market attractiveness rankings provide only limited guidance if one defines risk in this spirit. Take corporate and personal income taxes, for example. Other things being equal, high taxes tend to make a market less attractive for private equity investments. However, this says little about risk. As long as the tax system is predictable and nondiscriminatory—for instance, against foreigners—high taxes do not imply investment risk per se. Rather, it's the unforeseeable changes in tax rates that may lead to significantly lower investment profits. An often cited example in this regard is Ripplewood Holdings' investment in Shinsei Bank, the successor of the Long-Term Credit Bank of Japan (LTCB), an institution that enjoyed monopoly status with regard to the issuance of many long-term debt securities. With a significant share of its loan portfolio suffering from the bursting of the Japanese asset bubble, LTCB was delisted and nationalized in 1998. In March 2000, LTCB was sold to an international group of investors led by Ripplewood Holdings for JPY 121 billion. The agreement included a "defect warranty provision," committing the government to purchase any claims that had fallen by 20 percent or more from book value within the next 3 years. LTCB was relaunched as "Shinsei Bank" in June 2000, with new management and services. Shinsei used the defect warranty provision to dispose of all the worst debts owed to the bank. It then raised JPY 230 billion in an IPO in February 2004, implying a profit of over JPY 100 billion within 4 years. However, this profit escaped Japanese taxation through the use of a foreign investment partnership, whereas the government incurred substantial losses due to the purchase of nonperforming loans. Predictably, this deal led to an outcry from Japanese taxpayers. A subsequent Japan–US tax treaty in 2005 included what the *Wall Street Journal* (January 20, 2010) dubbed the "Shinsei provision," requiring investors to pay capital-gains tax on the sale of shares in a company that has received public money.

Tough luck for investors who had made similar investments in the belief that their profits would remain untaxed. Unexpected changes in the tax regime are just one risk investors are facing, however. So let us look at country risk more systemically. In developing a framework investors may employ to assess macro risk, we distinguish between three main risk categories: economic risk, political risk, and governance risk. Each risk category comprises different focus areas, which have proved to be of particular importance in private equity investments.

6.4.1 Economic risk

Economic risk encompasses three main areas. At the most fundamental level, investors are concerned about a sharp fall in economic activity and, hence, company earnings. There are plenty of examples of *GDP risk*, some of the most dramatic ones in recent history being Argentina (1999–2002: compound annual rate of decline in real GDP of more than 5 percent); Indonesia (1998: −13.1 percent); Korea (1998: −6.9 percent); Malaysia (1998: −7.4 percent), Russia (1998: −5.3 percent), Thailand (1998: −10.5 percent); Turkey (2001: −7.5 percent); and Venezuela (2002–2003: compound annual rate of decline of 9 percent). These large contractions in real economic activity were usually associated with *banking and currency crises*, often reinforcing each other in a downward spiral.

These crises explain to a considerable extent why private equity funds raised in the mid-1990s for investments in emerging market economies failed to meet investors' return expectations. In fact, around 50 percent of the partnerships formed between 1993 and 1996 generated losses for their investors (see Fig. 2.7 in Chapter 2), prompting them to substantially reduce their allocations to this market segment. In some cases, huge exchange rate changes erased investment returns without causing a large contraction in economic activity. For example, while the Brazilian Real lost more than 80 percent of its value against the US dollar when the authorities decided to allow the currency to float freely in early 1999, the economy still registered positive growth in the same year and gathered considerable momentum in the following year. In Chapter 10, we shall discuss the impact on currency movements on private equity returns in greater detail.

To be sure, large economic contractions are not confined to emerging markets. While in the postwar era recessions in the industrialized world had seemingly become shallower, lulling investors into the false belief that deep declines in output were a phenomenon of the past, the Great Recession of 2007–2009 has served as a shrilling wake-up call. Europe's sovereign debt crisis has the potential to cause similar, if not greater, economic damage. Nor are banking crises limited to emerging markets. There are plenty of episodes in industrialized countries that are reviewed in detail by Reinhart and Rogoff (2009). Among the most severe ones in recent history are those in Japan and the Scandinavian countries in the early 1990s that were also associated with huge output losses and exchange rate adjustments.

Inflation poses another important macroeconomic risk, despite a falling inflation trend in most countries over the last few decades, thanks to more credible monetary and fiscal policies. Sudden spikes in inflation may be caused, for example, by exogenous shocks, as was the case in the mid-2000s when sharply higher commodity prices led to a considerable increase in the general price level in many countries. In the emerging markets, average consumer price inflation surged to 9.2 percent in 2008 from 5.6 percent in 2006. In individual countries, the rise in the general price level was even more dramatic. For instance, in China consumer price inflation accelerated almost fourfold to 5.9 percent during this period, while inflation reached again double-digit levels in Russia and Turkey. To the extent that changes in prices are not anticipated, they may have a profound impact on real investment returns. However, inflation risk stems not only from unanticipated changes in the price level. Suppose, for instance, that the authorities in the investee country impose price controls on selected final products in an effort to curb inflationary pressures. To the extent that input prices, including nominal wages, increase in line with the general price level, price controls will squeeze margins and may even lead to losses.

6.4.2 Political risk

This leads us to political risk, which can be broadly categorized into three components—government risk, nationalization risk, and regulation risk. Under government risk, we understand political instability. More specifically, *government risk* may entail civil disturbances, war, and the risk that a government is overthrown, causing investment uncertainty and potentially resulting in a fundamentally different investment regime. Africa has a particularly notorious track record in this regard, with the online encyclopedia *Wikepedia* counting almost 100 coup d' états between 1952 and 2009 in 33 countries in the region. Of course, coup d' états are not just an African phenomenon. According to the same source, there were more than 30 coup d'états, including failed attempts, around the globe in the first decade of this century, and in mid-2010 there were 15 incumbent leaders of current regimes who had assumed power via a coup d'état. Not all coup d' états are violent nor are fundamental regime changes necessarily bad news for investors. For example, the fall of the Berlin Wall and the end of communism in Central and Eastern Europe in the late 1980s has opened up tremendous opportunities for private equity.

Outright expropriation has become a relatively rare event, and to the extent that *nationalization* does occur it is usually confined to a small number of strategic sectors, such as oil and gas. However, governments may take decisions that may otherwise cause substantial harm to investors. By changing the rules of the game, such decisions may fundamentally undermine the entire investment thesis and result in lower profits or even losses. The Shinsei provision we referred to earlier is a frequently cited example of this type of risk. Let us consider another—fictitious—example to illustrate the complexity of *regulatory risk*. A limited partner coinvesting alongside a private equity fund acquires shares in a company that produces alcoholic beverages. The company operates in an oligopolistic market with just one competitor. Oligopolistic profits of the incumbent firms are protected by government licensing that prevents other competitors from entering the market. The investment decision is taken under the assumption that the regulatory framework remains unchanged. However, 1 year after the investment is made, the government decides to dismantle the licensing system. The two incumbent firms face increased competition, resulting in price cuts and declining margins and eroding profits.

The literature on political risk is full of real-life cases where unanticipated changes in regulations had substantial return implications through their impact on production costs, market prices, and the repatriation of profits (e.g., Henisz, 2002; Moran, 1998; Pickford, 2001; and the literature surveyed in these sources). As diverse the individual cases reviewed in this literature are, there is one common denominator, which we call the "surprise factor." It is this factor on which investors should focus in their macro due diligence work instead of limiting their analysis to the assessment of the attractiveness of the status quo regime.

6.4.3 Governance risk

The surprise factor is equally relevant in assessing governance risk that stems from an unpredictable legal system, underdeveloped accounting standards and corrup tion. As far as *legal risk* is concerned, the key issue is the protection of investors' rights in case of disputes. The "law on the books" is one thing, but as many investors have learned the way how the law is applied can be quite another. There is a huge body of "finance and law" literature that finds that the effectiveness of legal institutions has a much stronger impact on external finance than does the law on the books, despite legal change in many countries aiming to enhance shareholder and creditor rights (see, e.g., Berkowitz, Pistor, & Richard, 2003; Pistor, Raiser, & Gelfer, 2000). This finding suggests that extensive legal reforms may not be sufficient for the evolution of effective legal and market institutions that are critical for the protection of investors. This applies in particular to minority investors who run the risk of being exploited by large shareholders. Other things being equal, the absence of well functioning and predictable legal institutions thus favors acquiring a controlling stake in a company or, at a minimum, mitigating legal risk through the representation on the board. We return to this issue in Chapter 7 where we examine private equity investment flows relative to mutual fund investments in emerging markets.

Accounting risk may result from the lack of appropriate accounting standards as well as the limited capacity to apply such standards. Some countries still use national accounting standards that create substantial uncertainty in the due diligence process. Other emerging markets are already more advanced in their convergence on the International Financial Reporting Standards (IFRS). However, this process is generally slow, and in some cases national and international standards exist side-by-side. But even where the IFRS have already been fully adopted, accounting risk may exist due to the lack of qualified accountants with sufficient experience.

Of all the macro risks we consider in this section, *corruption* is perhaps the most evil one. Corruption has many dimensions, including tax bribery, procurement bribery, and judiciary bribery. Flourishing particularly well in complex bureaucratic regimes, corruption severely distorts policy decisions in virtually all areas imposing huge macroeconomic costs. Contrary to the popular myth that grease money may speed up the wheels of commerce in the presence of red tape, there is overwhelming evidence that corruption imposes huge costs for firms as well (Kaufmann & Wei, 1999; Lambsdorff, 2007). Corruption creates enormous uncertainty for firms and renders any investment planning process more or less irrelevant. Making things even worse, corruption is virtually unquantifiable, forcing investors to rely on perceptions of corruption rather than on hard evidence in their risk assessment.

6.4.4 The risk heat map

Given the mix of quantitative and qualitative information that investors rely on to assess country risk, numerical country rankings may pretend a degree of accuracy the underlying data are unable to deliver. In light of this, it seems preferable to employ a cruder but more appropriate traffic light system, ranging from low risk (green) to medium risk (orange) to high risk (red). In Fig. 6.8, we show a heat map with a somewhat more nuanced gradation of different shades of grey, ranging from light grey (low risk) to dark grey (high risk). Similar heat maps have been used, for example, by the IMF (2009) in examining and visualizing macro and financial vulnerabilities in a sample of emerging markets as well as the volatility of asset prices in different asset classes.

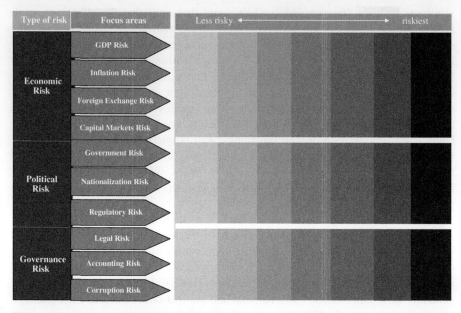

Figure 6.8 Heat map to assess country risk.

As far as economic risk is concerned, investors typically base their risk assessment to a significant degree on macro accounting. Standard indicators include, for example, past GDP growth and inflation rates, output and inflation volatility, budget deficit-to-GDP and public debt-to-GDP ratios. On the external front, macro risk assessments often focus on indicators, such as a country's foreign exchange regime, its current account-to-GDP and external debt-to-GDP ratios, short-term debt to foreign exchange reserves, and private and public external debt service payments. Finally, in scrutinizing the health of an investee country's banking system investors often look at ratios, such as bank regulatory capital to risk-weighted assets, bank capital to assets, bank nonperforming loans to total loans, and bank provisions to nonperforming loans. Although there is almost an infinite number of macro risk indicators investors can employ in their risk analysis, in determining a country's position on the heat map it is important to focus on those that have the greatest predictive power. In the academic literature that we review in Chapter 10, risk practitioners find numerous studies that attempt to identify key variables that have proved to have good predictive properties with regard to past currency crashes, banking crises, and sovereign debt crises.

There are also a considerable number of risk indicators in focus areas where investment risk is less quantifiable. Take legal risk, for example, where a key issue lies in the strength of minority shareholder protections against misuse of corporate assets by directors for their personal gain. At the country level, the World Bank's annual *Doing Business Reports* rank a large number of countries along three dimensions: (i) transparency of transactions; (ii) liability for self-dealing; and (iii) shareholders' ability to sue officers and directors for misconduct. Country scores on each dimension are based on expert readings of laws and regulations.

While these scores provide a first step in positioning a country on the heat map, in a more detailed due diligence exercise limited partners will blend publicly available information with their own intelligence sources, such as information they obtain from lawyers, accountants, and consultants who are familiar with the region or country in question. As far as coinvestments are concerned, the due diligence process needs to drill down to the deal level, taking into account the specific circumstances of the particular sector and industry in which the transaction falls. To what extent would a particular transaction be affected by a sizeable change in the exchange rate, in addition to the overall macroeconomic impact exchange rate variations bring about? And to what extent is the sector or industry in which a coinvestment is contemplated subject to specific regulatory risks? Finally, are there any potentially risk-mitigating factors and does the GP have the skills and the experience to deal with the risks identified in the due diligence process and visualized on the heat map?

6.5 Summary and conclusions

In this chapter, we have discussed the size of the global private equity market, its evolution, and its regional composition. With investors' private equity AUM having grown 16-fold between 1990 and 2009, financial-sponsor led acquisitions increased at a double-digit CAGR over the last couple of decades. Initially, much of private equity's global growth was driven by greater activity in the United States and later in Western Europe. More recently, activity has also picked up noticeably in other regions, including in many emerging economies. However, the catch-up process has been uneven. Although some national markets have enjoyed relatively rapid growth, in others the trajectory has been considerably flatter. This heterogeneity has been attributed to a complex set of factors. In venture capital, the existence of an active IPO market is generally found to play an important role. Corporate governance structures, especially minority shareholder rights, the quality of legal and labor market institutions and a country's capacity to innovate matter as well. In the buyout market, the potential for operational engineering, barriers to entrepreneurship, and barriers to international trade are identified as important factors explaining cross-country differences.

These observations have encouraged researchers to develop market attractiveness indexes. Although country rankings are relatively closely correlated with private equity investments in individual markets, they should not be taken as a shortcut for a proper country risk analysis. Country risk has many dimensions, which have in common that they subject investment decisions to additional uncertainty. Low corporate tax rates are generally considered as a positive factor in market attractiveness rankings, but this says little about the risk of unpredictable and potentially distortionary tax changes. The law on the books may provide a favorable investment climate, but is there an independent judiciary that applies the law in an unbiased and predictable manner in case of disputes? Assessing country risk is indispensable, especially in emerging and frontier markets whose institutions are still emerging. To the extent that these markets will continue to implement macroeconomic and institutional reforms, their risk profile will continue to improve, attracting a rising share of the world's private equity capital. Realistically, however, not all countries will follow the same trajectory in their catch-up process, and while some countries may soon be classified as *emergent* and become increasingly integrated, others might retain their status as emerging or frontier markets. Thus, it becomes increasingly important for investors to differentiate within the universe of nontraditional markets. Against this background, we now turn to cross-border capital flows, examining international investments by private equity funds.

Appendix 6.1: A brief guide to publicly available sources that may help investors assess the quality of the business environment

Investment returns and risk depend on the quality of the business environment, which is determined by a complex set of factors. Sound fiscal and monetary policies are critical conditions for investors to invest capital. However, these conditions are not enough. Today, it is well understood that a trusted and efficient legal context, a stable set of domestic institutions, and progress on social conditions contribute greatly to a healthy economy. Although macroeconomic data are readily available, for example, through the International Monetary Fund's *World Economic Outlook Database*, a growing number of publicly available sources allow investors to assess the institutional, legal, and social dimensions of the business environment in which they contemplate making investments. In the following, readers find a brief description of the most useful sources they can consult in their due diligence efforts.

The World Economic Forum's *Global Competitiveness Report* (GCR) is published annually. The report is freely available on the internet (http://www.weforum.org/pdf/GCR09/GCR20092010fullreport.pdf). Over the years, its coverage has continuously expanded, with the 2009/10 edition ranking 133 countries. The rankings are based on 117 indicators whose values are provided for each country in an extensive data appendix. Several indicators are based on "hard data" that measure objectively a particular quantity, such as GDP, main telephone lines per population, or the number of utility patents. Hard data also include quantified expert assessments, such as the "number of procedures and the time required to start a business." These data are imported from other sources, such as the International Monetary Fund, the World Bank (see below), and various United Nations agencies. What makes the GCR unique are the "soft" indicators that are based on an annual opinion survey of business executives (e.g., perceived intensity of local competition, burden of customs procedures, and the ease of access to loans). For each indicator (hard and soft), the GCR provides a country ranking. The individual indicators are then aggregated in 12 subindexes, or "pillars," of competitiveness. Four pillars—the quality of institutions, infrastructure, macroeconomic stability, and health and primary education—represent basic requirements for sustained economic growth in factor-driven economies in their early stages of economic development. Another set of five pillars serve to enhance efficiency—higher education, goods market efficiency, labor market efficiency, financial market sophistication, technological readiness, and market size. Finally, in more mature and innovation-driven economies a third set of pillars— business sophistication and innovation—becomes critical. The 12 subindexes are finally integrated in a single index, the Global Competitiveness Index. For each country, the GCR identifies competitive advantages and disadvantages, given the country's stage of development.

The *World Competitiveness Yearbook* (WCY), published annually by IMD, the business school, ranks 57 economies according to more than 300 criteria (http://www. imd.ch/research/publications/wcy/index.cfm). These criteria are grouped into four broad factors (economic performance, government, efficiency, infrastructure), each of which is composed of five subfactors. As is the case with the GCR, some indicators are based on hard data, while others reflect survey evidence. For each country, the reader finds a detailed profile summarizing the factors that determine its overall ranking.

In its report on *World Investment Prospects, The Economist* Intelligence Unit ranks countries according to the quality of their business environment. In its 2007 edition evaluating investment prospects until 2011, the report covers 82 economies that are analyzed regularly in The Economist Intelligence Unit's *Country Forecasts* (http:// www.vcc.columbia.edu/pubs/documents/WorldInvestmentProspectsto2011.pdf). Written in partnership with the Columbia Program on International Investment, the report employs a framework that is designed to mirror the principle criteria used by companies to formulate their global business strategies and investment location decisions. While the focus is thus different from the GCR and the WCY, its approach is in many ways similar. Blending hard data with survey evidence, the overall rankings are based on scores for 91 indicators, grouped into 10 categories. These are quality of the business environment; quality of the macroeconomic environment; market opportunities; policy toward private enterprise and competition; policy and attitudes toward foreign investment; foreign trade and exchange regimes; tax regimes; financing; labor market and skills; and infrastructure.

The World Bank's *Doing Business* report provides annual updates of the quality of institutions in 183 economies. The report is available online and can be downloaded free of charge from the World Bank's Doing Business website (http://www. doingbusiness.org/). The economies covered by the report are benchmarked in 10 areas: (1) starting a business; (2) dealing with construction permits; (3) employing workers; (4) registering property; (5) getting credit; (6) protecting investors; (7) paying taxes; (8) trading across borders; (9) enforcing contracts; and (10) closing a business. In each area, economies are benchmarked according to a number of indicators. For instance, as far as the protection of investors are concerned, economies are assessed with regard to the extent of disclosure requirements, the extent to which directors are liable and the ease at which shareholders may sue in court. Two types of data are used. The first comes from readings of laws and regulations. The second are time and motion indicators that measure the efficiency in achieving a regulatory goal (such as the time and the number of procedures required for registering a property).

A large set of governance indicators for 211 economies can be found at http://info. worldbank.org/governance/wgi/sc_country.asp. Compiled under a multiyear research project led by Kaufmann, Kraay, and Mastruzzi (2009), these indicators are based on responses on the quality of governance given by a large number of enterprise, citizen, and expert survey respondents in industrial and developing countries, as reported by survey institutes, think tanks, nongovernmental organizations, and international organizations. Countries are ranked according to each indicator, which are grouped into six categories: (1) voice and accountability; (2) political stability and absence of violence; (3) government effectiveness; (4) regulatory quality; (5) rule of law; and (6) control of corruption.

Focusing more narrowly on corruption, the most widely used source in this area is Transparency International. Its *Corruption Perceptions Index* ranks 180 economies and is available at http://www.transparency.org/policy_research/surveys_indices/cpi/2008. Transparency International does not conduct its own survey on corruption. Instead, the index is a statistical compilation of information collected by other sources, including the afore-mentioned GCR as well as private data providers, such as *The Economist* Intelligence Unit and Global Insights.

The *Economic Freedom Index* calculated by the Heritage Foundation for 183 economies is available at http://www.heritage.org/index/. Economic freedom is defined along 10 dimensions: (1) business freedom (the right to create, operate, and close an enterprise without interference from the state; (2) trade freedom (openness of an economy); (3) fiscal freedom (freedom of private agents to keep and control their income and wealth for their own benefit and use); (4) government size (burden of excessive government); (5) monetary freedom (stable currency and market deter- mined prices); (6) investment freedom (absence of restrictions on foreign invest- ment); (7) financial freedom (absence of excessive banking and financial regulation); (8) property rights (ability to accumulate private property and rule of law); (9) freedom from corruption; (10) labor freedom (ability of individuals to work as much as they want and wherever they want). Using a wide range of authoritative and internationally recognized sources, the 10 subindexes are integrated into one summary index.

The *eStandards Forum* (http://www.estandardsforum.org/) provides useful infor- mation about the extent to which governments comply with internationally recog- nized standards and codes of good practice in economic and financial affairs. The "12 Key Standards for Sound Financial Systems", developed by the international community, were compiled by the Financial Stability Forum in 1999 in response to the described need for a global set of best practices. They are divided into three areas: (1) macroeconomic policy and data transparency (Special Data Dissemination Standard, Code of Good Practices on Transparency in Monetary Policy, Code of Good Practices on Transparency in Fiscal Policy); (2) institutional and market infrastructure (Effective Insolvency and Credit Rights Systems, International Financial Reporting Standards, Principles of Corporate Governance, International Standards on Auditing, anti-Money Laundering/Combating Terrorist Financing Standard, Core Principles for Systemically Important Payment Systems); and (3) financial regulation and super- vision (Core Principles for Effective Banking Supervision, Objectives and Principles of Securities Regulation, and Insurance Core Principles). There are currently 93 economies being ranked according to their compliance with the standards.

Finally, a general source of information is the Central Intelligence Agency's *World Factbook*. Freely downloadable from the internet (https://www.cia.gov/library/publications/the-world-factbook/), the *World Factbook* provides information on the history, people, government, economy, geography, communications, transportation, military, and transnational issues for 266 world entities. The online factbook is updated biweekly.

Finally, a general source of information is the Central Intelligence Agency's World Factbook. Freely downloadable from the internet (http://www.cia.gov/library/publications/the-world-factbook/), the World Factbook provides information on the history, people, government, economy, geography, communications, transportation, culture, and transnational issues for 266 world entities. The online factbook is updated biweekly.

7 Private equity funds and cross-border acquisitions

Private equity plays an increasingly important role in financial intermediation in a growing number of countries. However, this says little about the extent to which the global private equity market has become more integrated. Some researchers (e.g., Megginson, 2004) have argued that regional private equity markets have developed more or less in isolation, with differences in national legal and regulatory regimes, differential access to information and behavioral biases discouraging cross-border transactions. Given the structural nature of these impediments, so the argument goes, market segmentation in private equity is set to be persistent.

From a limited partner's viewpoint, the degree to which private equity markets are integrated matters for at least three reasons. First, in segmented markets a limited partner's investment options are limited, and in constructing a geographically diversified portfolio, the LP is essentially confined to committing capital to a foreign fund operating in his target market. By contrast, in integrated markets where private equity funds deploy their capital across borders, LPs have a wider choice of tools through which they may get international exposure. Conceivably, this may even include capital commitments to private equity funds, which are domiciled in their home market (Fig. 7.1). Second, integrated and segmented markets pose different challenges in terms of due diligence on private equity funds. Internationally operating funds may have superior skills and experience with regard to financial engineering and company strategies and operations, but do they have the local market knowledge to identify attractive investment opportunities? Conversely, local funds are likely

International Investments in Private Equity. DOI: 10.1016/B978-0-12-375082-2.10007-2

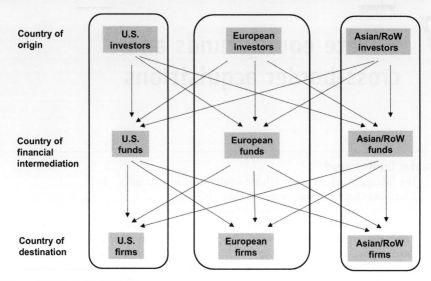

Figure 7.1 Global private equity flows.
Source: AlpInvest Research.

to have a competitive advantage in deal sourcing thanks to insider information and sometimes to government policies promoting domestic fund managers. However, especially in nontraditional markets, local funds often lack a track record, typically a key factor in LPs' investment decisions. Third, in segmented markets asset prices tend to follow different dynamics, which provides scope for portfolio diversification. As markets become more integrated because of increased cross-border investment flows, asset prices tend to move more closely together.

The extent to which private equity markets are integrated or segmented—the degree of financial globalization in private equity—is essentially an empirical question. However, measuring financial globalization is far from trivial. Although there is plenty of anecdotal evidence that GPs' investment strategies are getting increasingly global, market-wide cross-border flow and stock data have remained scarce. In this chapter, therefore, we use a proprietary data set, which helps us track international fund investments. More specifically, we focus on acquisitions by buyout funds raised in the United States, Europe, and Asia-Pacific and examine the degree to which they have deployed their capital outside their home region. This analysis allows us to estimate their home bias, that is, the ratio of the funds' investments in their respective home regions to their total investments. Furthermore, splitting our sample into two subsamples, we calculate how the home bias of fund investments has developed over time. Finally, we compare our results with mutual fund investments, which gives us valuable insights in the role of corporate governance in investment decisions.

7.1 The internationalization of private equity fund investments

7.1.1 Exporting the US venture capital model

Traditionally, VC investing has been a regional (if not local) business. Sørensen and Stuart (2001), for example, find that venture capital investments in the United States tend to be within a 500 miles radius.[1] This regional focus has been attributed to several factors. To begin with, start-ups have few tangible assets and, therefore, little, if any, collateral. They operate in new markets, where information about the nature of the market is generally poor. As start-ups do not have an established track record, the type of investor needed is an "active investor." Venture capitalists solve the corporate governance and monitoring problem through extensive initial due diligence and maintain a close relationship by frequently visiting and talking to company management. Furthermore, being well positioned in the VC network is found to be critically important for an investor's access to successful entrepreneurs and hence his fund performance (Hochberg, Ljungqvist, & Lu, 2007). To the extent that VC firms open new satellite offices, their decision is significantly driven by the success rate of venture capital backed investments in an area (Chen, Dai, & Schatzberg, 2009).

Expanding across national borders brings about a number of challenges for venture capitalists, with the single most important one generally seen in the legal protection of their investments. As Kaplan and Strömberg (2004) argue, venture capitalists face four critical agency problems: (1) the entrepreneur may not work hard enough to maximize value after the investment is made; (2) the entrepreneur may know more about his quality/ability than the venture capitalist; (3) after the investment is made, there may be circumstances when the venture capitalist disagrees with the entrepreneur and the VC will want the right to make decisions; and (4) the entrepreneur may "hold up" the venture capitalist by threatening to leave the venture when the entrepreneur's human capital is particularly valuable to the company. There exist different contractual solutions to mitigate such challenges, which, however, require a legal system that provides the basis for appropriate legal contracts and their enforceability. Although US law allows VC contracts to be specifically designed to address the afore-mentioned agency problems, there are doubts as to whether VC interests are sufficiently protected and enforceable in different legal environments.

Not surprisingly, therefore, the process of financial globalization in venture capital has been relatively slow. Early moves by US venture capitalists into Europe date back to the beginning of the 1980s, and interest in foreign investing surged during the tech

---

[1] However, Kogut, Urso, and Walker (2007) show that national networks of syndications across regions (such as Silicon Valley and New England) began to emerge relatively early.

boom in the late 1990s.[2] However, these waves proved relatively short-lived. A recent survey (Deloitte, 2008) shows that the majority of venture capital funds surveyed had actually less than 10 percent of their capital deployed abroad. In fact, more than 40 percent of venture capitalists participating in the survey had not invested outside their national home markets at all, and of those who did, many VC had made only one or two foreign investments.

Looking forward, are there any reasons to expect the globalization process to gain momentum on a sustained basis? A growing number of venture capitalists seem to think so. As Michael Moritz of Sequoia Capital has put it in a recent interview with Ernst and Young (2007, p. 30): "The near monopoly that the U.S. has enjoyed in the development of fresh and new technology companies is ending. That isn't to say for a moment that the U.S. or Silicon Valley is going to be a bad place to invest in over the next 20 years, but we need to have an expanded view of investment possibilities." Moritz's view is echoed in a recent survey of venture capitalists, who report a growing interest in chasing deals outside their home markets. This interest is motivated by a variety of considerations, such as the emergence of an entrepreneurial environment in a growing number of markets, the perceived increased capacity for innovation, and the desire to get access to foreign consumer markets (Fig. 7.2).

As a matter of fact, a growing number of VC firms have taken concrete steps to penetrate foreign markets, whereby their individual expansion strategies vary considerably (Fig. 7.3). Some VC funds deploy their capital across different geographies (e.g., Oak Investment Partners), with the country of management remaining the funds' home base. Partners may be required to travel more frequently, although it has become more common for VC firms to open offices abroad to source deals and work closely with their portfolio companies. The deal approval process is usually centralized, with investment decisions taken by a global committee.

Other venture capitalists have decided to raise specific country or regional funds (e.g., Accel Partners Europe, KPCB China, Benchmark Israel), a step that usually entails opening offices abroad.[3] However, others have developed strategic alliances

[2]One of the first movers was Atlas Venture, which began to operate in Europe in 1980, initially as a joint venture with IDG Bank of the Netherlands and later as an independent organization. Others followed, encouraged by the emergence of a hot VC market in Europe in the mid-1980s. However, this boom proved to be short-lived as returns substantially lagged expectations. Following the market crash in 1987, many US firms decided to close or sharply reduce their European presence. By the end of the 1990s, conditions in the European VC market seemed to have improved considerably, which motivated US venture capitalists to make another attempt to establish operations across the Atlantic. Importantly, new stock exchanges like Germany's Neuer Market, France's Nouveau Marché, or the United Kingdom's AIM offered additional exit options. Furthermore, a venture capital ecosystem had emerged, with an increasing number of support companies providing essential accounting, legal, and human resources services. However, this second wave came to an abrupt halt when the tech bubble burst and investors sharply reduced their allocations to venture capital around the world. An interesting case study about Accel Partners' venturing into Europe is provided by Hardymon, Lerner, and Leamon (2003).

[3]Sequoia Capital, one of the most global venture capital firms headquartered in Menlo Park in California, used to follow the regional fund model. More recently, however, Sequoia decided to move toward a more global model, a step motivated by its desire to have more flexibility in deploying its capital wherever it sees the best investment opportunities.

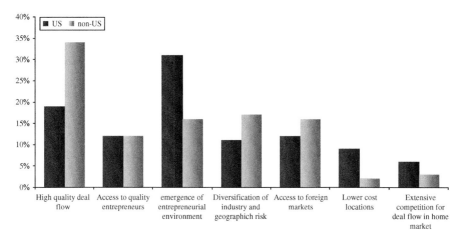

Figure 7.2 Reasons why venture capitalists want to become more global.
Source: Deloitte.

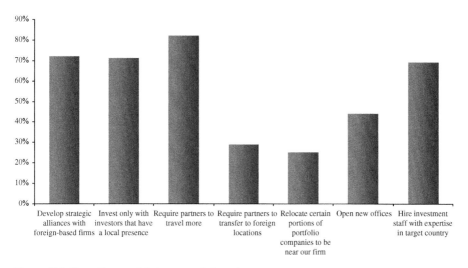

Figure 7.3 Operating models to expand abroad.
Source: Deloitte.

with foreign firms (IDG-Accel China). From an LP's perspective, such structures offer the advantage of being able to control the geographic allocation of his investments. For example, if an LP does not want to be exposed to the Chinese venture capital market, he can still remain in KPCB's main funds. Organizationally, some separate country-specific or region-specific funds are quite autonomous in their investment decisions and have their own carry. In other cases, however, investment decisions are more coordinated, with the individual funds of the VC firm offering the fund managers cross-carry. For instance, while Asian partners receive a share of the returns from US deals, the US partners receive a share of the returns from the deals managed by the firm's Asian fund.

To the extent that the growing interest in foreign investing is sustained, it should help the capital-importing economies build up their own venture capital industries. In countries, whose human capital base and institutional and financial infrastructure are already more advanced, this learning process is expected to be relatively faster (Aizenman & Kendall, 2008). By contrast, the global diffusion of venture capital investing will likely to be comparatively slow in countries where these factors are still emerging. Thus, foreign participation in venture capital transactions will need to remain relatively high for a sustained period of time for the domestic market to develop.[4]

7.1.2 The internationalization of buyout funds

Financial globalization in the buyout industry shows some commonalities with venture capital. First, the globalization process, which started in earnest in the second half of the 1990s, has been led by US GPs. Second, the greater outward orientation of buyout funds has initially focused on Europe, before expanding into other regions, such as Asia, Latin America, and the Middle East. Finally, there have been both push and pull factors motivating GPs to chase deals outside their home markets. In buyouts, an important push factor has been seen in the increasingly competitive market environment, with high company valuations undermining potential returns. On the pull side, Europe was perceived as a market with a substantial number of undervalued companies whose potential was waiting to be unlocked through a combination of superior governance structures, operational improvements, and financial leverage. Although the United States had already gone through a period of deconglomeration in the 1980s, Europe continued to have many underperforming conglomerates. Acquiring their noncore assets and running them as stand-alone companies promised to generate better returns than in the United States. Furthermore, a nontrivial number of European companies were owned by families who were assumed to face important generational transition issues and were thus open to sell to outside investors.

Today, virtually all large US buyout firms have opened offices in Europe, and several of them have raised specific European funds (see Chapter 12 on international expansion strategies by selected GPs). Over the past few years, US buyout firms have been involved in some of Europe's largest transactions (Table 7.1), thus helping private equity assume a significantly more important role in financial intermediation. In fact, at the peak of the last private equity cycle in 2006 and the first half of 2007, US buyout firms were involved in more than one-third of all European deals in terms of their overall value, with the most active investor in Europe being KKR.

---

[4]Aizenman and Kendall's findings are consistent with other research on the interaction between domestic financial development and financial globalization. According to this research, the development of domestic financial institutions facilitates asset trade among local residents and thereby potentially diminishes the role of external financial intermediaries. At the same time, however, domestic financial development is spurred by foreign investment in the domestic financial system, with the creation of domestic financial products fueling foreign demand for domestic liabilities (Martin & Rey, 2004). Thus, trade in financial services—involving commercial presence as well as cross-border supply—is found to be closely associated with cross-border capital flows.

Table 7.1 Top European deals involving US buyout firms

Year	Target	Country	Acquirer/member of consortium	Value
2010	Pets at Home	United Kingdom	KKR	£ 955 million
2009	Skype	Luxembourg	Silver Lake, Andreessen Horowitz, CPPIB, original owners	US$ 1.9 billion
2008	Expro	United Kingdom	Goldman Sachs/ Candover/AlpInvest	€ 3.6 billion
2007	Alliance Boots	United Kingdom	KKR	£ 11.1 billion
2006	VNU	Netherlands	Blackstone/Carlyle/ KKR/Hellman & Friedman/ Thomas Lee/AlpInvest	€ 8.7 billion
2006	NXP	Netherlands	Silver Lake/KKR/Bain Capital/Apax/AlpInvest	€ 8.4 billion
2006	Deutsche Telecom	Germany	Blackstone	€ 2.7 billion
2005	TDC	Denmark	Apax/Blackstone/KKR/ Permira/ Providence	US$ 12 billion
2005	TIM Hellas	Greece	Apax/TPG	€ 1.6 billion
2004	Eutelsat Communications	Luxembourg	TPG/Spectrum Equity Investors	€ 3.1 billion
2004	Maxeda	Netherlands	KKR/Change Capital Partners/AlpInvest	€ 1.5 billion
2003	Scottish & Newcastle	United Kingdom	TPG/Blackstone/CVC	£ 2.5 billion
2003	Debenhams	United Kingdom	CVC, TPG, Merrill Lynch Private Equity	£ 1.7 billion
2002	Legrand	France	KKR/Wendel	€ 4.97 billion
2002	Jefferson Smurfit	Ireland	Madison Dearborn	€ 3.7 billion
2001	Yell Group	United Kingdom	Hicks Muse/Apax	£ 2.1 billion
2001	Eircom Fixed Line	Ireland	Providence Partners et al.	€ 3 billion
2000	North Rhine Westphalia Cable	Germany	Blackstone et al.	€ 3 billion

Source: Capital IQ; company Web sites; AlpInvest Research

More recently, US firms have also expanded into other regions. Asia-Pacific, the world's third largest private equity market, has become a prime target thanks to a rapidly growing demand for private equity capital. However, this demand is fundamentally different from that in the more mature markets, in the sense that the majority of companies are seeking growth capital to expand. As a result, deal sizes in Asia-Pacific have generally been significantly smaller. Minority stakes are the norm in such deals (Fig. 7.4), which have little or no leverage. Although there have been a small number of more traditional LBOs—for example, Australia's retailer Myer acquired for US$ 1.1 billion in 2006 by a consortium led by TPG, Korea's Oriental Brewery bought

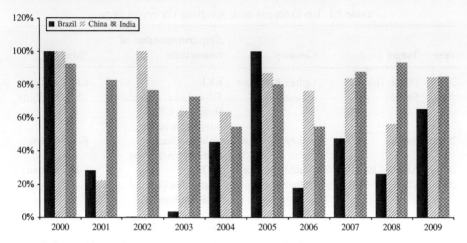

Figure 7.4 Minority investments as a percentage of country total deal value: Brazil, China, and India, 2000–2009.
Source: Dealogic.

by a KKR-led consortium for US$ 1.8 billion in 2009, and Japan's USJ Co purchased by Goldman Sachs Capital Partners and MBK Partners for US$ 1.4 billion in 2009—different demand dynamics have prompted US GPs to adopt new strategies.

Nontraditional investment strategies are also required in other emerging markets, such as Latin America or the Middle East where the acquisition of a majority position in a highly leveraged transaction represents the exception. In sourcing deals, US GPs are competing not only with indigenous private equity firms but also with a growing number of European buyout houses, such as Apax, CVC, and Permira, which have become significantly more outward oriented (Apax's expansion into Asia-Pacific is illustrated in an interview with former chairman for Asia, Max Burger-Calderon, in Chapter 12). Although European GPs have yet to achieve the same degree of market penetration in the United States as their American peers in Europe, they have made considerable efforts to gain a larger market share especially in Asia-Pacific and in their own backyard, Central and Eastern Europe. As their American counterparts, several European GPs have raised regional-specific or multi-regional funds and set up shop in different countries (Table 7.2). At the same time, global funds provide increased flexibility for GPs to chase deals across borders. As far as funds domiciled in the United States are concerned, the upper bound for foreign acquisitions typically varies from 15 percent to 50 percent. European buyout funds tend to have somewhat lower upper limits, ranging from 5 percent to 40 percent. Thus, it is expected that foreign funds continue to account for a sizable share in private equity activity in nontraditional markets, despite the development of an indigenous private equity industry (Fig. 7.5).

Regional or country-specific funds raised by foreign GPs have generally been denominated in US dollars or euros. In countries with freely convertible currencies, the currency in which the fund is raised should not matter (apart from exchange rate

Table 7.2 Large buyout/growth capital funds recently raised by foreign GPs[a]

Fund name and geographic focus	Fund manager	Location where GP is headquartered	Year	Capital raised (US$ million)	% of total capital raised for the region
Asia-Pacific					
Carlyle Asia Partners III	The Carlyle Group	United States	2010	2500	...
Mount Kellett Fund I	Mount Kellett Capital Management	United States	2009	2500	9.2
Carlyle Asia Growth Partners IV	The Carlyle Group	United States	2009	1040	3.8
TPG Asia V	TPG	United States	2008	4250	9.0
CVC Capital Partners Asia-Pacific Fund III	CVC Asia-Pacific Ltd.	Europe	2008	4100	8.7
HSBC Private Equity Fund VI	HSBC Private Equity	Europe	2008	1500	3.2
KKR Asian Fund	Kohlberg, Kravis, Roberts & Co	United States	2007	4000	10.3
Bain Capital Asia Fund	Bain Capital Asia LLC	United States	2007	1000	2.6
Carlyle Asia Partners II	The Carlyle Group	United States	2006	1800	7.4
Carlyle Japan Partners II	The Carlyle Group	United States	2006	1900	7.8[b]
Central and Eastern Europe					
Advent Central and Eastern Europe IV	Advent International	United States	2008	1587	28.5
Latin America					
LAPEV V	Advent International	United States	2010	1650	...
AIG Brazil Special Situations Fund II	AIG Capital Partners	United States	2008	692	15.5
LAPEF IV	Advent International	United States	2007	1300	29.4
Middle East					
Carlyle MENA Partners	The Carlyle Group	United States	2008	500	8.5
Multiregion					
Actis Emerging Markets Fund III	Actis	Europe	2008	2900	4.4
CIPEF V	Capital International	United States	2008	2250	3.4

[a]Capital raised refers to original amount of committed capital; in some cases, GP agreed with LPs on post-LPA adjustments.
[b]Percentage refers to capital raised for entire Asia-Pacific region.
Source: EMPEA, PREQIN, private equity firms' Web sites

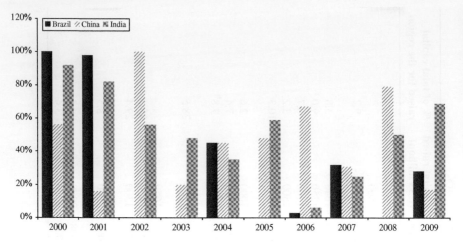

Figure 7.5 Foreign private equity acquisitions as a percentage of country deal value total: Brazil, China, and India, 2000–2009.
Source: Dealogic.

risk, of course, an issue we return to in Chapter 10). However, in some nontraditional markets, capital account convertibility is still restricted. China represents a particular important case, given the size of its economy and the growth outlook for its private equity market on one hand and its capital account regime on the other. Blackstone, the Carlyle Group, and First Eastern Investment Group have already launched their first renminbi (RMB) funds, and other large buyout houses are expected to follow. From their perspective, raising an RMB fund may have two important advantages. First, such funds represent a potential tool to tap into the huge pool of capital in China. Second, RMB funds may enhance deal flow as they may invest without having to obtain the government approvals required of offshore funds.[5]

There is concern, however, that the introduction of RMB funds may actually run counter to the interests of foreign LPs, who will be unable to commit to such funds under China's existing capital account regime. To the extent that RMB funds will find it easier than offshore funds to source attractive deals, foreign LPs who can commit capital only to the latter could be at a disadvantage. Although, in principle, potential conflicts of interest between RMB and offshore funds could be eliminated by ensuring that they invest together, pro rata to their capital commitments, in practice, regulatory hurdles still stand in the way of a full alignment of interests.[6]

---

[5]To foster the establishment of RMB funds, the Shanghai Pudong District government has reached an agreement with the State Administration of Foreign Exchange to waive Circular 142, a rule that prevents foreign GPs from making financial commitments to an RMB fund. The waiver applies to up to 1 percent of total capital commitments to a fund.

[6]For a detailed discussion of the legal and tax regime governing RMB funds, see Fadely and Gu (2009).

7.2   Measuring cross-border investment flows in buyouts

While there is considerable anecdotal evidence that general partners' investment strategies have become increasingly outward oriented, the analysis of intra-regional fund-raising and investment flows suggests that something more systematic is going on here. In Fig. 7.6, we compare regional flows for the two largest markets, the United States and Europe, between 1990 and 2008. More specifically, we calculate the ratio between commitments to buyout funds and equity investments made by such funds, which we then subtract from 100. Negative values imply that investments have been larger than fund inflows (and vice versa). Although the specific characteristics of the private equity market imply that aggregate fund-raising and investment flows will match only by accident in the short term, over the longer run investments can only be larger than fund commitments if private equity capital is imported from abroad.

This seems to be the case in Europe where we find a cumulative fund-raising gap of about 23 percent between 1990 and 2008. Other things being equal, the volume of LBOs would have been considerably smaller during this period, if the financing of such deals would have had to rely solely on European buyout funds. In reality, however, a significant share of European LBOs involved foreign buyout funds (Table 7.1). The mirror image is the US market where buyout funds raised considerably more capital than they deployed domestically between 1990 and 2008. During this period, US buyout funds show a cumulative fund-raising surplus of almost 20 percent. Notwithstanding variations in the stock of undrawn commitments (sometimes called "capital overhang" or "dry powder") of a fund, part of this surplus has been used to make acquisitions abroad. On a net basis, it seems that Europe has been an importer of private equity capital, whereas the United States has been a capital exporter.

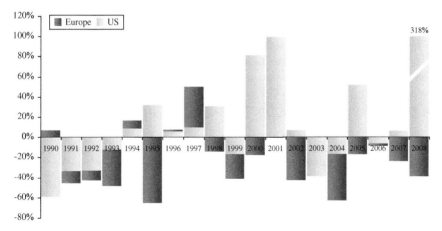

Figure 7.6 United States and Europe: LBO fund-raising-to-investment ratio (equity only), 1990–2008.
Source: TVE, EVCA, Capital IQ, S&P.

However, aggregate fund-raising and investment data are unable to answer a number of important questions. First, to what extent do individual private equity funds vary in terms of the share of capital they deploy abroad? Second, what is the gross stock of foreign investments made by private equity funds as opposed to net cross-border flows? Third, where do private equity funds invest when they make foreign acquisitions?

Recent research by Aizenman and Kendall (2008) attempts to address some of these issues, especially for venture capital investing. However, as Cornelius, Juttmann & Langelaar (2009) point out, their findings should be taken with caution. More specifically, Aizenman and Kendall make a number of critical assumptions to address important limitations in their raw data, which are provided by Thomson VentureXpert. Deals reported in Thomson VentureXpert are at the discretion of the investment firm, which means that a number of deals are likely to remain unreported. As a result, linking financial sponsor-led acquisitions to individual private equity funds is subject to considerable error. In club deals involving foreign investors, the name, the headquarters location of each investor, and the total investment amount are provided. However, there is no information as to how much individual club members have invested in particular deals.

Overall, the data situation is highly unsatisfactory. Against this background, we analyze information from AlpInvest Partners' proprietary database, one of the world's largest private equity investors with more than € 40 billion under management (for details, see Cornelius, Juttmann & Langelaar, 2009). This database allows us to link precisely individual portfolio companies with the buyout funds, which have acquired them, and unlike publicly available data sources, our database includes detailed information on the individual investment amounts. Specifically, our sample includes 102 buyout funds raised between 1995 and 2004. Only those funds are included that have already entirely, or at least to a large extent, drawn down the capital LPs have committed. In our sample, we have 48 US funds, 28 UK funds, 18 non-UK European funds, and 8 Asia-Pacific funds. At the end of June 2007, these funds had invested in 2260 portfolio companies that were valued at cost at around € 97 billion.

For these investment vehicles, we calculate the ratio of a fund's capital invested in its home region relative to the total amount of the fund's investments. Following Hau and Rey (2008), who study the home bias of mutual funds, we call this ratio the fund's *home bias*.[7] Consistent with EVCA's nomenclature, we use the *country of management* approach in defining whether a fund is a domestic or foreign fund. More

---

[7]Note that our definition deviates from the standard definition of home bias, which is typically calculated as 1 − (share of domestic equities in portfolio held by domestic investors/share of domestic equities in world portfolio) or as 1 − (share of foreign equities in portfolio held by domestic investors/share of foreign equities in world portfolio). The home bias literature has its roots in the seminal work by French and Poterba (1991). According to the International Capital Asset Pricing Model (ICAPM), individuals should hold equities from around the world in proportion to market capitalizations. However, empirical studies find that the share of foreign equities in domestic investors' portfolios is typically considerably smaller than predicted by the ICAPM. For example, the International Monetary Fund (2007) finds that foreign equities in US investors' portfolios accounted for 17 percent in 2005, substantially less than the 61 percent an unbiased investor would have allocated to foreign equities.

specifically, we consider a fund to be domestic if it is managed in the home market, irrespective of where the GP is headquartered. In principle, this definition may result in a higher aggregate home bias because funds raised by foreign GPs in the domestic market tend to have a clear investment focus on the market where they are managed and are less likely to invest outside the thus defined country of management. For example, a US GP deciding to raise and manage a fund out of its European office in London is less likely to deploy the fund's capital outside the European market. In practice, however, the risk of overestimating the degree of home bias (and hence underestimating the degree of financial globalization in private equity) seems to be rather small. In fact, in our sample, we have only a handful of funds whose country of management is different from where the GP is headquartered. Although these funds are relatively large, their reclassification according to the GP headquarters concept would not materially change our results.

Overall, we find substantial variation in the degree to which the funds in our sample are home biased: Although one-third of the funds in the sample have invested exclusively in their own region, 9 percent of the funds have invested only outside the region where they are managed (Fig. 7.7). Although some of these funds have a truly global investment focus, others target specific regions, especially in the emerging markets, but decide to manage their capital out of a major financial hub, benefiting, among other things, from a superior market infrastructure.

In examining the degree to which buyout funds in different regions are on average home biased, we calculate the ratio of the funds' capital invested in their respective home regions relative to the total amount of the funds' investment. We call this ratio the *aggregate buyout fund home bias* (Table 7.3). There are significant differences in the home bias across different regions. As far as US-based funds are concerned, 72.7 percent of their investments were made in the home market. Although UK-based

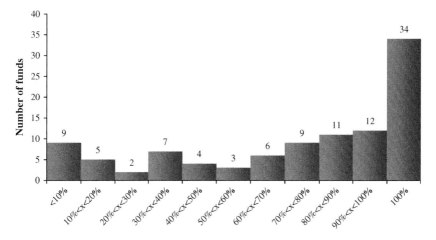

Figure 7.7 Histogram home bias at fund level.
Source: AlpInvest Research.

Table 7.3 Home bias statistics

	United States	United Kingdom	Europe	Asia-Pacific
Number of funds	48	28	18	8
Aggregate home bias (%)	72.7	44.6	100.0	92.7
Fund-level home bias				
Mean (%)	69.3	47.2	99.4	89.6
Median (%)	86.9	43.6	100.0	93.35
Upper quartile (%)	100.0	75.4	100.0	100.0
Lower quartile (%)	40.3	14.1	100.0	85.2
SD (%)	35.3	33.9	2.3	13.4

Source: AlpInvest Research

funds show a substantially smaller home bias, with less than half of their overall investments made in their home market, investments made by non-UK European funds and Asia-Pacific funds are highly focused on their home regions.

We also calculate the mean degree of home bias at the fund level. In the United States, the mean degree of home bias is somewhat smaller than the aggregate buyout fund home bias, suggesting a positive correlation with the size of funds. This is also true for funds in the Asia-Pacific region. In the United Kingdom, by contrast, the mean degree of home bias is comparatively larger, potentially indicating that our UK sample is biased toward more international funds.

To examine whether buyout funds have become more international over time, we split our sample into two subsamples, consisting of 39 funds raised between 1995 and 1999 and 63 funds raised between 2000 and 2004. As far as US-based funds are concerned, we observe a significant increase in their exposure in Europe. Whereas non-UK Europe accounted for just 5.2 percent of the capital deployed by US funds raised before 2000, its share rose nearly threefold to 15.3 percent in our subsample covering the vintage years from 2000 to 2004. Conversely, UK-based funds have expanded into the US market, whose share rose to 7.4 percent in 2000–2004 from 4.7 percent in 1995–1999. By contrast, non-UK European funds as well as Asia-Pacific funds in our sample do not exhibit any tendency toward greater interregional exposure during the period under investigation.

Importantly, we find no statistically significant relation between the size of private equity funds and the degree of their home bias (Fig. 7.8). At the one extreme, there are relatively small funds targeting buyouts in emerging markets but are managed in one the world's major financial hubs, notably New York and London. Their home bias is zero as they do not invest at all in the country where they are raised and managed. At the other extreme, there are a number of comparatively small funds especially in Europe, whose investment focus is often not even their home region but their local economy within that region (e.g., France, Germany, Italy, or United Kingdom). Their home bias is 100 percent. As far as large buyout funds are concerned, their home bias tends to vary between 40 and 80 percent, with US-based funds showing a somewhat stronger home bias than their European peers.

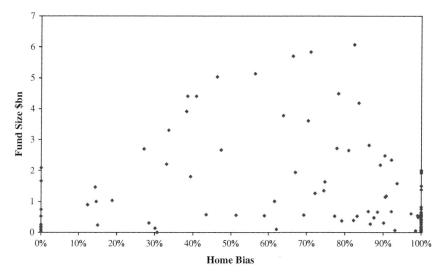

Figure 7.8 Fund size versus home bias.
Source: AlpInvest Research.

Finally, to the extent that buyout funds invest abroad, where do they deploy their capital? As far as our sample of buyout funds is concerned, we find that US funds are large net capital exporters, whereas all others are net capital importers. As Table 7.4 reveals, almost 53 percent of the acquisitions made by all buyout funds in our sample are due to US-based funds. However, less than 41 percent of the overall amount of capital deployed by the funds in our sample was actually invested in the United States. By contrast, although private equity funds based in non-UK Europe accounted for

Table 7.4 Investment value by origin of GP and destination market

Investor country	Recipient country											
	United States		United Kingdom		Non-UK Europe		Asia-Pacific		Latin America		Total	
	€ billion	%	€ billion	%	€ billion	%	€ billion	%	€ billion	%	€ billion	%
United States	37,398	72.7	4,098	8.0	5,865	11.4	2,521	4.9	1,542	3.0	51,424	100
United Kingdom	2,197	5.7	17,266	44.6	19,101	49.3	168	0.4	...		38,731	100
Non-UK Europe	26	0.4	2	0.0	5,882	99.5	...		...	...	...		5,909	100
Asia-Pacific	83	5.6	...		...	...	...		1,385	92.7	27	1.8	1,495	100
Total	39,704	40.7	21,365	21.9	30,848	31.6	4,074	4.2	1,568	1.6	97,559	100

Source: AlpInvest Research

only about 6 percent of global investments, their home market represented 31.6 percent of the equity value of global buyouts at the middle of 2007. The United Kingdom is clearly the most international market: Although only 21.9 percent of global private equity capital was invested in UK portfolio companies, UK-based funds in our sample managed almost 40 percent of private equity capital deployed worldwide. The broader European market (United Kingdom plus non-United Kingdom) represented 53.5 percent of the value of all buyouts in our sample, whereas funds domiciled in this region managed only 45.7 percent of the buyout capital worldwide.

Of the capital invested abroad by US buyout funds, non-UK Europe absorbed the relatively largest percentage, followed by the United Kingdom and Asia. By contrast, the Latin American market played a minor role for US-based funds, accounting for only 3 percent of their deployed capital. The vast majority of foreign investments made by UK-based funds have targeted firms in other European economies, underlining London's role as a major financial hub. In comparison, buyouts in the United States made by UK-based funds have remained rare. With funds managed in other European countries showing an extreme intra-European bias, Europe has been a significant net importer of private equity capital *vis-à-vis* the United States. This is also true for Asia-Pacific whose imports of buyout capital exceeded foreign investments made by domestic funds by a huge margin.

The funds' geographic allocations of their capital deviate significantly from the relative size of the respective regional markets. Table 7.5 shows the percentage US-based funds have allocated to individual regions relative to their total capital exports. The regions' shares are then compared with different market indicators, including the size of their respective private equity markets in terms of the volume of LBO transactions between 2000 and 2007, the size of their capital markets, and the size of their economies. Of the capital exported by the US-based funds in our sample, 71 percent was invested in (advanced and emerging) Europe. However, Europe

Table 7.5 Regional distribution of US-based buyout funds to individual regions and market size indicators

	Europe	Asia	Latin America	Middle East/Africa	Sum
Allocation (%)	71.0	18.0	11.0	–	100
Share in non-US buyout market (%)[a]	88.9	8.5	0.9	1.8	100
Share in non-US world equity market (%)[b]	39.9	49.1	5.4	5.7	100
Share in non-US world capital market (%)[c]	56.0	37.3	3.8	2.9	100
Share in non-US world GDP (%)[d]	36.9	43.0	11.1	9.0	100

[a]Ratio of volume of regional LBO transactions to volume of all non-US LBO transactions in 2000–2007.
[b]Ratio of regional equity market capitalization to market capitalization of all non-US markets in 2007.
[c]Ratio of regional amount of bonds, equities, and bank assets to total amount of bonds, equities, and bank assets in all non-US markets in 2007.
[d]Ratio of regional GDP relative to non-US GDP (in international dollars), 2007.
Source: AlpInvest Research; IMF WEO database; World Federation of Exchanges, Lerner, Sørensen, and Strömberg (2009).

accounted for almost 89 percent of the volume of LBO transactions outside the United States. Conversely, advanced and emerging Asia received 18 percent of the capital exports of US-based funds, whereas the region accounted for only 8.5 percent of non-US LBO transactions. Similarly, Latin America received substantially more capital from US-based funds than the size of its private equity market would have suggested.

Our observations, which are broadly consistent with Aizenman and Kendall (2008), suggest that the global diffusion of private equity is gathering momentum. Nontraditional markets are attracting more capital, whereby GPs weigh heightened governance risk against a less competitive deal environment and superior growth prospects over the medium to longer term. Furthermore, it seems that other factors, such as geographic proximity, language, and cultural relations, may also play a role.

7.3   Comparing cross-border private equity fund investments with mutual funds

How should we interpret the home bias in buyout funds? Is the bias large or rather small? In answering these questions, we first have to address the issue of choosing an appropriate benchmark. Earlier studies on home bias in portfolio investing have focused on cross-border holdings at the country level. Since 2001, the IMF conducts an annual "Coordinated Portfolio Investment Survey (CPIS)." Participation in the CPIS is voluntary, and some 75 economies currently participate in the survey. The CPIS provides information on individual economy year-end holdings of portfolio investment securities—equity securities and debt securities valued at market prices, cross-classified by the country of issuer of the securities.[8] The requirement to report a geographical breakdown of cross-border security holdings permits a time series analysis of the CPIS survey results. Importantly, it thus allows analyzing the reporting countries' holdings of portfolio investment securities, which highlights the changing extent of "home bias" in portfolio managers' decision-making.

The US Treasury conducts a similar survey collecting data on foreign holdings of US securities since 1974. However, both the CPIS and the US Treasury Survey are limited to portfolio investment. Foreign direct investment, which is typically defined as an acquisition of at least 10 percent of a foreign company's shares, is not captured by the two surveys. From our standpoint, this is an important shortcoming, as private equity funds typically seek to acquire controlling stakes or at least significant positions in a company. A more comprehensive data set on the gross liabilities and assets has recently been assembled by Lane and Milesi-Ferretti (2007, 2008). Covering 145 economies, this data set is based on investment flows reported in the balance of payments, which are adjusted for valuation effects. Although the Lane/Milesi-Ferretti data set captures FDI, it has in common with the CPIS and the US Treasury Survey that it does not identify individual classes of foreign acquirers, such as private equity funds.

---

[8]The coverage of the CPIS is augmented with information from two other surveys, namely "Securities Held as Foreign Exchange Reserves," and "Securities Held by International Organizations," although these data sets are not disclosed at a detailed level, as the data are reported on a confidential basis.

More recently, academic research by Chan, Covrig, and Ng (2005) and Hau and Rey (2008) has used more granulated data on investments by mutual funds, which are provided by Thomson Financial Securities. As the home bias in mutual funds mirror investment decisions by their fund managers, arguably these funds provide a superior benchmark for private equity funds. Recall that we have found that US buyout funds in our sample invested on average 27.3 percent of their capital abroad (Table 7.3). By comparison, Hau and Rey, who calculate the "aggregate mutual fund home bias" as the ratio between the total market capitalization of the domestic assets in which mutual funds invest and their total investment portfolio, find that foreign equities represent just about 15 percent of the investment portfolios held by US mutual funds (Table 7.6). Their results are virtually identical with those obtained by Chan et al., whose estimates are based on the same data set provided by Thomson Financial Securities, although for a different sample period.

In our sample, UK-based buyout funds show a significantly lower degree of home bias than their American peers, with 55 percent of their capital invested abroad. This is also true for mutual funds in the United Kingdom, which are found to be substantially less home biased than US mutual funds. However, the shares reported by Hau and Rey (2008) and Chan et al. (2005) differ significantly. While Chan et al. report a home bias in UK mutual fund investing similar to UK buyout funds, Hau and Rey find a substantially lower amount of holdings in the home market relative to the funds' overall holdings. Although Chan et al.'s UK sample of mutual funds is nearly twice as large as Hau and Rey's (2021 vs. 1186 funds), it remains unclear what explains the substantial difference in the home bias reported in these two studies. One

Table 7.6 Recent studies on home bias in equity investing

Study	Focus	Data source	Period	United States	United Kingdom
AlpInvest Partners	Buyout funds United States, Europe, United Kingdom, Asia-Pacific	AlpInvest proprietary data set	1995–2004	72.7	44.6
Hau and Rey (2008)	Mutual funds United States, Canada, United Kingdom, Europe, Switzerland	Thomson Financial Securities	1997–2002	85.1	22.8
Chan et al. (2005)	Mutual funds, 26 economies	Thomson Financial Securities	1999–2000	85.7	43.1
Hau and Rey (2008)	Portfolio investment, United States, Canada, United Kingdom, Europe, Switzerland	IMF CPIS	2001–2002	92.1	65.4

Source: AlpInvest Research

possible explanation Hau and Rey offer is that their sample is biased toward more international funds.

Hau and Rey also report the degree to which portfolio investors are biased at the country level, which they define as the ratio between the total investment made by domestic agents in the home market and the total domestic market capitalization. Their calculations are based on data from the International Monetary Fund's CPIS.[9] Importantly, the home bias at the country level is significantly higher than for mutual funds as well as for buyout funds, both in the United States and the United Kingdom. As far as buyout funds are concerned, the differences are quite dramatic. Although US buyout funds in our sample are found to have invested 27.3 percent of their capital abroad, at the country level holdings of foreign assets are reported to represent just 8 percent of total investments. Similarly, while UK-based buyout funds in our sample have deployed 55 percent of their capital abroad, at the country level foreign investment represents only about 35 percent.

Overall, our findings suggest that buyout funds are less home biased than mutual funds, a result, which is consistent with the "optimal ownership theory of the home bias" proposed by Kho, Stulz, and Warnock (2007). According to this theory, the home bias is largely a function of the quality of institutions, with weaker governance leading to a higher level of insider ownership and limiting portfolio holdings by foreign investors. This theory predicts that countries with poor governance standards tend to have a relatively higher share of foreign direct investment—typically defined as an acquisition of 10 percent or more of the shares, with the intention of participating in management—as information asymmetries make it more valuable for investors to expend resources in monitoring and enforcement.

7.4   Summary and conclusions

Financial globalization in private equity has gathered considerable momentum over the past one or two decades. Both venture capitalists and buyout firms have opened offices abroad to source deals, and while some general partners raise specific funds for individual regions or countries, others deploy a rising share of the capital they raise through a global fund in foreign markets. Led by US GPs, this process is radiating increasingly widely. Although initially US exports of financial services and private equity capital were concentrated on Europe, more recently GPs' expansion strategies have encompassed other regions, especially Asia but increasingly also Latin America, the Middle East, and Africa. Meanwhile, European GPs have also increased their efforts to expand abroad, focusing in particular on the rapidly growing economies in Asia.

The globalization of private equity has been fostered by financial globalization in other areas, and as equity and debt capital markets have become more integrated not

---

[9]In contrast to most other studies (e.g., Ahearne, Griever, & Warnock, 2004; Chan, 2005; Warnock, 2002), however, they choose not to normalize their numbers by the relative size of the domestic capitalization in the world market capitalization. This has the advantage that we can easily compare the thus calculated home bias at the country level with that at the mutual and buyout fund levels.

only globally but also regionally, the globalization of private equity has been accompanied by increased regionalization. In this process, a new class of fund managers has emerged whose investment focus is neither global nor local. Although the size of their funds allows them to target deals, which are often beyond the reach of purely domestic funds, regional fund managers do not normally compete with the mega global funds (e.g., Bridgepoint Capital and Cinven in Western Europe; Mid Europa Partners in central and eastern Europe; Pacific Equity Partners and Affinity Equity Partners in Asia-Pacific).

Financial globalization offers limited partners new investment opportunities. As global and regional private equity funds have emerged, limited partners seeking to diversify their portfolio internationally are no longer confined to local funds in the respective target markets. However, with the new opportunities come new challenges. To the extent that LPs commit capital to globally or regionally operating private equity funds, how can they control that their resulting geographic exposure is in line with their portfolio targets? Indeed, as we have seen in this chapter, this is an important question, given that LPAs provide GPs with a substantial degree of freedom where to invest, a freedom, fund managers usually take advantage of. As far as US-based buyout funds are concerned, our review of a proprietary data set compiled by AlpInvest Partners has revealed that around 27 percent of the funds' capital was deployed outside the US market. In the case of UK-based buyout funds, we have found that actually the bulk of capital was invested outside the United Kingdom.

The internationalization of private equity fund investments raises a number of important questions from the viewpoint of a limited partner's portfolio construction. Do GPs expanding into new markets have the right skills and experience to identify attractive investment opportunities and manage investments successfully in potentially complex business environments? Are the GP's decision-making process and the compensation structure consistent with his expansion strategy as well as the LP's risk appetite? Do global and regional funds offer additional diversification gains relative to domestic funds as they target different transaction sizes? We address these and other issues in the following chapter by looking at financial globalization in private equity from the standpoint of LPs' investment decisions.

8 Cross-border fund commitments, due diligence, and the allocation matrix

Chapter Outline head

As domestic private equity industries have emerged in a rising number of countries and private equity funds have become increasingly less home biased, the scope for limited partners to diversify their portfolios internationally has expanded substantially. In this chapter, we look at the globalization of financial intermediation in private equity from the GPs' fund-raising perspective. Specifically, we examine the extent to which inflows to private equity funds are due to commitments from foreign limited partners. The geographic composition of the GPs' investor base reflects the home bias of the limited partners, whose investment decisions may also be subject to capital barriers, informational gaps, and behavioral biases. In combination with our findings in Chapter 7, our analysis allows us to determine the degree to which the private equity market is integrated internationally between two extremes: In completely segmented markets, GPs raise capital only from domestic investors and deploy their funds in the same country. This was the situation in the early days of private equity, which is still applicable to many small funds, whose role in financial intermediation remains essentially confined to a national (if not subnational) market. Conversely, in a globally integrated market, GPs raise funds internationally and deploy the capital wherever they expect the best risk-adjusted returns.

In the first section of this chapter, we focus on the global integration of the fund-raising market. To get a more granular picture about the investor base of private equity funds, we slice the data in different ways, namely in terms of (i) geographies, (ii) investment stages (VC vs. buyouts), and (iii) the size of funds raised by GPs. Looking forward, Section 2 discusses the growing importance of institutional investors from emerging economies as suppliers of private equity capital. Our main

International Investments in Private Equity. DOI: 10.1016/B978-0-12-375082-2.10008-4

interest focuses on sovereign wealth funds (SWFs), who look set to continue to play a key role in recycling their home countries' current account surpluses. Section 3 debates the challenges that limited partners face in their due diligence work when contemplating commitments to foreign private equity funds. Finally, turning from the bottom-up fund selection process to the top-down construction of a global private equity portfolio, Section 4 develops an allocation matrix that links commitments to partnerships with deal-level exposures to different market segments.

8.1 Cross-border fund-raising: empirical evidence

As we have discussed in Chapter 2, the investor base of private equity funds comprises a wide range of institutions. In terms of the absolute amount of capital raised from individual investor classes, pension funds are by far the most important limited partners. Managing more than one-third of assets held by institutional investors in mature markets (International Monetary Fund, 2007, p. 68), pension funds allocate a comparatively high share to private equity. Insurance companies and banks follow. Although endowments show on average the relatively highest allocation to private equity funds (Chapter 4), their substantially smaller portfolios give them less weight in the overall investor base of private equity funds. Although some SWFs are large investors in private equity funds—and for some private equity funds SWFs belong to their most important LPs—as an investor class they still fall significantly behind pension funds, insurance companies, and banks reflecting their considerably smaller asset base.

Asset managers have become more outward oriented over time, in part thanks to the relaxation of regulatory restrictions as well as technological advances that have helped reduce informational deficits about foreign markets. Regulatory restrictions on foreign investment have traditionally applied to pension funds, but as such regulations have been relaxed, pension fund portfolios have gradually become more diversified internationally.[1] Between the mid-1990s and the mid-2000s, US pension funds doubled their holdings of foreign equities to 15 percent (International Monetary Fund, 2007; based on the OECD Global Pension Statistics project). While the share of foreign equities in UK pension funds' portfolios rose to 32 percent from 23 percent during the same period, Dutch pension funds more than tripled their foreign equity holdings to 43 percent. At the end of 2008, the share of foreign assets, including bonds, held by pension funds in the OECD area averaged about 30 percent (Organisation for Economic Development and Co-operation, 2010).

Alternative investments have gained substantially in importance in pension funds' portfolios. In Chapter 4, we have seen that some US pension funds have allocated 10 percent or more of their AUM to private equity. The largest US pension fund, CalPERS, raised its allocation target for private equity to 15 percent in the spring of

---

[1]The majority of OECD countries have abolished limits on foreign investment by pension funds. Although some countries still maintain restrictions on foreign investment, in several cases they only apply to investments in non-OECD countries.

2009. CalPERS' private equity portfolio is substantially diversified internationally. The most important portfolio segment includes commitments to buyout funds targeting large transactions (Table 8.1). These funds are raised by globally operating private equity firms, some of which (e.g., CVC and Permira) being headquartered outside CalPERS' home market, the United States. The funds themselves may be chasing deals on a global scale (Blackstone Capital Partners, TPG Partners), or they are raised to target specific regions (e.g., Carlyle Europe Partners, CVC Capital Partners Asia, and KKR European Fund). What is considered as a "large" transaction depends on the market where the funds are operating. For example, by US standards, a buyout with an enterprise value of, say, US$1 billion would have been classified as a mid-sized transaction in the US market prior to the market correction in 2007, whereas in Asia such a buyout would qualify as a very large deal.

In addition to its commitments to globally operating private equity firms specialized in large buyouts, CalPERS has also made considerable investments in buyout funds targeting mid-sized deals in Europe and in nontraditional markets. Although some of these funds are raised by local GPs (e.g., Bridgepoint in Europe, Polish Enterprise Fund in central and eastern Europe, and Affinity Equity Partners in Asia-Pacific), others are managed by GPs headquartered in the United States (e.g., Advent Latin America). At the end of 2008, commitments to non-US middle-market buyout funds totaled 12 percent of CalPERS' private equity portfolio. Finally, although US middle-market players typically target transactions in their home market, some of them have begun to operate in other regions, providing their LPs with additional international exposure.

How does CalPERS' private equity portfolio compare with AlpInvest Partners, Europe's largest private equity investor? In fact, AlpInvest Partners' exposure to globally operating buyout firms is even higher amounting to 41 percent. In addition, AlpInvest Partners has made considerable commitments to US middle-market buyout funds and private funds operating in nontraditional markets, totaling around 23 percent of its fund portfolio. Furthermore, a substantial share of AlpInvest Partners' commitments to venture capital, clean-tech, distressed, and secondary funds are managed by non-European private equity firms. In terms of invested capital in the

Table 8.1 Fund commitments by CalPERS and AlpInvest Partners, 2000–2008

	CalPERS	AlpInvest Partners
Large buyouts (%)	37	41
US middle market (%)	35	15
European middle market (%)	7	13
Nontraditional markets (%)	5	8
Venture capital (%)	8	14
Distressed (%)	4	4
Clean-tech (%)	4	2
Mezzanine (%)	1	3

Source: Investors' Web sites; author's calculations

underlying portfolio companies in AlpInvest Partners' portfolio, the United States accounted for around 44 percent at the end of 2008. Investments in nontraditional markets amounted to another 12 percent, implying that considerably more private equity capital had been invested abroad than in AlpInvest Partners' home region.

While the two examples of CalPERS and AlpInvest Partners suggest that private equity markets have become more integrated not only in terms of cross-border investments by private equity funds but also with regard to cross-border commitments to such funds, there are no aggregate data on the geographic composition of investors' private equity portfolios. Given the size of CalPERS' and AlpInvest Partners' private equity portfolios, one may have doubts whether their investment decisions can be generalized. Foreign funds, especially those raised and managed in economies whose institutions are still emerging, pose particular challenges in terms of due diligence and require resources smaller LPs might not have. This may entail opening offices in key foreign markets—just as GPs have opened offices abroad to identify attractive deals and help raise local capital. As far as AlpInvest Partners is concerned, for example, their office network now spans New York, Hong Kong, and London, in addition to the firm's headquarters in Amsterdam.

In the absence of aggregate data on the geographic composition of private equity investors' portfolios, what can we do to track investment flows at the LP level? The mirror image of LPs' commitments to private equity funds in different regions is the regional composition of private equity funds' investor base. Although information about the amount of individual capital commitments is confidential, thanks to data collected by PREQIN we know at least the geographic origin of LPs in a large sample of private equity funds. Table 8.2 depicts the investor base of private funds raised by GPs domiciled in the United States, Europe, and the rest of the world. Note that what matters here is where the private equity firm or the venture capitalist is headquartered and not where their funds are raised and managed. In other words, we look at a GP's entire LP base, taking into account that in their investment decisions many LPs focus

Table 8.2 Composition (%) of investor base of buyout and venture capital firms

	Limited partners from		
	United States	**Europe**	**Rest of the world**
Buyout firms focusing on large transactions headquartered in			
United States	57.3	29.5	13.2
Europe	48.8	41.1	10.1
Buyout firms focusing on middle-market transactions headquartered in			
United States	62.0	25.1	12.9
Europe	39.9	49.9	10.2
Rest of the World	40.9	30.6	28.5
VC firms headquartered in			
United States	73.7	16.9	9.4
Europe	38.2	56.4	5.5

Source: PREQIN; author's calculations

not only on their exposure to different regions but also to individual GPs. Although from a risk management standpoint, investors generally want to avoid an excessive exposure to single private equity firms, opportunities to coinvest often arise as a function of an LP's total commitment to a GP's funds rather than individual funds. Consistent with this approach, a commitment made by a European LP to KKR's European II Fund (which was raised in 2004) would be treated in Table 8.2 as a commitment to a US-based private equity firm. Similarly, if this LP had made a commitment to CVC's Asia Fund, he would be considered as part of the fund's domestic investor base.

A number of interesting observations can be made as follows:

- Buyout firms whose funds focus on large transactions enjoy a particularly international investor base. For instance, as far as US-based GPs are concerned, nearly 43 percent of the limited partners in their funds are from abroad. In absolute terms, more than 230 foreign LPs are reported to have committed capital to US-based GPs focusing on large buyouts, which is almost 10 percent of all non-US limited partners. This compares with around 220 foreign LPs, who are identified to have made commitments to European funds raised by GPs with a focus on large deals. Representing about 7 percent of all non-European LPs in the PREQIN LP data set, these investors account for nearly 59 percent of the investor base of these funds.

- The investor base of venture capital firms tends to be comparatively more domestic. In US venture capital funds, about three-quarters of the LPs are from the United States. We can only speculate whether this reflects LPs' portfolio decisions and their potential investment biases or instead access restrictions to such funds.

- US-based limited partners play an important role as capital providers around the world. In fact, they represent the largest group of investors in private equity funds managed by European GPs with a focus on large transactions. Although we only know the number of LPs from different regions, given the amount of capital US LPs manage we may suspect that they are also the most important group of investors in these funds in terms of their capital commitments.

- LPs from nontraditional markets account for a good 10 percent of the investor base of US and European buyout firms. In their home markets, they represent less than 30 percent of the investors in private equity funds managed by local GPs. This is low by US and European standards, which is likely to reflect the still comparatively small number of private equity investors outside the United States and Europe. However, in some markets, notably the Middle East and Emerging Asia, the true weight—weighed by their capital commitments—of domestic LPs in domestically managed private equity funds might be considerably higher, as some recent research on the geographic focus of SWF investments suggests (Bernstein, Lerner, & Schoar, 2009).

Overall, we find that buyout funds and venture capital firms around the world rely on an internationally diversified investor base. This suggests that the global fund-raising market has also become more integrated as a rising number of limited partners have been seeking to diversify their private equity portfolios internationally (as well as regionally, as we shall see in Chapter 9). This trend is likely to gain further momentum in the future, which, as we discuss in the following section, is at least in part thanks to the growing importance of institutional investors from emerging economies.

8.2 The growing importance of emerging economies as suppliers of private equity capital

In Chapter 6, we have already discussed the growing importance of private equity in nontraditional markets and their attractiveness as a destination for foreign private equity funds. However, nontraditional markets are not only increasingly important absorbers of private equity investments but also providers of private equity funds. This applies especially to emerging market economies, which have become large capital exporters in recent years (Table 8.3). On a net basis, there has been an outflow of almost US$ 2.8 trillion between 2002 and 2008, 70 percent of which in just 3 years. Although *private* capital inflows (direct and portfolio investments and bank loans and deposits) exceeded private capital outflows by almost US$ 1.3 trillion in 2002–2008, these net inflows were dwarfed by investments of foreign exchange reserves that the monetary authorities accumulated.

That emerging market economies are net capital exporters is in stark contrast with economic theory, which predicts that capital should be flowing from rich to poor countries, given that the capital productivity in the latter should be relatively higher because of comparatively lower wages. The so-called Lucas (1990) paradox has attracted substantial interest in the academic literature. One strand focuses on capital inflows, which have grown strongly in recent years but nevertheless failed to keep pace with sharply rising outflows. A key factor is generally seen in the inferior degree of investor protection in an environment where legal and regulatory institutions are still emerging. As we have discussed in Chapter 7, this factor is also relevant for cross-border private equity investors, which helps explain why penetration rates have generally remained significantly lower than in more mature markets.

A second strand of literature has focused on capital outflows from emerging markets, which to a large extent are a mirror image of the large current account surpluses these countries have been running. In the 4-year period from 2006 to 2009, emerging markets [including the newly industrialized economies in Asia (NIACs)] had a cumulative surplus of nearly US$ 2.8 trillion. This was almost entirely due to two regions: emerging Asia (US$ 1.9 trillion) and the Middle East (US$ 0.9 trillion) where high savings rates exceeded investment rates by a wide margin (Table 8.4) and pegged or quasi-pegged exchange rates prevented a greater demand for imports and a decline in foreign demand. In its World Economic Outlook, the International Monetary Fund (2010b) projects a more or less unchanged picture for the foreseeable future, with the aggregate current account surplus of emerging economies and the newly industrialized countries in Asia totaling almost US$ 1 trillion in 2015.

As a result, emerging economies (including the NIACs) look set to continue to accumulate foreign exchange reserves at a rapid pace. At the end of 2009, foreign exchange reserves stood at almost US$ 6.6 trillion, a more than tripling from the US$ 1.9 trillion at the end of 2003 (Fig. 8.1). If this pace is maintained, as the IMF

Table 8.3 Net capital flows to emerging markets

	1998	1999	2000	2001	2002	2003	2004	2005	2006	2007	2008
Direct investment	155.0	166.7	149.1	170.5	150.0	147.4	186.7	251.9	255.3	412.3	436.0
Portfolio investment	13.2	10.6	-32.5	-55.6	-42.2	-16.3	3.2	6.6	-116.3	10.8	-166.7
Other investments	-52.1	-93.1	-94.5	-23.2	-31.6	-6.2	-3.3	-75.5	-78.0	169.8	-219.6
Reserve assets	6.4	-37.8	-84.0	-90.3	-154.5	-303.9	-426.7	-540.1	-717.7	-1226.6	-668.0
Total capital flows	122.5	46.4	-61.9	1.5	-78.2	-178.9	-240.2	-357.0	-656.7	-633.8	-618.2

Note: Emerging markets comprises the group of 149 emerging and developing economies defined in the IMF's World Economic Outlook. Other investments include bank loans and deposits.
Source: International Monetary Fund (2010a, 2010b)

Table 8.4 Savings—investment and current account balances in different regions (percent of GDP)

	1988–1995	1996–2003	2004	2005	2006	2007	2008	2009	2015[a]
Newly industrialized Asian economies									
Savings	35.6	32.3	32.9	31.6	31.9	32.4	32.8	32.4	31.7
Investment	32.2	28.1	26.7	26.1	26.4	26.1	27.8	23.6	25.9
Current account	...	...	6.2	5.3	5.4	6.1	4.9	8.9	6.0
Developing Asia									
Savings	30.6	33.1	38.4	41.5	44.1	45.0	43.9	43.6	46.0
Investment	32.9	31.7	35.8	37.3	38.0	37.9	38.2	39.5	41.3
Current account	...	...	2.7	4.2	6.1	7.0	5.7	4.1	5.0
Middle East and North Africa									
Savings	20.2	27.3	35.5	41.2	42.8	41.6	42.4	29.6	34.6
Investment	24.3	23.4	25.3	23.9	24.0	26.0	26.8	27.8	26.6
Current account	...	...	10.4	17.2	19	15.7	15.5	1.8	7.7
Sub-Saharan Africa									
Savings	16.2	16.1	18.3	19.4	25.0	22.8	23.3	20.3	21.6
Investment	17.1	18.3	19.7	19.6	20.4	21.6	22.1	21.9	22.4
Current account	...	...	−1.5	−0.4	4.3	1.2	0.9	−2.1	−1.4
Latin America									
Savings	18.2	18.3	21.9	22.0	23.2	22.5	22.8	19.2	21.2
Investment	19.1	20.6	20.8	20.5	21.6	22.2	23.4	20.8	22.7
Current account	...	...	1.0	1.4	1.6	0.4	−0.6	−0.5	−1.6
Central and Eastern Europe									
Savings	22.1	18.2	16.4	16.6	16.9	16.9	16.9	16.5	17.7
Investment	24.1	21.4	21.8	21.5	23.5	25.0	24.8	18.8	21.8
Current account	...	...	−5.4	−5.0	−6.6	−8.0	−7.8	−2.3	−4.3
CIS									
Savings	...	25.4	30.4	30.5	30.7	31.1	30.8	22.6	26.5
Investment	...	20.8	22.1	21.7	23.4	27.0	26.0	19.9	25.2
Current account	...	...	8.2	8.7	7.4	4.2	4.9	2.6	−0.1
Advanced economies									
Savings	22.2	21.1	20.1	20.2	21.0	20.7	19.5	17.1	19.2
Investment	22.7	21.3	20.7	21.1	21.6	21.5	21.0	18.0	20.0
Current account	...	...	−0.7	−1.2	−1.2	−0.9	−1.3	−0.4	−0.7

[a]Forecasts for savings and investment ratios refer to averages in 2012–2015.
Source: International Monetary Fund (2010b)

expects, an amount of around US$ 800 billion pa will be added to the already very high stock of foreign exchange reserves in these countries.

The amount of foreign exchange reserves some countries hold has become far bigger than what would appear prudent from a macrorisk standpoint. While central banks typically hold their reserves in high-quality and highly liquid assets, several countries have created special funds that enjoy greater freedom in their portfolio choices. Owned by a sovereign government and managed separately from funds administered by the sovereign government's central bank or ministry of finance, or

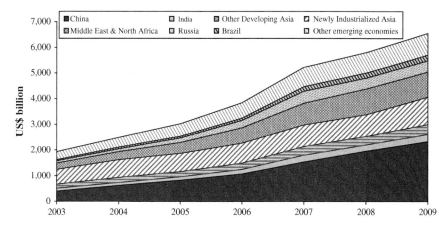

Figure 8.1 Foreign exchange reserves in emerging economies.
Source: International Monetary Fund (2010b).

treasury, SWFs invest in a broad range of asset classes with different risk profiles.[2] Although most SWFs are a more recent phenomenon, some were already founded in the 1950s and the 1970s. At the end of 2009, SWFs in emerging markets and newly industrialized countries in Asia managed around US$ 3.3 trillion, with the 13 largest SWFs accounting for almost 90 percent of this amount (Table 8.5).[3]

Many SWFs do not have liabilities to meet. Nor are they subject to withdrawals by external investors, two important factors that distinguish them from most other institutional investors. As a result, they tend to have long investment horizons and are able to allocate a greater share of their assets to riskier and less liquid alternative investments. Although little is known about the asset allocation of individual SWFs, Private Equity Intelligence (2010) reports that 55 percent of the funds are active in private equity. Eighty percent of those SWFs that make private investments do so through both commitments to private equity funds and direct investments. The remaining 20 percent undertakes only direct investments.

Bernstein et al. (2009) analyze the direct private equity investment strategies of SWFs. Their sample includes 2662 investments between 1984 and 2007 by 29 SWFs. Of these, Asian and Middle Eastern SWFs accounted for 2046 and 532 transactions, respectively. In terms of the geographic focus of their investment strategies, Asian

[2]Despite all the controversial debate about the growing influence of SWFs, there is no generally accepted definition of a SWF. In this book, we follow Blundell-Wignall, Hu, and Yermo (2008) who define a SWF as a pool of assets owned and managed directly or indirectly by a government to achieve national objectives. Typically, these objectives are to diversify and improve the return of foreign exchange reserves or commodity revenue and to shield the domestic economy from fluctuations in commodity prices. SWFs should be distinguished from other pools of capital governments have formed to finance public pension systems.
[3]There are some SWFs in industrialized countries. By far the largest one is the Norwegian Government Pension Fund, whose AUM stood at US$ 445 billion at the end of 2009. However, SWFs in industrialized countries account for less than 15 percent of the US$ 3.8 trillion SWFs are estimated to have held worldwide at the end of 2009.

Table 8.5 Largest SWFs in emerging markets and NIACs (end of 2009)

SWF	Country	AUM (billion)	Inception year	Source
Abu Dhabi Investment Authority	UAE	627	1976	Commodity
SAMA Foreign Holdings	Saudi Arabia	431	n/a	Commodity
SAFE Investment Company	China	347	n/a	Noncommodity
China Investment Corporation	China	289	2007	Noncommodity
Government of Singapore Invest. Corporation	Singapore	248	1981	Noncommodity
Kuwait Investment Authority	Kuwait	203	1953	Commodity
National Welfare Fund	Russia	168	2008	Commodity
National Social Security Fund	China	147	2000	Noncommodity
Hong Kong Monetary Authority Invest. Portfolio	China (HK)	140	1993	Noncommodity
Temasek Holdings	Singapore	122	1974	Noncommodity
Libyan Investment Authority	Lybia	70	2006	Commodity
Qatar Investment Authority	Qatar	65	2005	Commodity
Revenue Regulation Fund	Algeria	47	2000	Commodity

Source: SWF Institute, IFSL

funds have focused to a large extent (75.7 percent) on their home region. However, only 37.4 percent of the acquisitions by Asian SWFs were actually made in the home economy of the respective funds. As far as direct private equity investments outside Asia are concerned, Asian funds have focused mainly on Europe and North America. By contrast, SWFs in the Middle East are found to have invested only a small percentage in their respective home economies (9 percent) and not much more in their home region (16.5 percent). Investments outside their home region are concentrated on Europe, North America, and Australia, which have a combined share of 61.7 percent.

Assets under management held by SWFs in emerging economies and the newly industrialized countries in Asia are set to continue to grow. Given the IMF's current account forecasts, it would seem possible that AUM double to around US$ 6.5 trillion by 2015 (not counting assets held by SWFs in industrialized countries). Suppose SWFs aim to allocate 7.5 percent of their assets to private equity, not a particularly aggressive assumption, given the long-term nature of their investments.[4] This would imply that SWFs in emerging markets and NIACs would hold nearly US$ 500 billion in private equity assets in 2015.

This amount would be significantly larger than one could expect the emerging markets to absorb in global private equity investing, even taking into account that they are set to continue to grow significantly faster than the mature economies. As a result, emerging markets and the NIACs are anticipated to be large net exporters of private equity capital. A simple back-on-the-envelope calculation shows why; at the end of

---

[4]According to its first annual review, the world's largest SWF, the Abu Dhabi Investment Authority (2010), has a target range for private equity from 5 to 10 percent.

2009, the stock of private equity investments in emerging economies stood at around US\$ 170 billion (estimated as cumulative investment flows between 2005 and 2009 as reported by the Emerging Markets Private Equity Association (2010) and assuming an average holding period of 5 years). To increase the stock of private equity investments from US\$ 170 billion at the end of 2009 to US\$ 500 billion by 2015, the countries' investment-to-GDP ratios would need to more than double in 2011–2015 from their current levels, given the IMF's economic growth projections. Such an increase would seem rather unrealistic in light of the gradualism with which private equity has expanded its role in today's more mature markets. To the extent that investors in emerging markets commit more capital to private equity than their economies can reasonably be expected to absorb, private equity capital will need to be exported (Cornelius, 2007, p. 26).

Although SWFs are already the largest providers of private equity capital in emerging economies, there are other investor groups that are likely to become increasingly important investors in private equity. Among these, pension funds are of particular interest. Over the past couple of decades, many emerging markets have introduced pension reforms in response to political and demographic pressures threatening the financial stability of pay-as-you-go systems. Following the lead of Chile, which initiated the reform drive in Latin America, several other countries in the region have adopted variants of a funded, privately managed, defined-contribution personal accounts retirement system (Roldes, 2004). Similar reforms have been implemented in central and eastern Europe as well as in Asia. In general, these reforms have been far more extensive and bolder than those in Western industrialized countries and have generated important benefits for the development of domestic capital markets.

Allianz Global Investors (2008) estimates that pension assets in central and Eastern Europe and in Asia could reach almost US\$ 250 billion and around US\$ 1.05 trillion by 2015, implying a CAGR of about 19 percent and 17 percent, respectively, from their 2006 levels. Adding Latin America, where pension assets already stood at around US\$ 380 billion in 2008, total assets in the three regions could, thus, excess US\$ 2 trillion by the middle of the decade.[5] How much of this amount will be invested in private equity, depends no least on portfolio limits imposed by governments in individual countries. Remaining investment restrictions tend to be tighter with regard to commitments to foreign private investment funds (Table 8.6).[6] However, to the extent that domestic investments by pension funds in emerging economies crowd out commitments by other domestic investors who are less subject to such restrictions on foreign investments, they will still contribute to increasing net exports of private equity capital.

---

[5]Data on pension assets are from the International Federation of Pension Fund Management Companies (http://www.fiap.cl/prontus_fiap/site/edic/base/port/series.html), ABRAPP (http://www.abrapp.org.br/ppub/pef.dll?pagina=servscript&QUALS=home/home.html), and Allianz Global Investors (2008).

[6]Apart from private equity funds, private investment funds include hedge funds, real estate, and infra-structure funds and funds with similar structures.

Table 8.6 Portfolio limits on pension fund investments in selected emerging economies in private investment funds (as of 2009)

Country	Portfolio limits in private investment funds	Specific investment limits in selected foreign private investment funds
Africa		
South Africa	Not allowed	Not allowed
Asia		
India	–	–
Korea	• Personal pension: no limit • Corporate pension: Equity fund: DB 50%; DC not permitted Balanced fund: DB 50%; DC not permitted Bond fund: no limit	• Personal pension: no restriction • Corporate pension: DC: not permitted DB: not permitted
Central and Eastern Europe		
Czech Republic	If traded on OECD regulated markets: 70%; if not they can be included in 5% limit for other assets	–
Hungary	• Derivative fund: 5% • Risk capital: 5% • Conventional portfolio: 0% • Balanced portfolio: 3% • Growth portfolio: 5%	–
Poland	• Personal pension fund: no limit • Occupational pension fund: not allowed	• Personal pension fund: no limit • Occupational pension fund: not allowed
Russia	Not permitted	Not permitted
Turkey	Information not available	–
Latin America		
Brazil	No limit	Not permitted
Chile	Not permitted	Not permitted
Columbia	5%	5%
Mexico	Only through structured instruments, ranging up to 10%	Not permitted

Source: Organisation for Economic Development and Co-operation (2010)

8.3   Due diligence in cross-border commitments

8.3.1   General due diligence principles

Each individual commitment behind a private equity fund is (or should be) the result of the due diligence investors undertake before making investment decisions. In conducting their due diligence on GPs, investors are usually guided by a set of general principles, which are rooted in the performance dynamics of private equity partnerships we discussed in Chapter 2 (see also Gottschalg, 2010).

- *Past performance*: Private equity returns are found to be persistent over time (Kaplan & Schoar, 2005), suggesting that the past performance of a general partner is a possible predictor for his future performance.
- *Experience*: Successful private equity investments require specific skills, which are typically acquired through a learning process. As fund managers become more experienced, their performance is generally found to improve (Kaplan & Schoar, 2005). In conducting due diligence on a newly raised fund, it is, therefore, usually assumed that its future performance is positively related to the experience of the fund manager.
- *Access to deal flow*: Although experience is generally seen as a fund manager's competitive advantage in screening a given universe of investment opportunities, this universe is a function of a fund manager's access to deal flow. With information asymmetries representing an important determinant of success in private equity investments, limited partners will typically look at the stability of past deal flow of the fund manager when contemplating a commitment to a newly raised fund.
- *Diseconomies of scale*: As general partners raise larger funds, their performance is generally found to deteriorate, however (Lopez-de-Silanes, Phalippou, & Gottschalg, 2009). This deterioration is generally attributable to the limited pool of attractive investment opportunities that fall into the sweet spot of the fund manager. While acquiring more portfolio companies with a larger pool of capital, therefore, often implies investing in less attractive companies and thus compromising returns, acquisitions of larger portfolio companies require a different set of skills, and experience. As a result, the expected performance of a newly raised fund tends to be inversely related to the increase in fund size between the prior and the focal fund.

Although these general observations provide a good starting point in the due diligence process and have been used in econometric benchmarking studies (Gottschalg, 2010), in practice few investors will rely solely on a top-down approach in their fund selection. Instead, investment decisions are usually based on a more nuanced bottom-up due diligence process that focuses on fund-specific investment characteristics. For example, take the persistence of fund returns. Although past returns are found to have predicative power for the relative performance of newly raised funds, from Chapter 2 we know that this persistence is far from perfect. Let us reiterate the findings of a large-sample study we referred to earlier. According to this study, a limited partner committing to a newly raised fund has a 43-percent probability that he has invested in a top-quartile fund if the predecessor fund was a top-quartile fund. Conversely, this probability would drop to 16 percent if the predecessor fund had been in the lowest quartile. Although these findings support the notion of persistence, it is clear that there is no guarantee for outperformance just by looking at a fund manager's past performance. In fact, there is a 57-percent probability that a top-quartile fund will be succeeded by one whose performance will be second quartile or worse!

There are good reasons why a top-quartile fund manager may not be able to repeat his outperformance in a newly raised fund. For instance, individual people who had been instrumental for the success of previous funds might have left the firm or their influence in the internal investment decision process might have diminished. It is, therefore, imperative for limited partners to get a thorough understanding as to who exactly takes the investment decisions in the fund, how these decisions are made and how the carry and the management fee profits are shared among a fund's executives. Apart from adverse team dynamics, a GP might have ventured into market segments or industries beyond his traditional sweet spots. It is this sort of information a detailed due diligence process aims to unearth, which in a top-down cross-section benchmarking exercise would be lost.

Furthermore, a fund manager's past performance tells us little about the sources of his success. Two factors that cross-section studies have identified are deal flow and experience. However, how exactly do we measure these variables? For example, as far as deal flow is concerned, the simplest measure is the number of portfolio companies a GP has acquired in previous partnerships. This variable is relatively easily available for a large number of funds and, as Gottschalg (2010, p. 287) finds, is statistically significantly correlated with the performance of the focal fund. Such an approach ignores, however, the whole question of deal sourcing and hence the robustness of a GP's business model. For example, is one firm paying systemically higher multiples for its companies than its competitors, which, according to Fraser-Sampson (2007, p. 186), could be an indicator of a GP that is struggling for deal flow. Similarly important, investors should try to understand the reasons where GPs were chasing particular deals but failed to manage to close. Was the price a GP offered the only or dominant factor or did other considerations play a role?

Other things being equal, higher purchase prices will lead to lower returns. However, things may not be equal, and GPs paying higher multiples in buyout transactions may try to offset the negative impact on returns by leveraging deals more aggressively than their competitors. Unfortunately, risk increases proportionally as GPs use more debt, a factor that should be paid close attention to when benchmarking individual funds.

Another important issue to be addressed in the due diligence process concerns the concentration of returns in a private equity fund. Instead of looking at the overall performance of previously raised funds, it is important to analyze the contribution that each individual deal has made to this performance to gain a better understanding of the risk profile of different partnerships. Essentially, this analysis requires disaggregating investment returns into two components—the return on each investment in a fund and the size of individual transactions. In venture capital where a significant number of deals often lead to investment losses and a (very) small number of deals turn out to be home runs, this analysis is particularly crucial. Ideally, of course, one would like to see a positive correlation between the returns of individual deals and the capital allocated to them—which can be taken as a very good indicator of home run mentality: "a firm that is identifying and killing off its losers quickly and devoting its resources to those few companies which emerge as having home run potential" (Fraser-Sampson, 2007, p. 189).

The afore-mentioned points are just illustrative of the due diligence work investors should undertake before committing to a private equity fund. There is no one-size-fits-all approach, and although standardized questionnaires (e.g., Meyer & Mathonet, 2005, pp. 202–216) are designed to help collect relevant information and facilitate the comparison of alternative investment opportunities, they can only be the basis for more in-depth specific research, including reference calls with portfolio company managers. Due diligence is a costly and time-consuming exercise, and Meyer and Mathonet reckon that less than 20 percent of the initial proposals make it to the due diligence stage. Others are eliminated through so-called "quick-kills" at an early stage, for instance, because a fund's investment style and its industry and geographical focus do not fit into the limited partner's target portfolio, or because it is sufficiently clear that the fund manager's track record and experience fall short of the investor's requirements. As Fraser-Sampson (2007, p. 186) puts it, "(D)ue diligence should only follow a decision in principle to invest, and if you are not committing to at least two-thirds of the funds on which you perform due diligence then something is wrong."

8.3.2 Due diligence in nontraditional markets and real options

Committing capital to foreign partnerships poses additional challenges in terms of the fund selection process, which will render the due diligence process an even more exhaustive (and often exhausting) exercise. This applies in particular to nontraditional markets where it is usually significantly more difficult and costly to gather relevant information. Private equity markets in emerging economies have expanded particularly rapidly in recent years, reflecting the strong rise in capital expenditure to fuel economic growth. At the same time, private equity investors have been willing to provide substantially larger amounts of capital, expecting economic growth in these countries to bring about attractive investment returns.

Although the substantially larger capital flows to emerging markets suggest that many investors anticipate the tide to lift all boats, there is no guarantee that rapid economic growth will actually translate into superior investment performance. Perhaps the most critical variable in the equation is the quality of financial intermediation—do fund managers have the skills and the experience to identify attractive investments and generate returns for their investors through the right mix of operational, financial, and governance engineering? In identifying the best managers in nontraditional markets, investors usually follow the same due diligence principles as in the more mature markets. However, in conducting their due diligence on individual funds, investors face far greater challenges. These challenges arise to a large extent from the almost tautological fact that there is much less historical information about investment returns and their dispersion in these markets.

In general, limited partners know much less about nontraditional markets, for instance, with regard to the ownership structure of companies, the regulatory framework of private equity, the industry structure of private equity firms, the countries' private equity ecosystems, and the performance and return drivers of individual private equity funds. In this environment, an important amount of effort and time in the due diligence work will, therefore, need to be dedicated to the analysis of macro and industry factors and the selection of a benchmark. In the absence of quantitative information, limited partners have to rely to a much larger extent on qualitative factors. Some LPs have decided to open offices in key emerging economies to be closer to their target markets and better understand their structures and dynamics. While there already exist some highly respected private equity firms in these markets, which have been able to raise multibillion dollar funds, their success has encouraged an almost uncountable number of new fund managers to follow their path. Individual managers may have gained relevant investment experience in already more established domestic firms or subsidiaries of foreign financial institutions, but to what extent have they been able to assemble a team where their experience has reasonably good prospects to lead to attractive returns for the fund's limited partners?

In the mature private equity markets in the United States and in Western Europe, there is usually not much point in verifying stated IRRs by recalculating historic cash flows. Fund returns are audited by trustworthy accounting firms, and to the extent that the auditors fail to detect fraud, such as in the gigantic Ponzi scheme set up by hedge fund manager Bernhard Madoff,[7] it is difficult to see how a limited partner is able to find out that a fund's returns are largely or wholly fabricated. Although fraud is a serious risk that investors have to reckon with anywhere, that risk is usually perceived to be higher in countries whose legal and regulatory institutions are still emerging. In nontraditional markets, limited partners, therefore, often prefer to double-check what they take for granted elsewhere. Financial due diligence, thus, becomes an integral part of the overall due diligence process, trying to find answers to questions like these: To what extent have GPs followed generally accepted industry standards, such as the International Private Equity and Venture Capital Valuation Guidelines or the EVCA's Reporting Guidelines? To what extent may returns be overstated due to less stringent accounting rules and audits? And to what extent are performance differences across fund managers explained by accounting gimmicks? One of the biggest nightmares fund managers have in some countries is that the portfolio company they acquire turns out to be a Potemkin village (see the strategic conversion with Max Burger-Calderon, former Asia chairman of Apax Partners, in Chapter 12);[8] similarly, it is one of the biggest nightmares for limited partners that they might invest in a fund whose stated returns are more or less fantasy.

For investors in funds raised in emerging markets, especially frontier markets, it is, therefore, not uncommon to undertake thorough background checks of fund managers through specialized intelligence firms. Hiring intelligence advisors increases due diligence costs even further, however, and especially smaller LPs may decide to piggyback on commitments to partnerships made by national, regional, or international organizations, such as Britain's CDC, America's OPIC, Germany's DEG, the EBRD, the EIF, or the IFC. As we discussed in Chapter 6, these institutions have been instrumental in getting private equity markets off the ground in several countries, and

---

[7]In March 2009, Bernhard Madoff pleaded guilty to 11 federal crimes, admitting that he had turned his wealth management firm into a massive Ponzi scheme, under which returns to separate investors were paid from their own money or money paid by subsequent investors, rather than from any actual profit earned. The court-appointed trustee estimated actual losses to investors at US$ 18 billion. Having found guilty of having fabricated investment gains for at least 20 years, in June 2009 Madoff was sentenced to 150 years in prison.

[8]Legend has it that Russian minister Grigory Potyomkin, who had led the Crimean military campaign, instructed the erection of fake settlements along the banks of the Dnieper River to impress Catherine II with the value of her new conquests during her visit to Crimea in 1787.

private investors often take their commitments to a fund as a stamp of approval. Even in markets where a certain level of maturity has already been reached, such as the European venture capital market, do newer partnerships often still find it difficult to raise capital unless the EIF has decided to invest.

Other investors decide to shun local fund managers altogether. Instead, they invest in nontraditional markets only through international private equity firms they know well (which themselves routinely hire firms to conduct background checks on prospective portfolio company managers) or through a fund of funds. Although these investment strategies aim to mitigate the risk of fraud, they raise their own set of important issues.

Internationally operating private equity firms usually have extensive experience in private equity investments. However, this experience has typically been gained in fundamentally different business environments. That earlier attempts in the 1990s to develop a private equity market in Asia and elsewhere were not particularly successful is usually attributed to the failure of adapting investment strategies and business models to local circumstances (Leeds & Sunderland, 2003). Have international GPs learned from these lessons and developed more appropriate approaches in profiting from the dynamic economic environment while managing investment risks more effectively?

Investors who commit capital to a fund-of-funds to get exposed to nontraditional markets essentially outsource due diligence of local funds. This may make sense especially for limited partners with relatively small private equity teams. However, selecting the right fund-of-funds requires intensive due diligence to ensure that the manager has relevant investment experience and a deep understanding of the private equity landscape in nontraditional markets.

As we have seen in the previous chapter, international private equity firms follow different operating models in their global expansion strategies. Some firms have acquired or formed joint ventures with local investment companies, whereas others have decided to build their own presence in the nontraditional markets, sometimes led by experienced partners from their own organizations, sometimes by hiring local senior investment professionals. The jury is still out as to which model is superior in generating deal flow, managing an investment and finding an attractive exit. In the absence of more structural empirical evidence, limited partners will, therefore, need to rely to a larger extent on individual transactions in developing a view on committing to a particular fund.

Sourcing deals is a particularly critical issue in emerging markets that are often opaque and subject to government influence. Although auctions are becoming more common, smaller and middle-market transactions are still frequently proprietary. Local knowledge is, therefore, critical, especially where international GPs compete with a rapidly growing indigenous private equity industry, which may have a competitive advantage in this respect. A related issue concerns risk management. In leveraged buyouts, the traditional private equity model has been predicated on the acquisition of a controlling stake in a company. In emerging economies, however, where companies are predominantly seeking growth capital, incumbent owners—often families—are usually unwilling to give up control. In many deals, therefore, the traditional private equity model does not apply, and an important differentiating factor lies in the GP's ability to deal with corporate governance risk that minority positions inevitably entail. How does a fund manager ensure that the majority owner's interests are to a maximum degree aligned with the fund's interests and what are the mechanisms to resolve potential disputes once an investment is made? The recent experience suggests that such disputes are especially common with regard to exits, which, as a result, are sometimes considerably delayed.

These considerations suggest that limited partners face a trade-off in their investment decisions. While investment experience and skills favor internationally operating private equity firms, domestic firms may have a competitive advantage in terms of their local knowledge and their access to proprietary deals—a factor the former try to minimize by hiring domestic investment managers, forming joint ventures with local firms or forging partnerships in coinvestment transactions. Despite this trade-off, however, it is important to note that investments in partnerships managed by global and local firms are not necessarily substitutes. Recently raised mega funds by US and European GPs, such as KKR's, TPG's, or CVC's Asian partnerships (US$ 4 billion or more, see Table 7.2), typically target relatively large deals whose sheer size restrict competition from local players. Conversely, many small but potentially attractive transactions fall below the radar screen of global operators. Thus, getting exposure to such deals usually requires committing to local private equity firms.

There is another reason why limited partners may not want to rely entirely on funds raised by international private equity firms to achieve their desired exposure to particular regions. Although some large GPs raise regionally specific funds (such as those mentioned earlier), others do not. Instead, they chase deals across a variety of geographies—sometimes as heterogeneous as the entire universe of emerging markets. However, even within regions there can be a significant degree of heterogeneity. For example, limited partners committing to a Pan-Asian fund may end up with a portfolio encompassing deals in countries as diverse as Australia, Japan, and Vietnam. This may or may not be in the interest of a limited partner who will typically find it easier to control the geographical composition of his portfolio by committing to local funds investing in individual countries or strictly defined subregions.

In practice, most investors seeking exposure to nontraditional private equity markets will, thus, follow a combined approach of investing in international as well as domestic funds, despite the lack of a track record, which severely restricts a limited partner in his due diligence. This situation is not much different from early investments in US or European funds in the 1970s and 1980s, which had also lacked a track record at that time - with the important difference, of course, that in these markets investors could to a much greater extent rely on predictable institutions. As it has turned out, some of these funds have made spectacular returns for their investors, notably a small number of US venture capital funds. Today, these funds are heavily oversubscribed, and limited partners who had been investors at an early stage enjoy today superior access to GPs who severely restrict access to their funds for other investors.

In this sense, commitments to funds can be perceived as real options (Meyer & Mathonet, 2005, pp. 319–325). The real options approach has its roots in the financial option pricing models developed by Black and Scholes (1973) and by Merton (1973) in the early 1970s. Essentially, the real options approach represents an extension of such models to the valuation on real assets, helping managers formulate the future opportunities that are created by today's investments. Real options are typically used in areas where investment decisions are subject to a particularly high degree of uncertainty. In such situations, standard valuation methods, such as DCF, are often inappropriate to estimate the NPV of alternative investment projects as they introduce a significant rejection bias. Where uncertainty about future cash flows is high, DCF analysis requires them to be discounted at a high rate. Thus, the valuation of an investment captures the possibility that actual cash flows may be lower than forecast. By contrast, the possibility that cash flows may be higher than projected is not captured in the valuation, potentially leading managers to reject promising, if uncertain projects. As van Putten and McMillan (2004) show, this is where real options come in: They provide a method to recapture some of the value lost through the conservative DCF valuation while still protecting against the risk of pursuing highly uncertain projects.

Although developed for investment decisions under uncertainty in real, that is, nonfinancial assets, such as in oil and gas exploration (Cornelius, Van de Putte, & Romani, 2005), the broader idea behind the real options approach is applicable to limited partners contemplating investments in private equity funds raised by GPs with a limited or no track record. As Lerner, Schoar, and Wongsunwai (2007, p. 734) point out, "(o)nce an LP has invested in a fund, it generally has access to the subsequent funds raised by the GP." Thus, while a fund commitment can be considered as a real option, the decision not to invest in a fund implies exercising the option (assuming that the fund is successful and access to subsequent funds is restricted to LPs in the first fund). The real options approach provides a particularly appropriate mental framework for endowments, which enjoy greater flexibility to evaluate nonstandard investment opportunities. As Swensen (2009) argues, investors increase the likelihood of discovering the next big winner well before it becomes the next big bust by considering alternatives outside the mainstream. By evaluating managers without the requisite institutional characteristics, investors might uncover a highly motivated, attractive group of partners. Operating on the periphery of standard institutional norms thus increases opportunity for success.

8.4   The allocation matrix

In the preceding analysis, we have examined the extent to which private equity markets are globally integrated, both in terms of cross-border acquisitions by private equity funds and the geographic origins of the capital they raise. Our macro-observations reflect the sum of individual, or micro, investment decisions. At the same time, aggregate market data on capital flows provide useful information for individual investors constructing an internationally diversified private equity portfolio.

In principle, there are two approaches to build a robust private equity portfolio (see Chapter 5). Let us look first at the top-down approach, which starts with

Table 8.7 Asset allocation matrix

	Globally operating private equity firms specialized in large transactions (%)		Private equity firms targeting mid-sized and smaller transactions (%)			Venture capital and clean-tech firms (%)			Distressed fund managers (%)			Mezzanine fund managers (%)		Total (%)
	US GPs	European GPs	US GPs	European GPs	NTM GPs	US GPs	European GPs	NTM GPs	US GPs	European GPs	NTM GPs	US GPs	European GPs	
Large transactions in														**30.0**
US	10.5	2.5												13.0
Europe	4.0	8.0												12.0
NTM	3.5	1.5												5.0
Mid-sized transactions in														**37.5**
US	2.0		13.0											15.0
Europe	2.0	2.0		10.0										15.0
NTM	1.5	1.0			5.0									7.5
Seed/early stage/CT investments in														**17.5**
US						10.0								10.0
Europe						1.0	3.0							4.0
NTM						2.0		1.5						3.5
Investments in distressed assets in														**10.0**
US									5.0					5.0
Europe									2.0	1.0				3.0
NTM									1.0		1.0			2.0
Mezzanine investments in														**5.0**
US												2.5		2.5
Europe												1.0	1.5	2.5

a general analysis of macroeconomic and industry trends, the assessment of equity and debt capital markets, and the examination of regulatory and country risk factors. Suppose this analysis produces risk-adjusted return expectations for individual market segments consistent with the weights shown in the last column in Table 8.7. For example, let us assume that our investor expects smaller and mid-sized companies to outperform over the relevant investment horizon and allocates 37.5 percent of his capital to this market segment, with regional allocations to the US, European, and nontraditional markets amounting to 15 percent, 15 percent, and 7.5 percent, respectively. The question that immediately arises, however, is this: How does the investor achieve his target exposure to this asset class and the regional segments, given that his capital allocations are intermediated by private equity funds?

Until not so long ago, the answer would have been straightforward: commit capital to the respective buyout funds targeting these assets and select the best-in-class fund managers on the basis of a bottom-up analysis. Today, things are more complex, as we have learned in the previous chapters. For instance, small and mid-caps in Europe are not only targeted by specialized middle-market European funds, but they also face meaningful competition from US GPs and European managers who generally focus on large-cap transactions. Although LPAs define the general investment focus of a fund, they provide considerable flexibility for the GP to chase attractive deals. In the large cap market, this flexibility tends to be particularly significant, and unless LPs take into account that GPs pursue transactions across borders and across market segments, they will find it difficult to meet their allocation targets.

In the example given in Table 8.7 where we make assumptions about cross-border and cross-sectoral investment flows in accordance with our preceding market analysis, the LP would allocate 45.5 percent of his capital to the US market, 36.5 percent to the European market and 18 percent to nontraditional markets. The example is chosen in a way that it does not deviate too much from the actual relative size of the private equity markets in the three regions, but, of course, the investor's top-down analysis could lead him to deviate more substantially from a market-neutral allocation. In terms of the location of fund managers, the LP would allocate 62 percent to US-based GPs, 30.5 percent to European-based GPs, and 7.5 percent to GPs domiciled in nontraditional markets, a distribution, which again is broadly in line with the global fund-raising market.

Alternatively, the LP could allocate his capital from the vantage point of a bottom-up analysis of fund managers. In this case, his exposure to individual market segments (start-ups, small and mid-caps, large caps, distressed assets) and geographies would not be the objective but rather the unplanned outcome of this process. Suppose, for example, that the LP decided to allocate equal amounts to US and European GPs in both the large cap and mid-cap buyout markets (15.5 percent in each segment). Other things being equal (i.e., cross-border and cross-sectional investment flows are adjusted proportionally), the LP's exposure to small and mid-caps would rise by 5 percentage points at the expense of large caps. At the same time, his exposure to the European market would increase by 4 percentage points at the expense of both the US and nontraditional markets.

In practice, as we have argued earlier, portfolio construction is usually an iterative process. Starting with a top-down allocation that takes into account cross-border and cross-sectional capital flows, LPs will then see whether they can identify, and have access to, a sufficient number of fund managers who meet their return expectations in each segment. If not, they will need to revise their top-down allocations accordingly. Conversely, if an LP's bottom-up analysis results in a concentration of assets in individual market segments or geographies he is not comfortable with, he will need to reconsider his planned commitments to GPs operating in different market segments.

8.5 Summary and conclusions

This chapter has focused on the global integration of the fund-raising market. Examining the investor base of GPs in different regions, we have found that especially buyout firms specialized in large transactions raise funds from a geographically diversified class of investors. As far as large US private equity firms are concerned, we have found that 43 percent of their funds capital has been committed by non-US limited partners. In Europe, almost 60 percent of the fund commitments have come from investors outside the region. In fact, US limited partners have a larger share in the investor base of large European buyout funds than limited partners from the region. In the venture capital market, the investor base tends to be comparatively less international but still very significant.

Looking forward, institutional investors from emerging markets are likely to play an increasingly important role as global suppliers of private equity capital. Although private equity investments in emerging markets are generally expected to continue to rise, both in absolute terms and as a percentage of GDP, their economies will remain large net exporters of capital, mirroring their persistent current account surpluses. This applies especially to Asia and the Middle East, where SWFs play an important role in recycling these surpluses. Some SWFs already have a sizeable allocation to alternative asset classes, and as their AUM continue to grow, their role as LPs in private equity funds around the world look set to further gain in importance.

Individual investment decisions in private equity funds are usually based on thorough due diligence, which follows some general principles. The principles take into account that private equity returns tend to be persistent, suggesting that a GP's past performance has potential predictive power. While experience and access to deal flow matter, academic research finds diseconomies of scale in the sense that the expected performance of a newly raised fund tends to be inversely related to the increase in fund size between the prior and the focal fund. These general observations provide a good starting point for the detailed due diligence on individual funds, which may or may not entail a cross-border transaction.

While due diligence is generally a very exhaustive and exhausting exercise, this is even more the case in nontraditional markets. Given that these markets, as the name suggests, are relatively new, domestic fund managers typically lack the kind of track record, which would provide guidance to investors in the more mature markets.

Alternatively, limited partners may decide to invest in funds raised by globally operating GPs or in funds of funds to get exposure to nontraditional markets. However, as we have discussed, this approach raises its own set of issues. Although international GPs may have gained superior investment skills through their experience in their home markets, there is a question as to whether their standard business models can be easily transplanted to significantly different investment environments.

Furthermore, domestic and foreign GPs in nontraditional markets may not necessarily chase the same type of deals, for example, in terms of industry and size. Therefore, LPs may choose to commit to both groups of GPs rather than relying on just one type. Selecting funds in such an environment is obviously subject to a high degree of uncertainty, which favors a real options approach. This approach takes into account that an investment in a fund usually ensures that the investor is able to commit to the next fund whose performance is expected to improve as the GP gains in experience. Conversely, the decision not to invest may kill the option of investing in future funds with potentially attractive returns.

In the final part of the chapter, we have presented an asset allocation matrix as a simple tool to construct a robust private equity portfolio. Taking into account capital flows both across borders and sectors, the allocation matrix shows the investor's exposure to different asset classes as a result of their fund selection. This tool is of particular interest to those limited partners whose fund selection is driven by a top-down portfolio construction.

9 Regional integration: the case of Europe

In the two preceding chapters, we have discussed *interregional* fund-raising and investment flows to understand the emergence of new investment opportunities in increasingly integrated private equity markets. National markets may also integrate with the region where they are located. In this chapter, we focus on *intraregional* flows and the degree of regional market integration. For GPs, the integration of regional markets is of critical importance as it broadens their access to capital and the scope for investment opportunities. GPs who have built a successful track record in their home markets often grow beyond their national borders by raising larger regional funds. As these funds often target larger deal sizes than national funds but do not necessarily compete with the global powerhouses, they offer different risk/return characteristics to investors.

Much of the following debate focuses on the European private equity market, which provides a particularly interesting example. To begin with, Europe is the world's second oldest and largest market. Second, substantial progress has been made in establishing a single market in Europe since the 1985 Internal Market White Paper. A key factor in the process has been financial market integration, which has gathered substantial momentum thanks to the introduction of the euro. Within the Single European Market, cross-border mergers and acquisitions have risen markedly. Third, despite the overall progress with financial integration, the process has remained uneven, and although some market segments are now virtually fully integrated, others remain more fragmented. Private equity falls into the latter category, which can be attributed to a number of important impediments. Finally, several transition economies in central and eastern Europe (CEE) have joined the European Union (EU), with their product, labor, and capital markets becoming increasingly integrated. Overall, Europe's experience has important lessons not only for other regions, especially for Asia-Pacific where private equity

International Investments in Private Equity. DOI: 10.1016/B978-0-12-375082-2.10009-6

has gathered substantial momentum in recent years, but also for Latin America, Africa, and the Middle East.

We begin by briefly discussing the state of financial market integration in Europe, specifically within the European Monetary Union (EMU). Next, we review the empirical evidence of cross-border intraregional fund-raising and investment flows and identify impediments to market integration. Furthermore, we assess the progress that CEE countries have made in attracting private equity capital from the rest of Europe. Then, we discuss the factors that are responsible for the limited progress in establishing a single European private equity market and draw lessons from the European experience for other regions. Finally, we discuss investment implications from an LP perspective.

9.1   European financial integration

Financial and monetary integration has been a key pillar of Europe's single market project, which was launched in 1985. In its Internal Market White Paper, the European Commission set as a goal to establish a fully unified internal market by 1992 by abolishing barriers of all kinds, harmonizing rules and approximating legislation and tax structures, and strengthening monetary cooperation. The framework for the latter was provided by the European Monetary System (EMS), which came into effect in 1979. Under the Exchange Rate Mechanism of the EMS, participating countries agreed to maintain a system of fixed, though adjustable, exchange rates. Twenty years later, in 1999, 11 European countries (Austria, Belgium Finland, France, Germany, Ireland, Italy, Luxembourg, Netherlands, Portugal, and Spain) decided to introduce a single currency, the euro, delegating monetary policy to the newly established European Central Bank (ECB).[1]

According to the ECB (2008), "... the market for a given set of financial instruments or services (is) fully integrated, when all potential participants in such a market (i) are subject to a single set of rules when deciding to buy or sell those financial instruments or services; (ii) have equal access to this set of financial instruments or services, and (iii) are treated equally when they operate in the market." In monitoring the process of financial and monetary integration, the ECB has developed a set of price-based, news-based, and volume-based indicators for the euro area (Baele et al., 2008). Overall, these indicators suggest that national financial markets in the euro area have become more integrated. However, two important qualifications are in order: First, it is not entirely clear to what extent the integration process can be attributed to the introduction of a single currency. As Lane (2008) points out, the past decade has also been a period in which the pace of global financial integration has accelerated, and progress in promoting financial integration has been across the European Union, not just within the euro area. As a matter of fact, the United Kingdom, a non-euro member country, has played a key role in the promotion of a single market in financial services.

---

[1]Greece joined in 2001, Slovenia in 2007, Cyprus and Malta in 2008, and Slovakia in 2009, expanding the common currency area to 16 member states.

Second, the progress in individual market segments has remained uneven. The most integrated market is found to be the euro area money market, notwithstanding the severe market dislocations in the wake of the recent global financial crisis (ECB, 2008) and the subsequent sovereign debt crisis in the common currency zone. Until recently, government bond markets in the euro area seemed to have become highly integrated, too, as evidenced by the progressive narrowing of yield spreads to just a few basis points following the introduction of a single currency. Arguably, however, the spread narrowing was not fully justified by economic fundamentals. In the fall of 2009, spreads of bonds issued by governments in periphery of the euro area widened substantially against German benchmark bonds when investors took a more nuanced view on default risk in individual member countries amid growing budget and current account deficits. In the case of Greece, yield spreads reached pre-EMU levels in the spring of 2010, and with borrowing costs becoming prohibitively high, the Greek government had to revert to emergency funding provided by the EU and the IMF. As far as the corporate bond market in the euro area is concerned, country effects are found to play an increasingly less important role in explaining the variance of total yield spreads. This is consistent with the continuing growth in cross-border holdings of long-term debt securities issued by nonfinancial corporations, suggesting that investors are increasingly diversifying their portfolios across the euro area.

Comparatively less progress has been made in establishing a more integrated market for short-term securities in the euro area. The vast majority of short-term debt securities issued by residents of a particular member country continues to be held by residents of the same country, which is attributed to differences in market standards and practices. Similarly, the considerable dispersion of interest rates on loans and deposits from banks to nonfinancial corporations and households suggests that the euro area retail banking markets are still fragmented. The share of assets held in foreign branches and subsidiaries has generally remained limited, and although cross-border mergers and acquisitions in financial services in the euro area has increased in recent years, domestic M&A transactions have grown faster.

Turning to the equity markets, euro-wide—as opposed to local—factors are found to explain a rising proportion of the total domestic equity volatility. This implies that diversification through sector-based equity investment strategies should have become more important relative to country-based ones. At the same time, euro area residents have substantially increased their holdings of equity issued in other euro area countries, whereas the share of euro area equity assets held outside the common currency area has remained considerably smaller and increased only moderately.

Greater financial integration has fostered cross-border investments, both in the form of greenfield investments and M&A activity. Overall, Petroulas (2007) estimates that the introduction of the euro increased inward foreign direct investment (FDI) flows by approximately 15 percent within the common currency area. As far as M&A activity is concerned, Coeurdacier, De Santis, and Aviat (2009) find that EMU helped the restructuring of capital within the same sector of manufacturing among euro area firms. In fact, the adoption of the single currency is found to have increased both cross-border M&A between euro area countries and M&A from non-euro area countries toward euro area countries. The impact on horizontal M&A activity is found to be particularly large. While EMU is estimated to have increased intra-euro area horizontal cross-border M&As in manufacturing by about 200 percent, the estimated effect on euro area M&As from non-euro to euro area countries amounts to about 70 percent. As far as vertical M&A activity within the euro area is concerned, the impact of EMU is not statistically significant, suggesting that cross-border M&A activity has aimed at restructuring capital within the same sector of activity, rather than boosting the formation of conglomerates between euro area sectors. In the services sector, the impact of EMU on cross-border M&A activity has remained comparatively weaker. Coeurdacier et al. (2009) attribute this observation to the higher level of protection and barriers to entry in the services sector.

Cross-border listings of companies within Europe have also increased since the mid-1980s. However, cross-listings of European companies in the United States have risen considerably faster during this period, suggesting that factors such as market liquidity, trading costs, and the potential advantages of bonding a company to higher corporate governance standards have probably played a comparatively more important role (Degeorge & Maug, 2008). Within Europe, geographical and cultural proximity matters for cross-listing decisions (Pagano, Randl, Röell, & Zechner, 2001), a finding which is consistent with evidence on intra-European cross-border equity flows (Portes, Rey, & Oh, 2001).

Overall, the empirical evidence can be summarized as suggesting that European financial markets have become considerably more integrated over time, notwithstanding important setbacks especially with regard to the EMU sovereign debt markets. In principle, more integrated financial markets should foster the integration of the European private equity market. Although the introduction of a single currency eliminates foreign exchange risk in cross-border investments, broader and deeper capital markets facilitate the financing of deals. Exits become easier thanks to a more integrated M&A market, and to the extent that financial integration fosters economic integration, private equity portfolio companies benefit from enlarged supplier and product markets and economies of scale. So what do the data tell us?

9.2   How integrated is Europe's private equity market?

In examining the degree to which the European private equity market is integrated, price-based and news-based indicators are of little use. Although valuations of portfolio companies of buyout funds are generally marked-to-market and hence mirror changes in public markets, valuation adjustments take place relatively infrequently. In venture capital, valuations are even more difficult to interpret. This is especially true for seed and start-up capital provided to portfolio companies that have yet to generate revenues. Instead, we have to rely exclusively on quantity-based measures, which track cross-border fund-raising and investment flows. More specifically, we use data collected by the European Private Equity and Venture Capital Association, which allow us to distinguish between the geographic location of the GP ("Country of Management" concept), the geographic location of the limited partner ("Country of Origin" concept), and the geographic location where funds are deployed

("Country of Destination" concept). These data allow us to track capital flows to private equity funds raised in the same country where the fund is managed, in other European countries as well as outside Europe. Similarly, the data track where European funds deploy their capital: in their domestic market, in other European economies, and in the rest of the world.

However, EVCA's data set has some important limitations: First, the data make no distinction between different investment stages, preventing us from examining the degree to which individual segments of the private equity market—notably buyouts versus venture capital—are integrated. Furthermore, as far as cross-border fund-raising within Europe is concerned, no breakdown of individual countries is given. Therefore, we are unable to say to what extent European monetary unification might have accelerated the integration process in the private equity market. Another limitation lies in the lack of a breakdown of commitments by domestic LPs to other European versus non-European funds. All we know from the EVCA database is the total amount of LPs' commitments and the share that went into domestic funds. Finally, although the EVCA data tell us the amount of capital received by domestic portfolio companies from domestic funds, there is no geographic distinction between flows received from other European versus non-European funds.

9.2.1 Fund-raising

An important indicator of market integration is the degree to which domestic private equity funds rely on commitments from domestic as opposed to foreign investors. Figure 9.1 provides an overview for the entire European fund-raising market from 1995 to 2008. During this period, GPs became significantly more outward oriented, with commitments from foreign LPs rising to 70 percent from less than 25 percent.

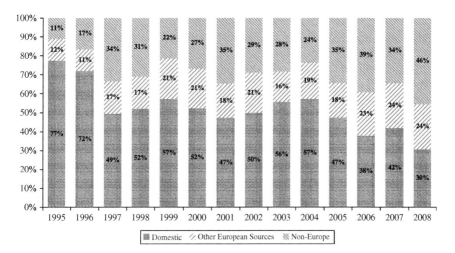

Figure 9.1 Geographic sources of European private equity funds raised.
Source: EVCA.

Importantly, the share of non-European investors—as opposed to foreign investors from other European countries—expanded particularly rapidly, becoming a major force in the recent private equity boom.

Table 9.1 provides a more granular picture by showing the funds that domestic GPs have raised in individual European countries. While the first column shows the total amount of funds managed, the next three columns provide country-specific information about the origins of these funds. However, domestic GPs compete with foreign investors for raising funds, with the total amount of funds committed by investors in the country of origin shown in the last column. The fund-raising flows are shown for three different years: 1991, 2000, and 2008.

An example may help illustrate the information in Table 9.1: In 2008, French GPs raised an amount of around € 10.8 billion, roughly twice as much as in 2000. Of this amount, almost 48 percent (close to € 5.2 billion) was raised from French investors. While another 23 percent was committed by other European investors, almost 30 percent came from foreign investors in third countries. From the perspective of the country of origin, French investors committed about € 6.3 billion in 2008. Because we know that French GPs raised nearly € 5.2 billion from domestic sources, French investors must have committed around € 1.1 billion (19 percent) to foreign funds. As explained earlier, however, we do not know how much of the € 1.1 billion went to funds in other European countries versus those outside Europe.

Overall, the EVCA reports that an amount of € 78.5 billion was raised by European private equity firms in 2008, an almost twenty-fold increase compared with 1991 and a more-than-doubling relative to 2000. This tremendous growth is all the more remarkable in light of the progressive deterioration in the fund-raising environment following the sudden market correction in 2007. Of the € 78.5 billion committed to European funds in 2008, less than one-third was raised from investors domiciled in the same country. This is significantly lower than in 2000 when almost 50 percent of the capital was still raised domestically, and it is much lower than at the beginning of the 1990s when more than three-quarters were committed by domestic LPs.

Where do the foreign funds come from? In 2008, almost 24 percent was raised from LPs domiciled in other European economies, a considerably larger share than the 18 percent in 2000 and the 13 percent in 1991. Although this increase suggests that the European fund-raising market has indeed become more integrated, we have to consider that commitments from LPs in non-European countries have actually risen considerably faster. Although inflows from third countries accounted for just 10 percent in 1991, their share rose to more than 45 percent in 2008. The United States represents the most important country of origin, with US LPs reported to have committed almost € 24 billion to European funds, or almost one-third of all funds raised by European GPs during this year.

There are considerable differences across European countries. By far the most important fund-raising market is the United Kingdom where private equity funds raised more than € 46 billion in 2008, accounting for almost 60 percent of all funds raised by private equity funds domiciled in Europe, twice the share UK funds had in the early 1990s. The United Kingdom has benefited in particular from inflows from third countries, which have become considerably larger than the combined amount of

Table 9.1 Geographic origin of capital managed by European private equity funds (€ billion)

	Country of management (funds managed by domestic firms) (1)			Funds managed by domestic firms originating from other European countries (2)			Funds managed by domestic firms originating from non-European sources (3)			Funds managed by domestic firms originating from domestic sources (4) = (1) − (2) − (3)			Country of origin (5)		
	1991	2000	2008	1991	2000	2008	1991	2000	2008	1991	2000	2008	1991	2000	2008
Austria	0	137	230	0	52	123	0	0	38	0	86	69	...	153	215
Belgium	93	651	582	2	71	3	0	0	0	91	579	579	...	714	1,025
Finland	9	407	903	2	60	259	0	0	1	7	347	643	...	418	1,458
France	1,203	5,492	10,778	171	1,008	2,464	157	810	3,160	875	3,673	5,154	...	4,197	6,330
Germany	842	3,714	2,400	197	463	436	82	190	125	563	3,061	1,839	...	4,339	3,517
Greece	9	51	20	...	12	11	...	0	9	...	39	0	...	41	189
Ireland	40	210	155	0	0	16	0	23	1	40	188	138	...	198	169
Italy	172	1,875	1,455	13	181	682	37	158	266	122	1,536	507	...	1,662	633
Netherlands	110	716	1,579	1	147	730	0	48	605	109	521	244	...	1,616	1,551
Portugal	12	117	15	1	0	15	0	0	0	11	118	0	...	133	30
Spain	145	751	2,224	74	238	979	23	20	92	48	493	1,153	...	520	1,444
Denmark	26	494	258	4	106	96	4	48	23	18	340	139	...	358	1,064
Sweden	107	1,815	6,597	32	853	3,297	0	335	2,709	75	626	591	...	740	1,371
United Kingdom	1,246	20,485	46,334	38	3,485	8,257	108	11,021	28,093	1,100	5,978	9,984	...	6,817	11,142
Norway	33	366	1,268	3	19	715	0	4	162	30	344	392	...	363	896

(continued on next page)

Table 9.1 Geographic origin of capital managed by European private equity funds (€ billion)—cont'd

	Country of management (funds managed by domestic firms) (1)			Funds managed by domestic firms originating from other European countries (2)			Funds managed by domestic firms originating from non-European sources (3)			Funds managed by domestic firms originating from domestic sources (4) = (1) − (2) − (3)			Country of origin (5)		
	1991	2000	2008	1991	2000	2008	1991	2000	2008	1991	2000	2008	1991	2000	2008
Switzerland	20	667	3,051	2	135	527	0	140	241	18	392	2,283	...	545	4,559
Czech Republic	...	24	19	...	15	17	...	6	0	...	3	2	...	3	3
Hungary	...	60	120	...	60	0	...	0	72	...	1	48	...	1	50
Poland	...	176	760	...	139	490	...	27	270	...	10	0	...	10	0
Romania	...	...	0	...	...	0	...	...	0	...	...	0	...	0	0
Unknown Europe	...	...	...	...	...	...	...	...	...	...	...	...	...	2,306	7,312
Total Europe	4,067	38,219	78,748	540	7,044	19,117	411	12,830	35,867	3,107	18,335	23,765	...	25,383	42,949
United States													...	9,594	23,777
Asia-Pacific													...	1,202	6,862
Other													...	2,040	5,160
Total		38,219	78,748										...	38,219	78,748

Note: 1991 data in millions of European currency units (ECU); 2000 and 2008 in millions of euros.
Source: EVCA, various yearbooks

funds raised from domestic and European LPs. Providing an environment that is particularly conducive to developing a private equity industry from the standpoint of taxation and fund structuring, the recorded capital flows underline London's dominant role as a Pan-European and global financial hub. However, the picture does not materially change if we exclude the United Kingdom from our analysis. Inflows of capital to non-UK private equity funds from LPs situated outside Europe still increased significantly faster than cross-border fund-raising flows within non-UK Europe. Thus, although European GPs rely to a decreasing extent on domestic investors in their home country, it seems that the European fund-raising market is becoming more rapidly integrated with the rest of the world than within the region itself.

Importantly, this observation is also true for the member states of the euro zone. Notwithstanding considerable progress in financial integration, cross-border fund-raising flows within the euro zone have increased less than inflows from the rest of the world since the introduction of a single currency. Although intra-EMU commitments in 2008 were still larger than inflows from LPs based in non-European economies, the gap is closing progressively.

Although we do not know how much capital European LPs have committed to non-European private equity funds, it seems that investors' allocations have shifted significantly from domestic toward Pan-European strategies. Of the capital that European LPs committed in 2000 to European funds, about 72 percent was allocated to funds domiciled in the same European country. By 2008, this percentage shrank to just 55 percent. The main beneficiaries were funds managed by GPs domiciled in the United Kingdom. That the United Kingdom decided not to adopt the euro seems to have had little, if any, impact. As funds have largely been raised in euros, there is no currency risk for euro area-based investors.

9.2.2 Investing

Unlike in fund-raising, domestic GPs in Europe have remained considerably more inward oriented in terms of their investment decisions (Fig. 9.2). Although the share of capital invested domestically fell significantly between the mid-1990s and the second half of the first decade of this century, it is still in the range of two-thirds. The mirror image of the gradual decline in the share of domestic investing is a gradual increase in cross-border investing in Europe. By contrast, investing capital outside Europe has remained very limited relative to the overall amount of capital European private equity funds have deployed in recent years.

Table 9.2 allows us to take a detailed view on the geographic investment pattern of European private equity funds.[2] Initially, there was very little variation in the home bias of private equity investments across individual countries, with GPs typically investing around 90 percent of their capital in their home markets. Although in most countries the home bias has fallen gradually over time, it seems that much of this greater outward orientation has already occurred in the 1990s. Since then, the European private equity firms' home bias has more or less stagnated at that level.

---

[2]This section follows Cornelius, Juttmann & Langelaar (2009).

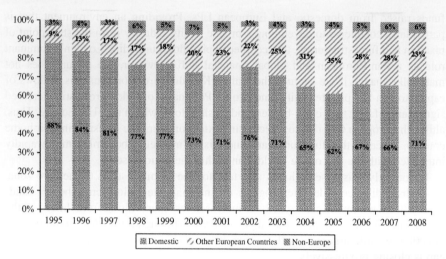

Figure 9.2 Geographic distribution of investments by European private equity funds.
Source: EVCA.

As far as individual countries are concerned, private equity funds domiciled in large economies tend to be particularly home biased in their investment decisions. Although their home bias varies in individual years, French, German, and Italian private equity funds generally invest 90 percent or more of their capital in their domestic markets. As a result, their investments account for the bulk of capital portfolio companies in their home markets have received. Apart from the United Kingdom, France, Germany, and Italy are Europe's largest individual private equity markets, with their companies having absorbed 18.5 percent, 14 percent, and 9 percent, respectively, of all investments made in Europe between 2000 and 2008.

By contrast, funds domiciled in the United Kingdom are particularly international, confirming our preceding observations. Individual funds tend to be considerably larger than the European average, and of the € 22.5 billion deployed by UK-based funds in 2008, more than 45 percent was invested abroad, with companies in other European countries having accounted for the bulk of foreign investments. In identifying investment opportunities abroad, several GPs have built an extensive network of offices in individual countries. CVC Europe, for example, has offices in no fewer than 12 different European economies. These offices represent spokes to source and manage deals, with the head office in London serving as the hub. London's role has been further strengthened by the arrival of US private equity firms, some of which have begun to create their own European hub-and-spoke systems. For instance, The Carlyle Group has already established eight European offices in six different countries, apart from their regional headquarters in London.

To the extent that non-UK European private equity funds have become more international in their investment decisions, they have focused on other European markets as well. However, to a large extent this integration process already occurred in the 1990s when the aggregate share of investments in other European countries

Table 9.2 Geographic destination of capital managed by European private equity funds (€billion, unless specified otherwise)

	Country of management investments managed by domestic funds (1)			Investments managed by domestic funds going to other European companies (2)			Investments managed by domestic funds going to non-European companies (3)			Investments managed by domestic companies (4) = (1) − (2) − (3)			Aggregate home bias (4)/(1) (%)		
	1991	2000	2008	1991	2000	2008	1991	2000	2008	1991	2000	2008	1991	2000	2008
Austria	3	163	231	0	19	107	0	0	0	3	144	124	100	88.3	53.7
Belgium	106	565	668	11	84	277	8	167	1	87	480	390	82.1	85.0	58.4
Denmark	22	274	482	0	63	54	0	22	47	22	164	381	100	59.9	79.0
Finland	19	384	480	1	97	45	2	18	16	16	271	419	84.2	70.6	87.3
France	1,003	7,841	8,772	55	1,632	466	10	1,532	55	938	5,794	8,251	93.5	77.4	94.1
Germany	593	4,767	7,082	29	442	367	10	428	171	554	4,154	6,544	93.4	87.1	92.4
Greece	1	195	344	0	125	115	0	11	0	1	70	229	100	35.9	65.1
Ireland	36	223	80	5	50	27	0	6	6	31	167	47	86.1	74.9	58.7
Italy	490	2,969	3,071	24	390	150	0	301	8	466	2,571	2,913	95.1	86.6	94.9
Netherlands	297	1,916	1,788	12	708	461	3	228	18	282	1,190	1,309	94.9	62.1	73.2
Portugal	43	183	396	0	13	39	0	0	5	43	165	352	100	90.2	88.9
Spain	153	1,127	1,842	1	24	118	1	11	11	151	1,092	1,713	98.7	96.9	93.0
Sweden	47	2,098	3,404	18	846	520	0	4	914	29	338	1,970	61.7	16.1	57.9
United Kingdom	1,635	12,918	22,525	123	3,032	8,536	80	1,013	1,744	1,432	8,142	12,245	87.6	63.0	54.4
Norway	47	299	756	0	23	83	5	16	26	42	250	647	89.4	83.6	85.6
Switzerland	34	646	1,307	17	446	815	8	39	123	9	77	369	26.5	11.9	28.2
Czech Republic	...	127	48	...	61	17	...	0	0	...	66	31	...	52.0	64.6
Hungary	...	52	34	...	0	4	...	0	0	...	52	30	...	100	88.2
Poland	...	220	719	...	98	213	...	0	6	...	116	500	...	52.7	69.5
Romania	...	15	100	...	0	0	...	0	1	...	15	99	...	100	99.0
Europe	4,529	36,622	54,129	296	8,153	12,415	127	3,790	3,151	4,106	25,318	38,563	90.7	69.1	71.2

Note: 1991 data in millions of European Currency Units (ECU); 2000 and 2008 in millions of euros.
Source: EVCA, various yearbooks

more than tripled. Since 2000, this progress seems to have slowed substantially, with intra-European investment flows in 2008 still accounting for less than 25 percent of total investments made by European private equity funds. This may seem surprising, given the introduction of the euro in 1999, which, as we have seen earlier, has fostered the integration of Europe's financial markets.

In general, there is a close geographical proximity of the fund management company to the investee companies. On the basis of information from AlpInvest's database, for example, Swedish funds have made most of their foreign investments in neighboring countries Denmark, Finland, and Norway (Table 9.3). As far as foreign investments by French buyout funds are concerned, they have deployed their capital in five other European economies, especially in Germany. Similarly, Swiss buyout funds have focused in particular on Austria and Germany.

How does the picture look like from the viewpoint of European portfolio companies? Companies in the United Kingdom received the largest share of private equity capital in Europe in 2008, totaling about € 13.5 billion. The bulk of the financing (€ 12.5 billion) was provided by UK-based funds. Similarly high ratios are found in other large European markets, such as France and Sweden. Italy represents an outlier, with nearly 50 percent of the capital of acquired companies provided by foreign funds. To the extent that domestic portfolio companies received capital from foreign funds, those were mainly located in other European countries. In some cases, however, a considerable share came from non-European funds. For example, of the € 1 billion of capital received by UK portfolio companies from foreign funds in 2008, € 725 million were invested by funds located outside Europe. This high share of private equity investments by non-European countries funds mirrors the high degree of network intensity of the UK private equity market, an observation that is found to hold more generally in global investing in private equity (Tykvová & Schertler, 2006).

9.2.3 Integrating central and eastern Europe

Over the past decade, several countries in CEE have joined the EU (Czech Republic, Estonia, Hungary, Latvia, Lithuania, Poland, Slovakia, and Slovenia in 2004 and Bulgaria and Romania in 2007) and two of them have already adopted the euro (Slovenia in 2007 and Slovakia in 2009). At the time of writing, Croatia, Macedonia, and Turkey were EU candidate countries. Those countries that have already joined the EU had a combined GDP of € 955 billion in 2008, contributing around 7.5 percent to the EU's total output. GDP in other CEE countries, including Turkey and the Commonwealth of Independent States,[3] totaled € 2.1 trillion. Thus, the combined size of the CEE economy is roughly equivalent to the three southern European economies of Italy, Spain, and Portugal.

In Tables 9.1 and 9.2, we reported fund-raising and investment flows for four CEE countries (Czech Republic, Hungary, Poland, and Romania) where private equity has

---

[3] Armenia, Azerbaijan, Belarus, Georgia, Kazakhstan, Kyrgyz Republic, Moldova, Russia, Tajikistan, Turkmenistan, Ukraine, and Uzbekistan.

Table 9.3 Geographic exposure of European buyout funds

Market	Fund located in								
	Denmark (%)	France (%)	Germany (%)	Italy (%)	Poland (%)	Spain (%)	Sweden (%)	Switzerland (%)	United Kingdom (%)
Austria	0.0	0.0	10.0	0.0	0.0	0.0	0.0	29.9	0.9
Belgium	0.0	2.7	5.9	0.0	0.0	0.0	0.0	0.0	1.1
Bulgaria	0.0	0.0	0.0	0.0	1.9	0.0	0.0	0.0	0.0
Czech Republic	0.0	0.0	0.0	0.0	0.0	0.0	0.0	0.0	0.1
Denmark	63.1	0.0	0.0	0.0	0.0	0.0	19.6	0.0	2.2
Estonia	0.0	0.0	0.0	0.0	0.0	0.0	0.0	0.0	0.1
Finland	24.7	0.0	0.0	0.0	0.0	0.0	8.7	0.0	1.7
France	0.0	52.2	0.6	0.0	0.0	0.0	0.0	0.0	7.2
Germany	0.0	44.1	66.2	0.0	0.0	2.0	0.0	13.1	10.7
Ireland	0.0	0.0	0.0	0.0	0.0	0.0	0.0	0.0	1.7
Italy	0.0	0.6	1.4	88.0	0.0	0.0	0.0	0.0	3.1
Luxembourg	0.0	0.0	0.0	12.0	0.0	0.0	0.0	0.0	2.3
Netherlands	0.0	0.1	7.0	0.0	0.0	0.0	5.1	0.0	8.8
Norway	0.0	0.0	0.0	0.0	0.0	0.0	16.0	0.0	0.6
Poland	0.0	0.0	0.0	0.0	63.2	0.0	0.0	0.0	0.0
Romania	0.0	0.0	0.0	0.0	17.3	0.0	0.0	0.0	0.0
Slovakia	0.0	0.0	0.0	0.0	7.7	0.0	0.0	0.0	0.0
Slovenia	0.0	0.0	0.0	0.0	0.0	0.0	0.0	0.0	0.1
Spain	0.0	0.0	0.0	0.0	0.0	98.0	0.0	0.0	4.3
Sweden	12.2	0.0	0.0	0.0	0.0	0.0	49.3	0.0	4.6
Switzerland	0.0	0.0	9.1	0.0	0.0	0.0	1.3	57.0	1.6
United Kingdom	0.0	0.2	0.0	0.0	0.0	0.0	0.0	0.0	42.9
Non-Europe	0.0	0.0	0.0	0.0	9.9	0.0	0.0	0.0	6.0
Grand total	**100.0**	**100.0**	**100.0**	**100.0**	**100.0**	**100.0**	**100.0**	**100.0**	**100.0**

Source: AlpInvest Research; author's calculations

already become more active in financial intermediation. By far the most important market is Poland, both in terms of fund-raising and investing. In 2008, private equity firms based in Poland raised € 760 million, considerably more than in a number of smaller more advanced economies in Europe. Importantly, none of this capital was raised domestically. While around two-thirds of the funds raised by private equity firms in Poland were committed by LPs situated in other European countries, non-European LPs accounted for the remainder. On the investment side, Polish funds are significantly more inward oriented. In 2008, their domestic acquisitions totaled € 500 million, or 70 percent of the total investments Polish funds made during this year. Thus, Polish funds accounted for nearly 80 percent of the total amount of € 628 billion private equity funds invested in 2008. Deal sizes have remained small, averaging just € 10 million. This reflects the dominance of venture capital deals (especially late stage), although buyout activity has also picked up appreciably.

The reliance of Polish companies on funds raised by domestic firms is fundamentally different from the financing patterns in Hungary, the Czech Republic, and Romania, whose corporate sector received € 476 million, € 441 million, and € 273 million, respectively, in private equity capital in 2008. Together with Poland, these markets accounted for almost three-quarters of the CEE region in terms of the investment volume (€ 2.5 billion) and two-thirds in terms of the number of deals (196) (EVCA, 2009). Unlike in Poland, however, domestic funds in Romania contributed only one-third of private equity investments, and in Hungary and the Czech Republic the respective shares were only 6 percent and 7 percent. This implies that private equity transactions in these countries are financed to a much larger degree by funds raised abroad, especially in the more mature markets in Western Europe.

Whether the Czech Republic, Hungary, Romania, and other CEE countries will eventually follow the Polish example is an open question. Much will depend on whether an indigenous private equity industry will emerge in these economies. Given the significantly smaller size of their economies—Poland's GDP in 2008 was almost as large as the GDP of the Czech Republic, Hungary, and Romania combined—it would seem more plausible to expect cross-border transactions to continue to play a comparatively larger role. In this scenario, Poland could increasingly assume the role of a regional hub, with funds raised from a geographically wide range of LPs, investing across the entire region.

9.3 Why has Europe's private equity market not become more integrated?

Complete integration is unlikely to be achieved as long as key investment parameters vary widely across individual economies in Europe. Several factors are structural and, therefore, tend to be persistent—such as the restrictiveness of labor laws, corporate governance regimes, and corporate and personal income taxation. These factors are important determinants of the attractiveness of national private equity markets (Apax Partners, 2007; Groh & Liechtenstein, 2009), which is mirrored in their respective

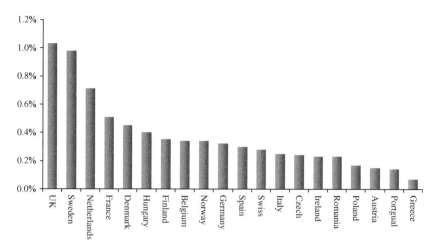

Figure 9.3 Private equity investments in Europe (in percent of GDP, 2004–2008). *Source:* EVCA.

degrees of private equity penetration. In fact, the degree to which national markets in Europe are penetrated varies almost as widely as the variation of penetration on a global scale. While private equity investments in the United Kingdom averaged about 1 percent of GDP in 2004–2008, Greece attracted only 0.1 percent of GDP during the same period. The Netherlands enjoyed a penetration rate more than twice as high as Germany's (Fig. 9.3).[4]

Cross-country differences in the economic structures of individual economies present important impediments to deeper integration in virtually all asset classes. However, there are also private equity-specific barriers that have prevented the European private equity market from becoming more deeply integrated. As a recent report of the Alternative Investment Expert Group (2006) points out, there is no specific EU level regime governing the regulatory approach to the private equity industry. Instead, the legal, tax, and operating environment of private equity is still largely determined at the national level, with little, if any, alignment across countries. The two areas that are found to be particularly important are fund structuring and selling funds across borders.

As far as fund structuring is concerned, requirements pertaining to the taxation of capital gains, VAT, management charges, and the deduction of losses continue to vary widely. Pension funds, the most important suppliers of private equity capital, may not enjoy their tax-exempt status when they invest in other EU Member States. Thus, any

---

[4]The penetration rates reported here refer to equity investments across the entire spectrum of private equity. In terms of transaction volumes, which also include leverage in certain types of deals, penetration rates are considerably higher. For example, based on the work by Lerner, Sørensen, and Strömberg (2009), Cornelius, Juttmann, and Langelaar (2009) calculate average LBO penetration rates for the United Kingdom, Scandinavia, and continental Europe of 3.6 percent, 2.1 percent, and 1.4 percent, respectively in 2001–2007.

tax imposition is likely to penalize and discourage cross-border investment to investment in local vehicles. For example, if an exempted pension fund invests in a private equity fund that in turn makes an investment in another Member State, it may be required that both the state where the private equity fund is domiciled and where the investment is made recognize the tax-exempt status of the investing pension fund. Otherwise, the pension fund's commitment to a private equity fund may be subject to a tax disadvantage relative to alternative investments, such as public equity or bonds.

Unless pension funds can be certain that commitments to private equity funds does not create any tax liability for capital gains in the country where the private equity funds deploy their capital, they will be reluctant to make such commitments. To be able to raise capital, private equity funds are, therefore, established offshore, which limits the actual activity in the local country to purely advisory services rather than actual decision-making regarding the making, managing, and disposing of investments. However, these structures are often inefficient, costly, and operationally complicated to construct and manage (Alternative Investment Expert Group, 2006).

By favoring investments in locally domiciled funds, the current regime has resulted in a significant degree of market fragmentation with a number of shallow national markets. It is difficult to see how the European private equity market can become fully integrated, unless each Member State treats capital gains realized in private equity funds as being taxed in the investors' home countries, regardless of where the funds are managed and invested. Unfortunately, the current tax treatment of capital gains is not the only challenge European private equity funds face when raising capital. Although private equity funds look to a regional or even global investor base, they operate in a rather heterogeneous regulatory and legal environment with respect to the marketing and selling of funds across EU borders. Placement rules differ and are often complex, notably with regard to the definition of the pool of eligible investors. Complying with a patchwork of legal restrictions tends to lead to higher legal and advisory fees, which imply higher hurdle rates before profits are made.

On the investment side, there remain important tax obstacles, too. Private equity investments generally require a local presence in the country of the portfolio company for the fund manager to source new deals and manage existing investments. Most Member States of the EU have agreed bilateral double taxation conventions between each other that are generally based on the Model Double Tax Convention of the OECD. However, when a fund manager operates in the state of the portfolio company, the manager's activities risk creating a permanent establishment for tax purposes for the private equity fund (or for its investors) in that state. To avoid the risk of double taxation, the fund manager has to limit its activities at the local level to the mere provision of advice. In fact, this advice is usually provided by separate advisory companies that analyze the local market, identify and evaluate investment opportunities, and prepare investment proposals. However, such advisory companies must not carry out management functions, which otherwise would qualify them as permanent establishments for tax purposes. According to a recent report by an Expert Group established by the European Commission (Venture Capital Tax Expert Group, 2010), the current situation creates substantial inefficiencies and potentially deters investments, a risk that is particularly serious in venture capital.

Recent regulatory initiatives provide little hope that the situation will be fundamentally improved in the foreseeable future. On the contrary, if implemented, they could further undermine the development of a vibrant and integrated private equity market in Europe. By far the most far-reaching consequences are expected to result from the new EU Directive concerning Alternative Investment Fund Managers (AIFMD), which was proposed in April 2009. While there remains much uncertainty about its final form as we go to press, the draft AIFMD stipulates that EU-domiciled GPs approved by national regulators may sell EU-domiciled AIF across the EU. However, the EU Directive fails to address the existing tax hurdles in cross-border commitments to private equity funds. Instead, it restricts the marketing of offshore funds in the EU to alternative investment fund managers (AIFMs) whose home authorities have equivalent regulatory legislation to the EU. Approved offshore funds receive a passport for the entire EU, but unless unapproved offshore AIFMs relocate to the EU, they will no longer be available for EU-based LPs. There is considerable concern that regulators in third countries may retaliate by restricting the marketing of EU-based AIFMs. Furthermore, the Directive is expected to result in significantly higher costs by imposing capital requirements, setting stricter disclosure rules and requiring AIFMs to have independent evaluators and a depositary.

Although estimates about the impact of the new regulations in Europe differ considerably, there is general agreement that the EU Directive will affect European investors' risk-adjusted return expectations for private equity as an asset class. Other things being equal, adjustments in return expectations and quantitative restrictions concerning the universe of available instruments could result in significant shifts in investors' asset allocations and the construction of their private equity portfolios.

9.4 Summary and conclusions

Over the past couple of decades, Europe's financial markets have become more integrated, despite recent setbacks in the wake of the sovereign debt crisis in the periphery of the European Monetary Union. While in some markets in the euro area full integration is virtually achieved, in other markets the integration process has been more gradual and uneven. For investors, economic and financial integration has important implications. In the common currency area, cross-border investments are no longer subject to currency risk. Debt capital markets are deeper and broader, with country effects on corporate bond spreads having diminished progressively. The consolidation of the European corporate sector has gathered considerable momentum thanks to significantly greater intra-European cross-border M&A activity, and with the business cycles in individual European economies converging, equity investments have shifted from country-focused strategies to sector-oriented ones.

Deeper and broader financial markets have fostered the development of the European private equity market, which has seen a substantial increase in investment activity over the past two decades, notwithstanding its cyclical correction in the context of the recent global financial crisis. However, Europe's private equity market has not benefited as much as it potentially could from financial integration. Instead, the market remains fragmented because of different regulatory and tax regimes. As a result, investors are confronted with a number of relatively small markets in countries whose economies basically follow the same business cycle. This observation is particularly important for large investors who would find it difficult, if not impossible, to pursue a purely domestically oriented strategy, given the size of their investment portfolios.

In this context, it is interesting to note that European private equity returns have remained far more widely dispersed than in the United States. More specifically, when we look at the difference in the performance between upper quartile and lower quartile funds (Figs 2.3. and 2.4 in Chapter 2) in Europe and the United States over the period from 1985 to 2005, we find the European spread to be on average almost 4 percentage points larger.

Presumably, the wider dispersion of returns is in part attributable to the fragmentation of individual markets and the informational advantages national fund managers may have in identifying and managing attractive deals. These advantages are particularly relevant in the smaller and middle-market segment, although larger Pan-European funds have taken important steps through their hub-and-spoke networks to take advantage of the continuous market segmentation. In the current environment, there is little evidence that European private equity returns are converging, and for European and foreign LPs alike, fund selection remains critical. This is particularly true for LPs who seek exposure to smaller and mid-sized companies, which are typically the domain of national or regional funds exploiting their competitive advantage thanks to their local market knowledge.

In many ways, these observations apply to other regions as well. Regional markets have largely remained fragmented, and despite some policy efforts to achieve more economic and financial integration, investors remain confronted with a set of national markets with their own regulatory peculiarities following their own dynamics. In general, market transparency has been low, and many international investors seeking exposure to private equity outside the US and Western European markets have concentrated their investments on funds raised and managed by global private equity firms.

Some regions have seen the emergence of indigenous regional players who have been able to raise significant amounts of capital, including from foreign investors (Table 9.4). Their competitive advantage lies in their special knowledge of local market conditions and their perceived familiarity with potentially thorny corporate and public governance issues. While these funds have already been able to establish a track record, their success in raising increasing amounts of capital has encouraged a growing number of new fund managers to enter the market. Their business model is usually predicated on providing investors with access to particular market niches, including in smaller frontier markets global and regional players do not cover.

As we have discussed in Chapter 2, the performance history of private equity outside the United States and Western Europe remains spurious. At the market level, time series data usually do not go beyond a few years, and at the fund level, few

Table 9.4 Large funds recently raised by regional private equity firms in selected emerging markets

Fund	Manager	Vintage year	Amount (US$ billion)
Asia			
CCCP II	CITIC Capital Partners	2010	0.9
Hopu USD Master Fund	Hopu Investment Management	2008	2.5
Hony Capital Fund IV	Hony Capital	2008	1.4
CCMP Asia Opportunity Fund III	CCMP Capital Asia	2008	1.2
Affinity Asia-Pacific Fund III	Affinity Equity Partners	2007	2.8
CDH China Fund III	CDH China	2007	1.6
Chrys Capital V	Chrys Capital	2007	1.3
SB Asia Investment Fund III	SAIF Partners	2007	1.1
Navis Asia Fund V	Navis Capital Partners	2007	1.0
Latin America			
Gávea Investment Fund III	Gávea Investimentos	2008	1.2
GP Capital Partners IV	GP Investimentos	2007	1.3
CEE			
Mid Europa Partners III	Mid Europa Partners	2007	1.5
Baring Vostok Private Equity Fund IV	Baring Vostok Capital Partners	2007	1.0
Middle East			
Abraij Buyout Fund III	Abraij Capital	2008	3.0
Citadel Capital SPV Fund III	Citadel Capital	2006	1.4
Swicorp Joussour	Swicorp	2006	1.0
Africa			
Ethos Private Equity Fund III	Ethos Private Equity	2006	0.8

Source: EMPEA; PREQIN

managers have been around for a sufficiently long time to allow meaningful conclusions about their performance. However, if Europe is to provide any guidance, we should expect individual fund returns to be substantially dispersed. As regional markets are likely to remain significantly segmented, performance differentials look set to continue to be relatively high in the foreseeable future. This expectation seems even more plausible in an environment where cross-border investments face the additional risk of currency movements, an issue we turn to in the final chapter of this part of the book.

Table 4.4 Large funds recently raised by prominent private equity firms in selected emerging markets

Fund	Manager	Vintage year	Amount (US$ billion)

(table content largely illegible/reversed in source)

managers have been around for a sufficiently long time to allow meaningful conclusions about their performance. However, if Europe is to provide any guidance, we should expect individual fund returns to be substantially dispersed. Accordingly, markets are likely to remain significantly segmented, performance difference look set to continue to be relatively high in the foreseeable future. This expectation seems even more plausible in an environment where cross-border investments face the additional risk of currency movements. An issue we turn to in the final chapter of this part of the book.

10 Fund investments and currency movements[1]

Chapter Outline

Exchange rates matter. A US-based investor is interested in returns in US dollars rather than in local currency returns, just as much as an investor based in the euro area is interested in returns in euros. In cross-border transactions, returns in the investor's home currency and in the currency of the recipient economy are identical only if the exchange rate remains unchanged. However, exchange rates tend to move, especially over longer time periods, reflecting, for example, inflation differentials and divergent monetary policies. While some countries maintain fixed exchange rate regimes, discrete jumps, for instance in the wake of balance of payments crises, may have a substantial impact on an investor's returns in his home currency.

Foreign exchange risk in private equity has several dimensions (Fig. 10.1). Sequentially, investors are first confronted with exchange rate risk when they commit to a foreign-currency-denominated private equity fund. Exchange rates may move between the point in time when an investor makes a commitment to a foreign-currency fund and when the GP draws down the committed capital. To the extent that the currency in which the fund is denominated has appreciated against the investor's home currency, he may face a liquidity problem. Conversely, depreciation may result in an underexposure relative to the investor's target allocation.

Second, movements in the exchange rate affect the performance of an investment in a foreign private equity fund expressed in the investor's home currency. The impact of the exchange rate may not only be negative but also positive. Third, GPs are exposed to currency risk if they acquire portfolio companies abroad. Exchange rate movements may result in investment losses, but they may also lead to windfall gains.

[1]This chapter is based on a joint work with my colleague Robert de Veer.

International Investments in Private Equity. DOI: 10.1016/B978-0-12-375082-2.10010-2

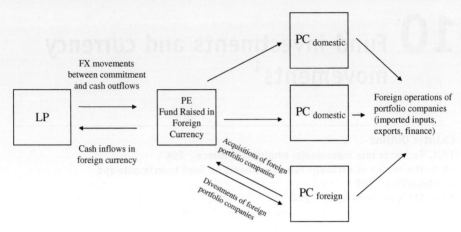

Figure 10.1 Foreign exchange risk in private equity.

In their due diligence, LPs may want to know the extent to which the performance of a fund was due to superior operational and governance skills and financial engineering as opposed to unpredictable exchange rate changes, which may be considered as sheer luck. Finally, to the extent that an LP coinvests alongside a private equity fund, which makes an acquisition in a foreign currency, he is directly exposed to currency risk.

In this chapter, we start by examining the global fund-raising market in terms of its currency composition. Examining the degree to which the main funding currencies have been subject to exchange rate volatility, we then estimate the impact of currency movements on the performance of private equity funds. Next, we look at cross-border investments made by internationally operating private equity funds and analyze the impact of currency movements on their performance. Finally, turning to the drivers of currency movements, we discuss their predictability and ask how limited partners may mitigate the foreign exchange rate risk that international investments inevitably bring about.

10.1   Exchange rate movements: empirical evidence

Our starting point is the currency composition of the global fund-raising market. In addressing this question, we concentrate on buyout funds raised during the last cycle. As we have seen before, buyout funds have accounted for the bulk of global fund-raising and are especially outward oriented both in terms of their investor base and their investment focus. In Table 10.1, we show the global amount of capital raised by buyout funds between 2003 and 2009, both in the currency in which individual funds were raised and in US dollars. For example, in 2003, a total amount of US$ 43.2 billion was committed to buyout funds. Around half of this amount was raised in US dollars (US$ 21.6 billion), while the rest was raised by funds in five other

Table 10.1 Global fund-raising in fund currency and US dollars (in million currency units), 2003–2009

	2003		2004		2005		2006		2007		2008		2009	
	FC	USD	FC	USD	FC	USD	FC	USD	FC	USD	FC	USD	FC	USD
USD	21,638	21,638	48,510	48,510	69,857	69,857	144,051	144,051	183,315	183,315	142,893	142,893	63,881	63,881
CanD	736	545	120	93	60	50	3,351	3,046	750	712	180	170	351	296
EUR	13,405	15,592	12,042	14,829	48,583	61,099	48,964	62,134	40,535	60,381	52,029	78,909	27,046	36,374
GBP	3,383	5,264	1,219	2,232	1,347	2,350	2,640	4,724	2,489	4,968	2202	4,105	175	256
DEK	...	...	273	46	4,000	647	...	...	1,413	262	...	...	...	...
SEK	...	...	2,350	322	...	...	...	749	6,000	918	...	...	225	28
NOK	...	...	...	...	...	...	4,850	...	...	...	6,000	1,019	...	...
CHF	...	...	...	...	...	...	...	...	218	183	25	21	...	...
JPY	...	...	106,500	979	155,400	1,476	23,100	196	171,154	1,387	37,875	370	140,000	1,473
AUD	115	78	1,500	1,057	4,326	2,913	3,436	2,558	2,326	1,930	5,093	4,591	...	...
NZD	...	...	...	...	195	135	...	...	...	...	250	136	322	229
RMB	...	...	...	...	...	...	20,000	2,563	...	...	...	...	...	...
INR	...	...	...	...	...	...	...	...	...	...	6,000	140	...	...
BRL	...	...	...	...	150	64	...	...	25	13	1,550	888	...	...
ZAR	553	73	350	56	...	...	6,578	944	5,000	710	875	107	...	...
Total		43,190		68,124		138,591		220,965		254,779		233,349		102,537

Source: PREQIN; author's calculations

Table 10.2 Global fund-raising: currency shares (%)

	2003	2004	2005	2006	2007	2008	2009	Total 2003–2009
USD	50.1	71.2	50.4	65.2	72.0	61.2	62.3	63.5
CanD	1.3	0.1	0.0	1.4	0.3	0.1	0.3	0.5
EUR	36.1	21.8	44.1	28.1	23.7	33.8	35.5	31.0
GBP	12.2	3.3	1.7	2.1	1.9	1.8	0.2	2.3
DEK	...	0.1	0.5	...	0.1	...	...	0.1
SEK	...	0.5	...	...	0.4	...	...	0.1
NOK	...	...	...	0.3	...	0.4	...	0.2
CHF	...	...	...	...	0.1	...	0.0	0.0
JPY	...	1.4	1.1	0.1	0.5	0.2	1.4	0.6
AUD	0.2	1.6	2.1	1.2	0.8	2.0	...	1.2
NZD	...	...	0.1	...	...	0.1	0.2	0.0
RMB	...	...	...	1.2	...	...	...	0.2
INR	...	...	...	...	...	0.1	...	0.0
BRL	...	...	0.0	...	0.0	0.4	...	0.1
ZAR	0.2	0.1	...	0.4	0.3	0.0	...	0.2
Total	100.0	100.0	100.0	1000	100.0	100.0	100.0	100.0

Source: PREQIN; author's calculations

currencies, namely the Canadian dollar (CanD), the euro (EUR), British pound (GBP), the Australian dollar (AUD), and the South African Rand (ZAR). At the peak of the cycle in 2007, buyout funds raised nearly US$ 255 billion. While US$ 183 billion was raised by funds denominated in US dollars (72 percent), the remainder was committed to funds in 10 different currencies.

Table 10.2 depicts the currency shares in individual fund-raising years and for the entire period under investigation. Essentially, the global LBO fund-raising market represents a bipolar world. While the US dollar accounted for 63.5 percent of the total amount of buyout capital raised between 2003 and 2009, the euro had a share of 31 percent. Although PREQIN reports that on a global basis buyout funds were raised in 13 additional currencies, their combined share was just 5.5 percent. The share of funds raised in emerging markets currencies [Chinese renmimbi (RMB); Indian Rupee (INR), Brazilian real (BRL), and South African Rand (ZAR)] totaled only 0.5 percent of all buyout funds raised in 2003–2009.

The share of emerging market's currencies is considerably lower than the share of emerging markets as a target region for LBO funds. This suggests that a nontrivial number of funds targeting emerging markets are raised in international reserve currencies, especially in US dollars. For example, this is the case for virtually all large buyout funds, which have been raised by global players targeting emerging markets, such as KKR's 2007 Asian Fund (US$ 4 billion), CVC Capital Partners' 2008 Asia-Pacific Fund III (US$4.12 billion), and TPG's 2008 Asia V Fund (US$4.25 billion). However, this is also the case for a nontrivial number of funds raised by GPs domiciled in emerging markets, such as Hopu's 2008 USD Master Fund I (US$

Table 10.3 Fund-raising in regions' currencies to overall fund-raising for region (%)

	2003	2004	2005	2006	2007	2008	2009	Total 2003–2009
North America[a]	109.7	115.7	116.1	112.4	114.4	124.7	110.5	115.7
Europe[b]	97.2	87.7	98.5	96.7	101.2	98.1	99.9	98.0
Nontraditional markets[c]	10.0	33.5	34.7	31.0	17.3	18.9	21.9	23.8

[a]USD, CanD.
[b]EUR, GBP, DEK, SEK, NOK, CHF.
[c]JPY, AUD, NZD, CNY, INR, BRL, ZAR.
Source: PREQIN; author's calculations

2.5 billion), Affinity's 2007 Asia-Pacific Fund III (US$ 2.8 billion), or Abraaj Capital's 2005 Buyout Fund II (US$ 500 million).

In Table 10.3, we present the ratio of fund-raising in the region's currency to the overall amount of capital raised by funds targeting the same region. We show these ratios for three regions, North America (United States and Canada), Europe (euro area, United Kingdom, Denmark, Norway, Sweden, and Switzerland), and the rest of the world (advanced economies outside of North America and Europe, plus all emerging markets). Importantly, funds raised in local currencies accounted for less than 25 percent in the rest of the world. North America presents the mirror image, with the US dollar being used as the fund-raising currency in a significantly larger number of LBO funds than just those targeting the region. In a small number of cases, the US dollar has also been used for LBO funds targeting Europe, which explains why the European currencies show a slightly below par ratio relative to LBO funds raised for the region. However, foreign currency funds are the exception in the mature markets. The overwhelming number of funds targeting North America and Europe are raised in the region's respective currencies. In fact, this is even true within regions. In Europe, for example, buyout funds targeting specifically the United Kingdom are raised in British pounds, while country-specific funds focusing specifically on Denmark, Norway and Sweden are usually raised in Danish, Norwegian, and Swedisch Krona.

As we have seen in Chapter 8, around 25–30 percent of the capital commitments to US-based buyout funds stem from European LPs. Conversely, around 40–50 percent of the capital raised by European buyout funds comes from US-based LPs. Inevitably, these investors incur currency risk. Within Europe, investors may also face currency risk. Although we do not have data on fund-raising flows between the euro area, the United Kingdom, and the Scandinavian countries (except for Finland which has adopted the euro), anecdotal evidence from individual funds suggests that their investor base includes a significant number of European LPs from outside their home markets. For instance, funds such as the Swedish middle-market fund Segulah IV that raised SEK 5 billion in 2007 or UK middle-market fund Graphite Capital Partners VII that closed at GBP 475 million in the same year count among their LPs a significant number of investors from other European countries.

Currency risk is also relevant for LPs based in the rest of the world who seek exposure to the mature markets in North America and Europe. Such investors,

Figure 10.2 Daily US dollar/euro exchange rate, January 4, 1999–December 31, 2009.
Source: Bloomberg.

a category that includes large sovereign wealth funds in Asia and the Middle East, account for 10–13 percent in terms of the total capital raised by buyout funds headquartered in North America and Europe. By contrast, US dollar funds targeting emerging and frontier markets in Asia, Latin America, the Middle East, and Africa offer US-based GPs the possibility to avoid currency risk at the fund level.

So how important is currency risk empirically? In Figs 10.2 to 10.4, we present bilateral exchange rates for the key funding currencies in the global buyout markets during the 11-year period from January 1999 to December 2009. As far as the US

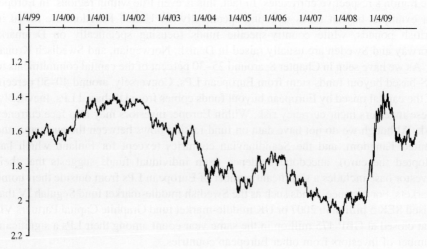

Figure 10.3 Daily US dollar/sterling exchange rate, January 4, 1999–December 31, 2009.
Source: Bloomberg.

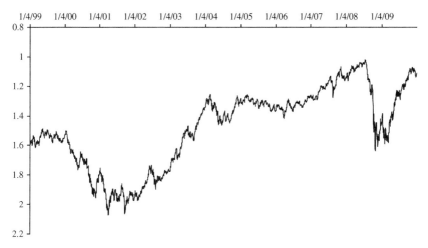

Figure 10.4 Daily Australian dollar/US dollar exchange rate, January 4, 1999–December 31, 2009.
Source: Bloomberg.

dollar/euro rate is concerned, the dollar peaked at 0.8252 on October 26, 2000. Since then, the dollar remained under downward pressure against the euro. On July 15, 2008, investors had to pay almost twice as much for one euro (USD/EUR 1.599), with a monthly standard deviation of 19.8 percent. For most of the time, the dollar also slipped against the British pound, although it recouped most of its losses in the wake of the financial crisis when the dollar gained more than 50 percent within a time span of just 14 months. On a monthly basis, the USD/GBP rate had a standard deviation of 19.1 percent. Finally, the Australian dollar appreciated to near-parity against the US dollar in July 2008 from a low of 2.07 in early April 2001. Over the entire period from 1999 to 2009, the AUD/USD exchange rate had a monthly standard deviation of 26.5 percent.

10.2 The impact of exchange rate movements on fund investments and benchmarking

These exchange rate movements may have material implications for investors. Let us take the example of an investor making a commitment to a single private equity fund. Suppose this investor is based in the euro area and committed US$ 100 million to a US buyout fund on December 3, 1999, when the USD/EUR rate was parity (1.0015, to be precise). Converted at the market exchange rate, his commitment thus was EUR 100 million. Suppose further that the LP's committed capital was drawn down in 2002-2003. The drawdowns are made in US dollars, and given an average exchange rate of USD/EUR 1.15, the LP's exposure therefore totaled EUR 87 million in his home currency, an exchange rate induced shortfall of EUR 13 million relative to his initial commitment. Finally, suppose that the fund had divested its portfolio companies in

2006 and the first half of 2007, achieving a money multiple of 1.75 (net of fees). In dollar terms, the LP would thus have received USD 175 million. In the meantime, however, the exchange rate has moved to USD/EUR 1.35. Other things being equal, our euro area-based investor would have received just EUR 130 million, that is, a multiple of only around 1.5 in his home currency.

For US-based LPs investing in buyout funds raised in euros, the opposite would have been true. Under the same assumptions, the LP would have had to come up with an additional amount of US$ 15 million due to the depreciation of his home currency between the time he made his commitment to the foreign fund and the GP's capital calls. The subsequent depreciation of the US dollar would have worked in his favor, however, magnifying the performance of the fund converted to the LP's home currency.

Let us now turn to the real world and consider the actual impact of exchange-rate movements on the performance of a private equity portfolio. For this, we need to know the cash flows of the underlying private equity funds and the transaction dates of the takedowns and distributions. This information is generally not available for individual funds. Luckily, however, Thomson VentureXpert provides cash flows on a pooled basis for individual years, that is, the cash flows of all funds in the database are lumped together, treating them as one huge fund. These cash flows are then used to calculate pooled average IRRs for individual market segments in different geographies in their respective currencies—US buyout and venture capital funds, and European buyout and venture capital funds. These pooled average IRRs are used as a standard private equity benchmark by many LPs.

Since we know the quarterly cash flows in the funds' currencies (USD and EUR), we can convert them to foreign currency using quarterly average exchange rates and recalculate the pooled average IRRs. Table 10.4 summarizes the results. In the first half

Table 10.4 Exchange rate effect on pooled mean IRR for European and US-based investors committing to USD- and EUR-denominated buyout funds, respectively, as of June 30, 2009 (in percentage points)

Vintage year	European investor investing in USD-denominated buyout funds	US investor investing in euro-denominated buyout funds
2000	−6.3	7.0
2001	−6.1	7.1
2002	−4.4	5.0
2003	−4.2	4.7
2004	−4.0	3.0
2005	−2.1	2.3
2006	0.7	−0.2
2007	2.2	−1.6
2008	2.0	−3.9

Note: Cash flows are converted using average quarterly exchange rates. NAV is converted based on the USD/EUR rate as per June 30, 2009.
Source: TVE; author's calculations

of the 2000s, the depreciation of the USD against the Euro shaved a considerable part off the performance of US-denominated buyout funds from the perspective of a Euro-based investor. Let us look more specifically at the early vintage years 2000 to 2002, which are more meaningful as they were largely divested as of mid-2009. In these vintage years, US buyout funds generated pooled average IRRs of 12.3, 15.3, and 14.1 percent, respectively. This implies that, other things being equal, around one-third to one-half of the returns would have been eaten up by currency movements!

The opposite is true for a US-based investor who committed capital to euro-denominated funds during this period. In local currency, the pooled average generated IRRs of 13.9, 24.1, and 17.9 percent in 2000, 2001, and 2002, respectively. With the cash flows converted in USD, a US-based investor would have received significantly higher returns than from investments in local buyout funds. As far as more recent VYs are concerned, euro-based investors have enjoyed moderate exchange-rate–induced gains. However, much of the capital of the funds raised after 2006 were not yet invested by the middle of 2009, preventing us from drawing any firm conclusions.

Unfortunately, TVE reports cash flow data only for the United States and Europe. While these regions still represent the largest private equity markets—with the USD and the EUR having an even greater market share in the global fund-raising market—other markets are catching up. To provide a more granulated and precise picture about the impact of exchange rate movements on investors' portfolios, we turn again to AlpInvest Partners' database. Between 2000 and 2008, AlpInvest Partners has made commitments to nearly 350 private equity partnerships worldwide across the entire spectrum of the asset class (venture capital and clean tech, buyouts, mezzanine, and distressed; for a breakdown, see Table 8.1). In terms of the number of fund investments, less than 25 percent was made in AlpInvest Partners' home currency, the euro (Table 10.5). The majority of commitments have been made to funds in US dollars, with the remainder of commitments denominated in sterling, Japanese yen, Australian dollars and Swedish Krona.

For all fund investments, we calculate pooled IRRs by combining the cash flows of the respective funds raised in the same currency. In a second step, we convert the combined cash flows of funds denominated in foreign currencies into euros at the

Table 10.5 AlpInvest Partners: number of fund commitments by fund currency, 2000–2008

Fund currency	Year of commitment									Total
	2000	2001	2002	2003	2004	2005	2006	2007	2008	
EUR	6	5	8	4	9	14	12	12	10	80
USD	18	7	15	11	19	37	57	37	36	237
GBP				2	1	4	3	4	3	17
JPY				1				2	1	4
AUD					1	1	1	2		5
SEK	1				1				1	3

Source: AlpInvest Research

market exchange rates at the time when the cash flows occur. Since we know the exact transaction dates, we can use daily exchange rates rather than quarterly average exchange rates as in the case of the TVE dataset. The differences between the pooled IRRs calculated in the respective fund currencies and the pooled IRRs calculated in euros represent the exchange rate effect on the performance of AlpInvest Partners' investments in private equity funds (Table 10.6).

The results confirm that currency risk in private equity is considerable. For example, returns on investments made in USD-denominated funds in 2002 are reduced by 5.2 percentage points, a similar exchange-rate effect as we have calculated on the basis of the TVE data. Exchange-rate losses have also been suffered from investments in private equity funds raised in British pounds. Conversely, investments in AUD-denominated funds have gained due to the appreciation of the Australian dollar against the euro. However, these losses and gains may not be the final outcome. At the cutoff date, many funds in AlpInvest Partners' portfolio had not yet fully returned the invested capital, with their reported performance reflecting—necessarily subjective—valuations by GPs. Their final performance will only be known once the funds have fully exited their investments. Until then, the funds' returns measured in their own currency remain subject to change. The same is of course true for exchange rates—for the worse or the better.

The importance of exchange rate changes for the returns of a globally diversified private equity portfolio raises a fundamental issue: How should an LP benchmark his performance? More specifically, should an investor benchmark his performance against a portfolio that isolates exchange-rate effects or should he allow currency movements to affect his relative performance? If he chooses the former, the LP would use performance data for individual markets in local currency, which are provided by TVE and other data vendors. Investments in US buyout funds raised in US dollars would be benchmarked against the pooled mean IRR calculated on the basis of takedowns, distributions, and NAV in US dollars. Similarly, investments in European buyouts would be benchmarked against the pooled mean IRR calculated on the basis of cash flows in euros. In benchmarking his foreign-currency investments in his home currency, he would convert the cash flows of his investments as well as the benchmark cash flows on the basis of fixed exchange rates.

Table 10.6 AlpInvest Partners: exchange rate effect on pooled IRR of funds raised in foreign currencies, percentage points (as of September 30, 2009)

$\Delta IRR_{fund\ currency}$ vs. IRR_{euro}	Fund vintage year								
	2000	2001	2002	2003	2004	2005	2006	2007	2008
USD	−5.8	−6.5	−5.2	−4.6	−5.3	−4.5	−3.0	−3.1	−3.1
GBP				−2.4	−7.0	−8.3	−8.9	−9.1	4.9
JPY				−0.4				7.7	0.0
AUD					1.3	2.7	3.4	2.3	
SEK	0.2				−3.1				−2.2

Source: AlpInvest Research

Alternatively, the investor may choose to convert foreign cash flows into his home currency by using market exchange rates. Other things being equal, his relative performance might not be affected in individual regional markets, as both the cash flows of his own fund investments and the benchmark cash flows are converted at the same market exchange rates. However, currency movements do play a role for the overall performance of the investor's portfolio, reflecting his allocation to individual foreign markets. This becomes clear when we look at Table 10.6: while from a European perspective foreign investments have suffered from adverse currency movements of most currencies, in some cases the (book) losses have been larger than that in others. For example, exchange-rate–induced performance effects have been particularly pronounced in the case of UK funds, and although the relative benchmarking in the UK market should be unaffected, the relative weight of UK fund investments in the overall portfolio affects the portfolio's performance relative to the global benchmark.

There are important arguments for and against isolating exchange rate effects in private equity benchmarking. Starting with the latter, one may take the view that the only relevant evaluation criterion is the returns an investor generates in his home currency relative to a global benchmark. Since exchange rate changes are a relevant performance driver, no attempt should be made to eliminate currency effects from the portfolio relative to the benchmark. After all, why should exchange rate movements be treated differently from other risk factors in international investing, such as political risk? Proponents of this approach may also point to public equity benchmarks, including listed private equity. For instance, the widely used global LPX 50 has 50 constituents in different markets, with daily exchange rates being used to calculate the index in EUR.

Opponents argue that foreign exchange exposure needs to be seen and managed from the perspective of the investor's total portfolio rather than in an isolated fashion for each portfolio component. In a portfolio context, currency risk in private equity may be hedged by offsetting positions in other asset classes. Private equity investing, so the argument goes, is about choosing the best fund managers, and it is the LP's selection skills that should be used as the sole benchmarking criterion.

There are also important arguments from a practical standpoint. Although TVE provides cash-flow data on a pooled basis, which allows investors to convert pooled mean IRRs into their home currency that can then be used as a benchmark, this cannot be done for individual funds. Because there is no publicly available information on the cash flows of individual funds, one would not be able to convert the cash flows of the upper-, median-, or lower-quartile funds in foreign markets into the investor's home currency. But even if we had access to cash-flow data for individual funds, how would we interpret the results? How would we evaluate an UQ fund in local currency, which had dropped to the median when converted into foreign currency (and vice versa)? For all these reasons, it is argued that benchmarking an LP's fund selection skills in individual foreign-currency markets can only be done in local currency.

There is no simple answer as to how currency risk should be treated in benchmarking the performance of private equity investors. Which approach is seen as more appropriate depends not least on the specific circumstances of the LP. Large institutional investors with global portfolios across many asset classes will find it easier to manage currency risk in their private equity portfolios than small funds of private equity funds. Regardless of the agreed benchmark, however, any private equity investor should closely monitor the impact of currency movements on their portfolios. This entails analyzing the impact on currency movements on the performance of individual funds, an issue we now turn to.

10.3   Skills or (bad) luck?

Limited Partners may be exposed to currency risk even if they commit capital only to private equity funds in their home currency. As we have seen in Chapter 7, private equity funds invest a nontrivial part of their capital in foreign markets acquiring assets in currencies different from the fund currency. Some funds have become truly global, chasing deals across different geographies and holding an international portfolio of companies. To the extent that private equity funds acquire foreign portfolio companies, their performance may be affected by currency movements.

Exchange rate changes work both ways, not just for LPs but also for GPs. Adverse movements may reduce returns on an investment a fund makes and may even turn a gain into a loss. But exchange rate changes may also enhance returns. This raises the question to what extent a fund's performance is strictly based on the GP's operational and financial qualities as opposed to factors that are arguably beyond his control. Whether (adverse) exchange rate movements are just (bad) luck is of course debatable—a GP who decides to invest abroad deliberately accepts currency risk, which should be an integral part of his investment (and divestment) decision process. In fact, GPs interviewed for this book (Chapter 12) confirm that the timing of their foreign investments and exits do reflect their exchange rate views. Furthermore, foreign acquisitions by private equity funds tend to be biased toward export-oriented companies,[2] which, other things being equal, helps mitigate exchange rate risk.[2] Skills or bad luck—inextricably intertwined with this question is, of course, the issue of compensation. Should profits due to exchange rate movements be excluded from the calculation of carried interest? While LPAs are generally silent on the exchange rate question, Meyer and Mathonet (2005, p. 127) argue that in the future "...investors could ask for a carried interest calculation on the underlying investments' currencies to strip off the effect of exchange rates."

The academic literature has little to say on this issue due to the lack of sufficiently detailed deal-level data and the fact that cross-border investments are a relatively recent phenomenon. To better understand the significance of exchange rate movements on investment returns, we look at individual transactions of private equity funds in AlpInvest Partners' database. More specifically, we concentrate on cross-border deals by buyout funds that have already been exited. For each deal, we convert the cash flows of foreign-currency transactions into the funds' currencies. As far as

[2]I owe this argument to Roger Leeds.

European funds are concerned, we identify 18 fully exited (and nonwrite off) deals in US dollars (Table 10.7); for buyout funds raised in USD, we have 24 deals undertaken in euros. The exchange-rate impact on the returns of the transactions is shown as the absolute difference between the money multiple calculated in the fund's and the deal's currency and as the deviation of the IRR in the deal's currency in percentage points of the IRR in the fund's currency.

Most USD-denominated deals by European funds were negatively impacted by the appreciation of the euro. The impact was sizable, with adverse exchange rate movements shaving around 4–5 percentage points off the IRR calculated in the funds' currency. In some cases, the currency effect was even larger, depending on the exact entry and exit dates of the deals. For instance, over the holding period from 2003 to 2008, a European fund saw the IRR of one of its US buyouts reduced by as much as nine percentage points when calculated in EUR, the fund's currency.

Conversely, in our sample, the overwhelming majority of transactions undertaken by USD-based funds in Europe benefited from the EUR appreciation. In some cases, the exchange rate effect added 10 percentage points or more to the IRR of individual European deals when converted into USD, the funds' currency. In other words, the performance of these transactions, and hence the performance of the buyout funds that have sponsored them, would have been considerably worse in the absence of— from their perspective—favorable exchange rate movements.

10.4 Are exchange rate movements predictable?

Since exchange rate movements have a material impact on private equity returns, the question arises whether such movements are predictable. As far as short-term changes over the next few days or weeks are concerned, the answer is "no." Exchange rates are found to be nonstationary, in the sense that exchange rate movements are not identically independently distributed.[3] Spot rates behave very much similar to random walks. In fact, numerous academic studies provide overwhelming evidence that (the log of) daily spot exchange rates are autocorrelated. The existence of unit roots, which indicates that daily exchange rates follow a wandering process without any long-term attractor value, means that statistical moments (mean, variance, skewness, and kurtosis) are meaningless in forecasting exchange rates.

If nonstationarity renders fundamental exchange rate models useless, what about technical analysis? Based solely on price information, technical analysis attempts to detect specific price patterns to extrapolate past trends. Supported by relatively simple computer models, this identification process usually applies moving averages, filters, or momentum. A related approach is known as chartism, which relies on the interpretation of exchange rate charts of the kind we presented in Figs. 10.2 to 10.4. Chartism is more an art than a science—some would even say a "black art" (Lo & Hasanhodzic, 2009)— which is why it is rejected by most academics. The problem with technical analysis is, of course, that the same technical models, such as moving averages, are constantly

[3]A good discussion about the statistical properties of exchange rates can be found in Sercu (2009).

Table 10.7 Impact of exchange rate changes on deal performance

Year of acquisition	Exit year	Impact on realized MM	Impact on IRR (% points)
USD deals by EUR buyout funds			
1999	2001	0.01	1
1999	2004	0.31	13
1999	2005	−0.44	−2
1999	2006	−0.81	−5
2000	2001	0.02	2
2000	2005	−0.01	−3
2000	2005	−0.01	−4
2000	2006	−0.19	−7
2000	2006	−0.40	−6
2000	2008	−0.78	−8
2003	2006	−0.29	−8
2003	2006	−0.09	−4
2003	2008	−2.33	−9
2003	2009	−0.01	0
2004	2008	−0.04	−3
2004	2008	−0.17	−5
2004	2008	−0.51	−6
2005	2008	−1.23	−7
EUR Deals by USD Buyout Funds			
1999	2001	−0.21	−12
1999	2001	−0.93	−26
1999	2003	0.19	3
1999	2004	0.34	4
1999	2006	0.24	3
2000	2004	0.27	9
2000	2007	0.87	5
2000	2008	0.22	5
2001	2004	0.59	12
2002	2005	0.85	14
2002	2007	1.53	16
2002	2008	0.70	10
2003	2006	0.02	1
2003	2007	0.34	6
2003	2007	0.32	4
2003	2008	1.71	11
2003	2008	0.25	4
2004	2006	0.05	2
2004	2007	0.23	3
2004	2008	0.27	5
2005	2007	0.28	10
2005	2007	0.25	10
2005	2008	0.6	3
2005	2008	0.59	10

Source: AlpInvest Research

calculated by a large number of investors. As a result, technical analysis typically fails to beat the market, since so many other analysts employ the same approach.

How good is the foreign exchange market itself in predicting future spot rates? Unfortunately, not good at all. In fact, the forward rate is found to have surprisingly poor predictive power. Early tests of the forecasting performance of the forward rate have centered on the uncovered interest parity hypothesis, which states that the difference in interest rates between two countries is equal to the expected change in exchange rates between the countries' currencies. If this parity does not hold, there is an opportunity to make a profit. This is exactly what several empirical studies find— the observed forward bias in the foreign market allows developing profitable trading rules involving carry trades. Although more recent models have focused on risk premia, they have failed to explain the excess return, a result that represents a second key puzzle in international finance (in addition to the home bias in international investing we discussed in Chapter 7). However, the view that the forward bias should be seen as a market inefficiency is not universally shared. That the forward bias puzzle has remained unresolved may say more about the models than about the markets. As Sercu (2009, p. 428) puts it: "It would be conceited, in short, to conclude that if academics do not understand reality, then reality is wrong."

From the standpoint of private equity, the forward market is of limited relevance anyway, as the market gets progressively thinner as we approach time horizons of relevance for this particular asset class. Private equity investors need to take a view on exchange rates over several years, which begs the question whether exchange rate models perform better over the long term. Here, the unfortunate answer is "not much."

According to the law of one price, the real price of a good must be the same in all countries. In a two-country world, if goods prices go up in country A, its exchange rate *vis-à-vis* country B must depreciate to maintain the same real price for goods in the two countries. If this is true for any particular good, it should also be true for the weighted average of the prices of all goods in the economy. In its absolute form, the theory of purchasing power parity (PPP) thus claims that the exchange rate should be equal to the ratio of the average price levels in the two economies.

Since the mid-1980s, *The Economist* has published a *Big Mac Index*, which compares the price of the MacDonald's Big Mac hamburger in a large number of countries. Over time, this index has become increasingly popular, including academic research on equilibrium exchange rates. There is a wide dispersion in the dollar prices of the Big Mac around the world. At the beginning of 2010, the price of a hamburger averaged US$ 3.58 in the United States. While it cost the equivalent of US$ 1.83 in China, the Big Mac was priced at the equivalent of US$ 7.02 in Norway. In the euro area, consumer had to pay on average the equivalent of US$ 4.84. On this basis, *The Economist* concluded that the Norwegian kroner was the most overvalued currency, with the price of a hamburger 96 percent above the currency's PPP rate. Conversely, the Big Mac Index implies that the Chinese currency was undervalued by nearly 50 percent.

The good thing about the Big Mac Index is that hamburgers are a largely homogenous good. Around the world, the same ingredients are used to produce it. But, of course, the index can only be a very rough approximation of the relative price levels in individual countries, which are determined by tens of thousands of goods and services. The IMF attempts to provide a more comprehensive picture based on a bundle of about 3000 goods. Figures 10.5 and 10.6 juxtapose implied PPP rates calculated by the IMF with NOK/USD and RMB/USD spot rates, the two most overvalued and undervalued currencies according to the Big Mac Index. The conclusions are similar to those drawn on the basis of the Big Mac index. Based on annual averages, the IMF estimates that the NOK was overvalued by nearly 50 percent in 2009, while the RMB was found to be undervalued by 84 percent. Importantly, deviations from PPP may be persistent. In current account surplus countries with (largely) fixed exchange rates, such as China, the reason for this is clear. It is less clear in countries with flexible exchange rates, such as Norway, whose currency has diverged increasingly from PPP since the beginning of the 2000s.

Although the IMF approach is probably the best approximation we have today, it is not free of important statistical problems.[4] In some countries, not all goods might be available or consumed by most agents. The quality of products, including related services, may vary. Prices may be highly heterogeneous even within countries, and they may not equalize (expressed in the same currency) if local taxes, rents, and labor costs are different.

These issues may help explain why market exchange rates fail to ensure that the *price* for a good—or a bundle of goods—is the same in two countries when expressed in the same currency. But how do market exchange rates perform in terms of off-setting *inflation* differentials between countries, which is known as relative PPP (RPPP)? This question has attracted a huge amount of interest in academic studies. However, the bottom line is not too encouraging: the variability of the RPPP rate is generally found to be small and explains little about the nominal exchange rate. In other words, the main driver of the real exchange rate is the nominal exchange rate

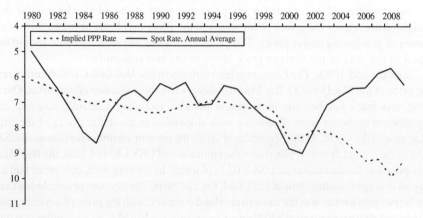

Figure 10.5 Norway: NOK/USD spot rate versus implied PPP rate, 1980–2009.
Source: Bloomberg; IMF.

---

[4]This became apparent when the IMF decided in 2007 to revise China's and India's price levels upward, which caused a drop by 40 percent in their respective GDPs measured at PPP rates.

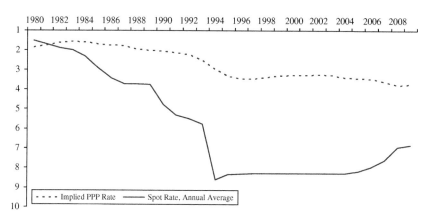

Figure 10.6 China: RMB/USD spot rate versus implied PPP rate, 1980–2009.
Source: Bloomberg; IMF.

and not the PPP rate. The exceptions are high-inflation countries, where inflation differentials are found to play a more significant role in explaining nominal exchange rate movements.

Yet other approaches, such as the monetary approach or real business cycle models, have been hardly more successful. The unfortunate conclusion we have to draw is that until now exchange rates have remained largely unpredictable. This is certainly true in the short run, but it is also true for time horizons relevant from the perspective of private equity. Deviations from PPP may persist for prolonged periods, and there is very little, if any, evidence that other economic fundamentals can explain exchange rate behavior.

10.5   Currency crashes and early warning systems

Thus far, our discussion has focused on currency movements, which may be considered as a fact of life in a world of flexible exchange rates. While over longer time spans such "normal" currency movements may add up to a significant change in bilateral exchange rates, it is useful to distinguish them from an abrupt currency crash. There is no universally agreed definition of what a currency crash constitutes, but a workable one has been suggested by Frankel and Rose (1996) who consider a crash as a change in the exchange rate by at least 25 percent within a year. Note that according to this definition, the USD actually crashed against the EUR between June 2002 and June 2003 when the value of the USD fell by 26 percent relative to the EUR.[5] As substantial as the depreciation of the USD was during this period, it looks rather moderate compared with the exchange rate crises in Mexico (1994), Asia (1997), Russia (1998), Brazil (1999), and Argentina (2001).

---

[5]The euro nearly "crashed" against the US dollar in the spring of 2010 when the sovereign debt crisis in Europe resulted in substantial Treasury buying in a pronounced flight to quality.

These crises are well documented in the literature (Collyns & Kincaid, 2003; Daseking, Ghosh, Lane, & Thomas, 2004; Goldstein, Kaminsky, & Reinhart, 2000; Hemming, Kell, & Schimmelpfennig, 2003; Kaminsky, Lizondo, & Reinhart, 1998; Reinhart, 2002; Reinhart & Rogoff, 2009; Rosenberg et al., 2005). In all these cases, the authorities maintained a regime of pegged or quasi-pegged exchange rates with limited flexibility, with growing macroeconomic imbalances resulting in the progressive depletion of foreign exchange reserves. The absence of exchange rate flexibility made the countries highly vulnerable to changes in investor sentiment, and when massive government intervention failed to prop up their currencies, a substantial devaluation became increasingly inevitable. This step was usually followed by the adoption of a new, more flexible exchange rate regime. Virtually all exchange rate crises were accompanied by steep output losses, a sharp rise in bankruptcies and a large decline in corporate profits. In this environment, the performance of private equity funds deteriorated substantially. For instance, the majority of Latin American private equity funds, which were raised between 1996 and 1998 and for which PREQIN reports return data, showed negative IRRs, failing to return the invested capital to their LPs.

Given the huge macroeconomic and social costs and the massive losses for investors, the recent currency crises have encouraged researchers to develop early warning system (EWS) models (Berg, Borenstein, & Patillo, 2004; Berg & Patillo 1999; Kaminsky et al., 1998). The number of these models has grown significantly in recent years. Today, EWS approaches are widely used as a part of investors' efforts to anticipate crises and of governments' and international organizations' efforts to prevent them. The different models have in common that they attempt to determine empirically the relationship between past crises and a range of explanatory factors, including country fundamentals, developments in the global economy, and political risks. In selecting potentially predictive variables, researchers are usually inspired by theories of balance of payments crises. Constrained by the availability of data, in the end, the models reflect what works best in fitting the data. Given the empirical relationship, the EWS models then predict the probability of future crises using the latest values of the explanatory variables.

Individual EWS models differ substantially in terms of (i) how they define a currency crisis; (ii) the time horizon they take; (iii) the statistical method they apply; and (iv) the variables they use. How successful have EWS models been in predicting sudden and large changes in the exchange rate? As Berg et al. (2004) find, the out-of-sample predictive power of the various models has been quite mixed. Short-horizon models have generally performed poorly, despite their excellent in-sample performance. In fact, their predictions have proved to be largely uninformative in the sense that the probability of a crisis was about the same whether the forecast probability was above a cutoff threshold or not.[6] This should not bother us too much, however, as the

---

[6]EWS models may fail in two ways—they may miss a crisis or they may signal a crisis that fails to materialize. The threshold probability for an alarm can be chosen to minimize a weighted sum of the share of missed crises and false alarms. In examining the goodness-of-fit of the models over the out-of-sample period, Berg et al. (2004) place equal weight on the share of crises that are missed and the share of alarms that are false. Thus determined, the threshold probability is then related to the actual probability of a crisis.

models' applicability in a private equity context would be extremely limited anyway. Taking a perspective of just 1 to 3 months, these models have been developed specifically for portfolio investors, hedge funds, and proprietary trading desks of financial institutions.

The long-horizon models, which take a perspective of 2 years, are found to perform comparatively better. For the Kaminsky et al. (1998) model, the out-of-sample forecasts proved to be statistically significant predictors of the crisis. Not only that, the model also outperformed alternative forecasts by agency ratings and currency crisis risk scores published by analysts as well as risk perceptions of market participants embodied in bond spreads. According to the Kaminsky et al. model, the variables with the best predictive power of currency crashes are the real exchange rate (deviations from trend), the ratio of the current account to GDP, export growth, and broad money to international reserves.

More recent work, which is reviewed in detail by Reinhart and Rogoff (2009), has focused on the interactions between different types of crises. For instance, banking crises are found to be powerful predictors of currency crises. Similarly, debt crises are often associated with currency crises (although the opposite is not true), which makes it useful to look at "rules of thumb" for sovereign debt crises, such as a country's total level of external debt or its short-term debt relative to its international reserves (Manasse & Roubini, 2005). However, notwithstanding the progress that has been made with EWS models, there remain important limits. None of the approaches that exist today is able to pinpoint the exact date on which a crash occurs. Nor do they provide a clear indication of the severity of an imminent crisis. Instead their usefulness lies in providing a framework that helps investors and other economic agents determine whether a country shows certain symptoms before a severe financial illness develops. Although this would be no small achievement, Reinhart and Rogoff (2009, p. 281) warn that "(t)he greatest barrier to success is the well-entrenched tendency of policy makers and market participants to treat the signals as irrelevant archaic residuals of an outdated framework, assuming that old rules of valuation no longer apply."

10.6   Should limited partners hedge their exchange rate risk?

An unhedged international equity investment corresponds to a long position in foreign currency equal to the equity holding. A fully hedged position corresponds to a net zero position in foreign currency—implying that currency hedging is similar to short selling. If currencies and equities are uncorrelated, full hedging is optimal since it substantially reduces risk without lowering returns (Solnik, 1974a, 1974b). Examining the performance of equities in Canada, Germany, France, Japan, Switzerland, and the United Kingdom from 1975 to 1988, Thomas (1990) compares hedged and unhedged results for a USD investor. He finds that the compounded annual returns were nearly identical—16.5 versus 16.4 percent. These results are largely consistent with those obtained by Jorion (1993) who calculates hedged and unhedged returns for an investment in the MSCI EAFE (Europe, Australia, and Far East). For the period from 1978 to 1988, he obtains average annual returns on unhedged and hedged foreign equities of 22.9 and 20.9 percent, respectively.

The apparent logic for hedging has been widely embraced by practitioners. While equity investors see themselves as being literate in terms of reading a company's balance sheet, few pretend to be able to read a country's balance sheet and understand currency valuations. Since the currency aspect of international investment entails substantial risk, which provides no additional average reward, hedging is often considered as a free lunch (Perold & Schulman, 1988). Not quite free, of course, since hedging involves costs. However, even if one takes into account typically hedge costs of, say, 3 percent per year, the substantial reduction in volatility makes hedging highly attractive.

Empirical studies on hedging strategies in international portfolios have generally focused on the short term using monthly and, in some cases, quarterly returns. Does hedging make similar sense for long-term investors as in private equity with a perspective of several years? Here, the evidence is less clear. Froot (1993) argues that currency hedges have very different properties at long horizons compared with short horizons. In fact, he finds that at long horizons fully hedged international investments actually have greater return variance than their unhedged counterparts.

Why? Consider an acquisition in the euro area by a US private equity firm. Suppose the euro depreciates in the short term due to unanticipated disturbances, resulting in a currency-induced loss in the value of the investment for the US-based investor. This risk could have been eliminated by selling short the euro. With the domestic price level remaining unaffected in the short term, the nominal depreciation of the euro means that the currency depreciates also in real terms.[7] However, if PPP holds in the long term, the price level in the euro area has to increase relative to the United States, resulting in a real appreciation of the euro. To the extent that the value of the investment is linked to the domestic price level, the price effect should compensate the currency effect in the long term. In other worlds, at long horizons, the investment is "naturally hedged," and currency hedging does little to reduce long-term return volatility.

In examining the horizon effect in currency hedging, Froot (1993) uses data for the US and UK markets. He interprets his empirical findings as suggesting that "… while complete hedging is the best strategy for investors who care primarily about short-term moments, no hedging at all is likely to be best for those who care primarily about long-horizon moments. The case for 'going naked' becomes even stronger if one considers the transactions costs and counterparty risks that hedging inevitably adds (p. 4)." As Froot argues further, "going naked" may become fashionable even in the short term: as markets continue to become more integrated and high-frequency currency fluctuations and local-currency returns become more highly correlated, then even the free lunch case for hedging could disappear (Froot, 1993, p. 24).

---

[7]The real exchange rate is defined as $Q = P^d/(P^f \times S)$ where P^d is the domestic price level, P^f the foreign price level, and S the nominal exchange rate. In empirical studies, this definition is usually expressed in log terms: $q_t = s_t - p_t^d + p_t^f$.

Although financial markets have become considerably more integrated since Froot's analysis, there is little evidence that the benefits of hedging in international portfolios have diminished. As a matter of fact, Campbell, Serfaty-de Medeiros, and Viceira (2010) who study seven major developed market currencies (USD, JPY, EUR, SFR, GBP, CanD, and AUD) are unable to detect any horizon effect. In contrast to Froot who finds that risk-minimizing foreign currency positions increase with the investment horizon, their results are robust to variation in the investment horizon between 1 month and 1 year. But even in the longer term, Froot's results raise a number of important questions. How can we reconcile his conclusions with our earlier observation that (relative) PPP does not hold even over periods of many years? And how can we explain that returns from cross-border private equity investments have been substantially affected by exchange rate movements, which seem to contradict Froot's findings?

If a natural hedge in private equity is less than perfect, the question arises whether investors have any instruments to hedge currency risk over longer horizons. This question may be less relevant for LPs with globally diversified portfolios where hedge ratios would need to be determined according to their effects on the entire portfolio rather than individual asset classes. However, it may be of considerable relevance for investors who are exclusively or largely exposed to private equity, such as funds of funds. Those investors may have at their disposal a broad range of hedging instruments and strategies, which have been developed in response to increased cross-border investments (Sercu, 2009; Solnik & McLeavey, 2009).

- *Forward contracts* allow economic agents to buy and sell foreign currency to be delivered at a specific date in the future for a price they already know today. Forward markets are over-the-counter (OTC) markets, with banks acting as market makers. Each forward contract is unique in terms of size, and the expiry date can be chosen freely. Contracts for up to a year are most common. Although for some currencies banks quote rates up to 10 years forward, these markets have remained very thin.
- *Futures markets* are organized markets where contracts are transferable among investors. Contracts are standardized in terms of their size and their expiration dates. The seller agrees to deliver a known amount of units of Currency A on a known future date. This amount is paid by the buyer in Currency B during the life of the contract via daily marked-to-market payments, with the remainder due at maturity. If prices go down, the buyer pays the seller, and vice versa. Daily payments occur through accounts the two parties hold with their brokers. The settlement price, which serves to determine the daily marked-to-market cash flows, is generally equal to the day's close price. On the last trading day, which is 2 working days before delivery, the futures price is equal to the contemporaneous spot price. In other words, following all intermediate cash flows between the buyer and the seller over the life span of the futures contract, the buyer holds a spot contract.
- *Currency swaps* are contracts to exchange streams of fixed cash flows denominated in two different currencies. For example, such streams may arise from interest payments on loans. Currency swaps differ from forward contracts in that there is not only an exchange of the agreed amount at the end of the contract period but also an exchange of interim interest rate payments at regular dates. Since in most cases the purpose of the swap is to transform a loan into a different currency, a spot deal is generally added. Currency swaps may be combined with interest rate swaps (floating vs. fixed rate), which are known as cross-currency swaps.

Banks quote swap rates for so-called plain-vanilla swaps, which are largely standardized. However, many swaps are customized products, reflecting specific characteristics of the parties' existing liabilities or assets.

- *Currency options* fundamentally differ from the three preceding instruments, whose payoffs are linear in the future spot rate in the sense that gains and losses are proportional to currency movements. Instead, the buyer of an option has the right, but not the obligation, to buy an asset at a specified price on or before a specified date from the seller of the option (call option) or to sell an asset to him (put option). Payoffs are nonlinear: If the asset price moves in the wrong direction, the option becomes worthless and the buyer will let it expire. Conversely, if the asset price moves in the right direction, the buyer makes potentially huge profits. Options may be traded, with the options market organized in a similar fashion as the futures market based on standardized contract sizes and expiration dates.

Are any of these instruments suitable for an investor in private equity funds whose cash flows are subject to currency risk? The fundamental problem with private equity investments is that cash flows are uncertain, both in terms of their timing and their size.[8] An LP makes a capital commitment of an agreed amount, but he does not know when the GP draws down the capital, nor does he know how large the individual drawdowns are. Similarly, the fund distributions are unknown. Cash flows from private equity funds to the LP may occur only in the distant future, usually several years. These characteristics render traditional currency hedging strategies more or less useless. It is only by accident that standardized contract sizes and expiration dates match the cash flow pattern of individual private equity funds. While hedging instruments can in principle be customized, this makes sense only if cash flows are predictable with a reasonable degree of confidence. Take currency options, for example, which provide the relatively greatest degree of flexibility in the sense that the buyer is not required to exercise his option. Nevertheless, the quantity risk makes options unsuited for hedging an LP's currency risk. The value of the option is contingent on the exchange rate, whereas the amount of the foreign cash flow is contingent on a different event, which the option's value has nothing to do with.[9]

Conceivably, the potential for managing currency risk might be somewhat greater in the context of an already established portfolio of foreign-currency-denominated private equity funds. First, cash outflows in foreign currency due to drawdowns may at least be partly offset by cash inflows in the same currency, with the mitigating impact being the greater the better the amount and the dates of the cash flows match. Second, although cash flows in individual funds occur at discrete and unpredictable points in time, at the portfolio level cash flows may exhibit a more continuous pattern. In portfolios with a significant share of foreign-currency-denominated funds, this may improve the scope for using different hedging strategies. However, any currency

---

[8]Our arguments are largely applicable to the secondary market as well. To the extent that an investor acquires in the secondary market the funded commitments from another LP, currency risk is limited to future distributions, as opposed to capital drawdowns. Furthermore, the investment horizon is considerably shortened to just a few years. Fundamentally, however, investors face the same challenge, which lies in the unpredictability of the timing and the amount of the cash (in)flows.

[9]Needless to say, the same applies to investors with exposure to foreign public equities (Sercu, 2009, p.283).

hedging in private equity will remain imperfect, and the probably limited benefits for the LP have to be considered in light of the nontrivial costs of such strategies. This may explain why currency hedging has remained largely unknown in private equity— even among LPs whose AUM are exclusively or largely held in this particular asset class.

10.7 Summary and conclusions

In this chapter, we have discussed currency risk investors in private equity funds face at different stages of the investment process. Currency risk in private equity is material, which becomes clear when we examine the impact of currency movements on fund returns. Depending on the perspective we take, changes in the exchange rate have on average increased or reduced private equity fund returns by a few hundred basis points. Similarly, cross-border investments made by individual funds have been subject to currency risk. Although some deals have benefited from favorable exchange rate changes, others have suffered from adverse movements.

As we have discussed further, exchange rate changes are largely unpredictable. Frustratingly, exchange rates are nonstationary and may deviate from PPP for prolonged periods. Forward rates are very poor predictors of future spot rates, and to make things worse, the specific investment characteristics of private equity strictly limits the potential for hedging currency risk through traditional strategies. However, these rather dismal observations should not lead us to abandon international investing. In fact, as markets become more and more integrated, it will become increasingly difficult to avoid foreign currency exposure. Instead, investors should embrace currency risk, in the same way as they face other investment risks. Importantly, this entails incorporating foreign exchange risk in the due diligence process and benchmarking approaches investors employ. Making foreign exchange risk transparent helps improve investment decisions and should therefore be considered as an important part of risk management.

Part Three

What's Next?

11 What's next? Private equity in the era of deleveraging

Chapter Outline

In Parts I and II, we have discussed investment strategies in private equity. Such strategies have changed considerably over time, as private equity has progressed from a small cottage industry to an increasingly global trillion-dollar industry in just a few decades. During this transition, private equity has gone through several boom-bust cycles, and as we go to press, one of the deepest downturns in private equity's still relatively short history appears to have just bottomed out. Following a massive contraction in economic activity, industrialized countries have returned to positive economic growth. Earnings expectations have improved as a result, and although asset prices remain subject to considerable volatility, risk appetite has recovered appreciably from extreme levels of aversion following the collapse of Lehman Brothers in the fall of 2008. In this environment, M&A activity has picked up again, with financial sponsor-led acquisitions contributing to this increase. In the first 9 months of 2010, the volume of announced LBO transactions totaled US$ 145 billion, a more than doubling from the previous year (on an annualized basis) to a level comparable with 2003.

However, huge uncertainties remain, which are related to the required deleveraging in most advanced economies. While substantial progress has already been made in financial sector deleveraging, total debt to GDP has fallen only slightly, and only in a few countries. As a recent study by McKinsey (2010) has pointed out, an important reason for the small overall deleveraging to date has been the increase in government

International Investments in Private Equity. DOI: 10.1016/B978-0-12-375082-2.10011-4

debt, which has offset declines in financial sector and household sector debt. In the past, deleveraging episodes have typically lasted 6 to 7 years, and if history is a guide, the ongoing process of debt reduction is likely to exert a significant drag on GDP growth.

The recent sovereign debt woes in the euro area and elsewhere have reminded policy makers and market participants that fiscal support for global growth is strictly time limited. As the process of deleveraging continues, there are considerable risks of economic and financial market shocks. Against this background, we ask in this chapter what the future may hold for private equity investors over the next few years. What interests us especially are the following questions: is the precrisis growth trajectory of private equity still intact, with the recent collapse in fund-raising and investing representing a typical, if particularly deep, cyclical correction around this trend? Or should we expect a "new normal" in private equity, consistent with the new normal view some investors (Gross, 2009) have proposed for the US and European economies? And to what extent will the recovery bring about structural changes in the private equity industry?

Our discussion concentrates on leveraged buyouts, the largest segment of the global private equity market. Buyouts are highly susceptible to changes in debt market conditions and while busts are usually caused by rising risk premiums in response to mounting default risk, past recoveries in the buyout market have always occurred on the back of improved conditions in the leveraged loan and high-yield bond markets (Axelson, Jenkinson, Strömberg, & Weisbach, 2007). Little suggests that this time is different. Therefore, our analysis starts by asking: what are the prospects for a sustained recovery in leveraged finance?

11.1   Global deleveraging and the future of leveraged finance

There are two basic sources of debt financing in buyouts—leveraged loans and high-yield bonds. These two forms differ in a number of important aspects. Leveraged loans are sold through a process of syndication to an institutional investor base. Loan contracts typically include covenants and provide for circumstances under which creditors can intervene and impose management changes if management fails to deliver on an agreed plan for the company (International Monetary Fund, 2007). By contrast, bondholders generally only have a say in the management of the company if it has defaulted. Since bondholders are usually numerous, they often face a collective action problem that makes it difficult to intervene effectively. Finally, there is a much more active secondary market for bonds than for leveraged loans.

In the past cycle, leveraged loans accounted for more than two thirds of the debt financing of buyout transactions, a considerably higher ratio than in previous buyout booms. To a significant degree, the dominance of leveraged loans as the preferred source of debt financing is explained by the rapid expansion of the collateralized loan obligation (CLO) market, which considerably broadened the investor base for leveraged loans.[1] In fact, at the peak of the cycle, more than three-quarters of leveraged loan issuance was held by institutional investors, eclipsing banks by a wide margin (International Monetary Fund, 2007).

However, the CLO market has remained essentially shut since the peak of the financial crisis in 2008. While doubts about the riskiness of CLOs have driven away buyers of new CLOs, liquidity pressures and regulatory constraints have affected reinvestments of existing CLOs. Thus, although the demand for leveraged loans has increased recently, the recovery has been relatively subdued. Inflows to high-yield funds and credit funds have risen appreciably, but neither institutional investors, such as pension funds and insurance companies, nor banks have been able to fully pick up the slack left by the CLOs.

By contrast, high-yield bonds have enjoyed strong demand since the middle of 2009. In the first 9 months of 2010, global high-yield bond issuance totaled US$ 172 billion, a 72 percent increase compared with the same period in the previous year. This growth has been driven to a considerable extent by the issuance of senior-secured high yield bonds, which have attracted in particular pension funds, mutual funds and other institutional investors seeking greater security while searching for higher yield in an environment of extremely low interest rates. Helping broaden the investor base of high-yield bonds, the share of senior-secured high yields rose to 40 percent in the first three quarters of 2010, much higher than the historical average of just 7 percent. As the demand for high-yield bonds has picked up, spreads have narrowed progressively, although at the time of writing they were still higher than prior to the crisis. In Europe, whose high-yield bond market has remained substantially smaller than in the US, high-yield bond issuance has also picked up appreciably, exceeding the volume investors had absorbed at the peak of the last buyout boom in 2006 – 2007.

While the improved availability of credit, especially in the high-yield bond market, has supported a moderate increase in buyout activity, it is important to note that more than half of the recent borrowing by private equity firms has been used to refinance existing debts of portfolio companies, helping keep defaults relatively low.[2] According to Thomas (2010) only 183 U.S. portfolio companies defaulted in 2008 – 2009 out of a sample of 3,269 companies substantially backed by private equity firms.[3] This implies a cumulative default rate of 5.6 percent or an annual default rate

---

[1]A collateralized debt obligation is a structured credit security backed by the performance of a portfolio of loans. Securitized interests in the portfolio's performance are divided into tranches with differing repayment and interest earning streams. In the event of nonpayment or default, the higher-risk tranche absorbs the first loss from anywhere in the portfolio, up to a limit. After this tranche has been exhausted, the next least-secured tranche then absorbs the additional principal loss, and so on (International Monetary Fund, 2007, p. 129).

[2]Other factors are a relatively high ratio of EBITDA to interest payments thanks to highly liquid debt markets in the last cycle; the prevalence of covenant-lite structures and PIK toggle notes at the peak of the boom; and the repurchase of debt at steep discounts in the secondary market.

[3]The 3,269 companies in the sample were acquired by private equity firms between 2000 and 2009, with the bulk having been purchased during the boom period from 2004 to 2007.

of 2.84 percent.[4] However, refinancing needs of portfolio companies remain high over the next few years, reflecting the huge volume of debt capital raised to fuel the last buyout boom. The wall of debt repayments coming due until 2014 still pose substantial challenges. As of the middle of 2010, leveraged loan repayments in the United States falling due until 2017 total US$ 470 billion, of which more than 75 percent will be due by 2014 (Fig. 11.1).

Given the substantial refinancing needs of portfolio companies over the medium term, a key question facing private equity investors is the following: Will there be sufficient demand in the high-yield bond and leveraged loan markets to continue to fuel a sustained recovery in new LBO transactions, and will banks be able to intermediate a rising amount of issuance of debt instruments?

Any attempt to find an answer to this question is necessarily fraught with a high degree of speculation, especially in light of the extraordinary degree of uncertainty facing the global economy. Nevertheless, several factors caution against simply extrapolating the recent recovery in leveraged finance.

As far as the high-yield bond market is concerned, it is important to note that spreads have already narrowed substantially and, at the time of writing, are relatively close to their long-term average. Therefore, the pace of fund flows into high-yield bonds is likely to slow as the sharp decline in spreads has eroded the return potential of this asset class. At the same time, there is a non-trivial risk that spreads could widen again in response to heightened risk aversion, for example, triggered by rising

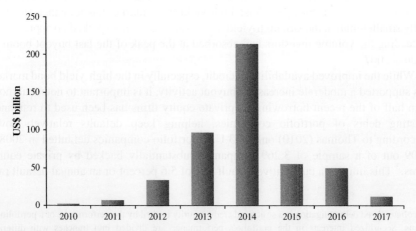

Figure 11.1 Leveraged loans: distribution by year of maturity (as of mid-2010).
Source: S&P 500.

[4]Kaplan and Strömberg (2009) find that 6 percent of the portfolio companies acquired during the first buyout boom between 1985 and 1989 went bankrupt. Their finding is based on the Capital IQ database. However, as the authors (p. 129) emphasize "(o)ne caveat is that not all cases of distress may be recorded in publicly available data sources; some of these cases may be "hidden" in the relatively larger fraction of "unknown" exits." In fact, Andrade and Kaplan (1998) find that 23 percent of the larger public-to-private transactions of the 1980s defaulted at some point.

defaults as the market approaches the maturity cliff or by renewed concerns about sovereign debt levels in the European periphery and elsewhere. Furthermore, there is considerable uncertainty about future benchmark yields. While aggressive monetary policies and the perceived risk of deflation in a possible double-dip recession have pushed 10-year government bond yields in the US and in core Europe to extremely low levels, the financing of huge budget deficits is expected to put considerable strain on the global capital markets. To the extent that benchmark bond yields increase as governments issue increased amounts of debt, other things being equal, borrowing costs for leveraged buyouts will increase.

Turning to the leveraged loan market, future CLO issuance is expected to be muted until the dormant market for arbitrage CLOs recovers (Bain & Company, 2010). However, at this stage there are few signs for this. According to S&P (2010), only 3 new arbitrage CLOs were issued in the US in the first 9 months of 2010, compared with 110 in 2006 and 98 in 2007. As far as existing CLOs are concerned, it is expected that only around 10 percent to 50 percent of the theoretical maximum will be available for reinvestment (Loan Syndication and Trading Association, quoted in Bain & Company, 2010, p. 28). Thus, a sustained increase in the demand for leveraged loans will be predicated on a profound shift in the market's investor base. High-yield funds and other relative value players as well as insurance companies have shown increased appetite thanks to attractive spreads in a low-return environment. Compared with high-yield bonds, leveraged loans are less susceptible to increases in benchmark rates, as interest rates are usually adjustable. However, whether these institutional investors will be able to offset the reduced demand by CLOs in the medium to longer term remains an open question.

This leads us to discuss the role of banks in the recovery process. Their role as providers of leveraged loans has diminished substantially over the past decade as institutional investors have absorbed a rapidly rising market share. In the US, banks accounted for only around 15 percent of the demand for leveraged loans in the first half of 2010, down from around 50 percent in 2000. Although European banks have retained a considerably higher market share than their US counterparts, their share shows a similar downward trend.

While little suggests that this trend will be reversed, there are important factors that may limit the role of banks as intermediaries in the leveraged loan market. To begin with, the global banking system still has to deal with the legacy of the recent economic and financial crisis. In its Global Financial Stability Review published in April 2010, the IMF (2010a) estimated the global bank writedowns in 2007 – 2010 at close to US$ 2.3 trillion, implying a loss rate of 4.1 percent (Table 11-1). Of this amount, U.S. banks were expected to write down almost US$ 900 billion on their loan and securities portfolios, with particularly high loss rates on consumer loans and mortgage securities. While the IMF estimated comparatively lower loss rates for the European banks, in absolute terms their required writedowns were expected to be higher than for U.S. banks. Asian banks, by contrast, are found to be less exposed, with an expected loss rate of 1.5 percent on a portfolio of nearly US$ 7.9 trillion.

To be sure, a significant part of the expected writedowns has already been realized or provisioned for. By the middle of 2010, U.S. banks had already written down, or

Table 11.1 Estimates of global bank write downs, 2007–2010

	Estimated holdings (US$ billion)	Estimated write downs (US$ billion)	Implied cumulative loss rate (%)
US banks			
Total	**12,561**	**885**	**7.0**
Loans	**8,059**	**588**	**7.3**
Mortgage	4,095	291	7.1
Corporate	1,104	65	5.9
Consumer	1,115	180	16.2
Foreign[a]	1,745	53	3.0
Securities	**4,502**	**296**	**6.6**
Mortgage	1,691	214	12.7
Corporate	1,115	17	1.5
Consumer	142	0.0	0.0
Governments	580	0.0	0.0
Foreign[a]	975	66	6.7
UK banks			
Total	**8,369**	**455**	**5.4**
Loans	**6,744**	**398**	**5.9**
Mortgage	1,980	68	3.4
Corporate	1,828	63	3.4
Consumer	423	64	14.0
Foreign[a]	2,514	203	8.1
Securities	**1,625**	**57**	**3.5**
Mortgage	276	19	6.9
Corporate	258	7	2.7
Consumer	58	2	2.8
Governments	360	0	0
Foreign[a]	672	29	4.4
Euro area banks			
Total	**22,901**	**665**	**2.9**
Loans	**15,994**	**442**	**2.8**
Mortgage	5,802	81	1.4
Corporate	5,018	79	1.6
Consumer	675	25	3.8
Foreign[a]	4,500	256	5.7
Securities	**6,907**	**224**	**3.2**
Mortgage	1,230	144	11.7
Corporate	1,316	0	0.0
Consumer	271	8	2.8
Governments	2,146	0	0.0
Foreign[a]	1,943	72	3.7
Other mature europe banks			
Total	**3,970**	**156**	**3.9**
Asian banks			
Total	**7,879**	**115**	**1.5**
Total global	**55,680**	**2,276**	**4.1**

[a]Foreign exposures of regional banking systems are based on BIS data on foreign claims. The same country proportions are assumed.
Source: International Monetary Fund (2010a)

made loss provisions for, US$ 709 billion. In Europe, where the total writedowns are expected to be larger, adjustments banks had already made to their balance sheets totaled US$ 929 billion by that date. Writedowns and loan loss provisions, which have already been realized, have to a considerable degree been offset by capital raisings, and thanks to improved earnings aggregate capital ratios have increased substantially.

Notwithstanding this progress, however, considerable further writedowns are expected. According to slightly revised figures published by the IMF (2010b) in its fall edition of the Global Financial Stability Report, these writedowns are estimated at about US$ 550 billion worldwide. The bulk of the remaining burden is expected to fall onto the European banks, which are projected to write down the value of the loans and securities in their portfolios by another US$ 287 billion. More than half of this amount is due to banks in the euro area, with banks in the United Kingdom and other non-euro area countries accounting for the remainder.

Actual writedowns could turn out to be lower, but they could also be higher. Note, for example, that the IMF projections (table 11.1) assume that there will be no need for banks to write down the value of their holdings of government bonds. However, in the spring of 2010 S&P and Moody's downgraded sovereign debt in the peripheral countries of the euro area by several notches. These downgrades were particularly severe in the case of Greece whose credit quality was lowered to junk status. At the same time, credit default swaps priced in a non-trivial default probability, despite a substantial rescue package of almost US$ 1 trillion put together by the European Union and the IMF. Should this package fail to prevent a debt restructuring, especially euro area banks would face additional writedowns on top of what is already estimated as a result of the Great Recession. In this downside scenario, a general rise in risk aversion would be likely to cause correlations to increase, resulting in further portfolio losses.

This risk has been priced into the cost of credit default protection for financial institutions. In fact, banking sector credit default swap spreads more than doubled in the recent European sovereign debt crisis. The increase in spreads was particularly pronounced for banks in the euro area, which are especially exposed to sovereign risks and face relatively greater pressure from wholesale funding strains. While the cost of credit default protection for financial institutions moderated somewhat in response to the EU/IMF rescue package, as we go to press it was still substantially higher than at the beginning of 2010.

Another risk factor are the substantial refunding needs that banks face over the next few years. Between the middle of 2010 and the middle of 2012, over US$ 4 trillion is due to be refinanced (IMF, 2010b), and by 2015 a total amount of nearly US $ 6 trillion will be due to mature. In addition, banks will have to refinance securities they structured and pledged as collateral at various central bank facilities that are expiring. In refinancing their debt that is coming due in the near- to medium-term, banks will operate under debt market conditions, which will be influenced by heavy government issuance.

While until now deleveraging has been driven primarily from the asset side, going forward new regulations look set to shift pressures to the liability side of bank balance sheets. Although the original draft of the Basel III framework was amended to reflect concerns that new and high capital requirements could hurt the recovery in economic activity, the general thrust of the proposed reform has remained intact. More specifically, in mid-September 2010 the Group of Governors and Heads of Supervision, the oversight body of the Basel Committee on Banking Supervision, announced agreement on the calibration and phase-in of new capital standards proposed by the Basel Committee. The capital standards and new capital buffers will require banks to hold more capital, predominantly in the form of common equity, than under current rules. The minimum Tier 1 common equity ratio (Tier 1 common equity to total risk-weighted assets) will be increased by Basel III from 2 to 4.5 percent.[5] In addition, Basel III introduces a new, additional capital conservation buffer to be used to absorb losses in periods of financial and economic stress. This buffer requires banks to maintain an additional 2.5 percent ratio of Tier 1 common equity, effectively implying that banks will have to have common equity equal to at least 7 percent of their risk-weighted assets. Moreover, the minimum Tier 1 capital ratio will be increased from 4 to 6 percent.[6] While the minimum total capital ratio – the sum of Tier 1 and Tier 2 capital ratios to risk-weighted assets – has remained unchanged at 8 percent, the addition of a capital conservation buffer increases the total amount of capital a bank must hold to 10.5 percent, of which 8.5 percent must be Tier 1 capital.

Whether retained earnings alone will lift banks to the new capital standards appears questionable. While banks have been greatly aided by high margins and the steepness of the yield curve in repairing their balance sheets, these factors are expected to peter out over the medium term as policy rates and liquidity conditions normalize and competition in the banking sector intensifies.

Furthermore, new regulations have been put in place with regard to securitizations and re-securitizations. Securitization is a process that involves repackaging portfolios of cash-flow-producing financial instruments into securities for transfer to third parties (Jobst, 2008). Re-securitization is defined as a "securitization exposure in which the risk associated with an underlying pool of exposures is tranched and at least one of the underlying exposures is a securitization exposure" (Basel Committee on Banking Supervision, 2009). In the last credit boom, securitization and re-securitization played a decisive role, as it allowed banks to actively manage their credit, funding and liquidity risk and leverage up their lending activity, since they were no longer required to keep the credit risk on their books. Risk weights for re-securitization exposures have been significantly raised for both the standardized approach and the internal-ratings based approach within the Basel framework for bank supervision. Under the standardized approach, re-securitizations now have a risk weight of 40 percent for the highest ratings (AAA to AA-), twice as high as for securitizations. As a result, many of the structured financial products prevalent in the credit boom have become substantially more expensive for banks to hold on their balance sheets in terms of regulatory capital.

---

[5]The ratio will be set at 3.5 percent as of January 1, 2013, 4 percent as of January 1, 2014, and 4.5 percent as of January 1, 2015 and will be calculated after applying certain regulatory adjustments, which will be phased in between January 1, 2014 and January 1, 2018.
[6]The ratio will be set at 4.5 percent as of January 1, 2013, 5.5 percent as of January 1, 2014, and 6 percent as of January 1, 2015.

Moreover, a bank may no longer recognize external credit ratings when those ratings are based on guarantees or support provided by the bank itself. For example, if a bank has purchased asset-backed commercial paper from a liquidity facility that it itself supports (and on whose support its rating depends), then the bank must treat that paper as if it were not rated. Similarly, a bank's capital requirement for exposures to structured financial products held in the trading book can be no less than the amount required under the banking book treatment. All these measures mean a tightening in capital charges, which requires holding more capital against securitizations, increasing banks' costs and reducing the attractiveness of holding securitized products.

At the same time, the U.S. Financial Accounting Standards Board (FASB) and the International Accounting Standards Board (IASB) have proposed new accounting standards requiring improved disclosure of off-balance-sheet entities and tightening requirements for moving assets off balance sheet. Moreover, the European and U.S. authorities have proposed to amend securitization-related regulations to incentivize issuers to retain an economic interest in the securitization products they issue. While the EU Parliament has already amended the Capital Requirements Directive to provide incentives for securitizers to retain at least 5 percent of the nominal value of originations, the U.S. government has called for similar risk retention requirements for US securitizers. Generally, incentives to retain skin in the game seem to be higher in more sophisticated areas of the market, such as CDOs/CLOs, where the decision to retain small, highly customized tranches has become part of hedging strategies. Should the retention scheme result in securitized loans remaining on balance sheet, there could be material effects, as the resultant increase in regulatory capital could deter securitization and make it more costly.

Finally, the recent financial crisis has reinforced calls for regulation of the credit rating agencies. Since the abolition of self-regulation in 2006, the U.S. SEC has limited oversight authorities over the credit rating agencies, which are required to publish a description of their rating methodologies and procedures, plus certain rating performance analytics. According to recent reform proposals, issuers will have to share with the other nationally recognized credit rating agencies all information they provide to any nationally recognized credit rating agency with respect to structured credit product ratings. Furthermore, it has been proposed to force credit rating agencies to rate structured credit products on differentiated rating scales. The proposed legislation also would require credit rating agencies to disclose preliminary ratings to reduce "rating shopping" whereby an issuer solicits ratings from multiple credit rating agencies but only pays for and discloses the highest rating. In Europe, where credit rating agencies are now required to register with and be supervised by the national authorities, reform proposals call for the disclosure of rating methodologies, procedures, and assumptions, as well as information about potential conflicts of interest, including compensation policies. Some proposals go even further and call for the abolishment of the major rating agencies' issuer-pay revenue model as a way of eliminating potential incentive conflicts.[7]

---

[7]However, as the IMF (2009) cautions, investor-pay revenue models are not immune to their own incentive issues, as many investors are incentivized by their overseers to seek out high-yielding, highly rated securities.

In summary, while the high-yield and leveraged loan markets are anticipated to continue to recover over the next few years, there are several reasons to expect credit growth to be more subdued than before the last boom. Risks remain firmly tilted to the downside. As the IMF (2010b) has pointed out, funding and capital pressures could reignite deleveraging pressures. For example, should banks find it difficult to secure all of the capital they need in markets, they may be forced to shrink balance sheets by selling assets to nonbanks or allow them to mature. This outlook will have important repercussions for the private equity industry, especially in the mature markets.

11.2   Ten trends shaping the future of private equity

Over the past three to four decades, the private equity industry has transformed itself from a cottage industry to a global asset class. This process has been evolutionary rather than revolutionary, although disruptive, new finance technologies (e.g., the emergence of the junk bond market in the late 1980s and the rapid proliferation of securitization since the late 1990s) and regulatory changes (especially the clarification of the "prudent man" rule by the US Department of Labor in 1979) have proved to be important game changers. David Rubinstein, managing partner and cofounder of the Carlyle Group, identifies four different stages through which the private equity industry had transitioned between the mid-1970s and mid-2007 (Table 11.2).[8] Since then, the private equity industry has entered a new era, which we label "The Great Deleveraging." In this new era, we identify 10 trends, some of which had already started in the *Golden Age* or even before. However, these trends are expected to gain considerable momentum as the global economy continues to deleverage.

11.2.1   *Increased equity contributions in leveraged buyouts*

The most immediate impact of less debt capital is the rise in the share of equity in leveraged buyouts. Between the second half of the1980s and the end of the *Silver Age*, the contribution of equity had already increased from less than 10 percent to around 40 percent, before falling back to around one-third in the Golden Age. Since then, the share of equity has reached more than 50 percent as it has become much harder for private equity firms to obtain leveraged loans and raise debt in the bond markets (Fig. 11.2).

With average purchase prices in buyouts having fallen from their peak in 2006–2007, debt multiples have thus declined significantly. Whereas in 2007 debt accounted in 30 percent of LBOs for at least seven times EBITDA, none of the few transactions in 2009 had debt multiples of six or higher (Table 11.3).

Given the short- to medium-term outlook for the debt capital markets, the share of equity in LBOs looks set to remain relatively high. As leverage declines, returns will likely be lower than otherwise. The deleverage effect on returns may be exacerbated

---

[8]Presentation entitled "The Post-Banana World of Private Equity" given at a conference of the National Bureau of Economic Research on April 5, 2008.

Table 11.2 The evolution of private equity

The Stone Age, 1974–1984	The Bronze Age, 1985–1990	The Silver Age, 1991–2001	The Golden Age, 2001–2007	The Great Deleveraging, 2008–?
An infant industry	More firms	Multibillion dollar funds	Dominant position in financial world	More equity in deals
Small firms	Wider investor base	Global investors and lenders	175 funds ≥ US$ 1 billion	Smaller funds, smaller deals
New technology of debt financing	Debt financing more mainstream	Many new funds	Fortune 500 companies go private	Increased focus on strategic and operational improvements
Small deals	Junk bonds	Public pension funds dominate investor base	Accounts for large percentage of M&A activity (40% in first half of 2007)	Minority positions and PIPEs
Not important to the financial world	Public companies taken private	Overseas investments	International expansion	Redefining GP/LP relationships
	Outsized returns	Talent drain from other financial companies	PE firms become large organizations	Increased coinvestments and direct investments by LPs
	RJR Nabisco		PE firms going public	Emerged markets and globalization
			Public/government scrutiny	CSR as risk management
				Private equity firms as the new merchant banks

Source: First four columns: David Rubenstein (2008); last column added by author.

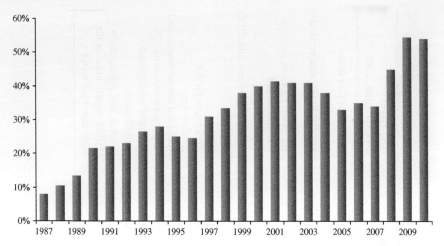

Figure 11.2 Average equity contribution to private equity acquisitions in the United States.   Note: 2010 refers to first half of the year.
Source: S&P LCD

Table 11.3 Debt multiples (Debt/EBITDA) in LBO transactions, 2002—first half 2010 (in %)

	Less than 4.0×	4.0–4.99×	5.0–5.99×	6.0–6.99×	7× or higher
2003	20	44	24	12	0
2004	20	26	45	8	2
2005	15	23	38	21	4
2006	12	19	28	37	4
2007	11	16	14	30	30
2008	31	16	28	9	16
2009	63	13	25	0	0
First half 2010	29	24	41	6	0

Source: S&P LCD

by lower earnings growth as governments and households continue to deleverage, resulting in flatter economic growth. However, to the extent that buyouts are less leveraged, they are also less risky, implying that on a risk-adjusted basis returns may be significantly less affected.

11.2.2   Smaller deals and smaller funds

While the more limited availability of debt capital is expected to affect the capital structures in individual deals, the experience with previous downturns suggests that average deal sizes will remain significantly smaller than during the last buyout boom. Although there exists a substantial capital overhang as a legacy of the huge capital inflows to buyout funds during the last boom, return considerations will be likely to prompt GPs to chase smaller transactions. As a result, the share of middle market deals is expected to rise at the expense of large buyouts. At the same time, the limited availability of debt may also limit the number of transactions, and to the extent that these deals are more carefully selected, this effect could at least partly offset the expected negative impact of reduced leverage.

Smaller and fewer transactions require smaller—and potentially fewer—funds. However, the inflow of capital to private equity funds may be limited not only by demand factors but also by constraints on the supply side. In a world where economic growth will be constrained by sustained deleveraging in the financial, government, and household sectors, investors' AUM look set to grow more slowly. To the extent that private equity allocations remain in the same ballpark in terms of total AUM, in nominal terms commitments to private equity funds will be likely to be more subdued.

11.2.3 Greater emphasis on company strategy and operational improvements

As debt financing remains more difficult to obtain, GPs will continue to put even greater emphasis on operational improvements and strategic initiatives to meet investors' return expectations. As we have discussed in the second chapter, this shift toward operational and strategic measures has already been underway for some time, as financial engineering has increasingly become a commodity and equity contributions have risen from their extremely low levels in the first buyout boom. This trend looks set to gain further momentum in an environment where the potential for value creation through financial engineering remains rather limited.

11.2.4 Growing share of PIPEs and minority deals

At the same time, private equity firms are likely to become more active investors in the PIPE market. In the United States, private placements by public companies to accredited investors made in reliance on Section 4(2) and/or Regulation D. Section 5 of the Securities Act of 1933 raised US\$ 194 billion between 1996 and 2007 (as reported by Dai, 2010). During this period, the number of transactions has more than quadrupled from 306 to 1249.

PIPE issuers are typically small, young, and risky companies, finding it difficult to obtain capital through more traditional means of financing, such as seasoned equity offerings (SEOs) (Brophy, Ouimet, & Sialm, 2009). The bulk of PIPE issuers are not covered by any financial analyst, the firms' stock bid-ask spread tend to be substantially greater than that of SEO issuers, and their operating performance is generally poor (Chen, Dai, & Schatzberg, 2009). PIPE issuances often represent the last resort for the firms with high information asymmetries, poor operating performance, and cash shortages.

Although hedge funds have traditionally been the largest investors in the PIPE market, accounting for around 30 percent of the total amount of capital invested in PIPEs, more recently, private equity firms and venture capitalists have become significantly more active. As long-term value investors, they are attracted by the steep discounts at which they may acquire stakes in a company whose potential for improving its operational performance over time is often substantial. To mitigate the high investment risk that PIPEs are typically subject to, investors usually seek contractional protection against dilution, redemption and investor registration rights and board representation. In 2008, a record year for the PIPE market, the combined share of private equity and venture capital funds increased to 40 percent.

Private equity firms are also becoming less strict in their views about governance engineering. Traditionally, a key pillar of private equity investments has been the acquisition of a controlling stake by the financial sponsor, a guarantee to be able to implement the strategic, operational, and financial measures deemed to be necessary to create value over the medium to longer term. However, as private equity firms are searching for investment opportunities in emerging markets, where companies are often controlled by families who seek growth capital without giving up control, GPs have increasingly accepted minority positions. Although control positions remain the norm outside the emerging markets, GPs have also become more open to consider acquiring minority stakes in the more mature economies. Although shareholder agreements are designed to ensure the alignment of interests between the majority and the minority shareholders, the more limited supply of debt (and equity) capital looks set to continue to de-emphasize the traditional role of governance engineering in private equity even further.

11.2.5 Redefining GP/LP relationships

In the LP community, there is a widely shared view that investors' interests have become increasingly misaligned with those of the GPs. This misalignment is mirrored in the industry's compensation structures, which ensures that around almost two-thirds of a GP's compensation is essentially unrelated to his performance (see Chapter 2). As funds have grown substantially bigger, this misalignment has gained even more importance.

To improve the organization of the relationship between LPs and GPs, the LP community, through its industry association, the Institutional Limited Partners' Association (2009), has made concrete proposals, which focus on three areas, namely (i) alignment of interests; (ii) governance; and (iii) transparency. As far as the *alignment of interests* is concerned, the *ILPA Private Equity Principles* foresee, for example, that

- management fees should be cost based;
- transaction and monitoring fees should accrue to the benefit of the fund;
- GPs should have a substantial equity interest in the fund, with a high percentage in cash as opposed to contributions based on waiving (part of) the management fee;
- fees and carry generated by the GP of a fund should be directed predominantly to the fund managers and expenses related to the success of that fund;
- a "distribution waterfall" should be followed that returns all contributed capital plus the preferred return to the LPs before carry is paid;
- if clawback situations do occur, clawbacks should be fully and timely repaid (gross of taxes); and
- possible changes in tax law that impact members of the GP should not be passed on to the LPs.

As far as improvements in *governance* are concerned, the Principles require, inter alia, that

- investments made by the GP be consistent with the investment strategy that was described when the fund was raised;
- the GP recognize the importance of diversification over time and across industries;
- a supermajority in interest of the LPs have the ability to decide to dissolve the fund or remove the GP without cause;
- a majority in interest of the LPs have the ability to elect to effectuate an early termination or suspension of the investment period without cause;
- a "key-person" or "for cause" event should result in an automatic suspension of the investment period;
- the fund be audited by an independent auditor, focusing on the best interests of the partnership and its limited partners;
- LP Advisory Committee meeting processes and procedures be adopted and standardized across the industry;
- the "gross negligence, fraud, and willful misconduct" indemnification and exculpation standard be the minimum in terms of what is agreed by the LPs.

Finally, with regard to improved *transparency*, the Principles suggest that

- fee and carry calculations be transparent and subject to LP and independent auditor review and certification;
- detailed valuation and financial information related to the portfolio companies be made available on a quarterly basis;
- investors have greater transparency with respect to relevant information pertaining to the GP.

By the middle of 2010, 140 limited partners had endorsed the Principles, among them the largest US and European pension funds, funds-of-funds, and sovereign wealth funds. The prospects for implementing the Principles are widely seen as a function of the state of the fund-raising market. There are now signs that the pendulum between the power of GPs and LPs, which had swung substantially in favor of the former during the last private equity boom, has begun to swing back toward the latter. To the extent that the investment and fund-raising environment remains subdued in the era of deleveraging, the ground should remain fertile for further rebalancing the interests of LPs and GPs.

11.2.6 A greater role for coinvestments and direct investments

One way to achieve a better alignment of interests includes offering coinvestment opportunities to a fund's limited partners. As we have discussed before, relatively few LPs have the capacity and the experience to act as coinvestors, but those who do may find coinvestments an attractive way to increase their net returns. Offering coinvestment opportunities to their LPs allows fund managers to invest in larger deals in a debt capital-constrained environment, which otherwise would be doable only by teaming up with other GPs.

At the same time, some LPs have also been looking to reduce fees and other money management payments by making more direct investments. Canadian pension plans have been leaders in boosting their in-house investment capabilities to directly acquire companies. In fact, pension funds such as the Canadian Pension Plan Investment Board (CPPIB), Ontario Teachers' Pension Plan (Teachers), and Ontario Municipal Employees Retirement System (OMERS) have been active private equity investors since the early 1990s. With deep pools of capital and an ability to hold investments for long periods, they are seen as a new breed of financial investors that compete with established buyout firms. For instance, in March 2010, Teachers agreed to buy Camelot, the British lottery operator, fending off the European buyout house CVC in the final stages of the GBP 389 million deal. More recently, some US and European pension funds have also begun to show an interest in direct deals as a means to reduce fees and improve their net returns. However, their private equity teams tend to be more sparsely staffed, and in order for direct investments by institutional investors to become a broader trend they will first need to establish the institutional and organizational requirements to successfully chase and manage such investments.

11.2.7 Emergent economies in a globalized private equity market

Globalization is set to continue, with mature and emerging markets becoming even more integrated. As regards the latter, several of them are likely to have emerged in the foreseeable future. As they continue to play catch-up and account for a rising share in world GDP (Fig. 11.3), deeper and broader domestic financial markets will allow an indigenous private equity industry to play an increasingly important role in financial intermediation. Soon, the label "emerging markets" will no longer be appropriate. Instead, markets such as Brazil, China, India, Korea, Poland, South Africa, Taiwan (ROC), and potentially some economies in the Middle East may be more accurately classified as emergent.

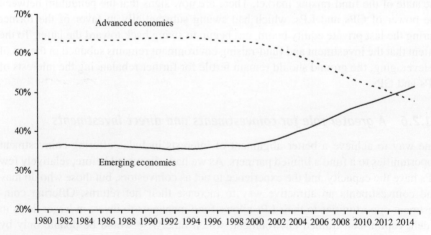

Figure 11.3 Share in world GDP by advanced and emerging economies (2010-2015 IMF projections).
Source: IMF WEO Database.

Importantly, as we have discussed earlier, globalization is a two-way street. While emergent markets are expected to become more deeply penetrated, in part thanks to growing investments from abroad, at the same time institutional investors in these markets are set to become increasingly important net suppliers of global private equity capital. As a result, the traditional investor base in private equity funds is likely to change significantly over the coming years.

11.2.8   Corporate social responsibility (CSR) in private equity investments

Responsible investing that considers environmental, social, and corporate governance (ESG) factors as well as ethical issues in addition to financial performance is increasingly attracting the attention of institutional and private investors. With investors putting greater weight on such criteria, companies are pressured to adhere to higher standards. This trend is set to gather further momentum, as the awareness for sustainability issues continues to increase. Some countries have already introduced mandatory reporting of ESG standards, and additional momentum comes from public initiatives to promote the efficient use of energy and to raise the share of renewables.

In response to heightened demands by large investors, especially large public pension funds, providers of traditional and specialized financial services are expanding the range of products offered to include ESG criteria. Increasingly, this includes private equity investments, with a rising number of investors taking ESG criteria into account when selecting individual funds. Although reliable ESG standards and uniform definitions are still lacking, investors are expected to pay even greater attention to nonfinancial issues as the private equity market is becoming increasingly globalized and integrated, with a rising share of funds being deployed in today's emerging markets. While a great number of LPs has already signed the *UN Principles for Responsible Investment*, the list of GP signatories is also getting considerably longer.

11.2.9   Private equity firms as the new merchant banks

The private equity industry will be likely to see important institutional changes. Some firms have started early to transform themselves from pure private equity players to alternative asset managers and financial services providers. Prime examples are The Blackstone Group and Kohlberg Kravis Roberts & Co (KKR) whose transformations are briefly described in the final chapter of this book. In fact, in 2009, The Blackstone Group was ranked among the top 10 M&A advisors in the US market in terms of transaction values.

Diversification remains a key motive as private equity firms may face important limits to grow in a market whose absorptive capacity is expected to be affected by the restricted supply of debt capital. Diversification is also likely to be an important motive for more private equity firms to go public. Rather than rely entirely on traditional funding sources, they are eager to diversify their fund-raising practices (Gogineni & Megginson, 2010). Furthermore, IPOs are the only way a private equity firm (more specifically, the founders) can realize value. The period from 2004 to 2007 saw a considerable number of IPOs, including that of The Blackstone Group in mid-2007. Although market conditions became increasingly hostile thereafter, KKR's listing on the New York Stock Exchange in July 2010 could be a sign that the precrisis trend has already begun to resume.

As a result, concentration in the private equity market looks set to increase further. At the upper end of the spectrum, globally operating alternative asset managers providing a wide range of financial services are likely to absorb an even larger share of private equity commitments, with their funds being managed by publicly listed management companies. However, whether the market will also become more bifurcated, as some expect, remains to be seen. Although at the lower end of the spectrum there are a significant number of small funds specialized in individual geographies and sectors, there are few signs that the traditional middle market players will be squeezed out. In fact, it is this segment that may benefit most from the private equity trends we have identified in this book.

11.2.10   Tightening regulation

Finally, the private equity is set to become subject to more stringent regulation. As we have discussed throughout this book, some initiatives focus specifically on private equity, whereas others will affect private equity more indirectly. The most important reforms are the following:

- In Europe, the *AIFMD* (see Chapter 9) is without a doubt the most important piece of regulation. Although its final form was still under debate as the manuscript of this book was finalized, the contours of the AIFMD suggest that it has the potential of profoundly altering the landscape for private equity as an asset class.
- In the United States, the Dodd-Frank Wall Street Reform and Consumer Protection Act, which was enacted in July 2010, is widely perceived to be the most sweeping financial sector reform since the 1930s. The Dodd-Frank Act includes concrete measures for the private equity industry. These measures fall in three areas, (i) registration requirements for investment advisors; (ii) limitations for banks as limited partners; and (iii) limitations for banks as general partners. As far as registration requirements are concerned, advisors with AUM of US$ 100 million or more will generally be required to register as investment advisors with the Securities and Exchange Commission (SEC). Advisors with AUM of less than US$ 100 million will be required to register with the state regulator in which they are located.

  Banks will be limited to a 3 percent investment in any private equity fund (or other private funds), and in the aggregate limited to 3 percent of their Tier 1 Capital in all private funds. These limitations apply to banks' own capital, but there are some exceptions for bank-managed funds for bank customers, such as separate accounts and high net worth wealth management clients. The new limitations do not apply immediately; instead, banks will have almost 4 years to comply, with the possibility of further extensions of up to 8 years. Finally, the legislation generally prohibits banks from "sponsoring" a private equity fund or a hedge fund, whereby "sponsoring" is defined to mean serving as a general partner, managing member or trustee. Notwithstanding the general prohibition, the legislation specifies a number of conditions under which a bank-owned firm can serve as a general partner of a fund.

- At the international level, as we have discussed above, *Basel III* will provide an enhanced framework for bank regulation, introducing a new set of requirements for banks' liquidity and capital, potentially affecting credit growth in the future.
- As far as the European insurance industry is concerned, newly proposed risk weights under *Solvency II* will affect the attractiveness of private equity as an asset class for these investors.
- Furthermore, in several countries, the tax treatment of carried interest is being debated, potentially resulting in higher tax payments and lower net returns.

Overall, it is safe to predict that private equity will be operating under substantially greater public scrutiny. Although earlier claims that private equity poses systemic risk have proved to be unfounded—in fact, private equity has been part of the solution to the recent financial crisis—the *Zeitgeist* in the post-Great Recession era calls for a greater role of government. Given the substantial role private equity plays in the broader macroeconomy, private equity is unlikely to escape from this spirit of the time.

11.3   Summary and conclusions

In its transformation from a small cottage industry to a trillion-dollar asset class, private equity has gone through pronounced cycles. These cycles have brought about important structural changes, requiring adjustments in investment strategies. This time is no different. As we go to press, the global financial markets are at a critical juncture, and although massive monetary and fiscal support has prevented a global meltdown in the wake of the collapse of Lehman Brothers, substantial challenges lie ahead. Private equity will be operating in an environment that is characterized by continued deleveraging, a process that is shifting from the financial sector to the household and government sectors.

Buyouts are particularly susceptible to changes in debt capital market conditions. In this chapter, we have identified 10 trends that are likely to shape the industry in the era of continued deleveraging. First of all, given the more restricted access to debt capital, private equity transactions will continue to see comparatively high equity contributions. While, other things being equal, less leverage dampens return expectations, on a risk-adjusted basis returns will be affected only to the extent that lower economic growth reduces earnings growth and limits multiple arbitrage. Second, less leverage means smaller deals, which, in turn, will probably imply smaller funds. Third, as GPs rely less on financial engineering, their focus will shift to an even greater extent to structural and operational improvements in creating value. Fourth, GPs may be more inclined to invest in PIPEs and take minority positions, in a significant departure from the traditional private equity model. Fifth, LPs will be seeking to redefine their relationships with GPs to achieve a better alignment of interest, improve governance, and increase transparency. Sixth, GPs are expected to offer their investors more coinvestment opportunities. While coinvestments allow GPs to target larger deals at a time when equity contributions remain high, LPs find coinvestments an attractive way to reduce fees. At the same time, some LPs may follow the example of large Canadian investors who have pursued direct investments, competing with private equity firms for deals. Seventh, globalization will further deepen, and as some emerging markets become emergent, markets will become even more integrated. This applies to both investments in today's nontraditional markets and fund-raising from investors situated in these economies. Eighth, CSR is expected to gain further momentum, increasingly affecting allocations to alternative asset classes. As more private equity capital is flowing into emerging markets, investors are set to watch even more closely whether their investments are compatible with CSR criteria. Ninth, the private equity industry itself is likely to remain subject to continuous structural change. Larger firms are becoming more and more alternative asset managers who seek public listings to diversify their business model and their funding sources. As a result, the private equity market is likely to become more concentrated. Finally, private equity is set to become subject to more stringent regulation, in part thanks to reforms affecting the industry directly, in part because of reforms targeting other financial intermediaries, especially banks and insurers. Overall, private equity, as a part of the broader financial sector, will be operating in an environment where governments assume a greater role in the post-Great Recession era.

Part Four

Strategic Conversations with General Partners

12 Chasing deals globally: expansion strategies and risk management of leading private equity firms

---

Much of this book has focused on the global proliferation of private equity in increasingly integrated markets, which has brought about new opportunities for portfolio managers. International investing also entails new risks, posing additional challenges to the due diligence work limited partners undertake. At the macroeconomic level, investment risks are generally a function of the quality of the business environment in foreign markets. Where cross-border investments involve transactions in different currencies, investors face foreign exchange risk. At the microeconomic level, limited partners have to assess whether the fund manager has the experience and skills to operate in potentially significantly more challenging macroenvironments. As impressive as a track record a fund manager may have established in his home market may be, will he be equally successful in outperforming his peers in a fundamentally different macro and governance context? On this dimension, a fund with local roots may have an important competitive advantage, but does the fund manager have the necessary operational and financial skills to undertake complex private equity transactions?

In illustrating the integration process of global and regional private equity markets and the opportunities and risks that arise from this process for limited partners, we have chosen seven cases, Abraaj Capital, Actis, Apax Partners, The Blackstone Group, Hellman & Friedman, Kohlberg, Kravis Roberts & Co (KKR), and Vestar Capital Partners (Table 12.1). All of them are leading fund managers in their respective markets and compete for global capital.

International Investments in Private Equity. DOI: 10.1016/B978-0-12-375082-2.10012-6

Table 12.1 Seven leading private equity firms: private equity funds raised since 2000[a]

Firm/fund	Year	Amount raised	Focus
Abraaj Capital			
Abraaj Buyout Capital I	2002	US$ 116 million	Buyout
Abraaj Buyout Fund II	2005	US$ 500 million	Buyout
Infrastructure and Growth Capital Fund IV	2006	US$ 2,000 million	Infrastructure/growth
Abraaj Buyout Fund IV	2008	US$ 2,000 million	Buyout
Actis			
Actis ASEAN Fund	2004	US$ 130 million	Buyout
Actis India Fund 2	2004	US$ 325 million	Expansion/buyout
Actis China Fund 2	2004	US$ 250 million	Expansion
Actis South Asia Fund 2	2004	US$ 150 million	Expansion/buyout
Actis Africa Fund 2	2004	US$ 355 million	Expansion/buyout
Actis Africa Empowerment Fund	2005	US$ 50 million	Buyout
Canada investment fund for Africa (CIFA)	2006	US$ 211 million	Expansion/buyout
Actis Africa Agribusiness Fund	2006	US$ 93 million	Expansion
Actis Umbrella Fund	2006	US$ 100 million	Fund of funds
Actis Emerging Markets 3	2007	US$ 2,868 million	Expansion/buyout
Apax Partners			
Excelsior VI	2000	US$ 1,100 million	Venture
Apax Europe V	2001	EUR 4,404 million	Balanced
Apax Europe VI	2005	EUR 4,310 million	Buyout
Apax US VII	2006	US$ 1,500 million	Buyout
Apax Europe VII	2007	EUR 11,200 million	Buyout
The Blackstone Group			
Blackstone Communications Partners I	2000	US$ 2 billion	Buyouts
Blackstone Capital Partners IV	2002	US$ 6.5 billion	Buyouts
Blackstone Capital Partners V	2007	US$ 21.7 billion	Buyouts
Blackstone Capital Partners VI[b]	*2010*	*US$ 13.5 billion*	Buyouts
Hellman & Friedman			
HFCP IV	2000	US$ 2.2 billion	Buyouts
HFCP V	2004	US$ 3.4 billion	Buyouts
HFCP VI	2006	US$ 8.4 billion	Buyouts
HFCP VII	2009	US$ 8.9 billion	Buyouts
KKR			
KKR Millennium Fund	2002	US$ 3 billion	Buyouts
KKR European Fund II	2005	US$ 5.7 billion	Buyouts
KKR Fund 2006	2006	US$ 17.6 billion	Buyouts
KKR Asia Fund	2007	US$ 4 billion	Buyouts
KKR European Fund III	2008	US$ 6 billion	Buyouts
KKR Mezzanine Fund	2010	US$ 350 million	Mezzanine
Vestar Capital Partners			
Vestar Capital Partners V	2005	US$ 3.65 billion	Buyouts

[a]Excludes real estate, natural resources, and special situations funds and private equity funds currently in formation.
[b]At the time of writing, the fund had raised USD 13.5 billion and was expected to have its final closing shortly.
Source: Information provided by the general partners

As far as US private equity firms are concerned, The Blackstone Group and KKR stand out as managing some of the world's largest pools of private equity capital and having invested in some of the largest buyouts in history. Although the roots of both firms lie in private equity, they have transformed themselves into alternative asset managers. Both firms are listed on the New York Stock Exchange. By contrast, Hellman & Friedman has remained a private partnership. Headquartered in San Francisco, Hellman & Friedman focuses on large buyouts and has been involved in some very large transactions on both sides of the Atlantic. In addition, the firm has been involved in some transactions in Asia-Pacific. Finally, Vestar Capital Partners is a leading player in the middle market, operating in its home market, the United States, and in Europe.

Although Apax Partners has both European and US roots, today the firm is generally considered as a European private equity house. Apax Partners has raised some of the largest European private equity funds targeting relatively large transactions. Headquartered in London, Actis is a globally operating private equity house focusing on mid-sized transactions in emerging markets. Abraaj Capital, finally, is one of the world's largest regional private equity firms. Operating from their headquarters in Dubai, Abraaj Capital's market encompasses the Middle East, North Africa, and South Asia.

As the strategic conversations with these private equity houses reveal, there are many commonalities as to how they identify and select investment opportunities and how they manage risk. However, there are also important nuances and variations, reflecting the firms' different business strategies and the markets they are operating in. Furthermore, the conversations provide important insights in the changing industry structure in local and regional markets, with domestic firms facing increased competition from global players.

12.1   US private equity firms

12.1.1   The Blackstone Group

The firm: The Blackstone Group was founded in 1985. Since its first private equity fund in 1987, Blackstone has raised more than US$ 46 billion in private equity capital. Blackstone's Capital Partners V fund had its final closing in 2007 raising US$ 21.7 billion, the largest private equity fund ever raised. Although Blackstone remains one of the world's largest private equity investors, the firm has transformed itself into a leading alternative asset manager. This transformation started in 1990 when Blackstone Alternative Asset Management was founded, managing funds of hedge funds, other institutional vehicles and publicly traded closed-end mutual funds. This step was followed by the formation of the financial restructuring advisory practice in 1991, the real estate group in 1992 and the corporate debt group in 1999, and the acquisition of GSO Capital Partners in 2008. Headquartered in New York, The Blackstone Group has several offices in the United States. In Europe, it has opened offices in London, Paris, and Düsseldorf. In Asia, Blackstone's office network includes Beijing, Shanghai, Hong Kong, Mumbai, Sydney, and Tokyo. In 2007, The Blackstone Group listed on the NYSE, with the offering totaling US$ 7.6 billion, including a US$ 3 billion investment by the China Investment Company (CIC).

Interview with Stephen Schwarzman, Chairman, Chief Executive Officer, and Co-founder. The interview was conducted in June 2010.

Question: What motivated you to expand abroad?

Stephen Schwarzman (SS): First of all, we saw new investment opportunities abroad. In Europe, a private equity industry had begun to emerge in the mid-1980s, and some U.S. firms, which had already decided to invest there, seemed to be quite successful in penetrating the European market by leveraging their experience gained in the United States. Europe faced tremendous challenges in terms of structural reform and corporate restructuring, and there was an important role for private equity to play in this process. In a way, it reminded us of what we had seen in the United States in the 1980s. We saw considerable potential for productivity gains, and, in fact, European private equity returns in the 1990s were considerably better than in the U.S. market.

Second, globalization was advancing progressively. There was a considerable increase in cross-border M&A transactions, and companies had become increasingly international, both in terms of their supply chains and their product markets. As markets became more integrated, it was important for us to expand internationally to take advantage of the globalization process. On a transatlantic basis, this process was already far advanced, but Asia and other parts of the world were rapidly playing catch-up.

You opened your first foreign office in London in 2000. Why haven't you taken this step earlier?

SS: A key reason for us was the lack of technology. Remember that high quality video conferencing became available only in the last decade. Of course, video conferencing had already been around before the turn of the century, but the quality was very poor. This made it virtually impossible to have global investment meetings where you really interact with others. Body language can be very revealing. Beyond the figures, I need to see whether someone is comfortable with an investment proposal. So the emergence of new technology was an important catalyst for us to expand internationally.

Was there any role your limited partners played in this decision?

SS: It was clear that our limited partners had a great interest in diversifying their private equity portfolios internationally. In the early days, U.S. private equity firms provided few opportunities, as their operations were concentrated on their home market. So in order to get exposure to foreign private equity markets, limited partners were largely restricted to committing capital to foreign funds. And that's what they did. In fact, large U.S. pension funds, such as CalPERS, have been large investors in European private equity funds. So clearly from a capital supply perspective there was substantial interest.

This doesn't mean, however, that our decision to expand into the European and other foreign markets was driven by diversification considerations of our limited partners. Instead, we took the decision, because we saw attractive investment opportunities abroad.

Instead of raising region-specific funds, Blackstone follows a different approach, forming global partnerships deploying capital across different geographies. What has been the rationale behind your global approach?

SS: Many limited partners like the regional-fund approach, since it may fit better with their asset allocation. If you set a certain target for individual geographies, such allocation targets are easier to achieve if you commit capital to funds that invest only in a particular region. GPs like it, because it facilitates fundraising. The amount of capital GPs may raise by launching different regional funds is probably larger than the amount if there was only one pool of capital. So from a fee perspective, that's great. The flipside though is that regional funds give you much less investment flexibility. By restricting the investment universe, regional funds are unable to respond to new investment opportunities that may emerge outside their target geography. The opposite is also true, of course. If investment opportunities dry up, for example, because the economic outlook deteriorates, investors get stuck. So I believe that our global approach is actually advantageous for our investors.

Your global expansion strategy started with Europe. What has been your experience there?

SS: We invested in a number of transactions early on, covering a broad spectrum of industries and deal sizes. In terms of industries, our acquisitions have included companies in the media and telecom, travel and leisure, healthcare and pharma, financial and business services and industrial sectors. In terms of size, some deals have been at the lower end of the middle market, such as *Kabel BW*, a cable television network operator in Germany we acquired in June 2003 for US$ 116 million. Other transactions we've been involved in have been far larger. For example, in 2005 we were part of a consortium that acquired *TDC*, the incumbent Danish telecom operator, for the equivalent amount of US$ 15.8 billion.

Generally speaking, we are quite pleased with these investments. However, we decided to stop investing in Europe basically in late 2006 when the risk/return balance became increasingly unfavorable. Prices were reaching very high levels, and the economy started to slow progressively, before falling off a cliff in 2008. By leaving the market, we were able to avoid the worst part of the bubble.

What is your outlook for Europe and especially the prospects for European private equity?

SS: We will stay on the sidelines for the time being. The outlook for the economy and for corporate earnings is clouded with substantial uncertainties. Several countries, especially those in the periphery of the euro area, face huge challenges in dealing with a debt crisis. Many governments have already announced tough fiscal adjustment measures. Will these measures work? Will they succeed in restoring market confidence? What role is monetary policy going to play in this? What will be the impact on economic growth? Will governments implement the right structural reforms to avoid repeating a crisis of the kind we've just seen? And will the euro area governments get their act together in putting in place a superior governance system supporting the single currency? These are fundamental questions, but asset prices do not fully reflect these uncertainties, in my view. So deals look expensive from a risk/return balance.

This is not to say that we have abandoned Europe, of course. When prices become more realistic, we will be getting back into the market. In fact, I expect some great deals to be had. So in the meantime, we watch the situation carefully and stand ready if and when investment opportunities arise.

What role does corporate governance play in creating value?

SS: Corporate governance is not an issue if you own a company. It becomes a huge issue if you take a minority stake in a company. This doesn't mean that we don't take minority stakes in the future. In fact, in Asia there are relatively few deals where investors are able to acquire a controlling position. Minority investments can generate attractive returns. However, our experience tells us how important it is to ensure that the majority stakeholder's interests are fully aligned with ours. Unless we are 100 percent satisfied that this is the case, we will not take a minority stake.

How do you manage exchange rate risk in international transactions?

SS: There isn't really much one can do in hedging equity exchange rate risk in international transactions. We do hedge currency risk in international debt transactions, but as far as equity is concerned, the potential to hedge our positions is extremely limited. Besides, hedging is very expensive. To the extent that international investments involve transactions in different currencies, their performance is subject to currency movements.

However, there is also upside risk, since the exchange rate can move both ways. The exchange rate is an important parameter in our investment and also divestment decisions. In that sense, we manage exchange rate risk, although we are unable to hedge it. Take, for example, our investment in *Orangina*, a transaction we completed, together with Lion Capital, in February 2006, with a transaction value of US$ 2.6 billion. At that time, the US$/EUR rate was around 1.20. When we decided to sell the company in November 2009, the dollar had depreciated to around 1.50. We thought that the dollar had become increasingly undervalued against the euro. In this case, the exchange rate actually influenced the timing of our decision to sell the business.

12.1.2 Hellman & Friedman

The firm: Founded in 1984, Hellman & Friedman LLC is headquartered in San Francisco and has offices in New York and London. Since its first partnership in 1987, the firm has raised over US$ 25 billion of committed capital. Its latest fund, Hellman & Friedman Capital Partners VII, had its final closing in 2009 raising US$ 8.9 billion. Since inception, Hellman & Friedman has invested in more than 60 companies primarily in the United States and in Europe. Seeking to invest long-term capital to support management teams operating businesses with defensible positions in growing markets, Hellman & Friedman has focused on business services, communications, consumer services, financial services, information services, media, and services. In terms of investment sizes, Hellman & Friedman targets equity investments of between US$ 300 million and US$ 1.2 billion.

Interview with Brian Powers, Chairman of Hellman & Friedman. The interview was conducted in July 2010.

When did you decide to expand internationally?

Brian Powers (BP): Actually, we had opened an office in Hong Kong in 1993. However, we decided to close our Hong Kong office in 1998 as we didn't really see enough investment opportunities that matched our criteria. For instance, while we generally look for opportunities where we can invest at least US$ 300 million in equity, few, if any, private equity transactions in the region were of that size. Besides, we felt that there was a profound lack of transparency, both at the market and company levels.

In the 1990s, we made several investments in Australia, sourced from our U.S. office. In 2004, we opened our London office. At that time, we had already been involved in three European transactions. This decision was essentially motivated by our desire to have better access to deal flow and to be closer to our European portfolio. We also opened an office in New York at about the same time. I would not rule out that we make a second move into Asia, but this decision will depend on our assessment of the quality of deal flow.

To what extent have your limited partners influenced your decision to invest outside the U.S. market?

BP: As a matter of fact, some investment opportunities were brought to us by our LPs. But there was no pressure on their side, in the sense that they wanted to get exposure to foreign markets through our partnerships. The decision to expand into Europe was solely our own. Needless to say, if we had not seen attractive investment opportunities there, we would not have taken this step.

More generally, we are agnostic about geographies. Our investment approach is very much opportunity-driven, and we don't have particular portfolio weights in mind. If all the attractive opportunities were in Europe, I don't see a reason why we shouldn't be disproportionately invested there. Conversely, if all the great opportunities were in the U.S., we would be comfortable with our portfolio consisting entirely of U.S. companies. In practice, though, U.S. buyouts account for around 70 percent of our current portfolio, and we are generally limited to putting 40 percent of our fund outside the U.S.

Consistent with our investment approach, we raise global funds, as opposed to either regional or specialized funds. In our view, the risk with regional or specialized funds is that you lock yourself in and unnecessarily limit your flexibility. If, for whatever reason, the flow of opportunities dries up, you're stuck. And you don't have the possibility to re-allocate resources to other regions or industries that may be more attractive. Our global fund approach allows us to deploy capital wherever we see the most attractive returns, which should be in the interest of our LPs.

What is your experience in Europe?

BP: In general, we are pleased with our European investments, although the earlier ones have probably been a bit more successful than those made more recently.

The fact that the European private equity market has become more challenging reflects in part the macro cycle. In that sense, the European market is not really different from other markets, which have also been substantially affected by the global recession and the turmoil in the financial markets. However, where we do see a structural difference are public-to-private transactions. In Europe, such transactions have become significantly more difficult than in the U.S. as incumbent shareholders have shown less willingness to sell to financial buyers in recent years. This has slowed the market considerably.

Turning to corporate governance, what is your position on club deals?

BP: We have been involved in a number of club deals, including in cross-border transactions. In one deal in Germany, we teamed up with four other U.S. GPs, and one U.S. individual investor. No European GPs participated in the transaction. This transaction worked out well.

Generally, though, I would see a risk that club deals may lead to inefficiencies in the decision-making process, and we would prefer to do proprietary deals. There may be important reasons why we do decide to be part of a joint transaction. Apart from the size of a transaction and risk concentration, club deals may be preferential in cases where a local partner brings specific knowledge and experience to the table.

Have you been involved in minority deals?

BP: In fact, Hellman & Friedman have been involved in minority deals since we raised our first fund in 1987. In a way, we may be considered as the "father of minority deals in private equity." However, whether or not we consider minority positions depends on the special circumstances in individual cases. Some industries are more conducive to acquiring non-control positions than others. Historically, we have been investing significantly in business services and other "asset-light" industries where capital investments are relatively limited. But, in any event, we need to be certain that the majority of other stakeholders' interests are fully aligned with ours—there is no room for compromises on this front. We really need to be on the same wave length. And, of course, we seek contractional protection in cases where we accept minority stakes. Thus far, we haven't really encountered any problems in deals where we don't hold a controlling position. True, if you are the controlling stakeholder, you can get things done more quickly. In one case, it was pretty clear that management needed to be changed. It took us four months to convince other shareholders. Had we been in the driver's seat, we would have implemented the necessary measures much faster. Overall, however, I don't see a difference in terms of the performance of our minority transactions versus ones where we have acquired a controlling stake.

As far as emerging markets are concerned, we haven't been involved in any minority transactions recently. The key issue there is, can you rely on the contractional agreement you have with the majority stakeholder?

As your investment universe has extended beyond the U.S. market, how do you deal with exchange rate risk?

BP: We have generally not hedged our exchange rate risk, as far as equity capital is concerned. Available hedging instruments are not suited for private equity transactions where the time horizon is relatively long and the cash flow patterns impossible to predict. That said, exchange rate risk does play a role in our assessment of foreign investment opportunities. Apart from the exchange rate exposure of the company itself, how vulnerable is a cross-border transaction to adverse currency movements? And exchange rate considerations could influence the timing of our investment and divestment decisions. It is much easier to effectively hedge a portfolio company's debt by making sure the debt is denominated in currencies corresponding to the company's earnings.

Moving from the investment to the fundraising side, how international is your investor base?

BP: Actually, our investor base is well diversified internationally. As far as our last fund is concerned—Hellman & Friedman Capital Partners VII—which had its final closing in 2009 at US$ 8.9 billion—U.S. investors account for approximately 60 percent of the capital raised while European investors account for approximately 12 percent.

In the previous fund, where we raised US$ 8.4 billion, U.S. investors played a comparatively larger role, accounting for approximately 70 percent of total commitments. A key principle that guides our fundraising process is that we only raise as much capital as we expect to be able to invest given our return expectations. Fund VI was significantly over-subscribed as was Fund VII when we began our fundraising, but as some domestic investors faced liquidity issues in the wake of the recent financial crisis, demand decreased and we were able to accommodate a greater amount of capital in Fund VII by new, overseas LPs.

Looking forward, what are the key trends, which will shape the industry over the coming years?

BP: We cannot really predict the future. For example, we had thought that 2009 would be a great year for investing. I believe many people in the industry shared that view. This view was predicated on the assumptions that prices would come down significantly, reflecting the sharp decline in economic activity and the resulting adjustment in earnings expectations, coupled with a re-pricing of risk equity. This was the experience from previous cycles. For example, investments made in the early 2000s when the market had just begun to recover have generally generated great returns. This time around, however, investment opportunities have been significantly rarer than we had anticipated. What we see is a kind of two-tier market: For outstanding companies, you've got several potential buyers, and deals are extremely competitive. By contrast, there are other companies where there is very little, if any, interest, given the quality of the business.

Predictions are also made more difficult by the speed at which market conditions may change. In the spring of 2010, debt capital markets rebounded dramatically. High-yield issuance was very buoyant, and the banks were willing again to underwrite leveraged loans at both higher multiples of EBITDA and at higher absolute dollar amounts than I think anyone would have predicted a year ago. However, this situation changed rapidly when investors became increasingly concerned about the sovereign debt woes in Europe and the possible implications for global growth. Banks became less willing to underwrite debt, as they feared that they would be unable to find buyers for the leveraged loans. While we are far away from the situation we had in the fall of 2008 when markets shut in the wake of the collapse of Lehman Brothers, the most recent episode shows us that things remain unsettled. Some potential transactions failed to materialize as the debt capital markets have become less accommodative again.

Since we cannot predict the future, we take a largely agnostic investment-by-investment approach. We look carefully for attractive investment opportunities in a given macro and financial environment, and when such opportunities arise, we stand ready to take a decision.

12.1.3   Kohlberg Kravis Roberts & Co

The firm: Founded in 1976 and led by Henry Kravis and George Roberts, KKR is a leading global investment firm with three primary business lines: private equity, fixed income, and capital markets.[1] Pioneers in private equity, KKR has built an extensive track record of creating value by partnering with management teams to build successful businesses across a wide range of industries. Today, the firm has US$ 54.7 billion in assets under management and more than 600 professionals in 14 offices around the world. Over the years, and through all economic cycles, KKR has executed some of the largest, most complex and innovative private equity transactions in the United States, Europe, and Asia. It has completed 62 deals larger than US$ 1 billion, led the first buyout of a public company, and participated in 6 of the 10 largest PE deals ever completed. Once acquired, KKR private equity professionals work with management on key strategic and operational issues. To support these efforts, KKR Capstone, a group of operational experts, was created in 2000 to work exclusively with senior company executives to help them manage and grow their businesses.

Although private equity continues to be KKR's core business, in recent years, the firm has leveraged its financial, industry, and operational expertise to develop new credit and capital markets capabilities that are complimentary to its private equity business. It has also expanded into new product areas in Infrastructure, Mezzanine, and Natural Resources.

In 2004, KKR launched its credit investing business and actively began pursuing debt investments as a separate asset class. This started with the formation of KKR Financial Holdings LLC, a publicly traded specialty finance company. Today, KKR has expanded this part of the business beyond KFN. With a team of more than 30 people, this team offers products and return profiles to satisfy a broad range of fixed-income investment mandates. It also offers tailored programs for institutional investors in accordance with such investors' investment criteria, targeted return and risk tolerance.

In 2007, KKR formed a capital markets business that supports the firm, its portfolio companies, and clients by providing tailored capital markets advice and developing and implementing both traditional and nontraditional capital solutions for investments and companies seeking financing. On July 15, 2010, KKR achieved another milestone when it listed on the New York Stock Exchange. Today, KKR has offices in the United States (New York, Menlo Park, San Francisco, Houston, and Washington, D.C.), Europe and the Middle East (London, Paris, and Dubai), and Asia-Pacific (Hong Kong, Tokyo, Sidney, Beijing, Mumbai, and Seoul).

Interview with Henry Kravis, Co-founder, Co-Chairman, and Co-Chief Executive Officer, KKR. The interview was conducted in July 2010.

Question: When did you consider expanding abroad? What was your main motivation?

Henry Kravis (HK): We had monitored the European private equity market since its emergence in the 1980s. At that time, the market was essentially limited to the

---

[1]The first two decades of KKR are discussed in detail in Baker and Smith (1998).

United Kingdom. As Europe's indigenous private equity industry developed and began to expand into Continental Europe and Scandinavia, we became increasingly convinced that there were interesting investment opportunities to be had. It was clear to us that sourcing attractive deals required opening an office in Europe. The two most critical questions we had to address were the office's location and its staffing. London, the cradle of the European private equity market, was already crowded with a significant number of private equity firms, and we actually contemplated opening an office in Germany. On the other hand, London had important competitive advantages, for example, in terms of its financial infrastructure, and in the end we decided to open an office there. In 1994, we founded Glenisla, which gave us a good window on Europe. In fact, we made our first European investment in 1996, and two years later Glenisla became part of KKR.

The second key decision we had to make concerned the recruitment of our European investment team. Basically, we had two options: hire someone locally to lead our European efforts or send someone from the U.S. to build a team in Europe. We decided to take the second route, as it was important that the firm's values and culture be engrained in our European operations. At first, Glenisla was run by Ian Martin and later by Neil Richardson. However, knowing the local markets and speaking the language are critical, and as we expanded our operations in Europe we added more and more local people. Since then, most people from the U.S. have moved back, and now our European leadership is almost entirely local.

More recently, you have also expanded substantially in Asia. Have you followed the same strategy?

A world class firm has to be successful globally, not just in the United States. Our European experience has shown us that there are good companies abroad, which motivated us to look for further investment opportunities in Asia. In fact, my first trip to Asia was in 1978, and since then I have visited the region numerous times. In Asia-Pacific, local market knowledge is absolutely critical, which is why we have decided to build an extensive office network spanning Australia, China, Hong Kong, India, Japan and Korea. While our presence in Asia-Pacific and in Europe allows us to penetrate local markets, as one global firm, we all work closely together to cross-fertilize our businesses in terms of geographies and business lines.

Why did you decide to raise private equity funds targeting specific regions?

HK: First of all, let me stress that one of the key pillars of KKR's culture is that we are one firm. Our investment approach is therefore global and we apply a uniform set of standards around the world in the deployment of our LPs' and our own capital.

That we have decided to raise regional funds rather than one global fund is largely driven by the investment preferences of our limited partners. Their asset allocation often favors a geographical approach. However, our global investment approach ensures consistency across all regions in which we operate.

I would add that our investor base has also become increasingly international. Apart from our traditional investor base in the United States and Europe, there are an increasing number of organizations from Asia and other parts of the world.

Are there any plans to expand further in regions where you have not yet invested?

HK: Recently, we have seen a significant increase in investment activity in Brazil. Looking forward, Brazil could be an interesting market. Elsewhere in Latin America, there may be interesting opportunities in Chile, although this market is considerably smaller. Outside of Latin America, I would mention South Africa, but at this point we do not have any concrete plans. We also continue to regularly engage in discussion in the Middle East, where we have an office and where there are some large companies and opportunities to consider.

What role does corporate governance play in your investment decisions?

HK: In terms of managing companies, our approach has been local. There are different corporate governance regimes around the world. Take Europe, for example, where in some countries workers are represented on the supervisory board. Our experience is that we can work well within the different systems. At the same time, we believe in active oversight of our portfolio companies including rigorous and involved boards comprised of industry experts as well as ensuring we have the right management at each of our companies.

As far as corruption is concerned, we have a zero-tolerance policy. We adhere to the laws of the Foreign Corrupt Practices Act. We would of course not do any deals that entail paying a company bribes and any portfolio company manager who is engaged in corruption would be immediately fired. In fact, we regularly work with our portfolio companies to ensure they understand the law in this area and have appropriate procedures in place to comply with the letter and spirit of anti-corruption laws around the world.

Traditionally, the private equity model is predicated on acquiring the majority of shares. What are the preconditions for KKR to accept minority positions?

HK: In China and India, virtually all transactions are minority deals. In these deals, the incumbent owner typically seeks growth capital. While there are very few investment opportunities where we can acquire a control position, it is important to note that our investments are usually significant—in some cases as large as 49 percent of a company's shares. Given the size of our investments, we are typically represented on the company's board. What is most important is that the majority owner's interests are fully aligned with ours. It is imperative for us to be involved in the company's strategic and operational decision-making process, and we work closely to ensure best practices and productivity improvements.

How do you manage currency risk?

HK: Monitored by KKR's Risk Management Committee, foreign exchange risk is managed through a currency overlay of our overall portfolio. More specifically, we hedge our currency risk on the basis of a basket of currencies that reflects our risk exposure against individual currencies. While we usually hedge individual portfolio companies' currency exposure with regard to debt capital, it is very difficult to hedge the foreign exchange risk of our equity in an individual company's capital, except through a basket of currency approach.

Looking forward, how do you see the prospects for private equity in the post-crisis era?

HK: In my career, private equity has been declared dead at least four times. From my experience over the last three or four decades, I am convinced that there will always be sufficient capital for the right deals. In the 1980s, deals tended to be much more leveraged. Take, for example, Safeway, which we acquired in 1986. The equity capital in this transaction was US$ 125 million, just a little more than two percent of the transaction value of US$ 5.5 billion. Other deals, such as Beatrice and RJR Nabisco, were also highly leveraged. This changed in the 1990s when equity ratios increased significantly.

In the most recent cycle, equity ratios remained substantially higher than in the 1980s, averaging around one-third. At the same time, however, the emergence of new markets, such as mezzanine ensured that overall there was a record amount of capital available. Whereas in the 1980s there had been just a few banks providing leveraged finance, more recently, there was a large number of institutions from which private equity firms could borrow. Importantly, the banks did not have to hold the loans on their balance sheets. Instead, securitization enabled them to tranche the debt and sell it to a diverse group of institutional investors, with CLOs playing a particularly important role in fuelling the last buyout boom. Since the banks did not hold the debt, however, due diligence was often not as stringent as it should have been, which was sowing the seeds for the financial crisis.

While credit became extremely scarce in the aftermath of the collapse of Lehman Brothers as banks had to write down their risky assets and de-risk their portfolios, more recently we have seen a remarkable recovery in the credit markets. Most notably, issuance of high-yield bonds has surged, and as the credit crisis has begun to ease, banks are more willing again to provide leveraged loans. In individual deals, debt multiples in the 5.5–6.5x range are possible. Investors are looking for yield, and banks need to find ways to do profitable business.

While I am not particularly worried about the availability of debt capital, in my view the most important challenge lies in finding and creating value. Competition for private equity transactions comes mainly from the stock market rather than from other private equity firms. We're also in a more regulated environment where there is likely to be more governmental and stakeholder scrutiny of many of the industries in which we invest. As a result, our understanding of regulatory trends and our engagement with key stakeholders on issues like our environmental footprint and relationship with the communities in which our companies operate will be important. Bottom line: the key challenge and goal is to identify attractive investment opportunities and create value through strategic and operational improvements.

12.1.4 *Vestar Capital Partners*

The firm: Vestar Capital Partners, a leading global private equity firm focusing on middle-market transactions, was founded in 1988. Headquartered in New York, the firm has offices in Boston and Denver, Paris, Milan, and Munich. Since inception, Vestar Capital Partners has raised five private equity funds, the most recent one managing a pool of committed capital of US$ 3.7 billion. As of mid-2010, assets under management totaled US$ 7 billion. Investing up to US$ 500 million in a single transaction, Vestar Capital Partners focuses on companies with a value ranging from US$ 250 million to US$ 3 billion in a broad range of industries.

Interview with Daniel S. O'Connell, Chief Executive Officer, Vestar Capital Partners. The interview was conducted in June 2010.

Question: As a leading middle-market private equity firm in the United States, what motivated you to expand into Europe?

Daniel O'Connell (DO'C): Vestar's roots go back to the First Boston Corporation, which was acquired by Credit Suisse in 1988, leading to the formation of Credit Suisse First Boston. We were seven principals in the Management Buyout Group of First Boston who decided to leave the firm and establish Vestar. Twenty-two years later, six of the original founders are still with Vestar. The seeds to move beyond the U.S. market were planted relatively early. In fact, we had a significant number of portfolio companies with highly promising markets abroad. While most large companies already had multinational operations, with a growing share of their earnings derived from exports and foreign production, we asked ourselves: How can we help medium-sized companies be successful internationally?

At that time, the European market appeared to be the most attractive market for us for two reasons. First, its size and the increasingly closer economic ties between the United States and Europe. Second, the emergence of a private equity market in Europe, with a rising number of local private equity firms. These conditions didn't really exist elsewhere. Although the Japanese economy had been growing strongly in the post-war period, it greatly suffered from the bursting of a massive real estate bubble in the early 1990s. There was virtually no private equity infrastructure in Japan. Obviously, this applied to the rest of Asia as well, with most Asian economies still in a relatively early stage of their development. So clearly any expansion outside of our home market had to focus on Europe.

Your expansion strategy differs from most other firms. Instead of expanding into Europe from London, Europe's major financial and private equity hub, you chose instead to open your first foreign office in Paris. Why?

DO'C: Before investing in Europe, we carefully studied the European market and what others had done. We wanted to learn from their experience. What had worked, what hadn't? We looked at European firms that were founded in the 1980s, such as BC Partners, CVC and Permira. We also studied several U.S. private equity firms that had moved into Europe, for example, KKR, Hicks, Muse, Tate & Furst and Madison Dearborn. One of the key lessons we drew from their experience was it was vital for deal sourcing, investing and monitoring to be locally present. Local presence is particularly key in the middle market, where many businesses are family- or privately-owned and do not want to go through the large traditional investment banking circles to find an investor for their company. Operating out of London and covering a diverse set of national economies and private equity markets did not seem to be a good strategy for us. Furthermore, the UK market already seemed to be well penetrated, efficient and highly competitive. Having studied the various firms and models, we decided to pursue the more European model.

It was not before the turn of the millennium we finally decided to expand abroad. We opened an office in Paris, which serves as our European headquarters. We have also opened offices in Milan and Munich. Eventually, our plan was to expand into other European markets, notably London and Scandinavia. So far, however, our

European office network has remained limited to three locations. Of course, in considering further expansions, we need to take into account our available resources. We only raise as much capital as we believe we can invest profitably. *Vestar Capital Partners V* closed in 2005 with a total commitment amount of US$ 3.7 billion. Our portfolio is managed by some 50 investment professionals, of which fourteen are based in Europe.

What are your key principles in organizing your international operations?

DO'C: We wanted to leverage our U.S. private equity model. And we wanted to have good quality control. This means a franchise operation was not the right model for us. Instead, our expansion strategy into Europe, and later into Japan, has been guided by the principle of "one firm—one fund." Our European operations are led by one of Vestar's founding partners, Rob Rosner, who carried the firm's culture to Europe. In that sense, Rob is our ambassador. Actually, his wife is French, so he is very comfortable living in Paris.

Consistent with our "one firm—one fund" approach, we make our investment decisions at the global level, as opposed to making decisions in a decentralized way for individual geographies. Further, our compensation model is also global to ensure that everyone works together and is incentivized to help the overall firm results—this creates a culture of teamwork across geographies.

When did you make your first investments in Europe?

DO'C: We didn't want to rush things. Instead, we decided to build a team first in one or two years. One of our first European deals was SAB Wabco, a Swedish manufacturer of brake systems, wheels and couplings for the railway industry we acquired in September 2002. This transaction originated in the United States, and we sold the business in November 2004 to a strategic buyer.

Another early deal was the acquisition of Selenia in October 2003, an Italian company producing lubricants for automotive, commercial and agricultural vehicles. A pan-European business, the company also had operations in the United States. We decided to sell Selenia in late 2005.

A final example is our investment in OGF, the leader in the French funeral services market owned by a U.S. parent company. Having bought the company in March 2004, we sold it in September 2007.

What has been your experience with your European portfolio?

DO'C: The clear differentiator in the European buyout industry has been our U.S. experience. Our early deals in Europe have been highly successful. The approximately US$ 400 million we had invested in four deals between 2002 and 2004 turned into a value of US$ 1.2 billion. During this period, we actually found the European market to be more attractive than the U.S. market.

Since 2004, the European buyout market became much more challenging. In this subsequent period, the European market ramped up significantly and deals became considerably more expensive. But as the economic environment deteriorated rapidly amid massive dislocations in the global financial markets, transactions we did pursue during this period face considerable challenges. This led us to redirect our strategy back to what had worked so well for us in the early years of our European investment experience. I believe it was important for us to go back to basics, which is to buy long-standing companies with leading market positions, run by experienced management teams. Our most recent European investment in AZ Electronics is a good example of investing in a very strong, highly international market leader.

In identifying investment opportunities, your focus has been on advanced economies. Are there any plans to expand into emerging markets?

DO'C: There is no imminent plan to invest in emerging markets. While countries like China and India enjoy rapid economic growth, this doesn't necessarily translate into superior returns, in our view. A key concern we have is: How much confidence can we have in the rule of law in these countries?

I wouldn't rule out in the future we will make investments in emerging markets. Currently, we do get exposure to these markets through many of our portfolio companies which are experiencing growth and expansion in such markets as China and Brazil. As far as central and Eastern Europe is concerned, these markets are already covered through our office in Germany. Overall, our interest in emerging markets will largely depend on the progress these economies make in establishing well-functioning institutions and a predictable legal system.

How do your limited partners view your globalization strategy?

DO'C: There are probably three groups of LPs: The first group of our LPs is very much in favor of our decision to move beyond the U.S. middle market. They see substantial potential for leveraging our expertise in other geographies. I would put the share of this group at roughly 50 percent. Then there is a second group that is more skeptical. These LPs show a sort of "wait-and-see" attitude. They represent perhaps 40 percent of our investor base. Finally, there is a small minority of around 10 percent who take a more negative view. In particular, they question whether we have the right resources and the right number of people with the right skills on the ground to ensure this strategy is successful. The fact, however, that these LPs are still part of our investor base indicates that they continue to be willing to support us.

How do you manage currency risk?

DO'C: As far as our latest partnership, *Vestar Capital Partners V,* is concerned, we actually contemplated a dual currency fund. However, our limited partners were not really enthusiastic about this idea. Instead, they want us to make the currency call a part of our investment and exit decisions. Exchange rate changes can significantly affect returns in the fund's currency, and hence the exchange rate is an integral part of our investment analysis. There is a natural hedge in some of our deals to the extent portfolio companies in foreign markets have opposite currency exposures. Suppose, for example, the dollar appreciates versus the euro. Other things being equal, an acquisition we made in euros will have a lower value in dollars. However, our portfolio company in Europe may be exporting to the United States and, as a result, benefit from a lower euro. In addition, some of the risk is significantly mitigated by borrowing our acquisition financing in local currencies. By matching cash flows with debt in the same currencies, we reduce the overall exposure of our investment. Apart from that, the exchange rate is a factor we take into account when considering an exit. While a favorable exchange rate may accelerate an exit, unfavorable currency movements may also delay the divestment.

12.2   European private equity firms

12.2.1   Actis

The firm: Actis is a leading private equity investor in emerging markets, with US$ 4.8 billion funds under management. Actis was created in early 2004 when its management and staff acquired a majority stake in the company from CDC Capital Partners, a UK government-owned fund of funds. Buyout and growth capital transactions typically have a minimum size of US$ 50 million and are sourced in countries in which investment opportunities arise from a growing prosperity from rising personal wealth and domestic consumer demand. To this end transactions focus on sectors such as consumer goods, business and financial services, and industrials. Apart from buyout and growth capital transactions, Actis is also investing in infrastructure and real estate. Specialized in Africa, Asia, and Latin America, Actis has offices in Egypt, Kenya, Nigeria, South Africa, China, India, Singapore, and Brazil. The firm's head office is in London.

Interview with Adiba Ighodaro (AI), a senior director with responsibility for leading and coordinating various fund-raising activities and investor relations, and Peter Schmid (PS), who as a partner is responsible for the leadership of Actis's private equity business in Africa. Peter is also a member of Actis's global investment committee as well as its executive management committee. The interview was conducted in October 2009.

Question: How is your current portfolio structured in terms of geographies?
Peter Schmid (PS): Our global portfolio of private equity, infrastructure and real estate investments is currently comprised of 58 companies in 23 countries. While the vast majority of these investments are growth capital and buyout transactions, we also have three active infrastructure and seven active real estate investments. In our most recent US$2.9 billion private equity fund that we closed at the end of 2008, we currently have 9 investments: 4 in Africa, 3 in China, 1 in India and 1 in south-east Asia. By the end of the fund's life, we expect to have a diversified portfolio of 30-40 investments across all of our markets including Brazil.

Adiba Ighodaro (AI): Overall, we believe that our portfolio is well balanced, reflecting the enormous growth dynamics in the individual markets we invest in. Besides, the LPA with our investors limits our capital exposure to any of India, China and Africa to 40 percent.

How does your portfolio structure look like in Africa, your most important host region right now?
PS: We're basically operating across the entire continent. Around 40 percent of our assets are in South Africa, with the remainder distributed almost evenly across East and West African markets. We've also made a number of investments in Egypt, by far the most important private equity market in North Africa.

Are there any countries where you do not invest categorically?
PS: For a number of reasons(e.g. sovereign risk) at any one time there are many countries in which we would not invest.

And in terms of sectors?

AI: In agreement with our investors, we do not invest in tobacco, defense, gambling, pornography and alcohol other than beer and wine. While this leaves a broad spectrum of industries we may invest in, we focus on those that are particularly important in driving and benefiting from the development process.

What drives your portfolio construction? To what extent does your portfolio mirror top-down considerations and to what degree is the composition a reflection of a bottom-up selection process?

PS: At Actis, a core principle of our investment policy is portfolio diversification. Specifically, our portfolio construction is based on a matrix approach that combines geographies and sectors. We don't want to be exceedingly exposed to any particular country or region, and we don't want to be exceedingly exposed to a particular sector. In that sense, our matrix approach is an important risk management tool. Our teams on the ground are aligned globally across the Firm into 4 focus sectors. Deal origination is driven both by systematic sector mapping and identification of target companies and businesses, as well as bottom-up building of relationship in the market. In terms of individual deals, transactions are limited to a maximum of 10 percent of the fund's capital. Let me emphasize in this context that our approach distinguishes us from local private equity firms. Whereas Actis operates as a single firm on a global basis and thus manages risk from a global perspective, local fund managers in emerging markets typically have highly concentrated portfolios. At the same time, however, we operate very locally when it comes to deal sourcing. In my view, it is impossible to over-emphasize the importance of being on the ground and maintaining personal networks, including with potential sellers and intermediaries. Different markets are subject to different cultural sensitivities. Apart from having access to proprietary deals, we need to be absolutely sure about the integrity of the seller. Nowhere is this more important than in emerging markets whose accounting rules tend to leave considerable room for interpretation and investor protection often remains inferior. In Africa, for instance, we have four regional offices, which serve as hubs from where we monitor investment opportunities in different clusters of countries. So risk management really starts bottom-up with every transaction we consider. Through our global investment committee, which consists of all regional heads, we ensure that our investment and risk principles are applied consistently and coherently across different regions, thus avoiding an undesirable concentration of risk in our overall portfolio.

Where in the investment process do you factor in currency risk as a key component of macro risk?

AI: First of all, individual deal teams access currency risk as part of their due diligence work. Is there risk of currency devaluation? Does the company have currency exposure? How would a devaluation affect the economics of the deal? So each investment is assessed for currency risk by stress testing the base case in our financial models. Second, currency risk is considered at the regional level. And finally, we assess currency risk at the global fund level. While we do not hedge individual currency positions, our global portfolio is substantially diversified, which gives us considerable protection against adverse currency movements at the global fund level.

Turning to individual investments, what are the key decision parameters?

PS: Our guiding principle is to invest in "best-of-breed" companies where we can add value in terms of management talent and strategy. The companies we invest in must have the potential of becoming world-class firms in their particular markets. Let me give you an example. In 1998, Actis invested US$ 75 million in Celtel, a start-up aspiring to become the first pan-African mobile phone company. Capitalizing on the growing political stability in Africa and avoiding the legacy challenges of fixed line telecom operators, the company acquired and built businesses in 13 countries across sub-Saharan Africa over the next eight years. By 2005, revenues had reached US$ 1 billion and the company was sold to MTC for US$ 3.4 billion.

There are two key questions we ask in every deal we consider: How can we add value to the company in order to reach its full potential? Does the management team possess the experience and the skills to allow the company to reach that potential?

The industry structure in private equity markets is changing rapidly. While there is a rising number of smaller local funds, large global players have begun to invest in emerging markets as well. To what extent does this affect your investment approach?

PS: Actis pursues a kind of hybrid model, which is rare and difficult to copy. While we are a firm with global reach, at the same time we are also very local. We do not compete with the large global buyout firms, which target considerably larger deal sizes. In the middle market, however, where we're operating, our hybrid model gives us an important competitive advantage relative to the local firms that lack the global perspective and the ability to bring deep industry knowledge to the table.

While Actis' local networks appear to be an important factor in sourcing deals, how do you assess governance risk?

AI: We believe that our local knowledge is an important risk mitigant in itself. But obviously that's not enough. Thorough background checks are an integral part of our due diligence process. We need to be absolutely confident about the quality of the assets we acquire. This includes the human capital factor. The quality of management is a particularly scarce factor in most emerging economies, and we always conduct detailed reference checks. We try in all cases to use psychometric testing. More generally, we need to be able to fully trust the seller. Many transactions in emerging markets are growth capital deals where the seller retains the majority of the company's capital. In such transactions, you've got to be 100 percent sure that the owner's interests are completely aligned with yours. Actis has a dedicated ESG team that focuses on governance and impact on the community. In all our investments we insist on world class corporate governance standards with the appropriate board structures, including non-executive directors and relevant sub-committees. Our experience is that this creates a lot of value for our investors on exit. Trade buyers know that any business they buy from Actis is clean and well run.

In your view, could club deals with local private equity firms play a role in mitigating political and governance risk?

PS: No, not really. In the majority of markets where we operate, notably in Africa, there are few deals of the size that require syndication. And even in markets where average deal sizes are comparatively larger, the need for teaming up with others is limited. In the few club deals we've seen, there will typically be a lead investor who controls a syndicate. For instance, this has been the case in the Alexander Forbes transaction, a diversified financial services company, which was one of the largest and most complex buyouts ever undertaken in Africa. In this US$ 1.2 billion transaction, we served as the lead investor. Apart from the size aspect of a transaction, I don't think that club deals would help us mitigate political and governance risk. Actis is perceived to be a local player in our markets, on par in terms of relationships with any domestic funds.

When are non-control positions acceptable and when are they not?

PS: In the rapidly growing markets we're focusing on, taking minority positions are a fact of life. If you are unwilling to take the governance risk that inevitably comes with minority stakes, there will be few investment opportunities in our markets. So our emphasis is on managing such risks effectively. While we do not have minimum thresholds below which we wouldn't invest, it is indispensable for us to be able to significantly influence decision making at the board level. In practice this means that we have seats on the board of virtually all our portfolio companies, regardless of the share of capital we hold. A recent example is our US$200 million investment in Egypt's CIB Bank. Holding 9 percent of the bank's capital, we are represented on the board and are members of some of the strategic board sub-committees. In mitigating risk, we also find it important to align ourselves with other likeminded shareholders to form blocks and to agree on veto rights on certain strategic decisions.

In non-control deals, how important are potentially conflicts concerning exits?

PS: The moment we consider making an investment in a company, we already think about our exit strategy. Unless we have a clear view about the timing of our divestment and the way we may divest, we wouldn't make the investment in the first place. In non-control deals, and this is really the default case in most markets, the alignment of our interests with those of the majority shareholder is an absolute precondition. That said, we generally hold our portfolio companies for several years, and, realistically, not everything is foreseeable over the course of the holding period. To minimize the risk of surprises, our investments usually include the possibility of a forced liquidity event.

AI: I would like to emphasize, however, that the execution of control deals varies from market to market and generally is on the increase. In South Africa, we have only ever invested in control transactions. In our most recent fund, 6 out of 9 investments made to date (including one in China) are control deals.

Once an investment decision is taken, how do you monitor risk?

PS: At the company level, risk monitoring is a continuous process, enabling us to detect any potential problems very early on and designing appropriate remedies. It is a key area of focus for the investment managers, and in particular for the specialist investment operations teams established to focus day to day on the implementation of 100-day plans and portfolio company strategy. As far as macro risk is concerned, this is the responsibility of the regional heads. Actis' Investment Committee then reviews risk factors on a semi-annual basis in formal investment reviews.

12.2.2   Apax Partners

The firm: Apax Partners is an independent global partnership. Although Apax Partners has a strong background in venture capital, it has transformed itself into a firm focusing exclusively on leveraged buyouts and growth capital transactions. Funds advised by Apax Partners typically invest in large companies with a value between € 1 billion and € 5 billion. Apax Partners' investment strategy is sector focused, with their funds investing in the tech and telecom, retail and consumer, media, healthcare, and financial and business services sectors. Apax Partners has offices in London, Guernsey, Madrid, Milan, Munich, Stockholm, Tel Aviv, New York, Hong Kong, Shanghai, and Mumbai. At the end of 2009, the total amount of capital raised stood at € 26.6 billion (US$ 37.7 billion).

Interview with Max Burger-Calderon. At the time of the interview, Max Burger-Calderon was Apax Partners' Chairman for Asia. Having been with Apax Partners since 1987, he co-founded the firm's German, Spanish, and Swiss offices. The interview was conducted in September 2009.

Question: How has your firm grown into the global platform it has become today?

Max Burger-Calderon (MBC): Apax's history has been very international, right from the beginning. Back in the early 1970s, Sir Ronald Cohen had co-founded Multinational Management Group (MMG), which provided advisory services to entrepreneurial companies. Originally, their partners were based in London, Paris and Chicago. In 1976, MMG teamed up with Alan Patricof Associates, a New York-based venture capital firm that also had a corporate-finance advisory business. Under the agreement, MMG continued as an advisory business, with a New York office for which Alan Patricof was responsible. Conversely, MMG's London office became the U.K. arm of Patricof's private equity firm. For several years, the two names co-existed, and while the U.S. firm raised its first fund of US$ 25.5 million in 1980, the U.K. firm raised its first fund of £ 10.2 million in 1981. In the second half of the Eighties, Apax expanded its European presence significantly. In 1989, Corporate Finance Partners, which I had co-founded in Zurich in 1986, became a member of MMG Patricof. We opened new offices in Spain in 1989 and in Germany in 1990, but it was increasingly felt that a unified, international brand was needed. In 1991, therefore, the name in Europe was changed to Apax Partners.

Under our new name, we opened additional offices in Tel Aviv in 1994 and in Milan in 2000 and, mirroring the growing regionalization of Europe's private equity market, raised our first pan-European fund in 1999. This fund succeeded a series of national funds. In 2002, finally, we merged our European and U.S. operating companies to become Apax Partners LLP.

As soon as we had created a single platform in the two most mature private equity markets, we began to think about "What's Next"? The decision to expand into Asia was taken in the Spring of 2005. China and India were the natural choices. Their markets are huge, and we thought that private equity could play an important role in helping companies realize their growth potential. Opening an office in Mumbai was comparatively easy, because we had a number of Indian professionals who were keen to take up this challenge. The Mumbai office thus opened in 2006. China was more difficult. Earlier on, we had decided not to hire new senior people for our "Expansion to Asia" project, but to grow organically using the resources we had in our firm. But unlike in the case of India, we had no Chinese professionals. So we first opened an office in Hong Kong in 2005, a step that was followed in 2008 by opening an office in Shanghai.

What were your motivations to expand into Asia?

MBC: Our Asian strategy is long-term oriented. We firmly believe that as a firm with global ambitions you've got to be in Asia. In the future, China will be in our view the most critical market, apart from the United States. So the first goal of our strategy was to get our feet on the ground by opening offices in China and India. Furthermore, we wanted to broaden our investor base, which we successfully did in the context of Apax Europe VII, a fund that closed in 2007 with €11.2 billion. Today, our investor base includes a number of important institutions from Asia as well as the Middle East. Moreover, we felt that our presence in Asia would help our portfolio companies in the United States and elsewhere, for example, in terms of sourcing production.

In our view, Asia may also provide interesting opportunities for us to exit deals. For instance, we sold our ownership stake in the Belgian wind turbine gearmaker Hansen Transmissions to India's Suzlon Energy, a market leader in Asia and the fifth largest wind turbine manufacturer in the world. Looking forward, I would expect interesting exit opportunities to come up in other sectors as well as Asian companies are teaming up to bid for foreign assets.

How many investments have you made in Asia so far?

MBC: Strictly defined, only one until now. In October 2007, we acquired an 11 percent stake in Apollo Hospitals, India's leading hospital chain. But this is very much in line with our expansion strategy, which foresees to grow our Asian franchise gradually over time. This strategy recognizes that in particular China is an incredibly competitive market, where local private equity funds are mushrooming, competing with regional and global players, state funds, insurance companies, corporations, and, of course, the public market. However, if you believe that China—besides the United States—will be the dominant market in the future, as I do, and if you want to be a global leader, you've got to be in that market at an early stage.

How does Apax take investment decisions?

MBC: As a global firm, all investment decisions are taken on a global basis by our Investment Committee. The same applies to portfolio reviews and exits. In fact, all issues are treated from a global perspective, including compensation and promotions of our investment professionals.

Are there any geographies you would not invest in?

MBC: We are fairly agnostic with regard to individual countries. We are organized according to industries, and should we see opportunities in countries where we are currently not present, for example, because a potential seller approaches us, we will consider such opportunities. In Japan, we haven't really looked at potential investments, and given the complexity of that market, we would probably make investments only in corporation with a local partner. In Australia, the private equity market has become substantially more active. However, competition is fierce, which limits the number of really good investment opportunities. In the emerging markets in Asia, country risk matters, of course, and where we believe that risk is too high, we will not consider making investments.

How important is governance risk for you? Is there a particular ownership threshold below which you would not invest?

MBC: Governance risk is of course of critical importance in any investment decision we take. If you want to invest in Asia, you've got to accept that in many cases you'll be unable to acquire a majority stake in the company. Someone who owns a business in a rapidly growing market and needs capital to exploit the growth opportunities will not be willing to sell you that company or the majority of its stakes. That's the way it is. So you've got to make sure that your interests are fully aligned with those of the seller. We don't really think in terms of what is the lowest share we can accept. Rather, we see this issue in absolute terms. At a minimum, we want to deploy US$ 100–150 million in any given deal. Is the owner willing to sell to us a stake of that size? Is the company big enough to absorb this kind of minimum amount? In the end, our investment approach as a global private equity house is to support the growth of global companies, this is where we believe we can best add value.

How do you deal with reputational risk?

MBC: This is a big issue for us. For example, I'm aware of a case where management had hundreds of phantom employees on the company's payroll in order to siphon off the profits. Having a very disciplined and rigorous due diligence process in place is absolutely indispensable. Routinely, we hire external consultants to do very thorough background checks. If these background checks produce the slightest doubts, this will be a deal breaker. In fact, we have rejected a significant number of deals because of this reason. Thus far, we haven't had any bad experience, but it is one of my biggest worries in making investments in countries whose governance standards are still emerging.

12.3 Private equity firms in nontraditional markets

12.3.1 Abraaj Capital

The firm: Abraaj Capital is one of the largest PE firms operating outside Europe and North America.[2] Headquartered in Dubai, its geographic focus spans from North Africa to the Gulf to Turkey and the Indian subcontinent, a region Abraaj Capital has labeled MENASA (Middle East, North Africa, South Asia). Apart from its headquarters, Abraaj Capital has offices in Riyadh, Cairo, Istanbul, Amman, Beirut, and Karachi. Since its inception in 2002, Abraaj Capital has raised around US$ 5 billion, including four buyout funds, one real estate fund, and two special opportunities funds. Abraaj Capital Holdings Limited has issued share capital of US$ 1.5 billion, with most shareholders being wealthy families and important regional institutional investors. Deutsche Bank has also acquired a stake in the management company.

---

[2]Background information on Abraaj Capital and private equity in the MENASA region can be found in a recent Harvard Business School case study prepared by Lerner and Bozkaya (2009).

Abraaj's investment ticket sizes in its last fully deployed buyout fund (a 2007 vintage US$ 2 billion fund) averaged US$ 150–175 million.

Interview with Omar Lodhi, Executive Director of Abraaj Capital. The interview was conducted in May 2010.

Question: As a regional private equity firm, Abraaj Capital's geographic focus appears to be unusually broad. What has motivated Abraaj Capital to define a region as heterogeneous as MENASA as its market?

Omar Lodhi (OL): Actually, MENASA is much more integrated than is often perceived. Within the Arab world of the Middle East and North Africa, there have always been close trade and investment links. While Turkey was westward focused in the 1990s as part of its EU accession process, the recent decade has seen a rekindling of trade and investment flows with the wider MENA block and GCC in particular. Historically, many merchant families in the Gulf region have also had tight links with the Indian sub-continent and often substantial business interests. Not to forget the large number of expatriate workers from Pakistan and India who are employed in the Gulf States.

The MENASA economies we consider as our market have in common that they are growing rapidly, both in terms of economic output and in population and have benefited in general from an economic reform process initiated earlier this decade. Furthermore, the Gulf region possesses the world's largest energy resources. Between 2002 and 2009, real economic activity in the Gulf States rose on average by more than 5 percent per year, in North Africa economic growth averaged more than 4.5 percent. The Turkish economy expanded at a similar rate, while real output in India rose by more than 7.5 percent per year in 2002–2009. Of course, MENASA was not entirely immune to the global economic and financial crisis, but overall it has weathered the storm reasonably well. While Dubai has recently faced considerable challenges in its financial and real estate sectors, the economic impact has remained largely contained and not impacted other regional countries which continue to present attractive growth opportunities. Economic prosperity brings about important needs across a wide range of sectors. Abraaj's investment strategy aims to capitalize on these growing needs, taking into account the close economic, financial and human capital ties within the region. In many instances we buy businesses not just for the growth opportunity they present in their home markets but indeed for the potential of expanding them into other markets in the region. These platform play strategies are synonomous with several of our investments including in the logistics, education and healthcare space.

What are your most important country markets in terms of capital under management?

OL: The countries within our region where we have been most active from an investment and capital allocation perspective are Turkey, Egypt, Saudi Arabia and the UAE, where many regionally focused businesses are domiciled. This is likely to remain the case going forward for our current vintage fund.

Which sectors and industries are you favoring?

OL: Generally speaking, we are fairly industry agnostic given the favourable demand/supply dynamics that exist in most sectors across the region. Given the rapidly rising economic prosperity in our region, demand growth for certain goods and services has outpaced supply growth by a considerable margin. This pertains, for instance, to health care and education. Other examples are energy and power, transportation, logistics and financial services. Furthermore, the rapid growth in the region's population brings about growing opportunities in sectors, such as food and agriculture and retail.

How do you source deals?

OL: Around two-thirds of our transactions are sourced on a proprietary basis. There are two important reasons for this. First of all, although the private equity eco system has become significantly more developed compared with just a few years ago, it remains less efficient than in today's more mature markets in the United States and in Europe. A growing number of foreign investment banks have set up shop in the region, competing with indigenous financial intermediaries. While their activities have certainly helped increase market transparency, personal ties remain critical. In our region, a large share of companies is controlled by families whose trust is critical to do business with and to identify attractive investment opportunities. Importantly, we see a new generation of entrepreneurs emerging. In taking their family businesses to the next level, they are not necessarily primarily interested in the capital we provide. Rather, they see us as partners in institutionalizing and corporatizing their companies.

Second, to the extent that deals come to market through auctions, prices are naturally more competitive. Where we see value in auction-led deals, we pursue that route, but our business model remains predicated on a sourcing model that's based on proprietary transactions.

Turning to corporate governance in your portfolio companies, are you willing to accept minority positions?

OL: Our investment strategy is to acquire control themed interests in stable, mature, well-managed businesses. In more than half of the transactions we have undertaken, we have been able to acquire a majority stake. Given that a large share of companies in our target region are owned or controlled by families who seek partnerships in growing their businesses rather than selling them, it is not always possible, however, to acquire the majority of the capital. In those deals where our share capital is less than 50 percent, we more often than not still achieve an equal position from a governance perspective thus allowing us to be deeply involved in the company's decision making process. Bearing in mind that sellers' interests often go beyond the capital we provide, it is critical that their interests are totally aligned with ours. Whether this is actually the case represents a core part of our due diligence work. Right from the beginning of this process, there must be absolute clarity and transparency, with the shareholder agreement documenting the agreed strategy to create value for the company's shareholders. This has worked well for us, and in none of our minority acquisitions to date have we had any negative surprises.

To what extent do you observe changes in the private equity industry structure in MENASA?

OL: The Middle East and North Africa are now widely considered as the world's fourth important private equity market, following the United States, Western Europe, and Asia. Abraaj Capital enjoyed a first mover advantage when we raised our first buyout and growth capital fund in early 2002. Closing at US$ 116 million in June 2003, this was actually the first Middle-East focused private equity buyout fund. Since then, a number of indigenous new players have arrived, some being independent, others being captive. Bahrain-based Investcorp, for example, which has traditionally raised funds in the region for acquisitions in the more developed markets, has in recent years started to focus on the Middle East as an attractive market to deploy capital. At the same time, some global players have shown increased interest in the region for the same reason. The Carlyle Group has also raised their first Middle-East fund and others have begun to explore similar strategies. The growing number of sophisticated firms naturally means more competition. We are confident, however, that we maintain our competitive edge thanks to our strong roots in the region, our track record and our human capital. Besides, as more players come to the market it is positive for the private equity industry overall as its helps the industry to grow and play a greater role in financial intermediation, and will also facilitate international investors increasing their allocations to the region.

As the private equity industry in your region grows, do you observe any changes in how private equity capital is intermediated?

OL: While firms like ours have always operated on the basis of fund structures, historically, several transactions were financed on a deal-by-deal basis. Once a deal was identified, capital was raised—predominantly from wealthy families and other important investors from the region—to finance that particular deal. However, as the industry has grown and become more sophisticated, fund structures of the type we know from other markets have become increasingly common.

What role does financial leverage play in creating value?

OL: Generally speaking, leverage plays a considerably lesser role than in the U.S. and European markets. More specifically, I would consider a structure where debt is equivalent to 3-4x EBITDA as quite aggressive by our regional standards. For instance, portfolio companies in our third (US$ 2 billion) buyout fund have an average debt-to-equity ratio of less than 0.6, compared with a ratio of around 2 during the last cycle in the more mature markets. When determining the appropriate amount of leverage in acquisitions, we always factor in the amount of debt that the company will need to fuel its growth through both organic and M&A means. In terms of the supply of debt, we work both with local and international banks as local bond markets in the region have remained more or less embryonic. While credit conditions have generally remained tight, the lesser reliance on debt in acquisitions has made our markets less susceptible to the global credit crunch than in other parts of the world.

How are deals exited?

OL: At Abraaj we have been able to exit our investments through multiple modes including IPOs, trade sales (to both strategic buyers as well as secondaries), and even management buyouts. With the economic reforms and liberalization of economies within the region there is an increasing level of both intra and inter regional M&A which will continue to strengthen going forward which bodes well for exits through the trade sale route. At the same time, capital markets in the region have reformed substantially and continue to do so, making them increasingly viable and attractive exit options for our recent vintage funds.

How diversified is your investor base?

Our investor base has become increasingly diversified. On a capital-weighted basis, around 20 percent of our limited partners are from countries outside the Middle East. This includes investors from the US, Europe and Asia. Looking forward, we seek to expand and diversify our investor base further. We regard our investors' commitments to our funds as long-term partnerships, and it is our strategic goal to forge new partnerships as Abraaj Capital continues to grow.

References

Abu Dhabi Investment Authority. (2010). *ADIA review* 2009. http://www.adia.ae/En/News/media_review.aspx

Acharya, V., Hahn, M., & Kehoe, C. (2010). *Corporate governance and value creation: Evidence from private equity*. http://papers.ssrn.com/sol3/papers.cfm?abstract_id=1354519

Ahearne, A. G., Griever, W. L., & Warnock, F. E. (2004). Information costs and home bias: An analysis of U.S. holdings of foreign equities. *Journal of International Economics, 62,* 313–336.

Aizenman, J., & Kendall, J. (2008). *The internationalization of venture capital and private equity (Working Paper 14344)*. Cambridge, MA: National Bureau of Economic Research.

Akerlof, G. (1970). The market for 'Lemons': Quality uncertainty and the market mechanism. *Quarterly Journal of Economics, 84*(3), 488–500.

Allen, F., & Song, W.-l (2003). Venture capital and corporate governance. In Peter Cornelius, & Bruce Kogut (Eds.), *Corporate governance and capital flows in a global economy* (pp. 133–156). New York: Oxford University Press.

Allianz Global Investors. (2008). *Pension trends in emerging markets—The rise of DC plans and its consequences* (International Pension Papers No. 2/2008). http://www.fiap.cl/prontus_fiap/site/edic/base/port/series.html

Alternative Investment Expert Group. (2006). Report. *Developing European private equity*. http://ec.europa.eu/internal_market/investment/docs/other_docs/reports/equity_en.pdf.

Andrade, G., & Kaplan, S. N. (1998). How costly is financial (not economic) distress? Evidence from highly leveraged transactions that became distressed. *Journal of Finance, 53*(5), 1443–1494.

Apax Partners. (2007). *Private equity in the public eye. 2007 global private equity environment rankings*. http://www.apax.com/EN/

Artus, P., & Teïletche, J. (2004). Asset allocation and European private equity: A first approach using aggregated data. In *Performance measurement and asset allocation for European private equity funds (Research Paper)*. European Private Equity and Venture Capital Association. http://www.cetraonline.it/file_doc/157/performance%20.pdf.

Axelson, U., Jenkinson, T., Strömberg, P., & Weisbach, M. S. (2007). *Leverage and pricing in buyouts: An empirical analysis*. http://papers.ssrn.com/sol3/papers.cfm?abstract_id=1027127

Axelson, U., Strömberg, P., & Weisbach, M. S. (2009). Why are buyouts levered? The financial structure of private equity funds. *Journal of Finance, 64*(4), 1549–1582.

Baele, L., Ferrando, A., Hördahl, P., Krylova, E., & Monnet, C. (2008). Measuring European financial integration. In Xavier Freixas, Philipp Hartmann, & Colin Mayer (Eds.), *Handbook of European financial markets and institutions* (pp. 318–341). Oxford, UK: Oxford University Press.

Bain &, Company (2010). *Global private equity report 2010.* Boston, MA: Bain & Company.

Baker, G. P., & Smith, G. D. (1998). *The new financial capitalists: Kohlberg Kravis Roberts and the creation of corporate value.* Cambridge, UK: Cambridge University Press.

Barro, R. J. (1998). *Determinants of economic growth. A cross-country empirical study.* Cambridge, MA: MIT Press.

Basel Committee on Banking Supervision. (2009). *Enhancements to the Basel II framework.* http://www.bis.org/publ/bcbs157.pdf?noframes=1

Berg, A., Borenstein, E., & Patillo, C. (2004). *Assessing early warning systems: How have they worked in practice? (International Monetary Fund Working Paper 04/52).* Washington, DC: International Monetary Fund.

Berg, A., & Patillo, C. (1999). Predicting currency crises: The indicators approach and an alternative. *Journal of International Money and Finance, 18,* 561–586.

Berkowitz, D., Pistor, K., & Richard, J. (2003). Economic development, legality, and the transplant effect. *European Economic Review, 47,* 165–195.

Bernstein, S., Lerner, J., & Schoar, A. (2009). *The investment strategies of sovereign wealth funds.* http://papers.ssrn.com/sol3/papers.cfm?abstract_id=1370112##

Bilo, S., Christophers, H., Degosciu, M., & Zimmermann, H. (2005). Risk, returns, and biases of listed private equity portfolios(*WWZ/Department of Finance Working Paper 1/05*). Basel, Switzerland: University of Basel.

Black, B. S., & Gilson, R. J. (1998). Venture capital and the structure of capital markets: Banks versus stock markets. *Journal of Financial Economics, 47,* 243–277.

Black, B. S., & Gilson, R. J. (1999). Does venture capital require an active stock market? *Journal of Applied Corporate Finance, 11*(4), 36–48.

Black, F., & Litterman, R. (1992). Global portfolio optimization. *Financial Analysts Journal, 48*(5), 28–43.

Black, F., & Scholes, M. (1973). The pricing of options and corporate liabilities. *Journal of Political Economy, 81*(3), 637–654.

Blundell-Wignall, A., Hu, Y., & Yermo, J. (2008). Sovereign wealth and pension fund issues. *OECD Financial Market Trends, 1*(94), 117–132.

Bongaerts, D., & Charlier, E. (2008). *Private equity and regulatory capital* (Center Tilburg University Discussion Paper 2008-52). http://papers.ssrn.com/sol3/papers.cfm?abstract_id=1140604

Boston Consulting Group, and IESE Business School. (2008a). *Get ready for the private equity shakeout.* http://www.iese.edu/en/files/PrivateEquityWhitePaper.pdf

Boston Consulting Group, & IESE Business School. (2008b). *The advantage of persistence. How the best private-equity firms "Beat the Fade."* http://www.bcg.com/documents/file15196.pdf

Bottazzi, L., Da Rin, M., & Hellmann, T. (2008). Who are the active investors? Evidence from venture capital. *Journal of Financial Economics, 89,* 488–512.

Brophy, D. J., Ouimet, P. P., & Sialm, C. (2009). Hedge funds as investors of last resort. *Review of Financial Studies, 22,* 541–574.

CalPERS. (2007a). *Statement of investment policy for permissible equity for emerging equity markets.* Retrieved May 14, 2007, from http://www.calpers.ca.gov/eip-docs/investments/policies/inv-asset-classes/equity/ext-equity/permissible-country.pdf

CalPERS. (2007b). *Statement of investment policy for permissible equity for emerging equity markets principles.* Retrieved November 13, 2007, from http://www.calpers.ca.gov/eip-docs/investments/policies/inv-asset-classes/equity/ext-equity/emerging-eqty-market-prinicples.pdf

Campbell, J. Y., Serfaty-de Medeiros, K., & Viceira, L. M. (2010). Global currency hedging. *Journal of Finance, 65*(1), 87–121.

CapGemini, & Merrill Lynch. (2009). *2009 world wealth report*. http://www.capgemini.com/insights-and-resources/by-publication/2009_world_wealth_report/

Chan, K., Covrig, V., & Ng, L. (2005). What determines the domestic bias and foreign bias? Evidence from mutual fund equity allocations worldwide. *Journal of Finance, 60*, 1495–1534.

Chen, H., Dai, N., & Schatzberg, J. (2010). The choice of equity selling mechanisms: PIPEs versus SEOs. *Journal of Corporate Finance, 14*(6), 104–119.

Chen, H., Gompers, P., Kovner, A., & Lerner, J. (2009). *Buy local? The geography of successful and unsuccessful venture capital expansion (Working Paper 15102)*. Cambridge, MA: National Bureau of Economic Research.

Cochrane, J. (2005). The risk and return of venture capital. *Journal of Financial Economics, 75*(1), 3–52.

Coeurdacier, N., De Santis, R. A., & Aviat, A. (2009). Cross-border mergers and acquisitions and European integration. *Economic Policy, 24*(57), 55–106.

Collyns, C., & Kincaid, G. R. (2003). *Managing financial crises. Recent experience and lessons for Latin America (Occasional Paper 217)*. Washington, DC: International Monetary Fund.

Committee of European Insurance, & Occupational Pensions Supervisors. (2009). *Draft CEIOPS advice for Level 2 Implementing Measures on Solvency II: Article 109 b equity risk sub-module* (Consultation Paper 69). http://www.ceiops.eu/media/files/consultations/consultationpapers/CP69/CEIOPS-CP-69-09-Draft-L2-Advice-Design-and-calibration-of-the-equity-risk-sub-module.pdf

Conroy, R. M., & Harris, R. S. (2007). How good are private equity returns? *Journal of Applied Corporate Finance, 19*(3), 96–108.

Cornelius, P. (2007). Emerging markets: Net importers or exporters of private equity capital? *Journal of Private Equity, 10*(4), 18–27.

Cornelius, P., Juttman, K., & Langelaar, B. (2009). Home bias in leveraged buyouts. *International Finance, 12*, 321–349.

Cornelius, P., Juttmann, K., & de Veer, R. (2009). Industry cycles and the performance of buyout funds. *Journal of Private Equity, 12*, 14–21.

Cornelius, P., Langelaar, B., & van Rossum, M. (2007). Big is better: Growth and market structure in global buyouts. *Journal of Applied Corporate Finance, 19*, 109–116.

Cornelius, P., Van de Putte, A., & Romani, M. (2005). Three decades of scenario planning in Shell. *California Management Review, 48*(1), 92–109.

Cornelli, F., & Karakas, O. (2008). *Private equity and corporate governance: Do LBOs have more effective boards?* www.ecgi.org/./Do%20LBOs%20have%20more%20effective%20boards,%20(Cornelli,%20Karakas).pdf

Cumming, D. (Ed.). (2010). *Private equity. Fund types, risk and returns, and regulation*. Hoboken, NJ: Wiley.

Cumming, D. J., & Johan, S. A. (2009). *Venture capital and private equity contracting: An international perspective*. Boston, et al: Elsevier and Academic Press.

Dai, N. (2010). The rise of the PIPE market. In Douglas Cumming (Ed.), *Private equity. Fund types, risks and returns, and regulation* (pp. 111–128). Hoboken, NJ: Wiley.

Da Rin, M., Nicodano, G., & Sembenelli, A. (2006). Public policy and the creation of active venture capital markets. *Journal of Public Economics, 90*(8–9), 1699–1723.

Dascking, C., Ghosh, A., Lane, T., & Thomas, A. (2004). *Lessons from the crisis in Argentina (Occasional Paper 236)*. Washington, DC: International Monetary Fund.

Day, S., & Diller, C. (2010). Benchmarking private equity investments. In Capital Dynamics (Ed.), *Risk management in private equity* (pp. 43–56). London: PEI Media.

Degeorge, F., & Maug, E. (2008). Corporate finance in Europe—A survey. In Xavier Freixas, Philipp Hartmann, & Colin Mayer (Eds.), *Handbook of European financial markets and institutions* (pp. 217–237). Oxford, UK: Oxford University Press.

Deloitte (2008). Global trends in venture capital 2008 survey. http://www.deloitte.com/assets/Dcom-Global/Local%20Assets/Documents/tt_2008GlobalVCSurvey_Global.pdf

Dembo, R. S., & Freeman, A. (1998). *Seeing tomorrow. Rewriting the rules of risk.* New York: Wiley.

Diller, C., & Kaserer, C. (2009). What drives private equity returns?—Fund inflows, skilled GPs, and/or risk? *European Financial Management, 15*(3), 643–675.

Dimson, E. (1979). Risk measurement when securities are subject to infrequent trading. *Journal of Financial Economics, 7*(2), 197–226.

Driessen, J., Lin, T., & Phalippou, L. (2009). *A new method to estimate risk and return of non-traded assets from cash flows: The case of private equity funds (Working Paper 14144).* Cambridge, MA: National Bureau of Economic Research.

Emerging Markets Private Equity Association. (2010). *Fundraising and investment review 2009.* Washington, DC: EMPEA.

Ernst & Young (2007). Acceleration. Global venture capital insights report 2007. http://www.indiavca.org/upload/library/29_E&Y_Global_VC_Insight_Report_2007.pdf

European Central Bank. (2008). *Financial integration in Europe.* Frankfurt: European Central Bank.

European Private Equity and Venture Capital Association. (2006). *Private equity fund structures in Europe.* An EVCA Tax and Legal Committee Paper. Ed. SJ Berwin LLP. http://www.evca.eu/uploadedFiles/fund_structures.pdf

European Private Equity and Venture Capital Association. (2009). *EVCA Yearbook.* Brussels: EVCA.

Fadely, J., & Gu, J. (2009). RMB funds—The current state and way forward: A legal and tax wish list. *Emerging Markets Private Equity Quarterly Review, 5*(3), 3–8.

Fama, E. F., & French, K. R. (1993). Common risk factors in the returns on stocks and bonds. *Journal of Financial Economics, 33*(1), 3–56.

Fama, E. F., & French, K. R. (1997). Industry cost of equity. *Journal of Financial Economics, 43*, 153–193.

Fenn, G. W., Liang, N., & Prowse, S. (1997). The private equity market: An overview. *Financial Markets, Institutions and Instruments, 6*, 1–106.

Financial Services Authority. (2006). *Private equity: A discussion of risk and regulatory engagement.* FSA Discussion Paper 06/6.

Financial Times. (2009). *I Love Competition…I Love winning' Lunch with the FT.* October 10/11.

Financial Times. (2009). *University funds take a course in liquidity.* October 16.

Fleming, G. (2010). Institutional investment in private equity. Motivations, strategies, and performance. In Douglas Cumming (Ed.), *Private equity. Fund types, risks and returns, and regulation* (pp. 9–29). Hoboken, NJ: Wiley.

Frankel, J. A., & Rose, A. K. (1996). Currency crashes in emerging markets: An empirical treatment. *Journal of International Economics, 41*, 351–368.

Fraser-Sampson, G. (2006). *Multi asset class investment strategy.* Chichester, UK: Wiley.

Fraser-Sampson, G. (2007). *Private equity as an asset class.* Chichester, UK: Wiley.

Freixas, X., Hartmann, P., & Mayer, C. (2008). *Handbook of European financial markets and institutions.* Oxford, UK: Oxford University Press.

French, K., & Poterba, J. (1991). Investor diversification and international equity markets. *American Economic Review, 81*, 222–226.

Froot, K. A. (1993). *Currency hedging over long horizons (Working Paper 4355)*. Cambridge, MA: National Bureau of Economic Research.

Gadiesh, O., & MacArthur, H. (2008). *Lessons from private equity any company can use*. Cambridge, MA: Harvard Business School Press.

Gogineni, S., & Megginson, W. L. (2010). IPOs and other nontraditional fund-raising methods of private equity firms. In Douglas Cumming (Ed.), *Private equity. Fund types, risks and returns, and regulation* (pp. 31–51). Hoboken, NJ: Wiley.

Goldstein, M., Kaminsky, G. L., & Reinhart, C. M. (2000). *Assessing financial vulnerability*. Washington, DC: Institute for International Economics.

Gompers, P. A., & Lerner, J. (1997). Risk and reward in private equity investments: The challenge of performance assessment. *Journal of Private Equity, 1*, 5–12.

Gompers, P. A., & Lerner, J. (2000). Money chasing deals? The impact of fund inflows on private equity valuations. *Journal of Financial Economics, 55*, 281–325.

Gompers, P. A., & Lerner, J. (2001). The venture capital revolution. *Journal of Economic Perspectives, 15*(2), 145–168.

Gompers, P. A., Kovner, A. R., Lerner, J., & Scharfstein, D. S. (2005). *Specialization and success: Evidence from venture capital*. Harvard Business School.

Gottschalg, O. (2010). Private equity fund selection. How to find true top-quartile performers. In Douglas Cumming (Ed.), *Private equity. Fund types, risks and returns, and regulation* (pp. 283–299). Hoboken, NJ: Wiley.

Groh, A. P., & Liechtenstein, H. (2009). How attractive is Central Eastern Europe for risk capital investors? *Journal of International Money and Finance, 28*(4), 625–647.

Groh, A., Liechtenstein, H., & Lieser, K. (2010). *The European venture capital and private equity country attractiveness indices. Journal of Corporate Finance, 16*, 205–224.

Gross, B. (2009, September). *On the course to a new normal*. PIMCO investment outlook. http://media.pimco-global.com/pdfs/pdf/IO%20Sept%2009%20WEB.pdf?WT.cg_n=PIMCO-US&WT.ti=IO%20Sept%2009%20WEB.pdf

Guo, S., Hotchkiss, E. S., & Song, W. (2009). Do buyouts (still) create value? *Journal of Finance, forthcoming*. http://papers.ssrn.com/sol3/papers.cfm?abstract_id=1009281.

Hardymon, F., Lerner, J., & Leamon, A. (2003). *Accel partners' European launch*. Harvard Business School. Case Study 0-803-021.

Hau, H., & Rey, H. (2008). Home bias at the fund level. *American Economic Review, 98*, 333–338.

He, G., & Litterman, R. (1999). The intuition behind Black-Litterman model portfolios. Goldman Sachs Quantitative Resources Group. http://papers.ssrn.com/sol3/papers.cfm?abstract_id=334304

Hemming, R., Kell, M., & Schimmelpfennig, A. (2003). *Fiscal vulnerability and financial crises in emerging market economies (Occasional Paper 218)*. Washington, DC: International Monetary Fund.

Henisz, W. J. (2002). *Politics and international investment. Measuring risks and protecting profits*. Cheltenham and Northampton, MA: Edward Elgar.

Hochberg, Y. V., Ljungqvist, A., & Lu, Y. (2007). Whom you know matters: Venture capital networks and investment performance. *Journal of Finance, 62*(1), 251–301.

Hwang, M., Quigley, J. M., & Woodward, S. E. (2005). An index for venture capital, 1987-2003. *Contributions to Economic Analysis & Policy, 4*, 1–43.

Institutional Limited Partners' Association. (2009). *Private equity principles*. http://www.ilpa.org/files/ILPA%20Private%20Equity%20Principles.pdf

International Monetary Fund. (2007). *Global financial stability report. Market developments and issues*. Washington, DC: Author.

International Monetary Fund. (2009). *Global financial stability report. Responding to the financial crisis and measuring systemic risk*. Washington, DC: Author.

International Monetary Fund. (2010a). *Global financial stability report. Meeting new challenges to stability and building a safer system*. Washington, DC: Author.

International Monetary Fund. (2010b). *Global financial stability report. Sovereigns, funding, and systemic liquidity*. Washington, DC: Author.

International Monetary Fund. (2010c). *World economic outlook. Rebalancing growth*. Washington, DC: Author.

International Organization of Security Commissions. (2009). *Private equity conflicts of interest. Consultation report*. http://www.iosco.org/library/pubdocs/pdf/IOSCOPD309.pdf

Jeng, L., & Wells, P. (2000). The determinants of venture capital funding: Evidence across countries. *Journal of Corporate Finance, 6*(3), 241–289.

Jensen, M. C. (1986). Agency costs of free cash flow, corporate finance and takeovers. *American Economic Review, 76*, 323–329.

Jensen, M. C., & Meckling, W. (1976). Theory of the firm: Managerial behavior, agency costs and ownership structure. *Journal of Financial Economics, 3*, 305–360.

Jobst, A. A. (2009). What is securitization? *Finance & Development, 47*(3), 48–52.

Johnson, E. (2009). 'Jump Ball' for limited LP capital: Assessing historical returns in Times of Crisis. *Emerging Markets Private Equity Quarterly Review, 5*(1), 1–9.

Jones, C. M., and Rhodes-Kropf, M. (2004). *The price of diversifiable risk in venture capital and private equity*. http://papers.ssrn.com/sol3/papers.cfm?abstract_id=342841

Kacperczyk, M., Sialm, C., & Zheng, L. (2005). On the industry concentration of actively managed equity mutual funds. *Journal of Finance, 60*(4), 1983–2012.

Kaminsky, G. L., Lizondo, J. S., & Reinhart, C. M. (1998). Leading indicators of currency crises. *IMF Staff Papers, 45*, 1–48.

Kaplan, S. N. (1989). Management buyouts: Evidence on taxes as a source of value. *Journal of Finance, 44*(3), 611–632.

Kaplan, S. N. (2009). *Private equity: Past, present, and future*. Presentation Given at the Second Private Equity Symposium at the London Business School, Coller Institute of Private Equity, Private Equity at the Cross Roads. A Vintage of Opportunities and Crises. http://faculty.chicagobooth.edu/steven.kaplan/research/kpe.pdf

Kaplan, S. N., & Lerner, J. (2009). *It Ain't broke: The past, present, and future of venture capital*. http://faculty.chicagobooth.edu/steven.kaplan/research/kaplanlerner.pdf

Kaplan, S. N., & Schoar, A. (2005). Private equity performance: Returns, persistence, and capital flows. *Journal of Finance, 60*, 1791–1823.

Kaplan, S. N., & Stein, J. (1993a). The evolution of buyout pricing and financial structure in the 1980s. *Quarterly Journal of Economics, 108*, 313–358.

Kaplan, S. N., & Stein, J. (1993b). The evolution of buyout pricing and financial structure (or what went wrong) in the 1980s. *Journal of Applied Corporate Finance, 6*(1), 72–88.

Kaplan, S. N., Sensoy, B. A., & Strömberg, P. (2002). *How well do venture capital databases reflect actual investments?* http://faculty.chicagobooth.edu/steven.kaplan/research/kss1.pdf

Kaplan, S. N., Sensoy, B. A., & Strömberg, P. (2009). Should investors bet on the jockey or the horse? Evidence from the evolution of firms from early business plans to public companies. *Journal of Finance, 64*(1), 75–115.

Kaplan, S. N., & Strömberg, P. (2004). Characteristics, contracts, and actions: Evidence from venture capitalist analyses. *Journal of Finance, 59*(5), 2173–2206.

Kaplan, S. N., & Strömberg, P. (2009). Leveraged buyouts and private equity. *Journal of Economic Perspectives, 23*(1), 121–146.

Kaufmann, D., Kraay, A., & Mastruzzi, M. (2009). *Governance matters VIII: Aggregate and individual governance indicators, 1996-2008* (World Bank Policy Research Working Paper 4978). http://papers.ssrn.com/sol3/papers.cfm?abstract_id=1424591

Kaufmann, D., & Wei, S. (1999). *Does 'Grease Money' speed up the wheels of commerce (Working Paper 2254)*. Washington, DC: World Bank Policy Research.

Kho, B., Stulz, R. M., & Warnock, F. E. (2007). *Financial globalization, governance and the evolution of the home bias.* http://papers.ssrn.com/sol3/papers.cfm?abstract_id=911595&high=%20kho#PaperDownload

Kogut, B., Urso, P., & Walker, G. (2007). Emergent properties of a new financial market: American venture capital syndication from 1960 to 2005. *Management Science, 53*(7), 1181–1198.

Korteweg, M., & Sorensen. (2009). Risk and return characteristics of venture capital-backed entrepreneurial companies. http://papers.ssrn.com/sol3/papers.cfm?abstract_id=1108610. Review of Financial Studies, forthcoming.

Lambsdorff, J. (2007). *The institutional economics of corruption and reform: Theory, evidence, and policy.* Cambridge, UK: Cambridge University Press.

Lane, P. R. (2008). *EMU and financial integration (Discussion Paper No. 272).* Institute for International Integration Studies.

Lane, P. R., & Milesi-Ferretti, G. M. (2007). The external wealth of nations mark II: Revised and extended estimates of foreign assets and liabilities, 1970-2004. *Journal of International Economics, 73,* 223–250.

Lane, P. R., & Milesi-Ferretti, G. M. (2008). The drivers of financial globalization. *American Economic Review, 98,* 327–332.

La Porta, R., Lopez-de-Silvanes, F., & Shleifer, A. (1999). Corporate ownership around the world. *Journal of Finance, 54*(2), 471–517.

La Porta, R., Lopez-de-Silvanes, F., Shleifer, A., & Vishny, R. (1997). Legal determinants of external finance. *Journal of Finance, 22*(3), 1113–1155.

La Porta, R., Lopez-de-Silvanes, F., Shleifer, A., & Vishny, R. (1998). Law and finance. *Journal of Political Economy, 106*(6), 1131–1150.

La Porta, R., Lopez-de-Silvanes, F., Shleifer, A., & Vishny, R. (2002). Investor protection and corporate valuation. *Journal of Finance, 57,* 1147–1170.

Latin American Venture Capital Association. (2010). 2010 scorecard. *The private equity and venture capital environment in Latin America.* http://lavca.org/wp-content/uploads/2010/05/scorecard2010-updated-for-web-1.pdf

Leeds, R. (2006). Do labels matter? *Private Equity International, 5,* 63–65.

Leeds, R., & Sunderland, J. (2003). Private equity investing in emerging markets. *Journal of Applied Corporate Finance, 15,* 8–16.

Lerner, J. (2007). Yale University Investments Office: August 2006. *Harvard Business School Case Study.* 9-807-073.

Lerner, J. (2009). *Boulevard of broken dreams: Why public efforts to boost entrepreneurship and venture capital have failed—And what to do about it.* Princeton, NJ: Princeton University Press.

Lerner, J., & Bozkaya, A (2009). "Abraaj Capital." Harvard Business School 9-809-008 (Rev: May 20, 2009).

Lerner, J., Hardymon, F., & Leamon, A. (2009). *Venture capital and private equity: A casebook* (4th ed.). Hoboken, NJ: Wiley.

Lerner, J., & Schoar, A. (2005). Does legal enforcement affect financial transactions? The contractional channel in private equity. *Quarterly Journal of Economics, 120,* 223–246.

Lerner, J., Schoar, A., & Wongsunwai, W. (2007). Smart institutions, foolish choices: The limited partner performance puzzle. *Journal of Finance, 62*(2), 731–764.

Lerner, J., Sørensen, M., & Strömberg, P. (2009). *Does private equity create value globally? (Working Papers Volume 2). The Global Economic Impact of Private Equity Report.* Geneva: World Economic Forum.

Lintner, J. (1965). The valuation of risk assets and the selection of risky investments in stock portfolios and capital budgets. *Review of Economics and Statistics, 47*(1), 13–37.

Ljungqvist, A., & Richardson, M. P. (2003). *The cash flow, return and risk characteristics of private equity* (New York University Finance Working Paper 03–001). http://ssrn.com/abstract=369600 or DOI: 10.2139/ssrn.10.2139/ssrn.369600

Lo, A. W., & Hasanhodzic, J. (2009). *The heretics of finance. Conversations with leading practitioners of technical analysis.* New York: Bloomberg Press.

Lopez-de-Silanes, F., Phalippou, L., & Gottschalg, O. (2009). *Giants at the gate: Diseconomies of scale in private equity.* http://papers.ssrn.com/sol3/papers.cfm?abstract_id=1363883##

Lucas, R. E., Jr. (1990). Why doesn't capital flow from rich to poor countries? *American Economic Review, 80*(2), 92–96.

Manasse, P., & Roubini, N. (2005). 'Rules of Thumb' for sovereign debt crises *(Working Paper WP/05/42.* Washington, DC: International Monetary Fund.

Markowitz, H. (1952). Portfolio selection. *Journal of Finance, 7*, 77–91.

Martin, P., & Rey, H. (2004). Financial super-markets: Size matters for asset trade. *Journal of International Economics, 73*, 335–361.

Mathonet, P., & Meyer, T. (2007). *J-Curve exposure.* Holbroken, NJ: Wiley.

McKinsey Global Institute. (2007), *The new power brokers: How oil, Asia, hedge funds, and private equity are shaping global capital markets.* http://www.mckinsey.com/mgi/publications/The_New_Power_Brokers/index.asp

McKinsey Global Institute. (2008). *The new power brokers: Gaining clout in turbulent markets.* http://www.mckinsey.com/mgi/publications/The_New_Power_Brokers/index.asp

McKinsey Global Institute. (2009a). *The new power brokers: How oil, Asia, hedge funds, and private equity are fairing in the financial crisis.* http://www.mckinsey.com/mgi/reports/pdfs/the_new_power_brokers_financial_crisis/MGI_power_brokers_financial_crisis_full_report.pdf

McKinsey Global Institute. (2009b). *Global capital markets: Entering a new era.* http://www.mckinsey.com/mgi/publications/gcm_sixth_annual_report/executive_summary.asp

McKinsey Global Institute. (2010). *Debt and deleveraging: The global credit bubble and its economic consequences.* http://www.mckinsey.com/mgi/reports/freepass_pdfs/debt_and_deleveraging/debt_and_deleveraging_full_report.pdf

Megginson, W. L. (2004). Towards a global model of venture capital? *Journal of Applied Corporate Finance, 16*, 89–107.

Metrick, M. (2007). *Venture capital and the finance of innovation.* Holbroken, NJ: Wiley.

Metrick, A., & Yasuda, A. (2007). The economics of private equity funds. http://ssrn.com/abstract=996334. Review of Financial Studies, forthcoming.

Merton, R. C. (1973). Theory of rational option pricing. *Bell Journal of Economics and Management Science, 4*(1), 141–183.

Meyer, T., & Mathonet, P. (2005). *Beyond the J-Curve.* Holbroken, NJ: Wiley.

Moerel, W. (2008). The linkage between the secondary and primary markets,. In Campbell Lutyens (Ed.), *The private equity secondaries market* (pp. 43–52). London: Private Equity International.

Moran, T. H. (Ed.). (1998). *Managing international political risk.* Malden and Oxford: Blackwell Publishers.

Mossin, J. (1966). Equilibrium in a capital asset market. *Econometrica, 34*(4), 768–783.

NVCA & Cambridge Associates. (2009). *National Venture Capital Association and Cambridge Associates Partner to Deliver Venture Capital Performance Data.* http://www.nvca.org/ index.php?option=com_content&view=article&id=78:latest-industry-statistics&catid= 40:research&Itemid=102

Organisation for Economic Co-operation and Development. (2010). *Survey of investment regulation of pension funds.* Paris: OECD.

Pagano, M., Randl, O., Röell, A., & Zechner, J. (2001). What makes stock exchanges succeed? Evidence from cross-listing decisions. *European Economic Review, 45,* 770–782.

Pastor, L., & Stambaugh, R. (2003). Liquidity risk and expected stock returns. *Journal of Political Economy, 111*(3), 642–685.

Peng, L. (2001). *Building a venture capital index (Yale Working Paper 00-51).* Boulder: University of Colorado.

Perold, A., & Schuman, E. (1988, May/June). The free lunch in currency hedging: Implications for investment policy and performance standards. *Financial Analysts Journal, 44,* 45–50.

Petroulas, P. (2007). The effect of the Euro on foreign direct investment. *European Economic Review, 51,* 1468–1491.

Phalippou, L. (2008). *The hazards of using IRR to measure performance: The case of private equity.* http://papers.ssrn.com/sol3/papers.cfm?abstract_id=1111796

Phalippou, L. (2009). Beware of venturing into private equity. *Journal of Economic Perspectives, 23*(1), 147–166.

Phalippou, L., & Gottschalg, O. (2009). The performance of private equity funds. *Review of Financial Studies, 20,* 1747–1776.

Pickford, J. (Ed.). (2001). *Mastering risk. Volume 1: Concepts.* Harlow and London: Financial Times and Prentice Hall.

Pistor, K., Raiser, M., & Gelfer, S. (2000). Law and finance in transition economies. *Economics of Transition, 8,* 325–368.

Porter, M. E. (1990). *The competitive advantage of nations.* New York: Free Press.

Portes, R., Rey, H., & Oh, Y. (2001). Information and capital flows: The determinants of transactions in financial assets. *European Economic Review, 45,* 783–796.

Private Equity Intelligence. (2010). *The 2010 Preqin sovereign wealth fund review.* London: Private Equity Intelligence.

Quigley, J. M., & Woodward, S. E. (2002). *Private equity before the crash: Estimation of an index (Working Paper).* Berkeley: University of California.

Reinhart, C. M. (2002). Default, currency crises, and sovereign credit ratings. *World Bank Economic Review, 16,* 151–170.

Reinhart, C. M., & Rogoff, K. S. (2009). *This time is different. Eight centuries of financial folly.* Princeton and Oxford: Princeton University Press.

Roldes, J. E. (2004). *Pension reform, investment restrictions, and capital markets (Policy Discussion Paper PDP/04/4).* Washington, DC: International Monetary Fund.

Roll, R. (1977). A critique of the asset pricing theory's test. Part I: On past and potential testability of the theory. *Journal of Financial Economics, 4*(2), 129–176.

Rosenberg, C., Halikias, I., House, B., Keller, C., Nystedt, J., Pitt, A., et al. (2005). *Debt-related vulnerabilities and financial crises. An application of the balance sheet approach to emerging market countries (Occasional Paper 240).* Washington, DC: International Monetary Fund.

Ross, S. (1976). The arbitrage theory of capital asset pricing. *Journal of Economic Theory, 13* (3), 341–360.

Rubenstein, D. (2008). *The post-banana world of private equity*. Presentation given at a Conference of the National Bureau of Economic Research, April 5, 2008.

Sercu, P. (2009). *International finance: Theory into practice*. Princeton. NJ: Princeton University Press.

Sharpe, W. F. (1964). Capital asset prices—A theory of market equilibrium under conditions of risk. *Journal of Finance, 19*(3), 425–442.

Sharpe, W. F. (2007). *Investors and markets*. Princeton and Oxford: Princeton University Press.

Shiller, R. J. (2005). *Irrational exuberance* (2nd ed.). Princeton, NJ: Princeton University Press.

Sørensen, O., & Stuart, T. (2001). Syndication networks and the spatial distribution of venture capital investments. *American Journal of Sociology, 106*, 1546–1588.

Solnik, B. H. (1974a). An equilibrium model of the international capital market. *Journal of Economic Theory, 8*, 500–524.

Solnik, B. H. (1974b). Why not diversify internationally rather than domestically? *Financial Analysts' Journal, 30*, 48–54.

Solnik, B., & McLeavey, D. (2009). *Global investments* (6th ed.). Boston, et al: Pearson, Prentice Hall.

Spence, M. A. (2009). *Periodic systemic risk and investment strategy*. http://media.pimco-global.com/pdfs/pdf/WP032-Periodic%20Systemisc%20Risk_FINAL.pdf?WT.cg_n=PIMCO-US&WT.ti=WP032-Periodic%20Systemisc%20Risk_FINAL.pdf

Standard and Poor's (2010). LCD's Leveraged Lending Review 3Q10.

Strömberg, P. (2008). *The new demography of private equity (Globalization of Alternative Investments, Working Papers Volume 1)*. The Global Economic Impact of Private Equity Report. Geneva: World Economic Forum.

Swensen, D. F. (2009). *Pioneering portfolio management: An unconventional approach to institutional investment. Fully Revised and Updated*. New York: Free Press.

Thomas, J. M. (2010). *The credit performance of private equity-backed companies in the 'Great Recession' of 2008–2009*. Private Equity Council.http://www.privateequitycouncil.org/wordpress/wp-content/uploads/PEC_Default-Rate-Study-03-31-10-FINAL.pdf

Thomas, L. R. (1990). *The currency-hedging debate*. London: IFR Books.

Treynor, J. L. (1962). Toward a theory of market value of risky assets. Unpublished manuscript finally published in 1999. In Robert A. Korajczyk (Ed.), *Asset pricing and portfolio performance: Models, strategy and performance metrics* (pp. 15–22). London: Risk Books.

Tykvová, T., & Schertler, A. (2006). *Rivals or partners? Evidence from Europe's international private equity deals (Discussion Paper 06–091)*. Germany: ZEW—Center for European Economic Research.

van Agtmael, A. (2007). *The emerging markets century: How a new breed of world class companies is overtaking the world*. New York: Free Press.

van Putten, A. B., & MacMillan, I. C. (2004, December). Making real options really work. *Harvard Business Review, 82*(12), 134–141.

Venture Capital Tax Expert Group. (2010). *Report of expert group on removing tax obstacles to cross-border venture capital investments*. http://ec.europa.eu/enterprise/newsroom/cf/document.cfm?action=display&doc_id=5797&userservice_id=1

Warnock, F. E. (2002). Home bias and high turnover reconsidered. *Journal of International Money and Finance, 21*, 795–805.

Index

Printed and bound by CPI Group (UK) Ltd, Croydon, CR0 4YY

08/05/2025

01864768-0003